Cabrini College Library

Radnor, Pa. 19087

SO-BRV-247

THE GIFT OF
THOMAS JOSEPH WHITE
M.D., L.H.D., F.A.C.P.
TO THE LIBRARY OF
CABRINI COLLEGE
1981

PEARL HARBOR

FDR Col.

PEARL HARBOR

The Story of the Secret War

GEORGE MORGENSTERN

1947 - *The Devin-Adair Company* - New York

397835

FDR
D
767.92
. M6
1947

COPYRIGHT 1947 *by George Morgenstern. All rights reserved. No part of this book may be reproduced in any form without permission in writing from the publisher, except by a reviewer who may quote brief passages or reproduce not more than three illustrations in a review to be printed in a magazine or newspaper. Manufactured in the United States of America.*

SECOND PRINTING JANUARY, 1947

But one of the weightiest objections to a plurality in the Executive, and which lies as much against the last as the first plan, is that it tends to conceal faults and destroy responsibility. Responsibility is of two kinds—to censure and to punishment. The first is the most important of the two, especially in an elective office. Man, in public trust, will much oftener act in such a manner as to make him obnoxious to legal punishment. But the multiplication of the Executive adds to the difficulty of detection in either case. It often becomes impossible, amidst mutual accusations, to determine on whom the blame or the punishment of a pernicious measure, or series of pernicious measures, ought really to fall. It is shifted from one to another with so much dexterity, and under such plausible appearances, that the public opinion is left in suspense about the real author. The circumstances which may have led to any national miscarriage of misfortune are sometimes so complicated that, where there are a number of actors who may have had different degrees and kinds of agency, though we may clearly see upon the whole that there has been mismanagement, yet it may be impracticable to pronounce to whose account the evil which may have been incurred is truly chargeable.

"I was overruled by my council. The council were so divided in their opinions that it was impossible to obtain any better resolution on the point." These and similar pretexts are constantly at home, whether true or false. And who is there that will either take the trouble or incur the odium of a strict scrutiny into the secret springs of the transaction? Should there be found a citizen zealous enough to undertake the unpromising task, if there happen to be collusion between the parties concerned, how easy it is to clothe the circumstances with so much ambiguity, as to render it uncertain what was the precise conduct of any of those parties?

THE FEDERALIST (No. 70)—*Alexander Hamilton.*

Cabrini College Library
072259
Radnor, Pa. 19087

072559

FOREWORD

THIS BOOK is intended to give the facts and examine the meaning of Pearl Harbor. The facts have come to the American public in disjointed form, from many sources, and with many interpretations, over a period of four and one-half years.

Pearl Harbor is already a chapter in history. Historians of World War II cannot escape its implications. At this date, so soon after the end of a victorious war, there has been a reluctance to appraise these implications. The mores of a victorious nation dictate that the whole of the war guilt be attached to the defeated adversary. Pearl Harbor, as a study of war origins, is thus a national embarrassment.

For the United States World War II—"the most unpopular war in history," to use the apt descriptive phrase of Lieut. Gen. Hugh A. Drum[1]—officially began December 7, 1941, with the Japanese attack upon Pearl Harbor. The assault which brought America into the war was the greatest naval disaster in American history. It was originally investigated solely as a failure of the commanders of the fleet and garrison at Hawaii. As more and more facts came to light, it became clear that any balanced study of the events of December 7 could not be thus restricted.

Pearl Harbor was the terminal result of a complex of events moving in many parallel courses. National ambition and international intrigue, diplomacy, espionage, politics, personalities, and the personal responses of men to crisis—all of these were of equal or greater importance than purely military considerations. Finally, Pearl Harbor reduced itself to a study of the reasons for which the United States was taken to war, the methods by which it was taken to war, and the motives of those who determined that course.

Of some dozen investigations and studies of Pearl Harbor, most were plainly partisan, undertaken either in defense of President Roosevelt and his administration or of certain members of the civil government or of the Army and Navy high command.

An inquiry by Army intelligence for Mr. Roosevelt was so secret that its existence is known only by hearsay.[2] A second investigation was authorized but never occurred. Col. Charles W. Bundy and Lieut. Col. George W. Ricker of the War Department general staff, who were commissioned to undertake the project, were killed while flying to Hawaii when their plane crashed December 12, 1941, in the Sierra Nevadas near Bishop, California.

Other investigations and studies were conducted by the late Secretary of the Navy Frank Knox, by a Presidential Commission headed by former Associate Justice Owen J. Roberts of the United States Supreme Court, by an Army Board of Inquiry,[3] by a Naval Court of Inquiry,[4] by Adm. Thomas C. Hart,[5] by Adm. H. Kent Hewitt, by Maj. Gen. Myron C. Cramer, Army judge advocate general, by Maj. Henry C. Clausen, by Col. Carter Clarke, and by a Joint Congressional Committee.

Throughout these investigations the administration was in a strategic position, because of its control of Congress and the executive departments, its control of records, its influence on rank and status in the services, its power to initiate investigations, to appoint the investigators and counsel, to define the limits and control the course of the investigations, and, during the war and the continuing period of emergency, to exercise powers of censorship.

The administration has done its utmost to discourage examination of the acts and intentions of the men who were in the vanguard of the march toward war. It has suppressed relevant documents and permitted important papers to "disappear" or be destroyed. It has even sought legislation which, on threat of penal confinement and heavy fines, would have forbidden discussion of the vital intelligence which came into its possession as a result of penetrating the Japanese code.

There could be no guaranty of impartiality and disinterestedness when men who were in the position of defendants were empowered to investigate and to appraise their own conduct and that of their close associates. This generalization is particularly applicable to a political party which is in the process of canonizing a party leader whose name has had a peculiar efficacy in maintaining that party in power.

Mr. Roosevelt was at pains to protect his reputation and political tenure by forestalling any thorough examination and report during his lifetime. When the Army Pearl Harbor Board submitted embarrassing findings six months before his death, his Secretary of War, resorting to the pretext of "national security," used the censorship to suppress the entire report for ten months. When, after both Germany and Japan were defeated, the report was finally released, 52 pages of it were still suppressed. They were made public two and one-half months later, when the hearings of the Joint Congressional Committee provided a convenient diversion to obscure their meaning.

The congressional committee, through the enterprise and resourcefulness of the minority members, made valid contributions to history, but the course of this investigation in itself provides discouraging evidence of the forces which were at work. On September 6, 1945, a concurrent resolution calling for an investigation of the Pearl Harbor disaster was submitted by Alben W. Barkley, the Senate majority leader. The purpose was described in section 2:

> The committee shall make a full and complete investigatio
> of the facts relating to the events and circumstances leading up
> to or following the attack made by Japanese armed forces upon
> Pearl Harbor in the Territory of Hawaii on December 7, 1941,
> and shall report to the Senate and the House of Representatives
> not later than January 3, 1946, the results of its investigation,
> together with such recommendations as it may deem advisable.[6]

The spirit and intentions supposed to animate the inquiry were described by Senator Barkley in his address. He said that reports of previous investigations "are confusing and conflicting, when compared to one another, and to some extent contain contradictions and inconsistencies within themselves." He referred to the "widespread confusion and suspicion" that prevailed "among the American people and among the members of Congress."

Senator Barkley said that the congressional investigation should fix responsibility "upon an individual, or a group of individuals, or upon a system under which they operated or co-operated or failed to do either," and that it should determine what corrective action might tend to prevent a recurrence of the disaster.

The inquiry, Barkley said,

> should be conducted without partisanship or favoritism toward
> any responsible official, military, naval, or civilian, high or low,
> living or dead. . . . Congress itself should make it own thorough,
> impartial, and fearless inquiry into the facts and circumstances
> and conditions prevailing prior to and at the time of the Pearl
> Harbor attack, no matter how far back it may be necessary to

go in order to appraise the situation which existed prior to and at the time of the attack.[7]

The resolution as so interpreted passed the Senate unanimously and was concurred in by the House on September 11. The administration then candidly confessed the partisan nature of the project by allotting six of the ten places on the committee to members of its own party and installing the Senate majority leader as chairman.* The majority established committee rules retaining control in its own hands and foreclosing important areas of inquiry. The effect of executive orders promulgated by President Truman was to deny minority committee-men the right to search government files.

Under these favorable auspices, witnesses with a direct concern in the proceedings were permitted to absent themselves, while those with a similar interest who appeared were emboldened to cover up what they could. In a courtroom many would have been adjudged reluctant if not hostile. The record of the hearings is filled with shabby and transparent evasions, special pleading, changes in sworn testi-mony, and unbelievable lapses of memory.[8] In significant respects it fails to satisfy the general standards of credibility. A minority of wit-nesses displayed not only candor but courage, but there were few who did not have some particular ax to grind, who were not trying to justify their actions or protect someone, or who had not been thor-oughly coached in advance.

Any show of independence in searching out the facts during the investigation provoked vituperative outbursts from New Deal spokes-men and the pushbutton press. There was an evident fear that some-one might pursue the facts to their logical conclusion. A campaign was instituted to intimidate the minority with the argument that if they gave an exact description of the methods and motives of Presi-dent Roosevelt and his administration in following the road to war, they could properly be pilloried as defenders of Hitler and Tojo. The investigators were exposed to the threat that by imputing censure to the nation's wartime leadership, they would be depicted as blaming the United States for starting the war.

This defense was mercilessly exploited by the Roosevelt-Truman administration. It was reduced to the lowest common denominator by Senator James A. Tunnell of Delaware, who implied that any in-

*Democratic members of the committee were: Senator Barkley, chairman; Repre-sentative Jere Cooper, vice-chairman; Senator Walter F. George, Senator Scott W. Lucas, Representative J. Bayard Clark, and Representative John W. Murphy. Republican members were: Senator Homer Ferguson, Senator Owen Brewster, Representative Frank B. Keefe, and Representative Bertrand W. Gearhart.

vestigation of Pearl Harbor must necessarily be partisan and an apol-
ogy for Japan.

"In their desperation," said Mr. Tunnell, "Mr. Roosevelt's oppo-
nents have in effect put on Japanese kimonos and said, 'Honorable
Roosevelt and Honorable Hull teased us into attacking.' "[9]

No one with the courage and capacity to confront facts need be
deterred by such abuse.

The committee reports,[10] submitted July 20, 1946, constituted three
separate statements of opinion. The majority report was signed by all
six Democrats and was adhered to without express qualification by
Representative Gearhart. The minority report was submitted by
Senators Ferguson and Brewster. Representative Keefe, although
signing with the majority, filed a supplementary statement which, in
essential respects, placed him with the minority.[11]

The record of diplomacy which so vitally influenced the Pearl
Harbor tragedy is admittedly incomplete. It is, however, far more
complete than it would be if there had been no investigation.[12] Some
day, when the passions of partisan apologists have cooled, when the
archives are opened and candid statesmen (if such there be) have provided a more adequate account of motives and events, more may be
known of the hidden history of our times. Enough of the truth is
known now so that judgments may be formed and conclusions offered.

With all of the elements at hand, the reader has the ingredients
of a mystery story. There are victims—3,000 of them in the Pearl
Harbor attack. There are a variety of clues. There are a multitude
of false leads. There are numerous possible motives. Innumerable
obstructions are put in the way of the discovery of truth. Many of
the characters betray guilty knowledge.

Only the writer of detective fiction, with full control over his plot
and his characters, can hope to achieve a complete examination of
motive and solve every subsidiary puzzle in the major mystery. The
Pearl Harbor record ends with no signed confessions.

August 23, 1946

ACKNOWLEDGMENTS

PERMISSION HAS been granted to quote from the following books:

How War Came by Forrest Davis and Ernest K. Lindley, by permission of Simon and Schuster, Inc., New York. Copyright, 1942, by Forrest Davis and Ernest K. Lindley.

Ten Years in Japan by Joseph C. Grew, by permission of Simon and Schuster, Inc., New York. Copyright, 1944, by Joseph C. Grew.

They Call It Pacific by Clark Lee, by permission of The Viking Press, Inc., New York. Copyright, 1943, by Clark Lee.

The Armed Forces of the Pacific by Capt. W. D. Puleston, USN, by permission of the Yale University Press, New Haven. Copyright, 1941, by W. D. Puleston.

The Devil's Dictionary by Ambrose Bierce, by permission of Albert and Charles Boni, Inc.

Battle Report: Pearl Harbor to Coral Sea by Commander Walter Karig, USNR, and Lieutenant Welbourn Kelley, USNR, by permission of Rinehart & Company, Inc., New York. Copyright, 1944, by Farrar and Rinehart, Inc.

Memoirs of a Superfluous Man by Albert Jay Nock, by permission of Harper & Brothers, New York. Copyright, 1943, by Albert Jay Nock.

The Case against the Admirals by William Bradford Huie, by permission of E. P. Dutton & Co., Inc., New York. Copyright, 1946, by William Bradford Huie.

Permission has also been obtained to quote from the following article:

"An Adventure in Failure" by E. Stanley Jones, by permission of *Asia and the Americas.* Copyright by Asia Press, Inc. This article appeared as a special supplement to *Asia and the Americas,* Volume XLV, No. 12, December, 1945.

PEARL HARBOR

The author wishes to express his gratitude to Charles A. Beard for a scholarly appraisal of this work; to Mary D. Alexander, who prepared the manuscript for the printer; to Mrs. Adelaide Ohlendorf, who made the index; to Kathleen King, who designed the jacket; to Gary Sheahan, who drew the maps; and to Leon Stolz, who read the manuscript and gave valuable criticism.

TABLE OF CONTENTS

PEARL HARBOR

Chapter One

WAR

At 7:58 A.M. on Sunday, December 7, 1941, a radio warning was broadcast to all ships in Pearl Harbor. "Air raid, Pearl Harbor!" the radio screeched. "This is no drill! This is no drill!" Three minutes before, Japanese warplanes had come in over the great naval base at Oahu, launching their first torpedoes and dropping their first bombs.

Almost at once a second warning was broadcast by the commander-in-chief of the Pacific fleet: "From Cincpac to all ships Hawaii area: Air raid on Pearl Harbor. This is no drill." The Navy radio station at Mare Island Navy Yard, San Francisco, intercepted this message. The country soon knew that it was at war.

For a year and a half a debate had raged the length and breadth of America over going to war or staying out. It was bitterly fought in Congress, in the newspapers, over the radio, in public forums, in private homes, by propagandists, by politicians, and by the plain people—and all the words, if people had but known it, were futile. Long before December 7 the United States was in fact at war. That decision had come at the policy-making level of the government and of the Army and Navy high command, and it had been put into execution without anybody asking a vote from Congress or bothering to let the people in on the secret.

For more than two years there had been war in Europe, and for more than four years war in the Orient, but, so far as the people knew, the United States was not a party to either war. In Europe, Germany and Italy, with their satellites, were at war with Russia, Britain, and the nations of the British commonwealth, supported by a group of paper allies, the governments in exile of Poland, Norway, Belgium, Yugoslavia, Greece, Ethiopia, Holland, and the De Gaullists of France. In the Far East Japan and China had been fighting since July 7, 1937,

3

but neither chose to call it a war. To the Japanese it was "the China Incident." The Chinese didn't have a name for it until two days after the attack on Pearl Harbor, when they finally declared war.

The debate over American intervention was emotional and none too well informed. The totalitarian governments of Germany and Italy, with their scurvy and cutthroat leadership, had nothing to commend them, while the brutal efficiency of the German army terrified the timid. The saber-rattlers of Tokyo were no more ingratiating. The Japanese military, in the course of a long harassment of the inoffensive mass of the Chinese people, had earned the condemnation of civilized men, and, in such outbreaks of mass insanity and violence as accompanied the fall of Nanking, had aroused horror and revulsion.

On the other hand, the forces in opposition were hardly able to pin the sanctions of high-minded morality or abstract justice to their banners. Even the Chinese, who had suffered long and had a legitimate claim upon the sympathy of the outside world, were afflicted with a corrupt, devious, and scheming central administration under the domination of a leader whose methods had frequently been discreditable, exercising his will ineffectively through the one-party Kuomintang government. China was disorganized, shot through with internal dissension, and more an anarchy than an organized state.

The faults of Britain and France were of another order. The French and British Munichmen had been guilty of the betrayal of national self-interest—the cardinal sin in the conduct of statesmen— and were now appealing to America to bail them out. They had sacrificed whatever hope there might have been in collective security by their selfish and cynical policy, accepting the extinction in turn of Austria, Ethiopia, Czechoslovakia, Albania, and the legal Spanish government, and calling these sell-outs "appeasement" and "peace for our time."[1] The judgment of Winston Churchill after Munich was prophetic: "France and Britain had to choose between war and dishonor. They chose dishonor. They will have war."

The Nazi and Fascist slave states were abhorrent to decent people, but it was not easy to forget that the British Empire rested upon the exploitation of hundreds of millions of natives, sweating out their lives in the steaming mines of the Rand at 7 cents a day or in the jungles of New Guinea at less than $5\frac{1}{2}$ cents a day, or subsisting, as 400 million of them did in India, with famine always half a step from the threshold.

Shocking as were Hitler's concentration camps, his calculated campaign against the Jews, and his dictum that the conquered were "sub-human," fit only for slavery or the charnel house, the barbaric government by terror, purge, and enslavement conducted by Stalin over his fellow-Russians was no more exemplary. The two tyrants had had no scruples in striking a bargain on August 23, 1939, when the ten-year "nonaggression" pact signed by them turned the German army loose eight days later upon Poland and western Europe, and permitted Stalin to roll up eastern Poland. Moral distinctions were difficult to perceive between this pair.

For its part, Britain, in guaranteeing to defend the corrupt Polish government of colonels and feudal gentry, had committed itself to a decision which was on a par with all of the other stupidities achieved in London. At any time up to the dismemberment of Czechoslovakia on October 1, 1938, the British and French, if they had been so minded, could have stopped Hitler.[2] When they finally chose Poland as the issue over which to fight a war, they assumed a task which was militarily impossible. They had waited too long and Hitler had grown too strong. Moreover, their commitment was neither complete nor candid.

Britain's guaranty to Poland was first announced in the House of Commons March 31, 1939, by Prime Minister Neville Chamberlain. The Prime Minister stated that consultations were in progress between the two governments, but in the meantime, before their conclusion, "I now have to inform the House that during that period, in the event of action which clearly threatens Polish independence, and which the Polish government accordingly considered it vital to resist with their national forces, his Majesty's government would feel themselves bound at once to lend the Polish government all support in their power." Chamberlain added that the French government had adopted a parallel policy.

On April 6 a communique released by Chamberlain stated that "the two countries were prepared to enter into an agreement of a permanent and reciprocal character to replace the present temporary and unilateral assurance given by his Majesty's government to the Polish government."

"Like the temporary assurance," the communique stated, "the permanent agreement would not be directed against any other country but would be designed to assure Great Britain and Poland of mutual assistance in the event of any threat, direct or indirect, to the independence of either."

On August 25, six days before Germany invaded Poland, the tentative Anglo-Polish arrangement was converted into a formal agreement of mutual assistance, pledging each party to give the other "all the support and assistance in its power" in the event of either "becoming engaged in hostilities with a European power in consequence of aggression by the latter against that contracting party." Eight articles of the treaty were made public. The first seemed to be an unequivocal pledge to fight any aggression. Such was not the fact.

Despite Chamberlain's statement in Parliament and the clear commitment in the published articles that Britain would come to Poland's defense in the event of aggression by any European power, it would later be discovered that strings were attached to the British guaranty, and that Britain had escaped from any commitment to defend Poland against aggression by Russia or to rectify any grabs Russia might subsequently make. It was finally disclosed on April 5, 1945, that the first article of a secret protocol to the Anglo-Polish treaty of mutual assistance provided, "By the expression 'a European power' employed in the agreement is to be understood Germany."[3] This escape clause paved the way for the Yalta and Potsdam deals handing over eastern Poland to Russia, thereby permitting Stalin the fruits of aggression under his deal with Hitler in August, 1939.

As the capstone to this edifice of bad faith, Hitler and Stalin, through the uneasy twenty-two-month existence of their "nonaggression" treaty, dickered for a full military alliance and a four-way partnership dividing up three continents among themselves, the Italians, and the Japanese. All that prevented the consummation of this deal was the cupidity of the tyrants in Berlin and Moscow, whose greed and distrust confirmed the validity of the definition that an alliance is "the union of two thieves who have their hands so deeply inserted in each other's pockets that they cannot separately plunder a third."[4]

The memoirs of Prince Konoye, who committed suicide on December 16, 1945, provide evidence that Russia late in 1940 agreed "in principle" to broaden the tripartite alliance of September 27, 1940, among Germany, Italy, and Japan into a four-power entente. Konoye said that Iran and India were to be Russia's "future sphere of influence" under a secret agreement accompanying the proposed entente. Japan was to receive the South Seas area, Germany would have taken central Africa, and Italy northern Africa.

Konoye stated that Von Ribbentrop, Nazi foreign minister, advanced the plan for a four-power agreement, providing:

> Firstly, the Soviet Union will declare that it agrees with the principle of the tripartite pact in the sense of preventing war and swiftly recovering peace.

Secondly, the Soviet will recognize the leading position of Germany, Italy, and Japan, respectively, in the new order in Europe and Asia, and the three nations will pledge respect of Soviet territory.

Thirdly, the three nations and the Soviet Union pledge not to assist any nation being the enemy of the other, nor to join such a group of nations.

The Japanese government promptly approved the plan, which was handed to Foreign Commissar Molotov of Russia during his Berlin visit in November, 1940. Then Tokyo heard nothing further until March, 1941, when the Japanese foreign minister, Yosuke Matsuoka, visited Berlin. Matsuoka was told that Molotov had agreed in principle, but proposed "exchange conditions of over 30 articles which Germany could in no way recognize." By then, Matsuoka told Konoye, German officials were openly talking about the inevitability of a Nazi-Soviet war.[5]

Additional light on this cynical deal was supplied through captured German documents, now in the possession of the American government, tracing Molotov's conversations with Ribbentrop. These documents disclosed that Russia's appetite for more and yet more of the earth's surface was all that prevented the formation of a Berlin-Moscow-Tokyo-Rome plunderbund.[6]

These intrigues are sufficient to demonstrate that there was not a major power involved in the mess in Europe or Asia that could come to the United States with clean hands, or represent itself as either a democracy or an exemplar of justice. The knowledge of all of this chicanery was, of course, withheld from the American people until after the war, and the debate on the question of intervention versus nonintervention was thus not illuminated by any perceptible degree of understanding or truth.

The American people, who thought that the issue of whether it was to be peace or whether it had to be war was still subject to democratic debate, did not know in the closing months of 1941 that the decision had long since passed them by. They did not know that already a state of war existed by executive action. Not for four years would they hear the admission from President Roosevelt's chief of naval operations that by October, 1941, the American Navy was "in effect, at war" in the Atlantic,[7] and that this shooting war against Germany and Italy constituted a direct invitation to Japan to attack the United States under the tripartite pact.[8]

On December 7, 1941, the policy-makers and war-makers in Washington were confidently awaiting the hour when their undeclared war would be regularized by the logic of events. On that same December 7, the people were still hoping that the peace which had already been lost could be preserved.

The previous day Pope Pius had said that the world needed faith more than great statesmen. In one American city there was a Christmas expression of such faith: a great "star of peace" emblazoned in lights 132 feet wide and 150 feet high on the side of a skyscraper office building. Even Lord Halifax, the British ambassador, had a kind word for peace as he busied himself talking up war. Lasting peace, he said, was foreshadowed "explicitly and implicitly" in the Atlantic Charter;[9] but he implied that to catch up with the shadow Americans would first have to fight; otherwise the professed objectives of the charter could not be realized.

The war, so far, had made little impact upon civilian life in America. The national debt, after eight and one-half years of the New Deal, stood at 55 billion dollars. There were fifteen shopping days until Christmas and the display advertisements told of peace-time abundance. No one yet had imposed rationing, although some of the more vocal proponents of war in and out of the administration were impatient that consumer's goods were still available, when, so these gentlemen thought, the nation's entire production should be devoted to rearmament and lend-lease for Britain and Russia. Secretary of Commerce Wallace was later to pay his peculiar tribute to American industry and management, which outproduced all other belligerents combined, friends and foes alike, by saying that plant managers were "sheer Fascists" and that it had been necessary "to take industry by the scruff of the neck" to get it into war.

If war crept into the advertisements, it was only in the form of fifty-piece soldier sets offered as a Christmas gift for the children: twenty-four soldiers, one cannon, twelve shells, a popgun, and twelve corks—all for $1.

There was another kind of advertisement. The United States Army Recruiting Service was calling for volunteers. The appeal said:

> Throughout the regular Army, there are thrilling jobs to be mastered—jobs that provide splendid technical training, combined with adventure, useful service to your country, and the opportunity to provide for a successful future career. More than a third of all enlisted men volunteer because of the recommendations of their friends in the Army. Most of them re-enlist after their first three years.

The actual war still seemed far away to those who read the morning newspapers of December 7, telling of a million and a half German troops, eight thousand tanks, and one thousand guns massed before Moscow. Hitler was talking as if the fall of the Soviet capital was a matter of a few days, if not of hours, and no one—least of all the Japanese whom he had been at pains to impress—knew that his armies had already been beaten by the terrible Russian winter and were even then preparing to retreat.

What hints there were that America would soon be committed to the slaughter were oblique. The people knew that relations with Japan had been deteriorating, but knew nothing of the course of the seemingly interminable diplomatic negotiations in Washington between Secretary of State Cordell Hull and the Japanese emissaries, Adm. Kichisaburo Nomura and Saburo Kurusu. Washington encouraged the notion that as long as the negotiations continued, there was still a substantial hope of achieving a settlement and keeping the peace. Not a word was let drop that the negotiations had come to an end and that war was inevitable, though the leaders of our government were fully aware of these facts.

True, Mr. Hull's pronouncements were not encouraging, and President Roosevelt's latest contribution—a personal appeal cabled December 6 directly to Emperor Hirohito—seemed, even for Mr. Roosevelt, a little frantic and somewhat excessively flamboyant. On Saturday Mr. Hull had acknowledged that relations with Japan were grave. He had called the President's attention to the presence of an estimated 125,000 Japanese troops in French Indo-China, which Japan had effectively taken over after the fall of France, and manifested disquiet because 18,000 of them were loaded aboard troopships in Camranh Bay. That suggested that they were going somewhere, and the only places to which they could go were the property of nations other than Japan.

Mr. Roosevelt, in an ill-advised moment in April, 1939, had addressed a personal message to Hitler asking him to pledge respect for the territorial integrity of thirty of Germany's neighbors in Europe and the Near East,[10] only to be rewarded with a sarcastic response. Hitler pointed out that although there were interlopers in many lands, they were not Germans, and that although many peoples were oppressed, their complaints were directed, not against Germany, but against nations which were prone to parade their virtue, among them the United States.[11]

Despite the dubious success of this venture in personal diplomacy, Roosevelt in his message to Hirohito followed virtually the same for-

mula, and laid himself open to much the same retort he had received
from Hitler. Hirohito's advisers, however, did not see fit to present
Roosevelt's message to the Emperor until twenty minutes before the
first bombs dropped at Pearl Harbor.[12] If Hirohito thought anything
of Roosevelt's message, which in itself is doubtful, he probably reflected that the President didn't have much understanding of protocol, for not even presidents communicate with gods.

The State Department on the morning of December 7 did not disclose the nature of the note that Roosevelt had dispatched, but later
it would become known that the message had appealed for Hirohito's
aid in "dispelling the dark clouds" of a possible Japanese invasion of
Malaya, Thailand, the Dutch East Indies, and the Philippines. The
Japanese might have conceded Roosevelt's right to discuss the Philippines, which were under the protection of the American flag, but
when the President also projected himself as the defender of British
and Dutch imperialism, he merely confirmed the Japs in a belief they
had entertained all along: that the United States would go to war to
preserve the white empires. Inasmuch as the time would never be
more propitious than the present, the new government of Gen. Hideki
Tojo had determined, in the general's own phrase, to answer Roosevelt "by quick action, not words."[13]

Mr. Roosevelt knew this quite as well as Gen. Tojo and the other
sword-rattlers in Tokyo. His appeal to Hirohito so late in the day
was dispatched with an eye toward the justification of history, although originally the President had had another purpose in mind. A
few weeks earlier Roosevelt might easily have succeeded in avoiding
embroilment in a war with Japan, but by December both Tojo and he
were equally intent that there should be no turning back.

By the final month of 1941 the western proprietors of colonial empires in East Asia and the Southwest Pacific were in no position to
safeguard their title. Japan had found how easy the pickings were
when, after the fall of France, Japanese forces had seized the defenseless French holding of Indo-China. Holland, occupied by Germany,
was impotent to defend the Netherlands East Indies, while the British had been driven off the European continent and were on the defensive in their home island and engaged in an inconclusive see-saw
war in North Africa. Britain could exact no great price from any
invader which went after its colonies in Southeast Asia and the Pacific.

This, so it must have seemed to the Japanese militarists, was the
opportunity of a lifetime. More than avarice prompted a program

of conquest. The Japanese military machine was bogged down in China in a war now well into its fifth year. With the military needing vast amounts of war material in order to continue functioning, the United States had cut off critical supplies by embargoing the export to Japan of oil and steel.* It had then frozen Japanese credits,† threatening Japan with economic strangulation. Hull, although even his countrymen did not know it, had set a stiff price if Japan was to restore itself to the good graces of the United States. He demanded nothing less than that Japan evacuate Indo-China, get out of China, repudiate its alliance with Germany and Italy, and accept equality and no more in the trade of the Far East.‡

Such terms confronted Japan with a dilemma. All that had been gained in four and one-half years of struggle in China would be lost if Japan gave in. The Japanese war lords could look upon lands not far removed which were possessed by the absentee white proprietor and see all of the oil, rubber, tin, and other materials which were so highly prized by a Japan which was denied them. The Japanese people, bound in uncomplaining bondage to the military, could follow that same glance and see rice and opportunity denied them in the home-land.

In the last estimate, Japan was confronted with the option of strik-ing out for a rich new empire or abandoning its conquests and resign-ing itself to the future of a third-rate nation. It made the natural if mistaken choice. Adm. Nomura and other intelligent Japanese knew that the choice meant the ruin of Japan; yet, there certainly seemed a chance of success in December, 1941, and a chance, which, very likely, would never again be so favorable. Nomura's estimate proved correct. Japan now is not a third-rate nation. It is, by the description of a perspicacious general of B-29's, a fortieth-rate nation—a Bulgaria or less.

The Japanese had hoped that the tripartite pact would serve to warn the United States off the "Greater East Asia Co-Prosperity Sphere" which Japan had staked out for itself. This alliance pledged Germany and Italy to respect Japan's position of leadership in the "new order" in East Asia, while Japan respected the ascendancy of Rome and Berlin in Europe. More important, it specified that if any of the partners was attacked by a nation not then involved in their respective wars, the other two should render all possible military, eco-nomic, and political assistance. Inasmuch as Russia had been specifi-

*Cf. pp. 99, 132-36.
†Cf. pp. 99, 132.
‡Cf. p. 160.

cally excepted when the pact was executed, and the United States was the only remaining powerful nation in the world, the alliance obviously was intended to caution this country against interfering either in Europe or the Pacific.

The purpose had failed, but at the time of the Pearl Harbor attack the tripartite pact still offered considerable insurance to Japan, especially in view of Roosevelt's preoccupation with the task of defeating Hitler and saving the British. The Japanese military government knew that if it had to fight the United States, it would fight with the support of a still powerful Germany, which could be expected to engage a substantial proportion of the American Army, Navy, and Air Force in a theater far distant from the Pacific.

Furthermore, the Japanese militarists determined that, if they must fight America, they should seize every possible initial advantage, especially that of surprise. They had a precedent for their strategy. In 1904 Japan had broken off relations with Russia on February 5, but war was not declared until February 10. Not even waiting for the declaration, Adm. Togo sent his torpedo boats into Port Arthur the night of February 8-9 and caught the Russian fleet by surprise in harbor.

The Russians had played into Japan's hands by splitting their fleet, and then splitting it again. Russia had a powerful fleet in the Baltic, in addition to its Far Eastern fleet. If the two could unite, they would decidedly outnumber the Japanese fleet, but the union was never permitted to take place. Russia had further divided its Far Eastern fleet. Four of its first-class cruisers were at Vladivostok, a fifth at Chemulpo, and the remaining four at Port Arthur, so that the Russian Port Arthur fleet under Vice-Adm. Starck was in no way equal to the fleet under Togo, which promptly put Port Arthur under blockade.

In 1941 the Jap high command could not but notice a striking parallel to this situation when it contemplated the American fleet dispositions. Roosevelt and the high command not only had split the fleet between the Pacific and the Atlantic, but had split the Pacific fleet further into an Asiatic fleet based upon Cavite, in the Philippines, and the main fleet body based upon Pearl Harbor. In the week preceding the December 7 attack, the Pearl Harbor fleet was split again when the only two carriers in Hawaii, with six heavy cruisers and fourteen destroyers, were sent to ferry a few Marine Corps planes and crews to Wake and Midway Islands, a mission which could easily have been performed by freighters.

In addition, a third task force, consisting of one heavy cruiser and

five destroyer minesweepers, was off Johnston Island, 700 miles southwest of Oahu, while one heavy cruiser and four destroyer minesweepers were 25 miles south of Oahu. Meanwhile, the battleship
strength of the Pacific fleet was bottled up in Pearl Harbor. All that
had changed in the thirty-seven years since the Port Arthur incident
was that the airplane had replaced the torpedo boat as the instrument
of attack.

In the event of war, it was a foregone conclusion that the Japanese
would seek out the American adversary for surprise attack at whatever
place American fleet strength was concentrated.[14] Pearl Harbor was
the only possible objective because that was where the fleet was. The
Japanese objective was simple. By attacking the fleet wherever it was
to be found, Japan would destroy the ships of greatest range and fire
power and thus prevent interference with its advance in Asia and the
Western Pacific.

With the exception of the British battleship "Prince of Wales" and
the battle cruiser "Repulse," which arrived at Singapore only a week
before Japanese planes were to seek them out and sink them as they
steamed without air cover in the East China Sea, the only element
that could possibly interfere with Japan's program of conquest was
the American fleet. Once it was immobilized, the Jap fleet and army
could move at will on their mission of capturing American possessions
and imperial colonies.

These strategic considerations alone were sufficient to have demonstrated to Roosevelt and the high command that war against the United
States would be inaugurated by a Japanese surprise attack at Pearl
Harbor and no place else. For years afterward the story was carefully
cultivated that the Japanese attack was a treacherous surprise, launched
when there was no remotest reason for expecting it, and therefore a
great shock to the leaders of government. The excuse has been made
that Japan's success in attaining surprise was the result of striking at
a time when the administration was engaged in peaceful negotiation
and war was remote from its thoughts. And even if the administration
had known that war was coming, the apologists say, it could not have
known at what time or what place.

Nothing was then known of the interception by American intelligence of Jap secret messages which, decoded, pointed unmistakably
to attack at Pearl Harbor December 7. Four years later it would become known that the Jap secret code had been cracked many months
before Pearl Harbor, and that the men in Washington who read the
code intercepts had almost as good a knowledge of Japanese plans

and intentions as if they had been occupying seats in the war councils of Tokyo.*

But in the last month of 1941 the American people knew nothing of this. If war was close—indeed, was here—the people were ignorant of it. They had not read the intercepts, tracing the gradual deterioration of relations with Japan. They did not know of warnings sent out by Tokyo to its diplomatic corps that after November 29 "things were automatically going to happen,"† of statements that by the beginning of December negotiations in Washington would be "de facto ruptured,"‡ of instructions to destroy code machines and burn ciphers in the Japanese embassy in Washington,§ of Japanese confidences to Hitler at the end of November that a Japanese war with the United States might come "quicker than any one dreams."‖ They had never heard then of "east wind rain."¶ They knew nothing of last-minute instructions to the Japanese emissaries to hand in their reply to Hull at 1:00 P.M., Washington time, on December 7.**

Roosevelt, the inner circle of the war cabinet, and the Army and Navy high command knew all of this and more, but the stage had been set that December Sunday to convey the impression that no one was more surprised than the President himself. That day Roosevelt and Harry Hopkins, with whom he shared state secrets, were in the oval study on the second floor of the White House. The scene has been described by Forrest Davis and Ernest K. Lindley.[15] Their account runs:

> Mr. Roosevelt had dedicated this day to rest. Today, tieless and in shirtsleeves, he hoped to catch up with his neglected stamp collection. The President might have been any one of a million Americans putting in a loafing Sunday with a crony and a hobby. Mr. Roosevelt expected war—but not this weekend.

That was the scene. That is the frame of mind which it was desired that the American people would remember. The President himself vouched for the fact that this was his attitude and these his thoughts.

All of the telephone lines through to Roosevelt had been shut off. A "do not disturb" order had been placed with the switchboard. "Mr. Roosevelt was topping his dinner with an apple," his personal chroni-

*Cf. p. 390 [Note 7].   §Cf. pp. 192-94, 197.
†Cf. p. 184.   ‖Cf. p. 190.
‡Cf. p. 188.   ¶Cf. pp. 183, 198-222.
        **Cf. pp. 196-97, 275-76, p. 400 [Note 56].

clers report, "when his desk telephone jangled disobediently." It was Secretary of the Navy Knox who had insisted on disturbing his tranquillity.

In his annual report, published that morning, Knox had been reassuring. He said:

> I am proud to report that the American people may feel fully confident in their Navy. In my opinion, the loyalty, morale, and technical ability of the personnel are without superior. On any comparable basis, the American Navy is second to none.
>
> The international situation is such that we must arm as rapidly as possible to meet our naval defense requirements—simultaneously in both oceans—against any possible combinations concerting action against us. Our aim always must be to have forces sufficient to enable us to have complete freedom of action in either ocean while retaining forces in the other ocean for effective defense of our vital security.[16]

At Oahu the Japs were revising Secretary Knox's report, and now the crestfallen secretary was obliged to call Roosevelt and make some emendations.

"Mr. President," Knox began, "it looks like the Japanese have attacked Pearl Harbor. . . ."

"No!" Roosevelt is supposed to have cried.[17] The reaction would suggest that he was surprised.

Chapter Two

MOUNT NIITAKA

THE NIGHT of December 5, 1941, the Japanese naval radio sent the code message, "Climb Mount Niitaka." That message meant war.[1] To the 1st Japanese air fleet, 800 miles north of Oahu in the Hawaiian Islands, it meant that there was no turning back. To Vice-Adm. Chuichi Nagumo, the fleet commander, it conveyed the order to attack Pearl Harbor with his carrier planes at dawn the second day following. Adm. Nagumo put on full steam, and all that night, all the next day, and all the second night his powerful task force forged southward at forced draft.

At 6:00 A.M. December 7, the Japanese striking force, then 200 miles north of Oahu, began launching its planes from six carriers—the "Kaga," "Akagi," "Hiryu," "Soryu," "Shokaku," and "Zuikaku." The planes, 351 in all,[2] took off in three waves. All had cleared the flight decks by 7:15. They rendezvoused to the south and then flew in for co-ordinated attacks on Pearl Harbor and the Hawaiian air fields.

The 1st air fleet had left Hitokappu Bay, Etorofu Island, in the southernmost part of the Kuriles, at 9:00 A.M., November 26, Japan time—1:30 P.M., November 25, Hawaii time. The striking force, commanded by Adm. Nagumo, consisted of twenty-seven warships: the six carriers, two battleships, the "Hiei" and "Kirishima"; two heavy cruisers, the "Tone" and "Chikuma"; one light cruiser, the "Abukuma," and sixteen destroyers. Eleven vessels were in the supply train.

The Japanese 6th fleet, under command of Vice-Adm. Mitsumi Shimizu, formed an advance expeditionary force. His fleet consisted of two light cruisers, the "Isuzu" and "Yura"; one training light cruiser, the "Katori," twenty submarines, five midget submarines of 45 tons, with a range of only 200 miles, and six vessels of the fleet train.

The plan of attack had originally been proposed early in January, 1941, by Adm. Isoroku Yamamoto, commander-in-chief of the combined imperial fleets. Rear Adm. Takijiro Onishi, chief of staff of the 11th air fleet, had been ordered by Yamamoto at that time to study the requirements of such an operation. It is not to be supposed from these facts that Japan even then was committed to war with the United States. The United States, as is now known, had also prepared war plans which were to be executed upon the decision to go to war, and at one stage, by the statement of former Secretary of War Stimson, even meditated a "sneak attack" such as the Japanese carried out at Pearl Harbor.*

The basic Japanese plan for an attack upon Pearl Harbor had been evolving ever since 1931. Its theoretical possibilities had been explored by all graduates of the Japanese naval academy, who, each year were asked on the final examination: "How would you carry out a surprise attack on Pearl Harbor?"[3] Ironically, however, it was the United States Naval Planning Board which helped the Japs perfect the plan.

In 1932 an American battle force assembled in the Pacific to test Pearl Harbor's defenses. One section of it was to attack, while the other, with coast artillery, a division of troops, one hundred planes, and a number of submarines, was to defend the naval base. The attacking force, commanded by Adm. Harry E. Yarnell, an air-minded officer who had made many flights with his squadrons—unusual in the Navy of that day—revolutionized naval strategy by leaving behind all his battleships and cruisers and using only two aircraft carriers, the "Lexington" and "Saratoga," and four destroyers. This was the first appearance of a new naval grouping, afterward to be known as a task force.

When twenty-four hours off Oahu the attacking force encountered heavy weather. This, from Adm. Yarnell's viewpoint, was all to the good, for the weather conditions made it less probable that the shore defenders, on the lookout for a great invasion fleet, would spot so small a flotilla.

By the evening of February 6, a Saturday, Adm. Yarnell's force was in a position to reach Oahu by dawn. Yarnell surmised that if he attacked early on Sunday morning the defenders would be less alert than usual. Thirty minutes before dawn on February 7, when the carriers had approached within 60 miles of Oahu after a forced run all night, they launched 152 aircraft—bombers, fighters, dive bombers, and torpedo planes.

*Cf. pp. 294-96.

Adm. Yarnell's planes, coming in from the northeast, exactly as the Japs were to do nine years later, were undetected until they darted out of the clouds into clear weather over Pearl Harbor. Simulated machine gun fire theoretically destroyed all defending planes on the ground. Not one got into the air during the attack. All of the hypothetical vessels in the harbor were "sunk."

Japanese observers watched the maneuver and forwarded full details to Tokyo. It was evident that Yarnell's maneuver had upset all existing naval concepts. Some American officers who participated later in the critiques when the lessons of the operation were evaluated argued that the Navy should be reorganized so that the striking force of the fleet should be built around its air arm, and the battleship and other surface craft relegated to the subordinate mission of protecting the air striking force and its carriers. As might be expected, the battleship admirals opposed, and, inasmuch as they held the positions of power in the naval hierarchy, they won. It was left for Japan to adopt Yarnell's brilliant concept.[4]

In late August, 1941, Adm. Yamamoto ordered all fleet commanders and key staff members to Tokyo for war games, preliminary to a final formulation of plans for a Pacific campaign which comprehended a surprise attack on Pearl Harbor in the event of war. Between September 1 and 12, the outline of a basic plan of operations was drafted at the naval war college in Tokyo.

As early as October 5 part of the attack plan was revealed to officer pilots of the task force who had been called together aboard the carrier "Akagi" in Shikishi Bay. About one hundred pilots who were present were told of the design to strike the American fleet at Pearl Harbor. Adm. Yamamoto informed them that "although Japan never wanted to fight the United States, the Japanese were forced to do so or they would be defeated regardless." American aid to China and the American embargo on oil shipments to Japan, the admiral said, were seriously affecting the progress of the imperial arms in the China war.

Yamamoto predicted to the pilots that the United States fleet would take two or three years to recover from the intended attack and that meanwhile Japan would occupy Sumatra, Java, and other territories from which critically needed materials could be extracted. The admiral described the American fleet as Japan's "greatest enemy."

Premier Prince Konoye's cabinet failed, so it was announced, to "agree on national policy," and, upon Konoye's resignation October 16, War Minister Tojo received the imperial command to form a new cabinet. The war party was now fully in control, and, although there was still a prospect of settling American differences with Japan, Tojo was taking no chances. On October 17, without even waiting to form his cabinet, he issued orders for the first and second squadrons of the 6th fleet's submarines to put to sea. This force represented some fourteen of the submarines which were to be a part of Adm. Shimizu's advance expeditionary force in the Pearl Harbor operation. That night they left Kure under cover of darkness and advanced to Kwajalein, in the Marshall Islands, where they found the cruiser "Katori." Fearing discovery, the flotillas dispersed temporarily to nearby Wotje and Maloelap, in the Marshalls.

On November 4 combined fleet top secret operation order No. 1 was promulgated to all fleet and task force commanders. It provided for subsequent designation of Y-day as the approximate date for the attack on Pearl Harbor, and of X-day as the actual date for execution. Operation order No. 2, issued by Yamamoto November 6, set Y-day as Dec. 7, Hawaii time.

On November 13 Yamamoto ordered the Pearl Harbor attacking force to assemble in Hitokappu Bay and remain there until November 22 taking on supplies. On November 21 Adm. Osami Nagano, chief of the naval general staff, instructed Yamamoto that fleet units in Hitokappu Bay might use force if they encountered any interference from British, Dutch, or American forces, but later the same day he amended the order in certain significant respects.

Nagano's revised order read:

> If American-Japanese negotiations are successful, forces will be ordered back immediately. Use of force mentioned above will be limited to three cases: if American, Dutch, or British surface forces appear in Japanese waters for reconnaissance, if same forces approach Japanese sea waters and jeopardize our forces, if aggressive action is taken by same forces outside Japanese territorial waters.

This was still far from reflecting an assumption that war was bound to ensue. It indicated that Japan was hopeful that some diplomatic compromise would enable a showdown to be avoided. By then, however, the hands of the clock of diplomacy were approaching midnight.

On November 24 the order was issued by Yamamoto to the striking force to leave Hitokappu Bay the following day and proceed in secret to Hawaiian waters. The order read:

(A) The task force, keeping its movements strictly secret and maintaining close guard against submarines and aircraft, shall advance into Hawaiian waters and, upon the very opening of hostilities, shall attack the main force of the United States fleet in Hawaii and deal it a mortal blow. The first air raid is planned for dawn of X-day (exact date to be given by later order).

Upon completion of the air raid the task force, keeping close co-ordination and guarding against enemy counter-attack, shall speedily leave the enemy waters and then return to Japan.

(B) Should it appear certain that Japanese-American negotiations will reach an amicable settlement prior to the commencement of hostile action, all the forces of the combined fleet are to be ordered to reassemble and return to their bases.

(C) The task force shall leave Hitokappu Bay on the morn- of 26 November (Japan time; 25 November, Hawaii time) and advance to 42 degrees N. and 170 degrees E. (standing-by position) on the afternoon of 4 December (Japan time; 3 December, Hawaii time), and speedily complete refueling.

The task force stood out to sea on November 25 and cruised eastward at 13 knots, held down by the low speed of the supply vessels. Lookouts were posted, but no searches or combat air patrols were flown. It had been calculated that North Pacific weather would cause difficulty in refueling at sea; so those ships whose capacity was small were loaded with oil in drums for emergency use. The weather, however, proved calm, and fueling from the tankers was carried out as planned.

The progress of the striking force was skilfully covered by a barrage of false warship call signs, padding of radio circuits, and similar deceptive tactics to simulate the presence of the principal carriers and carrier air groups in the Inland Sea. So successful was this program that in his intelligence roundup for December 1 Vice-Adm. Theodore S. Wilkinson, chief of naval intelligence, said of Japanese fleet dispositions, "Major capital ship strength remains in home waters, as well as the greatest portion of the carriers." This estimate could not have been more misleading to the fleet and Army commanders in Hawaii.

In order further to allay American suspicions, Premier Gen. Tojo announced that the Asama Maru would be sent to repatriate Jap residents in Malaya and British Borneo, and that the Tatsuta Maru would touch at Mexico to bring Japanese nationals back from the United States. The captain of the "Tatsuta Maru" had orders to take an eastward course in North Pacific waters, and, on reaching 180 degrees longitude, to turn southward. On the morning of the attack at Oahu his ship was back off Chosi, Japan.

Meanwhile, Japanese spies in Hawaii were busy feeding back reports to Tokyo on the movements and disposition of the American fleet. Although American intelligence was intercepting Tokyo's instructions to the spies, together with the responses of these agents, the intelligence chiefs of our Army and Navy later professed to see nothing alarming in Japan's preoccupation with the berthing of the Pacific fleet.*

Twice after its departure from Hitokappu Bay the Jap striking force received code messages from Tokyo giving dispositions of the fleet in Pearl Harbor. The second of these was received three days before the attack. In addition, an officer aboard the "Akagi" was detailed to listen to Honolulu broadcasts and decode them for last-minute information on fleet movements in and out of Pearl Harbor. A broadcast that "the German attaché has lost one dog" would mean that a carrier had left the harbor. If the attaché wanted a cook or a house boy, that would mean that a battleship or a cruiser had entered.

The war council in Tokyo had recognized December 7 as suitable for attack. Tuesday, December 9, was also considered suitable for a dawn attack, because it would then be the dark of the moon. It was expected, however, that the Pacific fleet, in accordance with its custom during maneuvers, would enter the harbor on Friday and leave on Monday. Adm. Yarnell's plan, moreover, had demonstrated that conditions on a Sunday were propitious for attack. Therefore, Sunday was chosen. Another consideration favoring an attack on Sunday around 8:00 A.M., was, in the view of Adm. Nagano, that "American officers were inclined to sleep late on Sunday morning."[5]

On December 1 an imperial naval order fixed X-day, stating that "hostile action against the United States shall be commenced on 7 December." This order thereby confirmed the date originally fixed in the Y-day order of November 6. On December 2, however, Nagano again inquired if the fleet could be recalled in the event of a belated settlement being reached in the Washington negotiations. He was assured by Yamamoto that it could.[6] That same day Adm. Yamamoto fixed "Tora" as the code word by which the attacking fleet would signal a successful outcome.

Upon receipt of the order setting December 7 as X-day, all ships in the Japanese striking force were darkened and condition 2 (second

*Cf. p. 262.

degree of readiness, gun crews stationed) was ordered. On December 4 the rendezvous point about 2,350 miles east of Tokyo and 1,460 miles northwest of Pearl Harbor was reached. The combat ships of the fleet fueled to capacity from the tankers, which were dropped that night.

The task force then turned southeast at increased speed. The carriers "Hiryu" and "Soryu," whose fuel capacity was small, had been oiled daily while in company of the tankers and now had to be fueled by bucket brigade from the oil drums taken on board. The cruise from the beginning had been uneventful. The route lay beyond the patrol sweeps of any American land-based planes. The Great Circle route through the vast and lonely North Pacific, between Midway and the Aleutians, was far from the commercial ship lanes and well out of waters which American patrol ships might be expected to prowl. No ships or planes had been sighted and no false alarms had been sounded.

Although the progress of the task force was unexpectedly smooth, the Japs were fearful of failure almost to the last. According to an official United States Navy account, the striking force, if detected before X minus 2 day, was to withdraw without executing the attack. In the event of being discovered on X minus 1 day, the question of whether to make an attack or to return would have been decided in accordance with local conditions and at Adm. Nagumo's discretion.

If contact had been made at sea with the main body of the United States fleet, the Jap operational plan called for a reserve group of heavy naval units to sortie from the Inland Sea of Japan to support the carrier striking force in a decisive engagement. The Japanese assumed that, with 180 or more combat vessels in the Pacific as against 102 warships in the United States Pacific fleet, their numerical superiority would be sufficient to bring them victory.

While the pilot and officer personnel of Adm. Nagumo's fleet knew the objective was Pearl Harbor, the crews of the six carriers thought until the day before the assault that they were on a training cruise. When the men noticed that the bows were heading east, according to the account of Capt. Mitsue Fuchida, commander of the flight groups aboard the carriers, they began to wonder and speculate. On December 3 the fleet personnel learned that Japan might enter the war and "the men became kind of excited," but they "calmed down when given the order to attack."[7]

On the night of December 5 the task force received the "Mount Niitaka" code signal. The run-in toward Hawaii the night of December 6-7 was made at top speed, 26 knots. At 5:00 A.M. two Zero reconnaissance planes were launched to survey Pearl Harbor and Lahaina anchorage. They reached their destination an hour before the arrival of the attack planes from the Japanese carriers, reported that the "fleet was in," and completed their mission without having been detected.

On the night before the attack the twenty large submarines of Adm. Shimizu's advance expeditionary force had reached the waters in the vicinity of Pearl Harbor under orders not to attack until the carrier planes had made their assault. The five midget submarines were launched from specially fitted fleet submarines between 50 and 100 miles off Pearl Harbor as a "special attacking force." Their task was to prevent the escape of the American fleet through the harbor entrance during the air raid, but two actually entered Pearl Harbor before the attack. One of these made an extensive reconnaissance and probably reported back to the fleet by radio.

Planes were launched from the large submarines after the attack to survey the extent of the damage. The operation plan provided that if the American fleet was virtually destroyed, one Japanese submarine division or less would be placed between Hawaii and the west coast of the United States to destroy sea traffic. In fact, at least one submarine was dispatched to the Oregon coast about December 14.

Weather was taken into consideration. Most of the winter the trade wind in Hawaii blows steadily from the northeast against the 2,800-foot Koolau Range, where it discharges its moisture. An air force which escapes being picked up by detection apparatus can approach hidden in the towering wall of rain clouds and then emerge suddenly into clear weather over Pearl Harbor before defending planes can rise to intercept. Adm. Yarnell's attacking force in 1932 had taken advantage of these conditions, and the Japs also counted on this cover.

The weather at Pearl Harbor on December 7 was officially logged by the Navy as: "Averaging partly cloudy, with clouds mostly over the mountains. Cloud base at 3,500 feet, visibility good. Wind north, 10 knots." These conditions favored a surprise attack. The planes bearing the Rising Sun were screened by the cumulus banks over the mountains until the aircraft were ready to split up and make predetermined approaches on their targets.

The Japanese had expected to lose 33 per cent of all participating units. Specifically, they thought they would lose at least one "Akagi" class carrier and one "Soryu" class carrier. They also expected to lose all of the midget submarines, whose "personnel had been prepared for death," and were correct in this estimate.[8] No attempt was made preliminary to the attack to reckon probable losses in planes, but losses were far less than even the most optimistic estimate could have suggested. Only twenty-seven aircraft failed to return to the carriers.

At no time was a landing in Hawaii contemplated. The Japanese high command believed that a landing operation would involve insuperable problems in logistics. Troop transports and cargo vessels carrying the huge volume of supplies necessary to sustain an expeditionary force would have required a great convoy, while the progress of the striking force would have been held to the pace of the slowest vessel. If speed were sacrificed, it was thought unlikely that surprise could be achieved.

The Japanese thought it impossible to follow up the air raid with a landing in less than a month. They apparently had underestimated the damage they would inflict and did not know how ill prepared Hawaii was to resist a landing in strength following closely upon an attack. After the surrender of Japan, Capt. Ryonosuke Imamura, secretary of the naval ministry, said, "We had expected a much greater defense at so important a base. We were amazed. Our fleet was told to bomb and leave. We had no troops with which to make a landing. If we had, perhaps we could have taken Hawaii, but we had no plan to do so."[9]

On the first anniversary of the attack, Secretary Knox asserted that the Japanese could have returned and taken Hawaii.[10] The statement must be regarded with a certain skepticism, inasmuch as Knox advanced it in justification of the concealment of American losses for a full year. Maj. Gen. Walter C. Short, commander of Army forces in Hawaii in 1941, estimated five years afterward that Japan would have required a force of 200,000 men to have taken Hawaii, and thought that, even so, the operation could have been successfully brought off only if the American fleet were not present to help defend the island.[11]

The Pearl Harbor attack was executed by Japan for the purpose of immobilizing the American fleet while the Japs expanded southward, and his fleet, in the opinion of Adm. Nagano, achieved "far greater success" on this mission than had been expected.[12] Gen. George C. Marshall, wartime chief of staff, later testified,

> If the attack had been repulsed successfully, the Japanese would have had to proceed more conservatively. Instead of striking south (to Malaya and the Dutch Indies) without protecting their lines of communication from flank attacks, they would not have dared to proceed as they did—a major part of

the United States fleet would still have been in effective condition.[13]

There were other and graver mistakes in Japanese strategy than failure to attempt to seize Hawaii. One was in the selection of the very targets at Pearl Harbor. The Japs went after our battleships. In order to carry out that attack without hindrance, they also went after the planes parked on the Hawaii airdromes. Planes are easily replaced, especially types which are obsolete or obsolescent, as most of those at Pearl Harbor were. The battleships which were knocked out were so old as to be of slight value. The records show that during the entire course of the Pacific war battleships fired at other surface craft on only four occasions.[14]

After the war Rear Adm. Husband E. Kimmel, who was in command of the Pacific fleet on December 7, said that proper Japanese strategy would have knocked the fleet out of action for a long time even if there had been no ships in harbor that day to attack. He said:

> Even if they had not sunk a ship, the Japs might have crippled the base and destroyed all the fleet's fuel supplies, which were in the open. The result might have been worse than it actually was, because this would have forced the fleet to return to the West Coast. As it was, our fuel was left intact at Hawaii and the base could still be used.[15]

He added that the Japs failed to immobilize the fleet because his three carriers and most of his fast cruisers—the most valuable vessels of his command—were not in harbor.[16]

Vice-Adm. W. W. Smith, chief of staff to Kimmel, said that the attack upon the fleet was Japan's "greatest mistake." The Japs, he said, knocked out only battleships, which were of less value than the two carriers which were at sea and escaped damage. Adm. Smith said that the Japs could have crippled the Pacific fleet for months if they had destroyed the oil supplies and machine shops at Hawaii instead of the battleships. By doing so, he said, the base would have been rendered untenable.[17]

Adm. Raymond A. Spruance, commander-in-chief of the Pacific fleet from November, 1945, to February, 1946, said that the attack demonstrated that the Japs did not appreciate sea power as an offensive weapon. "Instead of following up his initial successes," said Spruance, "the enemy diverted the navy, which then far outclassed ours, to the Southwest Pacific. The Japanese might have won a quick and decisive victory had the base at Pearl Harbor been smashed."[18]

Another error was the failure of the Japs to seize Midway Island in the first days of the war. They contented themselves with shelling Midway the night of December 7, but the defending garrison scored three hits on a destroyer with shore guns and at least two on a cruiser before the attacking force withdrew. If the Japanese wanted to take Midway, they would have found the island's defenses at their weakest in the first few days or few weeks after Pearl Harbor. But not until six months later did Japan make a serious effort to seize the island, and by then it was too late. The crushing defeat imposed upon the imperial fleet in the battle of Midway, June 4-6, 1942, was a turning-point in the war and one of the decisive battles of history.

After the attack upon Pearl Harbor the Japanese striking force was under orders to withdraw from Hawaiian waters with all possible speed. All except twenty-seven planes returned safely to their carrier decks between 10:30 A.M. and 1:30 P.M., and the task force withdrew to the northwest. The carriers, according to the flight group commander, Capt. Fuchida, had intended to bomb Midway on the homeward journey, but changed plans because the weather grew bad. On the way back to Japan, Fuchida said, two carriers left the fleet to assault Wake Island, which fell to a Japanese landing force on the evening of December 22, after a fifteen-day siege.

The remainder of the Pearl Harbor striking force returned to Japan by a circuitous course, arriving at Kure on December 22. Japanese officers said that there was no particular excitement or celebrations aboard the ships, but that "the pilots had a good drink after returning to their carriers." Any celebrations which might have seemed in order would, in any event, have been short lived. Four of the carriers which attacked Pearl Harbor—the "Kaga," "Akagi," "Soryu," and "Hiryu"—were sunk six months later in the battle of Midway. The "Shokaku" was sunk in the battle of the West Marianas, and the "Zuikaku" in the second battle of the Philippine Sea. Fuchida said he believed that he was the only flyer from the sneak attack group who survived the war.

Chapter Three

THE RISING SUN

ON WEDNESDAY, December 3, the carrier "Enterprise," commanded by Vice-Adm. William F. Halsey, Jr., was some 1,900 miles west of Pearl Harbor. She was the flagship of a task force consisting of three heavy cruisers and nine destroyers. The force had left Pearl Harbor November 28 to deliver a dozen Marine fighter pilots in Grumman Wildcats to Wake Island. The pilots had received such short notice of their departure that some had reported aboard with only the clothes they were wearing.

Adm. Halsey had enjoined radio silence and sailed with his ships darkened. Not until the second day out did the task force learn that its destination was Wake. On December 3 the Marines went into Wake and the "Enterprise" turned and headed back toward Pearl Harbor. Navy pilots aboard the carrier were flying scouting missions in all directions from the ship. A young officer aboard the "Enterprise" who was keeping an unofficial log noted: "Vogt says he saw a large fleet at the end of his scouting leg, but it was hazy and his tanks were low, so he isn't sure. Some imagination!"[1]

Whatever Pilot Ensign John H. L. Vogt, Jr., saw through the overcast will never be known. He may have sighted the main Jap striking force en route to Pearl Harbor. If so, it was far off its charted course. He may have seen part of Adm. Shimizu's advance expeditionary force, although that seems equally unlikely. He may have seen other Jap fleet units advancing for the attack on Wake. Because of radio silence, no report of Vogt's statement was sent to Pearl Harbor. At dawn on December 7 Vogt took off from the "Enterprise" and flew into a formation of enemy planes attacking Pearl Harbor. He was killed.

There were other portents that something was afoot. The cruiser

27

"Boise," convoying American merchantmen 3,400 miles from Pearl Harbor, to the northeast of Guam, sighted a darkened ship at about 16,000 yards on the night of November 27. The "Boise" challenged, but received no reply. On the following night the cruiser again sighted a darkened ship, hull down, at 5:33 P.M. "She appeared to be 'Atago' type [a class of Jap cruiser]," the log stated.

Battle stations were manned and the "Boise's" speed and course changed on each occasion, but the identity of the strange ships was never confirmed, nor was any other action taken. The vessels sighted were 1,400 miles off the reported course taken by the Jap task force bound for Pearl Harbor. No report was radioed to the fleet base.[2]

On the night of December 6 the aircraft tender "Wright" sighted another unidentified ship without lights west of Hawaii, but again made no report because of orders to keep radio silence. The "Wright," a unit of Halsey's task force, challenged the strange vessel between 8:00 P.M. and midnight, but the ship did not respond and slipped out of sight. It was later surmised that the vessel may have been a Japanese submarine.[3]

Navy department records provide another mystery. On December 5, an American patrol ship was operating north of Hawaii directly in the path of the Jap striking force. The Navy's chart of ship locations for the following day omitted the patrol ship and no accounting has ever been made for its "disappearance."[4]

While all of these incidents together might have suggested some event out of the ordinary, they were not reported to Pearl Harbor before the attack. Other contacts made by naval ships in the fleet-operating area about Pearl Harbor in the early morning hours of December 7 were reported.

The first of these was made at 3:58 A.M., when the minesweeper "Condor" flashed a blinker signal to the destroyer "Ward" that a suspicious object, believed to be a submarine, had been detected in the darkness westward of her sweep area.[5] Lieut. William W. Outerbridge, commanding the "Ward," sounded general quarters and combed a wide pattern for nearly an hour, but found nothing. Outerbridge returned to his bunk and Lieut. (j.g.) O. W. Goepner, a reservist from the Northwestern University Naval R. O. T. C., took over as officer of the deck.

At 6:37 A.M. Goepner awakened Outerbridge and pointed out a submarine conning tower between the "Ward" and the target ship "Antares," towing her raft to Pearl Harbor. A Navy PBY, returning from patrol, dropped a smoke bomb to mark the submarine's location.

The silhouette of the conning tower was unfamiliar, and for a good reason. This was one of Adm. Shimizu's midget subs.

At 6:45 the "Ward," on Goepner's order, opened fire from its number 1 gun in the bow. Number 3 gun from the waist then opened up and, at point-blank range of 75 yards, scored with its first shot, striking the conning tower. The "Ward" followed up with four depth charges dropped in pattern, but the number 3 gun had done for the sub.

At 6:51 it was adjudged sunk, and Outerbridge radioed Pearl Harbor, "We have dropped depth charges upon sub operating in defensive area." In order to underscore this startling intelligence, Outerbridge two minutes later sent a second message: "We have attacked, fired upon, and dropped depth charges upon a submarine operating in the defensive area." The operator at Bishop's Point naval radio station acknowledged receipt.[6]

This was a full hour before the Japanese air attack on Pearl Harbor. Two messages which should have warned the forces ashore had already been dispatched, and a third report was now radioed by the PBY flying boat which had circled overhead. This message was received by Comdr. Knefler McGinnis, commander of patrol wing 1 at Kaneohe Naval Air Station. Alarmed lest an American submarine had been sunk, McGinnis was still checking up an hour later when planes bearing the Rising Sun insignia came in and shot up every one of his flying boats in the bay or on the ramps. Only three patrol planes still in the air escaped this first attack, and one was badly shot up in landing.[7]

Outerbridge's message was received at 7:12 A.M. or earlier by the Pearl Harbor base watch officer, who immediately notified his chief of staff. No change to a higher condition of readiness, however, was ordered as a result of the report. The Army Board of Inquiry which investigated the disaster in 1944 observed, "This was one of the most important of a succession of mistakes made during this fateful morning. The Navy admits that it did not advise Gen. Short as it should have done."[8]

Meanwhile, the "Ward," inbound to Pearl Harbor, sighted a motor-driven sampan which had no business in the restricted area. As the destroyer charged down upon this craft, three Japanese came to the rail, two with their hands in the air and the third waving a white flag. These were the attitudes of surrender. They suggested war. The sampan was taken in tow by a Coast Guard cutter, but no further warning was dispatched to shore.[9]

There was at least one other episode at sea which justified an all-out alert if word had been passed to the base. While the "Enterprise" was still 200 miles from Pearl Harbor, it launched its planes to fly into Oahu. One of the flyers who took off was Ensign Manuel Gonzalez, of bombing squadron 6. Somewhere the fringe of the flight intercepted the course of the Japanese attacking formation. Back on the carrier listeners heard the cry of Gonzalez over the radio, "Don't shoot! This is an American plane." That was all. He was shot down. Again no warning was radioed to the fleet base.[10]

Ashore there was a still more inexplicable failure. The Army radar aircraft warning system had been operating between 4:00 and 7:00 A.M., the hour when the stations were to shut down on December 7. Two privates, Joseph E. Elliott and Joseph L. Lockard, were manning the station at Opana, on Kahuku Point, clear across Oahu from Pearl Harbor, at the extreme north of the island. Lockard was operating the detector and Elliott was plotting the information.

Between 6:45 and 6:59 A.M. Lockard and Elliott spotted ten or more unidentified planes northeast of Hawaii and 100 miles or less distant. Elliott's recollection four years later was that these planes had been reported to the Army Information Center,[11] which that morning was in charge of Lieut. Kermit A. Tyler, an Air Corps pursuit officer, but if they were no action was taken.

When it was time for the two privates to go off duty, Elliott asked that the station be kept open for further operation after 7:00 A.M., so that he might learn to operate the detector. Lockard acquiesced and, while adjusting the machine to begin the instruction, noticed on the radar screen an unusual formation, suggesting the approach of a large number of planes. These unknown planes, picked up at 7:02 A.M., were 137 miles distant and approaching Oahu from 3 degrees east of north.[12]

Lockard reported the discovery within seven minutes to the Information Center. Tyler was absent at the moment, but the switchboard operator located him, and Tyler, within two or three minutes, was listening to Lockard's report. "Tyler's answer," the Army Board report stated, "was disastrous. He said, in substance, 'Forget it.' Tyler's position is indefensible in his action, for he says that he was merely there for training and had no knowledge upon which to base any action; yet he assumed to give directions instead of seeking someone competent to make a decision."[13]

Not only did Tyler fail to act, but the Army neglected until two days after the attack to inform Adm. Kimmel of recording the ap-

proach of the attacking force by radar. This threw Navy search planes
completely off the track when they attempted to trail the Jap striking
force. The search planes made their sweeps to the south and southwest, not knowing that the enemy planes had come in from the
north.[14]

Meanwhile, Lockard and Elliott continued to follow and plot the
approaching aircraft until they came within 20 miles of Oahu at
about 7:35 A.M., when radar reception failed. From fifteen to twenty
minutes later the first enemy planes appeared over Hawaiian air
fields and burst through the clouds upon the Pearl Harbor base.

Tyler's subsequent explanation was that he believed that Lockard
and Elliott had picked up a flight of 12 B-17's which he knew were
coming in from Hamilton Field, California.[15] Some of these planes
did, in fact, arrive during the attack and were destroyed by the Japanese, but Tyler's defense took no account of the fact that if these had
been the planes spotted by the two privates, they would have been
flying 200 miles off their course at the time the formation was reported from Opana.

The greatest error of all, however, was that the Army garrison
and fleet base had not been alerted properly against attack. The Army
on November 27 had put into effect its alert number 1—defense
against sabotage and uprisings; no threat from without. This was
farthest removed from an all-out war footing of any of its three degrees of alert.[16] The Navy had instituted its number 3 condition of
readiness, providing a means of opening fire with a portion of the
anti-aircraft and secondary batteries in case of surprise encounter.
This was the minimum degree of readiness possible under its three
standing classifications.[17]

These limited conditions of readiness were in response to orders
from higher authority in Washington and represented what the
field commanders thought was required of them, but neither the
Army nor Navy in Hawaii was prepared on December 7 to cope
with a determined surprise attack in force. The Army's preparations
against sabotage, in particular, played into the hands of the Japs. All
of its planes, with a few exceptions, were lined up wing to wing, in
order that they might be more easily guarded by a cordon of sentries.
They presented a perfect target for bombs and machine gun bullets.

The situation prevailing December 7 under the conditions of
readiness in effect was thus summarized by the Army Board:

No distant reconnaissance was being conducted by the Navy;
the usual four or five PBY's were not out; the anti-aircraft artil-

lery was not out on its usual Sunday maneuvers with the fleet
air arm; the naval carriers with their planes were at a distance
from Oahu on that Sunday; the aircraft were on the ground,
were parked, both Army and Navy, closely adjacent to one another; the fleet was in the harbor with the exception of task
forces 9 and 12, which included some cruisers, destroyers, and
the two carriers "Lexington" and "Enterprise."

Ammunition for the Army was, with the exception of that
near the fixed anti-aircraft guns, in ordnance storehouses, and
the two combat divisions as well as the anti-aircraft artillery
were in their permanent quarters and not in battle positions.
Everything was concentrated in close confines by reason of the
[Army's] anti-sabotage alert number 1. This made of them
easy targets for an air attack. In short, everything that was done
made the situation perfect for an air attack and the Japanese
took full advantage of it.[18]

In addition to sending reconnaissance planes over Pearl Harbor
one hour before the arrival of their attacking planes, the Japanese
resorted to submarine reconnaissance for last-minute information. The
log of a Japanese two-man submarine showed that the craft entered
the harbor and made a complete run around Ford Island. Entry
apparently was effected about 4:10 A.M., when the submarine net
across the harbor mouth was open to permit a garbage scow to leave
the harbor.

The submarine commander roughed in the ships at their berths
as well as he could in the uncertain pre-dawn light, but he failed to
identify a single vessel correctly. He completed the circuit of the
harbor at 4:30 and turned down the channel for the open sea. The
submarine net had been opened again at 4:58 to permit the entrance
of two minesweepers and remained open until 8:40, when it was
closed by order as a result of the attack; so the submarine had no
difficulty in getting out of the harbor.[19]

Because the plottings of fleet units in harbor and the positions
they occupied, as shown on the map of the submarine commander,
varied considerably from the ships actually in harbor December 7
and their true locations, there has been disagreement as to whether
the submarine made its run in the hours directly preceding the attack,
or on some day before December 7.[20] Rear Adm. T. B. Inglis, chief
of naval intelligence, doubted in 1945 that the submarine ever entered
the harbor. He said "there was confusion in translating the Japanese
present and future tenses," and that the log may have shown what

the Jap commander intended to do, rather than what he had done.[21]

The admiral's statement, however, fails to explain why the Jap officer, if he never made the harbor circuit, wrote at one point on his chart, "I saw it with my own eyes!" when he thought he had located the aircraft carrier "Saratoga."[22] The "carrier" which he had erroneously identified was in reality the old battleship "Utah," which had been stripped and converted into a target ship. The fact that it later received special attention from Jap raiding planes suggests that the enemy submarine not only did tour the harbor, but communicated its findings by radio to the attacking force.

Another Japanese sub was indisputably in Pearl Harbor on December 7. It entered sometime after the anti-submarine net was opened at 4:58. At 8:35 A.M., 40 minutes after the attack had begun, it came up for a look. Half a dozen ships opened fire on the conning tower, and the craft was finished off when it was rammed and depth charged by the destroyer "Monaghan" after surfacing under her bows. Later, the submarine, with its crew of two still inside, was used as part of the fill-in for a new landside pier at the Pearl Harbor submarine base.[23]

The submarine believed to have made the circuit of Ford Island later ran on a reef in the open sea near Bellows Field, southeast of Kaneohe Bay. While it was stuck on the reef, a bomb dropped from a Navy plane knocked the submarine over to the other side of the reef. Gen. Short later said that Army troops threw a rope around the craft and pulled it ashore, capturing both members of the crew,[24] but Army intelligence four years after the attack acknowledged the capture only of the commander, Sub-Lieut. Kazuo Sakamaki.[25]

The remainder of the five enemy midget craft all were lost, as was confirmed by a subsequent Japanese citation granting "posthumous" promotion to all ten men of the crews.[26]

Sunrise was at 6:26 A.M. on December 7 at Pearl Harbor.[27] At least three civilian planes were in the air early. Roy Vitousek, a lawyer, suddenly found himself in formation with strange planes. Cornelia Fort, a civilian instructor, was aloft with a student. James Duncan, member of a flying club, was taking a lesson from Thomas Pomerlin, a commercial pilot. All three planes got down safely under pelting Jap machine gun fire.

The attacking force made three approaches. One group from the north came directly across the island, attacking the Army's Wheeler Field on its way to assault Pearl Harbor. A second force from the east attacked the Navy's Kaneohe Bay flying boat base, the Bellows

Field Army airdrome, and Pearl Harbor. The third Japanese force made its approach from the south, attacking Pearl Harbor and Hickam Field, the adjacent Army air field. The Marine air base at Ewa Plantation was destroyed, apparently by the force which darted in from the east on Kaneohe air station.

The enemy opened fire at Kaneohe about 7:50 A.M.[28] Five minutes later the attack hit Pearl Harbor. At Kaneohe the Japs knocked out twenty-seven flying boats and an observation plane. At Ford Island Naval Air Station twenty-six planes were destroyed on the ground—nineteen patrol bombers, three scout bombers, and four fighters. Only three planes were later able to take to the air from Ford Island. At Ewa, the Marine air base, nine fighters, eighteen scout bombers, three utility planes, two transports, and one training plane—thirty-three—were destroyed.[29]

At Hickam Field the Japs destroyed four B-17 bombers, twelve B-18 bombers, and two A-20 light bombers—eighteen planes. Forty pursuit and two observation planes were destroyed at Wheeler Field, and an observation plane and two pursuit aircraft at Bellows Field. Eleven planes of scouting squadron 8 which had flown in from the "Enterprise" were shot down over Pearl Harbor, and of eighteen dive bombers which left the carrier and flew into the attack five were lost. Ten of the sixteen carrier planes lost were believed to have been shot down or forced to crash by anti-aircraft fire from American guns.[30]

The Hawaiian air fields were hit first in order to eliminate any possible interference in the air. The attack was concentrated on the aprons where the planes were parked, upon hangars, and upon repair shops. Almost two hundred American aircraft were lost.[31]

Only a few fighter aircraft at the Army's remote Haleiwa Field, which was apparently unknown to the Japs, escaped the enemy attack. A squadron was practicing short landings there on Sunday morning.[32] Two flights, each consisting of four P-40's and one obsolescent P-36, got into the air from this field to engage the Japs in combat. Maj. (then Second Lieut.) George S. Welch and his wing man, Second Lieut. Kenneth M. Taylor, both got their planes off the ground from Haleiwa, Welch shooting down four enemy planes and Taylor two.

Enemy planes appeared over the Pearl Harbor fleet base at 7:55 A.M., just as the morning signal flag was being broken out from the signal tower atop the Navy Yard water tank, calling for morning colors to rise in five minutes. From the tower all of Pearl Harbor was spread out before the signalmen. That morning there were ninety-four ships in harbor: eight battleships, two heavy cruisers, six light cruisers, twenty-nine destroyers, five submarines, one gunboat, eight destroyer minelayers, one minelayer, four destroyer mine-sweepers, six minesweepers, and twenty-four auxiliaries.[33]

The battleship "Pennsylvania" was in drydock number 1 with the destroyers "Cassin" and "Downes." To the left, in drydock number 2, was the destroyer "Shaw." The light cruiser "Helena" was moored alongside 10-10 dock, with the minelayer "Oglala" moored outboard of her. The light cruiser "Honolulu" was in one of the yard berths to the northeast of the "Helena."

In Battleship Row, on the south side of Ford Island, were drawn up in order the "California," then "Neosho," a 21,000-ton oiler; the "Oklahoma" and "Maryland," tied up in a pair; the "West Virginia" and "Tennessee," also paired; the "Arizona" and 9,400-ton repair ship "Vestal," with the "Arizona" inboard, and, finally, the "Nevada." On the north side of the island were moored the light cruiser "Raleigh" and the target ship "Utah," with the seaplane tender "Curtiss" across from the "Utah," off Peninsula Point.

Of these nineteen ships, only the "Neosho" came through the Japanese attack unscathed.

Most of the damage, both to aircraft and ships, was done in the first few minutes of the attack, which was over in one hour and fifty minutes. The attack developed in the following rough phases: I. 7:55–8:25 A.M. Combined torpedo plane and dive bomber attack. II. 8:25–8:40. Comparative lull. III. 8:40–9:15. Horizontal bomber attack. IV. 9:15–9:45 Dive bomber attacks. V. 9:45. Waning of attack and completion of raid.[34]

Twenty-one planes took part in the initial torpedo attack, covered by thirty dive bombers and fifteen high-level bombers. The Japanese torpedo planes had been assigned definite targets among the heavy fleet units and had been provided with torpedoes particularly adapted to the shallow waters of Pearl Harbor. The torpedoes were fitted with wooden vanes so that they would not sink too deeply when launched from the planes, while detonators had been designed to operate after a short run so that they would be effective in the limited confines of the harbor.[35] The warheads of the Japanese torpedoes at that time were larger and more powerful than in any torpedoes in use by other navies of the world.

All of the battleships moored outboard in Battleship Row were torpedoed, while one torpedo passed underneath the "Oglala" and exploded against the "Helena," the blast caving in the side plates of the "Oglala," which capsized an hour later. On the north side of Ford Island the "Raleigh" was struck by one torpedo and the "Utah" turned turtle after taking two. All of these attacks were made by planes which came in at a height of 100 feet or less above the water and launched their torpedoes at very short distances.

In the simultaneous dive-bombing runs, one Jap pilot put a bomb down a stack of the "Arizona," whose forward boilers and magazine blew up. Other successful attacks were made on the "Pennsylvania," "California," "West Virginia," "Tennessee," "Helena," "Shaw," "Curtiss," and "Oglala." High-level bombers scored on the "California," "Utah," "Shaw," and Navy Yard docks. During the comparative lull between 8:25 and 8:40 an estimated fifteen planes continued dive-bomber attacks, directed against the "Pennsylvania," "Oklahoma," "Maryland," "Nevada," "Honolulu," "Helena," "Cassin," "Downes," "Shaw," and "Oglala."

The horizontal bomber attacks which followed were centered on the "Pennsylvania," "West Virginia," "California," "Helena," "Oglala," and the three destroyers in drydock. About thirty planes participated in these attacks, with eighteen dive bombers also in action. The dive bombers registered hits on drydocks numbers 1 and 2, "Tennessee," "West Virginia," "Nevada," and the three destroyers.

In the fourth phase, between 9:15 and 9:45, the three destroyers were again attacked, as was the "Raleigh." Bombs also fell on installations on Ford Island, the battleships on the south side of the island, and destroyers and other ships moored north of the island. Twenty-seven dive bombers were estimated to have participated in this closing phase. All enemy planes had retired by 9:45.

In addition to the specially fitted torpedo, the enemy force was provided with another novel weapon which produced unexpectedly good results. This was a large armor piercing shell of 15 or 16 inches, fitted for use by high-level bombers. Hits were scored with these improvised bombs on the battleships "California" and "Tennessee" and the light cruiser "Raleigh."[36]

One of these shells penetrated to the "California's" second deck, where a large part of the ship's company was assembled. Many of the men were killed and the explosion resulted in a raging fire between-decks. Two more of these projectiles each struck main turrets of the "Tennessee." One of the shells exploded and a fragment from it mortally wounded Capt. Mervyn S. Bennion, commander of the nearby "West Virginia." The other blew out its base plug and its detonating charge burned out on the deck without exploding. Despite these hits, only five men aboard the "Tennessee" were killed. The "Raleigh" was struck on the port side aft by a projectile which went through several decks and came out through the side of the ship to explode 50 feet away.

The defenders, although surprised and off balance, fought the Japanese attack with great courage, but losses were high. The attack cost the lives of 2,326 officers and men. The Navy's losses were 2,086 dead and 749 wounded, while the Army suffered 240 dead and 360 wounded. Total casualties thus were 3,435.[37] Of fifteen congressional medals of honor for heroism during the attack, eleven were posthumous awards.

The damage to the fleet consisted of:

Sunk: Five battleships, the "Arizona," "Oklahoma," "West Virginia," "California," and "Nevada"; three destroyers, the "Cassin," "Downes," and "Shaw"; the target ship "Utah," the repair ship "Vestal," the minelayer "Oglala," and floating drydock number 2.

Damaged but afloat: Three battleships, the "Pennsylvania," "Maryland," and "Tennessee"; three light cruisers, the "Helena," "Honolulu," and "Raleigh," and the seaplane tender "Curtiss."*

After the attack the Japanese estimated they had sunk four battleships and damaged four others and that they had wrecked about half of the 900 planes they estimated to be on Oahu.[39] They were conservative in estimating warship losses but exaggerated the number of American planes destroyed.

*Damage to these vessels individually is given in Appendix.[38]

Chapter Four

THE SCAPEGOATS

In the excitement and confusion on December 7, 1941, it was not immediately noticed that the leaders of the Roosevelt administration were frantically scurrying about proving their surprise and injury, shouldering the blame for the disaster at Pearl Harbor away from themselves. Events were moving too fast for citizens to detect that the disengaging tactics of the politicians were far more successful than had been those of the Pacific fleet.

The Japanese declaration of war was announced by imperial headquarters two hours and thirty-five minutes after the attack.* Premier Shidehara explained after Japan's surrender four years later that an "error in procedure" prevented the declaration from reaching the State Department in Washington before the attack.[1] Adm. Nagano, commander of the combined imperial fleets, said the Japanese plan was to send notification to the United States at 7:30 A.M., Hawaii time, on December 7, 1941. The necessary time lapse, he explained, between dispatch of such a message, its decoding by the Japanese embassy in Washington, and its delivery to the State Department, would mean at best a notification virtually simultaneous with the attack.

"At first," Nagano said, "we were going to give a one-hour notice before the attack, but the United States was fully prepared and its communications excellent, so it was shortened to thirty minutes' notice."[2]

On Monday Mr. Roosevelt sent his message to Congress calling for a declaration of war. The declaration was approved by both houses with one dissenting vote—that of Representative Jeanette Rankin of Montana, who had also voted against war with Germany in 1917.[3]

*At 6:00 A.M., Dec. 8, Tokyo time: 10:30 A.M., Dec. 7, Hawaii time; 4:00 P.M., Dec. 7, E.S.T.—N. Y. Times, Dec. 8, 1:2.

Britain, Canada, Australia, and Holland had already declared war against the Japanese.[4] On Thursday, December 11, Germany and Italy, acting under their tripartite pact commitments to Japan, declared war against the United States.[5] The same day Congress passed resolutions declaring the existence of a state of war with these two nations[6] after receiving a message in which President Roosevelt said: "The long known and the long expected has taken place."[7] This equivocal expression implied that Germany and Italy had long been meditating an attack upon the United States. Again the vote was unanimous for war, with the exception of Miss Rankin, who voted "present" in each instance.

Meanwhile, there had been ominous reports of the losses at Pearl Harbor. The first Japanese claims were that the battleships "West Virginia" and "Oklahoma" had been sunk and that four other capital ships and four cruisers had been damaged.[8] The first report from the American government came from the White House on December 8. About 3,000 casualties, equally divided between dead and wounded, were acknowledged by Roosevelt, while it was said that one old battleship had capsized, a destroyer had blown up, several other smaller ships had been seriously damaged, a large number of planes had been put out of commission, and several hangars destroyed in the bombing of Army and Navy air fields.[9]

The President on December 7 knew the true extent of the losses. Some of his alarm and dismay were communicated to the Cabinet members and congressional leaders who attended him in the White House that night. Roosevelt told them:

> The casualties, I am sorry to say, were extremely heavy. I cannot say anything definite in regard to the number of ships that have been sunk. It looks as if out of eight battleships, three have been sunk, and possibly a fourth. Two destroyers were blown up while they were in drydock. Two of the battleships are badly damaged. Several other smaller vessels have been sunk or destroyed. The drydock itself has been damaged. . . .
>
> Now I think that is all there is in the way of information, but it has been suggested that the Army and Navy losses, and the rather definite statements I have made about these ships, could not be spoken of outside, because we must remember that detailed military information, such as the damage to ships, or even the loss of personnel—that information is of value to an enemy. I think that is a matter of discretion, which all of you will accept.[10]

The first "official" report on the damage was to come from Secretary Knox. At 8:00 A.M., December 9, Knox left Washington in his own plane, "conscious," as Davis and Lindley put it, "of his share in the blame for the surprise attack at Pearl Harbor. . . . The Secretary of the Navy regarded his mission as an expiation."[11]

Upon his return to Washington, December 15, Knox hurried to the White House and conferred with Roosevelt. Later he called the press to his office and announced a total of 2,897 Army and Navy dead, 879 wounded, and 26 missing. The "Arizona," "Utah," "Shaw," "Cassin," "Downes," and "Oglala," he said, had been sunk; the "Oklahoma" was capsized but salvageable, and other vessels had suffered damage requiring repairs of a week to several months.[12]

Knox's published report had been prepared with the assistance of Comdr. Leland P. Lovette, whom the Secretary found at Pearl Harbor, where Lovette was commander of Destroyer Division 5, which included the "Cassin," "Downes," and "Shaw," all of which had been wrecked in the Jap attack.[13] Lovette, subsequently to be named director of Navy public relations by Knox, was an officer-author of some reputation. The statement which he and Knox drew up for submission to the public emphasized the heroism of the men at Pearl Harbor, but carefully refrained from giving the American people anything like a true accounting of the damage suffered by the fleet.

More important than what Knox chose to tell the people was the decision which he and Roosevelt reached at their conference preceding the release of the report. It would not be known for another four years that, although Knox in a private report to Roosevelt at this very meeting did not impute exclusive or even specific blame to the Hawaiian commanders,[14] Kimmel and Short were then assigned the role of scapegoats for the disaster. Adm. Stark, chief of naval operations in 1941, testified at the Congressional investigation in 1945 that the first thing Knox did after conferring with the President was to issue orders for the removal of Adm. Kimmel as commander of the Pacific fleet. Asked whether Knox's action was based on orders from Roosevelt, Stark said, "You always need the President's permission to remove a fleet commander."[15]

At his press conference, however, Knox made no admission that any such action would be taken. "The United States services were not on the alert against a surprise attack on Hawaii," his report stated. "This fact calls for a formal investigation which will be initiated immediately by the President. Further action is, of course, dependent on the facts and recommendations made by this investigating board."

Knox sought to create the impression that any assessment of blame would await later investigation by an impartial commission. The impression he gave the press and the nation was wholly disingenuous. He and the President had already decided to put the onus on Kimmel and Short. The commanders were relieved of their posts, but the announcement was held up for two days, until December 17. Maj. Gen. Martin, commander of the Army Air Forces in Hawaii, was relieved at the same time.[16]

On December 16 Roosevelt, moved by a rising tide of indignation in Congress which made it apparent that an investigation by that body was likely, forestalled independent inquiry by appointing his own investigating commission.[17] This was a five-man board of inquiry headed by Associate Justice Owen J. Roberts of the United States Supreme Court, who had been a proponent of war as a means of achieving world-government.[18]

The other members were two retired admirals, Rear Adm. William H. Standley, former chief of naval operations, and Rear Adm. Joseph M. Reeves, former commander-in-chief of the United States fleet, Maj. Gen. Frank R. McCoy, retired, and Joseph T. McNarney, a brigadier general on the active list of the Army Air Corps. McNarney later was promoted to the rank of four-star general, became deputy chief of staff, second only to Gen. Marshall in the Army hierarchy, and, finally, commander of all occupation forces in Europe. The selection of these men was not accidental. Reeves was the first commander-in-chief of the fleet to take it to Pearl Harbor. He was therefore disqualified from criticizing the selection of Pearl Harbor as its base. Standley, retired in 1937, was recalled to active duty March 6, 1941, and would not be disposed to criticize the decisions of the Navy leadership in Washington, of which he had formerly been a ranking member as chief of naval operations. McCoy, as president of the Foreign Policy Association, per se was a staunch supporter of Roosevelt's diplomacy. McNarney was a member of the Marshall clique which ran the War Department. Since 1939 he had been a member of the general staff, which was responsible for the failure to build up the defenses of Pearl Harbor and which withheld knowledge of Japanese designs and intentions from the field commanders.

Four of these men later were the recipients of honor and favors from the Roosevelt administration. Five and one-half years after his retirement with the rank of rear admiral, Reeves was promoted to admiral on the retired list June 16, 1942. This was five months after he had signed the Roberts report. Standley was decorated by Roosevelt with the Distinguished Service Medal after signing the report, and was appointed ambassador to Russia, a post which he held in 1942 and 1943. McCoy was appointed chairman of the Far Eastern Advisory Commission when allied control was established following the surrender of Japan. McNarney's meteoric rise in the Army has been described.

Roosevelt, in fixing jurisdiction, charged the commission with determining whether "any derelictions of duty or error of judgment on the part of United States Army or Navy personnel contributed to such successes as were achieved by the enemy" in "the attack made by Japanese forces upon the territory of Hawaii." These instructions were intended to exclude consideration of the behavior of official Washington.

Roosevelt had already tried the case. Without calling witnesses, he found Kimmel and Short guilty, condemned them, and carried out his sentence. He announced their removal from command the very day that the Roberts Commission assembled in Washington. Under the circumstances, it was hardly surprising that the President's hand-picked commission should report findings to order. On January 24 it submitted a report to Roosevelt which held that Kimmel and Short were guilty of "dereliction of duty."*[19]

The report ignored many vital considerations and its findings on points of major importance were contradicted in both the Army and Navy reports of a later day and in testimony before the Congressional Investigating Committee. In addition, the findings of the commission were based upon misinformation and errors in fact. The minority report of the Joint Congressional Committee (p. 3) remarks:

> It is extremely unfortunate that the Roberts Commission report was so hasty, inconclusive, and incomplete. Some witnesses were examined under oath; others were not. Much testimony was not even recorded. The commission knew that Japanese messages had been intercepted and were available, prior to the attack, to the high command in Washington. The commission did not inquire about what information these intercepts contained, who received them, or what was done about them, although the failure of Washington to inform the commanders in Hawaii of this vital intelligence bears directly on the question of whether those commanders performed their full duties. Mr. Justice Roberts testified before this committee: "I

*The record of the commission's proceedings and exhibits covers 2,173 printed pages.[20]

would not have bothered to read it [the intercepted Japanese traffic] if it had been shown to us (Tr., Vol. 47, p. 8836)."

If it were necessary to do so, detailed examples of the many short-comings of the Roberts Commission could be set forth. . . . It should be noted, however, that Justice Roberts had sufficient legal experience to know the proper method of collecting and preserving evidence which in this case involved the highest interests of the nation. The facts were then fresh in the minds of key witnesses in Washington. They could not then have been ignorant of their whereabouts at important times or have forgotten the details of events and operations. No files would have been "lost" and no information would have been distorted by the passage of time. The failure to observe these obvious necessities is almost as tragic to the cause of truth as the attack on Pearl Harbor itself was a tragedy for the nation.

For example, although the report did not mention that the United States had cracked the Japanese code months before Pearl Harbor, the commission had been informed by the chief of naval intelligence, Adm. Wilkinson, that all of the information from Jap code intercepts had been sent to the Hawaiian commanders. In fact, only a few of the hundreds of these messages, and none of major importance, had been relayed to Kimmel and Short. Four years later, when he was examined by the congressional Pearl Harbor investigating committee, Wilkinson "corrected" the statements he had given the Roberts Commission.[21]

The report held that Short's alert against sabotage "was not adequate," but had only the gentlest sort of criticism for his superiors in Washington, who had been informed by him of the action he had taken and had not even responded, let alone ordered him to go on an all-out alert. It criticized Kimmel for not taking "appropriate measures" in view of "war warnings," but held that in ordering attacks to be made upon Japanese submarines found in operating areas around Oahu, he had exceeded the authority given him by the Navy Department.

The commission greatly emphasized such information as could be construed to have given the Hawaiian commanders warning that war was imminent, but it withheld reference to the far more vital intelligence which was not transmitted to Hawaii. Of seven warning messages from Washington to Short and Kimmel which were recorded in the Roberts report, no less than four referred to the danger of sabotage. Not one suggested the possibility of surprise air attack.

These so-called warnings were so qualified by hampering instructions that the Army Board of Inquiry in its report, drafted in October,

1944, called them "do-don't" messages. The actual effect of the messages was to transfer responsibility from Washington to the field commanders if anything went wrong, but so to tie the hands of the commanders and restrict the course of action open to them that they were in no position to meet the attack when it came. The Roberts report devoted no attention to the fact that Washington had definite and detailed intelligence in the days preceding the attack that war was coming within predictable limits of time and had ample reason to believe the Jap blow would fall on Pearl Harbor.

On December 7, Gen. Marshall had opportunity to warn the Hawaii commanders that all evidence available to Washington indicated that an attack was coming. He sent a message, but its transmission was so botched that it reached Gen. Short seven hours too late. The Roberts report stated that at about 6:30 A.M., Honolulu time, Marshall dispatched "an additional warning message indicating an almost immediate break in relations between the United States and Japan." It continued, "Every effort was made to have the message reach Hawaii in the briefest possible time, but due to conditions beyond the control of any one concerned, the delivery of this urgent message was delayed until after the attack." The message, the report said, was "intended to reach both commanders in the field at about 7:00 A.M., Hawaii time," but the report adds that even "if the message had reached its destination at the time intended, it would still have been too late" because dispositions made by Kimmel and Short "were inadequate to meet a surprise air attack." By such statements, the commission glossed over Marshall's mishandling of a crucial dispatch which could have averted much of the damage suffered at Hawaii.*

The commission, although charged with seeking derelictions of duty and errors of judgment only among Army and Navy officers, was at pains to state that Gen. Marshall, Adm. Stark, and Secretaries Hull, Stimson, and Knox had discharged their responsibilities. In Conclusion 17, however, it implied that these officials did bear some responsibility, after all. It said that the dereliction of Kimmel and Short consisted of failing to "consult and confer . . . respecting the meaning and intent of the warnings" dispatched from Washington. It need hardly be said that such action would not have been necessary if the warnings were clear and precise.† By a curious exercise of inverted logic, the commission also advanced the contention that because Washington was keeping them in the dark on the vital intelligence obtained from Japanese code intercepts, Kimmel and Short by some

*Cf. pp. 238-39, 241, 253.
†Cf. pp. 240-41.

process of clairvoyance should have realized the necessity of placing a more urgent degree of readiness in effect. The report said in this connection, "Both commanders were handicapped by lack of information as to Japanese dispositions and intent. The lack of such knowledge rendered more urgent the initiation of a state of readiness for defense." Kimmel and Short did not know until much later that Washington even possessed information of the character which was being withheld from them.

Adm. Kimmel said that the Roberts Commission had informed him that he was not on trial. Kimmel, upon later inspection of the record of his own testimony, said that he found so many errors in the record that he spent two days correcting it, only to have the board refuse to change his statements as recorded originally. All that the investigators would do finally was to attach the corrected statement to the minutes. He said of the commission, "It permitted me to testify—that's all."[22]

Gen. Short said that upon his relief from command in Hawaii he had reached Oklahoma City when he read the report of the Roberts Commission in the press. He said:

> When I read the findings of the Roberts Commission, I was dumbfounded. To be accused of dereliction of duty after almost 40 years of loyal and competent service was beyond my comprehension. I immediately called Gen. Marshall on the telephone. He was an old and trusted friend of 39 years' standing. I asked him what I should do—having the country and war in mind should I retire? He replied, "Stand pat, but if it becomes necessary I will use this conversation as authority."

Short said that, having faith in Marshall's "judgment and loyalty," he wrote Marshall a personal letter and inclosed a formal application for retirement, to be used only if Marshall thought it desirable. His covering letter was not produced in evidence before the congressional committee, but a memorandum from Marshall to Secretary Stimson on January 26, 1942, reporting Short's telephone call of the day before, stated, "I am now of the opinion that we should accept Gen. Short's application for retirement today and do this quietly, without any publicity at the moment. Adm. Stark has requested me to advise him if we do this, as he proposes to communicate this fact to Kimmel in the hope that Kimmel will likewise apply for retirement." This correspondence demonstrates that, the day after reassuring Short, Marshall took steps in secret to get rid of him.

The War Department's order accepting Short's application for retirement was drafted after Stimson consulted Attorney General Francis J. Biddle as to how it should be worded. As finally phrased, Short's retirement was "accepted without condonation of any offense or prejudice to any future disciplinary action." The implication of this language was that Short faced court-martial action at some future date, and its effect was to seal his lips and to prevent him from making any defense of himself until he should be called for trial.[23]

Once in possession of Short's resignation, Roosevelt, Knox, and Stimson proceeded to use it as a lever to induce Kimmel to retire. Adm. Stark notified him on orders from Secretary Knox that Short had asked to be retired. "I took this as a suggestion and I submitted a similar request," Kimmel said. "Up to that time I never considered retiring. It had not even entered my head, but I thought it over and decided that if the Navy wanted it that way, I would not stand in the way."

Kimmel thereupon forwarded a request for retirement to Washington, but two days after sending his application was informed by Stark that the notification of Gen. Short's application was not meant to influence him. Although he then modified his request for retirement by telling the Navy he wanted to do whatever would best serve the country, he received a letter from Knox on February 16 peremptorily ordering him to retire as of March 1, also "without condonation of any offense or prejudice to future disciplinary action."

Six days afterward, in a letter to Stark, Kimmel said of this qualifying clause,

> I do not understand this paragraph unless it is to be published to the country as a promise that I will be disciplined at some future time. I stand ready at any time to accept the consequences of my acts. I do feel, however, that my crucifixion before the public has about reached the limit. I am in daily receipt of letters from irresponsible people all over the country taking me to task and even threatening to kill me. I am not particularly concerned except as it shows the effect on the public of articles published about me.
>
> I regret the losses at Pearl Harbor just as keenly, or perhaps more keenly, than any other American citizen. I wish that I had been smarter than I was and able to foresee what happened on December 7, but I do think in all justice the department should do nothing further to inflame the public against me.[24]

Gen. Short expressed similar resentment before the congressional committee. He said:

I do not feel that I have been treated fairly or with justice by the War Department. I was singled out as an example, as the scapegoat for the disaster. My relatively small part in the transaction was not explained to the American people until this joint congressional committee forced the revelation of the facts. I fully appreciate the desire of the War Department to preserve the secrecy of the source of the so-called "Magic" [cracking of the Japanese code], but I am sure that could have been done without any attempt to deceive the public by a false pretense that my judgment had been the sole factor causing the failure of the army to fulfill its mission of defending the navy at Pearl Harbor.

I am sure that an honest confession by the War Department general staff of their failure to anticipate the surprise raid would have been understood by the public, in the long run, and even at the time. Instead, they "passed the buck" to me, and I have kept my silence until the opportunity of this public forum was presented to me.[25]

Senator Ferguson asked him what meaning he wished to convey when he said he had been made the "scapegoat."

"I meant just exactly what the common usage meant, that it was some one that they saddled the blame on to get it off of themselves."

"In other words," suggested Ferguson, "they were in this position —that some one had to take some blame for what happened at Pearl Harbor, that certain people in Washington that you had named in your opinion were to blame, that they shifted that blame over to you as the commanding general at Hawaii, and therefore made you, in the common language, a scapegoat?"

"That is exactly what I want to convey."[26]

Thus the Pearl Harbor commanders were driven in disgrace from their professional careers, having been identified thoroughly in the minds of the public as bearing the sole blame for the Pearl Harbor disaster. The leaders of the Roosevelt administration and of its Army and Navy high command, who were in possession of the untold story of the catastrophe, saw to it that no hint of the concealed facts should leak out. Censorship and the pretext of "national security" enabled them for four years to suppress all facts which could damage them.

These men never confessed that they were in any way at fault or that the slightest blame attached to them. None of them resigned, and in less than a year they went to the country in a national election with the slogan that any political opponent "who had not been right before Pearl Harbor" should be retired by the electorate.

Representative Keefe, in "additional views" appended to the majority report of the Joint Congressional Committee (Maj., pp. 266-Q to 266-S), said of the process employed in retiring the Hawaiian commanders:

The President personally directed the method of handling the requests for retirement of Kimmel and Short. On Jan. 29, 1942, he instituted a three-point program for dealing with the matter. The Army and Navy were to act together. After a week's waiting they were to announce that Kimmel and Short had applied for retirement and that their applications were under consideration. After another week had passed, public announcement was to be made that the applications had been accepted with the condition that acceptance did not bar subsequent court-martial proceedings. Court-martial proceedings, however, were to be described as impossible without the disclosure of military secrets. The wording of the condition in the acceptance was troublesome to the administration. The President, Secretary Stimson, Secretary Knox, and Attorney General Biddle labored over the language (Tr., pp. 8462, 8464, Ex. 171). The administration wanted to avoid public criticism for having barred court-martial proceedings. On the other hand, it did not wish to stimulate the public or the two officers to expect or demand court-martial proceedings (Tr., p. 8464, 8467). Finally language as suitable as possible was agreed upon. The phrase to be used in accepting the retirement applications was "without condonation of any offense or prejudice to future disciplinary action." Adm. Kimmel and Gen. Short were each retired by letters so worded, dated respectively, Feb. 16 and Feb. 17, 1942. The Secretary of the Navy, in announcing the Navy's action, stated that he had directed the preparation of charges for court martial of Adm. Kimmel alleging dereliction of duty. The public were informed that a trial could not be held until such time as the public interest and safety would permit.

The public reaction was as planned. Kimmel and Short were considered solely responsible for Pearl Harbor. The Roberts report, considered by Justice Roberts as only an indictment, became, in effect, a conviction. The two officers were helpless. No court martial could be had. They had no way of defending themselves. They remained in ignorance of what evidence the Roberts Commission had heard. Adm. Stark wrote to Adm. Kimmel on Feb. 21, 1942:

"Pending something definite, there is no reason why you should not settle yourself in a quiet nook somewhere and let

Old Father Time help the entire situation, which I feel he will —if for no other reason than he always has (Ex. 121)."

The high civilian and military officials in Washington who had skillfully maneuvered Kimmel and Short into the position of exclusive blame knew at the time all the hidden facts about Pearl Harbor, at least as much and probably more than this investigation has been able to uncover. As the two-year statutory period for instituting court-martial proceedings was about to expire, Kimmel and Short were requested by the Secretaries of War and Navy to waive the Statute of Limitations. Adm. Kimmel did so but with the provision that any court martial be held in "open court" (exhibit 171). Gen. Short did likewise (Tr., pp. 8496–99). Similar requests were not made of other officers, not even of those who before this committee publicly accepted responsibility for certain failures of the high command in Washington.

In June of 1944 the Congress directed the Secretaries of War and Navy to conduct investigations into the Pearl Harbor attack. The War Department denied the Army Board of Investigation access to the intercepted messages. Gen. Miles, director of military intelligence at the time of Pearl Harbor, was ordered by Gen. Marshall not to testify on the subject of the intercepts (Tr., p. 11843). For a considerable period the Navy Court of Inquiry was denied access to the same material (exhibit 195). After repeated demands by Adm. Kimmel, the Navy Department released this restriction upon its own court. The War Department finally followed the same course. For the first time, late in the board's proceedings, Army officers were permitted to testify before the Army Board as to all details regarding the intercepts (Tr., p. 12035). But many important Army witnesses had already testified under the limitations previously ordered.

In the fall of 1944 the Army Board and Navy Court made their reports to the Secretaries of the War and Navy. These reports were critical of the conduct of Adm. Stark and Gen. Marshall. The findings were not made public. The Navy Court exonerated Adm. Kimmel. Adm. Kimmel's request to read its report was refused by the Secretary of the Navy (Tr., p. 6811). The Secretaries of War and Navy instituted further secret investigations dispensing with the services of the three-man board and court previously established, and each entrusting the conduct of proceedings to a single officer. Adm. Kimmel's request to be present at the further Navy investigation, to introduce evidence, to confront and cross-examine witnesses, was denied by the Secretary of the Navy (Tr., p. 6812). The affidavits and testimony at the further investigations contain many instances where witnesses gave evidence materially different from that which they had previously sworn to before the army board and the naval court. These changes were especially marked in testimony of certain key witnesses on the subject of the dissemination and evaluation of the intercepted messages in Washington. Again, before this committee these same witnesses further changed their testimony from that sworn to twice previously, or pleaded lapses of memory.

The record of the high military and civilian officials of the War and Navy Departments in dealing with the Pearl Harbor disaster from beginning to end does them no credit. It will have a permanent bad effect on the morale and integrity of the armed services. The administration had ample opportunity to record and preserve all the facts about Pearl Harbor, even if their public disclosure needed to wait upon the war's end. This was not done. The policy adopted was to place the public responsibility for the disaster on the commanders in the field, to be left there for all time. The policy failed only because suppression created public suspicion, and the Congress was alert.

Chapter Five

THE BASING OF THE FLEET

WHY, AND at whose command, was the Pacific fleet based at Pearl Harbor, within reach of the air striking arm of the Japanese navy?

The American fleet was started westward to the Pacific after World War I by President Wilson. The creation of a separate Pacific battle fleet was first announced in June, 1919. At the time it was said that stationing a strong fleet in each ocean would stimulate a spirit of rivalry within the service, and thus promote the efficiency of the entire Navy. But even then the notion seemed to be entertained that the fleet in the Pacific would constitute a "deterrent" to Japan, whose star was rising with the acquisition, under League of Nations mandate, of the German islands north of the equator.

By the end of 1919 the United States had assembled a fighting fleet of two hundred units in the Pacific, a force almost as large as the entire Japanese Navy of that day. Early in 1921 the Atlantic fleet was sent to the Pacific for joint maneuvers. In June of that year, after a Republican administration had returned to Washington, it was announced that it had been decided on the advice of naval authorities to station most of our fighting ships permanently in the Pacific, but to base them upon southern California.

In 1932 the security of the Pearl Harbor base was tested in Adm. Yarnell's mock attack. Yarnell's surprise should have resulted in serious misgivings as to the safety of the fleet while anchored in harbor.* In 1936, however, the American fleet was again taken to Pearl Harbor by its commander, Rear Adm. Joseph M. Reeves, subsequently a member of the Roberts Commission. On May 27 the battleship divisions and supporting craft—a fleet of one hundred sixty-five ships —moved into Pearl Harbor for a test of the base as an anchorage for the entire fleet. Because the harbor entrance was being dredged, three

*Cf. pp. 17-18.

carriers, the "Lexington," "Saratoga," and "Ranger," were left off-shore. The Roberts report, to which Reeves subscribed, recognized that there were diverse views respecting the basing of the entire fleet at Pearl Harbor, but stated, "We feel that the national policy in this matter is one that has been settled by those responsible for such decisions and that it is not within our province."

In 1939 the fleet shifted its war games from the West Coast to the Caribbean in what was regarded as a gesture of warning to Hitler and Mussolini that the United States would stand behind the nations opposing their ambitions. While the fleet was on the East Coast it was planned to hold a grand review in connection with the New York world's fair.

On April 16, 1939, however, the fleet unexpectedly was ordered back to the Pacific without explanation. This was about a month after Hitler had violated the Munich pact by absorbing all of Czechoslovakia, and eight days after Mussolini had marched into Albania. The return of the fleet to the Pacific was regarded at the time as evidence of an agreement with Britain under which the British fleet would safeguard the Atlantic in the event of war, while the American fleet stood watch over the Pacific.

After its return from the Caribbean, the main body of the fleet remained at San Diego until January, 1940, when it proceeded to Hawaii for war games. On February 3 the first step was taken to convert Pearl Harbor into the permanent base for a substantial number of fleet units. It was reported that the base would become the home port for a Hawaiian detachment consisting of thirteen ships: the heavy cruisers "Indianapolis," "Northhampton," "Houston," "Pensacola," "Salt Lake City," "Minneapolis," "Astoria," and "New Orleans," the light cruiser "Raleigh," the destroyer tender "Dobbin," and the minesweepers "Kingfisher," "Partridge," and "Turkey."

On May 7, 1940, the Navy announced that the entire fleet would remain at Pearl Harbor indefinitely. This represented a radical departure in American naval policy. Until this time it had been the Navy's policy to keep the fleet on the West Coast and to send it into blue water only in a period of tension. Not until the congressional investigation of 1945–46 would it be explained why this policy was abandoned and at whose behest.

On May 10, three days after the announcement that the fleet would be concentrated at Pearl Harbor, the German blitzkrieg in the west roared over the frontiers of Holland, Belgium, Luxembourg, and France. On the same day Winston Churchill succeeded Neville

Chamberlain as prime minister. As the Germans surged on toward completion of the conquest of all western Europe, it might have seemed to Mr. Roosevelt that he had his fleet in the wrong ocean. But he was inclined to dismiss the proposal for creation of a two-ocean navy as a crackpot idea.

At his press conference on May 14 he said that a two-ocean navy was "an entirely outmoded conception of naval defense."[1] He asked Congress for 50,000 airplanes, authority to muster the National Guard into federal service, and appropriations of a billion dollars for the Army and Navy. After that, he said, Congress could adjourn.

Congress, however, insisted on staying in session. It voted 5 billion dollars for defense and, on July 19, authorized a two-ocean navy. The Atlantic forces rapidly grew so large that a separate Atlantic fleet was created. But, to bolster this fleet, which was soon to enter into an undeclared war against Germany by executive order, the Pacific fleet was stripped of many of its major units. Steadily weakened, it still remained at Pearl Harbor—a temptation to Japan when the time would be ripe. This policy of splitting the fleet was severely criticized in 1941 by Capt. W. D. Puleston in his book, *The Armed Forces of the Pacific.*

"Until the two-ocean navy is completed," Puleston said, "the Navy should be concentrated in one fleet and kept in one ocean. At their present strengths the Pacific and Atlantic fleets would need to be brought together before undertaking a major campaign in either ocean."[2]

In June, 1940, national attention was focused on the Pacific fleet when it made a sudden and mysterious dash from its base. It is now known that the high command in Washington, after losing radio contact with the Japanese fleet, which unaccountably had gone into radio silence, had secretly alerted the Hawaiian garrison against the possibility of a trans-Pacific raid. Gen. Marshall, the Army chief of staff, ordered the troops of Gen. Herron's Hawaiian command to go on an all-out alert, occupying field positions with full equipment and ammunition.*

The fleet, under command of Adm. J. O. Richardson, had put to sea, not only to increase its security through freedom of maneuver, but to intercept any enemy fleet which might be approaching. At the end of a week the fleet returned to Hawaiian waters. The only explanation offered for its unexpected departure was that it had been engaged in routine training exercises. The Army, however, main-

*Cf. p. 246.

tained its alert for more than six weeks, although the fact was not made public for more than a year.

The congressional investigation in 1945 disclosed that the 1940 alert was based on the premise that an attack at any time on Hawaii by Japan "could not be ruled out because a large part of the fleet was based there." This estimate had been submitted to Chief of Staff Marshall by Maj. Gen. George V. Strong, chief of Army war plans in 1940.[3] It reduced to its simplest terms the obligation of the high command to put Hawaii on a full alert whenever available information indicated that there was a possibility of a sudden stroke against the fleet. Wherever the fleet was, so Gen. Strong reasoned, there would the danger be greatest. The conclusion was obvious.[4] It persuaded Gen. Marshall in 1940, for he promptly directed an all-out alert. Why, in November and December, 1941, when he knew the danger to be far greater, he did not follow a similar course is one of the unanswered mysteries.

Gen. Strong's view as to the inevitability of the place of attack was echoed by Capt. A. H. McCollum, head of the Far Eastern section of naval intelligence. He testified before the congressional committee that he had felt for many years that the Japanese would open hostilities by attacking our fleet wherever it was.[5]

The story of who sent the fleet to Pearl Harbor and why it was ordered there was first explained in testimony before the congressional committee in November, 1945, by Adm. Richardson.[6] Richardson had taken up his duties as commander-in-chief of the United States fleet on January 5, 1940. The fleet at that time was based at the California ports of San Diego, San Pedro, and Long Beach. It proceeded to sea on spring maneuvers, arriving at Lahaina Roads in Hawaii on April 10. It was supposed to depart on May 9, but two days before the scheduled date Richardson was notified by Adm. Stark that there would be a delay of two weeks.

In explaining this decision, Stark wrote Richardson:

> Just hung up the telephone after talking with the President and by the time this reaches you, you will have received word to remain in Hawaiian waters for a couple of weeks. When the fleet returns to the coast (and I trust the delay will not be over two weeks, but I cannot tell) the President has asked that the fleet schedule be so arranged that on extremely short notice the fleet will be able to return concentrated to Hawaiian waters.[7]

Stark explained that, with Italy expected to enter the European war at any moment, nobody could guess what lay ahead, and that the decision to retain the fleet at Pearl Harbor was related to the uncertainties of the situation. The letter shows that Roosevelt, using his "commander-in-chief" powers, was making decisions for the Navy, and that the order to keep the fleet at Oahu was his.

Richardson, in response to this communication, wrote Stark,

> It seems that, under present world-conditions, the paramount thing for us is the security of the western hemisphere. This, in my opinion, transcends everything—anything certainly in the Far East, our own or other interests.
>
> South America is the greatest prize yet remaining to be grabbed. Until the outcome in Europe can be more clearly seen, security in the western hemisphere seems to be the most important consideration to us.
>
> I feel that any move west [toward Japan and Asia] means hostilities. I feel that at this time it would be a grave mistake to become involved in the west, where our interests, although important, are not vital, and thereby reduce our ability to maintain the security of the western hemisphere, which is vital.
>
> If the fleet is to go west it can only start, properly prepared, from the West Coast where it can be docked, manned, stocked and stripped, and a suitable train assembled.[8]

On May 22, still at Pearl Harbor, Richardson sent another letter to Stark demanding to know why the fleet was being kept in Hawaii. He asked:

> Are we here primarily to influence the actions of other nations by our presence, and if so, what effect would the carrying out of normal training . . . have on this purpose? . . . Are we here as a stepping off place for belligerent activity? If so, we should devote all our time and energies to preparing for war. . . . This could more effectively and expeditiously be accomplished by an immediate return to the West Coast. . . . As it is now, to try to do both (train and prepare for belligerent action) from here and at the same time is a diversification of effort and purpose that can only result in the accomplishment of neither.

Stark on May 27 replied to the question of why Richardson was in the Hawaiian area by saying,

> You are there because of the deterrent effect which it is thought your presence may have on the Japs going into the East Indies. . . . You would naturally ask—suppose the Japs do go into the East Indies? What are we going to do about it? My answer to that is, I don't know and I think there is nobody on God's green earth who can tell you.

On June 22 Stark advised Richardson that the fleet was to remain "tentatively" in Pearl Harbor. Richardson continued his protests against retaining the fleet in Hawaii. On September 12 he filed a memorandum with Stark listing his objections as follows:

1. Difficulty, delay, and cost of transporting men, munitions, and supplies.

2. Inadequacy of Lahaina as operating anchorage because of lack of security.

3. Inadequacy of Pearl Harbor as an operating anchorage because of difficulties of entry, berthing, and departure of large ships.

4. Congested and restricted operating areas in the air and on the surface.

5. Inadequate facilities for fleet services, training, recreation, and housing.

6. Prolonged absence from mainland of officers and men in time of peace adversely affects morale.

7. In case of war, necessary for fleet to return to mobilization ports on west coast or accept partial and unorganized mobilization measures, resulting in confusion and a net loss of time.

Richardson continued:

If the disposition of the fleet were determined solely by naval considerations, the major portion of the fleet should return to its normal Pacific coast bases because such basing would facilitate its training and its preparation for war.

If factors other than purely naval ones are to influence the decision as to where the fleet should be based at this time, the naval factors should be fully presented and carefully considered, as well as the probable effect of the decision on the readiness of the fleet. In other words, is it more important to lend strength to diplomatic representations in the Pacific by basing the fleet in the Hawaiian area, than to facilitate its preparation for active service in any area by basing the major part of it on normal Pacific coast bases?

In case our relations with another Pacific nation deteriorate, what is the State Department's conception of our next move? Does it believe that the fleet is now mobilized and that it could embark on a campaign directly from Hawaii or safely conduct necessary training from the insecure anchorage at Lahaina, which is 2,000 miles nearer enemy submarine bases than our normal Pacific coast bases?

Adm. Richardson felt so strongly about these matters that when he was called to Washington, he took them up directly with the

President. On October 8 he was received by Roosevelt for a White House luncheon conference. Adm. William D. Leahy, then governor of Puerto Rico, who later became Presidential chief of staff, was also present.

Richardson had felt for a long time that the President's disposition to ignore competent professional advice and formulate his own war strategy was dangerous to the nation and to the fleet. On January 26, before the fleet was ordered to Pearl Harbor, he had expressed himself vehemently in a private letter to Adm. Stark:

> I strongly feel that you should *repeatedly impress on the boss* that an Orange [Japanese] war would probably last some years and cost much money, my guess is five to ten years, 35 to 70 billion dollars. . . . We ought not to go into a thing like this unless we expected to see it through.
>
> I hesitate to write you because the written word is so easily misunderstood. *Also I do not know what your ideas are,* what you are telling the boss, what is the meaning of our diplomatic moves, or our senators' talks, or our neutrality patrol. But you are *the principal and only Naval adviser* to the boss and he should know that our fleet cannot just sail away, lick Orange, and be back home in a year or so. Also the probable cost of any war should be compared [to] the probable value of winning the war . . . .
>
> All of this letter may be needless, but I know that if you do not tell the boss what you really know and feel about the probable cost and duration of an Orange war, NOBODY WILL.*

Asked before the congressional committee who "the boss" was, Richardson retorted, "The President of the United States, known by (*sic*) the Constitution as the commander-in-chief of the Army and Navy!"[9]

Stark, in response to these promptings, made a half-hearted attempt to talk sense to the commander-in-chief, but was rebuffed. Describing his lack of success, he said, "I asked the President several times what our Navy's role would be if Japan made war on British possessions. He just didn't answer. Once he said, 'Don't ask me those questions'. I don't think he knew the answer."[10]

Richardson was well aware when he came to Washington that no one else had been able to deter Roosevelt from his career as a one-man general staff, working through intuition. He determined, however, to make one last attempt himself. The admiral said:

*The two words were capitalized and underscored.

My mission was primarily to find out what was back of our intentions in the Pacific and to ascertain the duration of the stay of the fleet in Pearl Harbor. I took up with the President the question of returning to the Pacific coast all of the fleet except the Hawaiian detachment. The President stated that the fleet was retained in the Hawaiian area in order to exercise a restraining influence on the actions of Japan.

I stated that in my opinion the presence of the fleet in Hawaii might influence a civilian political government, but that Japan had a military government which knew the fleet was undermanned, unprepared for war, and had no train of auxiliary ships, without which it could not undertake active operations. Therefore, the presence of the fleet in Hawaii could not exercise a restraining influence on Japanese action.

I further stated we were more likely to make the Japanese feel that we meant business if a train were assembled and the fleet returned to the Pacific coast, the complements filled, the ships docked and fully supplied with ammunition, provisions, stores, and fuel, and then stripped for war operations.

The President said in effect, "Despite what you believe, I know that the presence of the fleet in the Hawaiian area has had and is now having a restraining influence on the actions of Japan."

I said, "Mr. President, I still do not believe it and I know that our fleet is disadvantageously disposed for preparing for or initiating war operations."

The President then said, "I can be convinced of the desirability of returning the battleships to the West Coast if I can be given a good statement which will convince the American people and the Japanese government that in bringing the battleships to the west coast we are not stepping backwards!"

Later I asked the President if we were going to enter the war. He replied that if the Japanese attacked Thailand, or the Kra Peninsula, or the Dutch East Indies, we would not enter the war; that even if they attacked the Philippines he doubted whether we would enter the war, but that they could not always avoid making mistakes, and that as the war continued and the area of operations expanded, sooner or later they would make a mistake and we would enter the war.[11]

Within a month the nation would vote on Roosevelt's third-term aspirations. He was telling Adm. Richardson that in the end Japan "would make a mistake and we would enter the war," but three weeks later he would address the parents of the nation and, in his Boston broadcast, make his famous pledge, "I have said this before, but I shall say it again and again and again: Your sons are not going to be sent into any foreign wars."[12]

Although he was now telling his fleet commander that the United States would not even fight in defense of the Philippines, an American possession, let alone in defense of Siam or the British and Dutch colonies, within three months he would commission his Army and Navy high command to initiate staff conversations with the British and Dutch which committed this country to fight in defense of their colonies.*

He was frank only when he expressed belief that some Japanese "mistake" would serve as the *casus belli*.

Two days after this meeting at the White House, Adm. Richardson learned more about Roosevelt's plans concerning the Pacific fleet. He was summoned to a conference in the office of Secretary Knox, together with Adm. Stark, Adm. Royal E. Ingersoll, deputy chief of operations; Capt. Charles M. Cooke, of Stark's staff, and Comdr. Vincent R. Murphy, Richardson's aide. Richardson related:

The Secretary stated that he had important information bearing on the employment of the fleet. He stated that he had just talked to the President and that the President was concerned about the Japanese reaction to the British decision to reopen the Burma road October 17.

In the event of drastic Japanese action, Knox said, the President was considering shutting off all trade between Japan and America and establishing a patrol of light ships in two lines, one from Hawaii west to the Philippines, and the other from Samoa to the Dutch East Indies.

The question was raised whether this included stopping Jap ships as well as others. The view was expressed that this would be an act of war. I asked if the President was considering a declaration of war. The Secretary said the President hadn't said.

"All I know is what I've been told," the Secretary said. I was amazed at the proposal. I said the fleet was not prepared to put such a plan into effect and war would be the certain result of such a course of action. I said we would be certain to lose many ships.

There was further discussion that such a line of ships would disperse the units and leave them exposed to destruction. It was said that the best way to control shipping would be to control the source of the trade by control of the relatively few ports involved. I, in particular, protested.

The Secretary appeared displeased at the general reaction,

*Cf. pp. 104-16, 367-69.

and mine in particular and said, "I am not a strategist; if you don't like the President's plan, draw up one of your own to accomplish the same purpose." The interview ended with Adm. Stark and I agreeing to draw up a tentative plan of operations in connection with the reopening of the Burma road.[18]

The plan drafted by Stark and Richardson provided for the transfer to the Pacific of an aircraft carrier, planes, one or two cruisers, and some destroyers. "Adm. Stark," said Richardson, "was not prepared to approve the plan. He said he would talk with the President and let me know later. When the plan was completed, both Secretary Knox and the President were away from Washington. All I ever heard of the plan after that was a directive from Adm. Stark to send a copy of it to Adm Hart, commander of the Asiatic squadron."

This astonishing scheme to put Japan under blockade was advanced by Roosevelt three weeks before his "again and again and again" speech and a month before the national election. He could not have been unaware that it inevitably would have led to war. Yet, while keeping such projects secret from the country, he was busy assuring the electorate that he firmly intended to stay out of war.

The plan shows Roosevelt as a reckless amateur naval strategist who thought that ships could be disposed about the oceans in the way that a child places dominoes on a board. If the plan had ever been put into effect, Japan would have been able to destroy the fleet piecemeal, for it would have been so dispersed that no warship could support any other. Hitler at his intuitive worst never engaged in such fantasies.

While in Washington, Richardson related, he was subjected from many sides to the theory that the fleet at Pearl Harbor was a deterrent to Japan. The State Department, it seemed to him, was the leading exponent of this school of thought. Secretary Hull, he said, "felt we should take a very strong position in regard to Japan. And he felt that the retention of the fleet in Hawaii reflected that strong attitude."

Adm. Richardson said he gathered the impression from his Washington visit that Dr. Stanley Hornbeck, then adviser to the State Department on Far East relations and now ambassador to Holland, was regarded by the administration as the unofficial commander-in-chief of the fleet. The admiral said:

Whether wrong or not, after talking with Dr. Hornbeck I was distinctly of the impression that he was exercising greater influence over the disposition of the fleet than I was. In my notebook at the time I wrote my impression that he was "the strong man on the Far East and the cause of our staying in Hawaii, where he will hold us as long as he can." He was, however, unwilling to accept the responsibility for the retention of the fleet in Hawaii. I told him he was completely wrong, even though he was the State Department's adviser on foreign affairs and had written many books on the subject.[14]

The evidence is abundant that the State Department, together with Roosevelt, was running the Navy, although it did not trouble to take the field commanders who would be forced to bear the brunt of the consequences of its action into its confidence by keeping them abreast of diplomatic developments.*

Adm. Stark said that a year before the war began the State Department wanted to extend its policy of using the Navy as a "deterrent" to Japan by sending a naval detachment to the Philippines. He said that facilities were lacking in the Philippines to maintain a sizable naval force. "The Navy," he said at the time, "already is faced with enough difficulty maintaining the Pacific fleet at Pearl Harbor." In letters to Adm. Kimmel, he referred to State Department suggestions as "childish."[15]

Stark said, however, that he did agree to a scheme cooked up in combination by Roosevelt and the State Department to keep naval vessels "popping up" at various points in the Western Pacific so that the Japs would be left guessing.

"Did the State Department want to use the Navy in a diplomatic way?" Stark was asked.

"They wanted to use it in supporting diplomacy in any way they thought effective," the admiral replied.[16]

In a letter to Richardson on March 15, 1940, Stark indicated that the State Department had had a hand in sending the original Hawaiian detachment of thirteen warships to Pearl Harbor. "I still think that the decision to send the detachment to Hawaii under present world-conditions is sound," he asserted. "No one can measure how much effect its presence there may have on the Orange foreign policy. The State Department is strong for the present setup and considers it beneficial; they were in on all discussions, press releases, etc."

Sumner Welles, Undersecretary of State, said that the only dis-

---

*The irresponsibility of the State Department in military matters is reflected in the statement in the minority report of the Joint Congressional Committee (p. 29): "The State Department seemed to labor under the impression that the United States could defeat Japan in a few weeks." The minority adds that the same kind of thinking permeated the annual report of Secretary of the Navy Knox, released December 6, 1941.

cussion of Pearl Harbor in numerous State Department conferences was of its strategic position in the Pacific. No one in the department, he said, regarded Pearl Harbor as an object of attack, but he said he recalled conversations with Richardson in which the fleet commander expressed "grave concern" because the fleet was not secure in the base.

He said the State Department opposed Richardson's suggestion that the fleet be moved to the Pacific Coast because such a step, in the opinion of department officers, would have given the Chinese the impression that we were withdrawing from the Pacific and would have been an invitation to the Japanese to "move in." When he talked to Richardson, Welles said, he did not believe that Pearl Harbor was in danger of attack. That, he said, was a question for the President and the Navy Department to decide.

"So the President had the Navy Department and State Department views before him and it was up to him to make the decision about moving the fleet, basing it on the information before him?" Welles was asked.

"That is correct," Welles said.[17]

Joseph C. Grew, former ambassador to Tokyo, also echoed the State Department opinion that the fleet, in Hawaii, was a "deterrent." He said that he hadn't been consulted on the subject of basing the fleet at Pearl Harbor, but that he did think it had a restraining influence on Japan and was "more or less useful there."

"What restraining influence did it have on December 7, 1941?" Grew was asked.

"Definitely no effect," he replied.

Grew explained that he did not know that the fleet was undermanned, undersupplied, and totally unprepared for war, as Richardson testified, and that keeping it bottled up in harbor would have no effect in deterring Japan from aggressive action.[18]

Under examination by members of the congressional committee, Adm. Richardson was asked, "Was the fleet in Pearl Harbor a restraining influence, as the President contended?"

"I didn't think so when I was talking to him and I haven't changed my mind!" Richardson responded.

"Did the Japs know the deficiencies of our Navy?"

"I never had any doubt that they did," Richardson replied. "The Secretary of the Navy told me the Japs knew more about our fleet than I did!"

"Was any definite order issued to keep the fleet in Pearl Harbor after it arrived there from fleet maneuvers in May, 1940?"

"There was never a definite order," Richardson replied. "We just gradually drifted into staying."

"After your argument with the President in October, 1940, over the basing of the fleet, when did you next hear from him?"

"I never heard from him again," the admiral said. "I never saw him again."[19]

Returning to Hawaii, Richardson wrote a memorandum to Stark from Bremerton, Washington, in which he said that he wanted to stress his firm conviction that "neither the Navy nor the country was prepared for war with Japan." He stated:

It now appears that more active, more open steps aimed at Japan are in serious contemplation and that these steps, if taken now, may lead to hostilities. The present Orange plan [for attack against Japan] is believed beyond the present strength of the United States fleet and beyond the present resources of the United States Navy. The strength of the fleet is not sufficient. We cannot at this time, even with Great Britain assuming responsibility for our Atlantic interests, denude the ocean of sufficient forces to protect our coastal trade and to safeguard our more vital interests in South America. Nor can we neglect the protection of our own and the interdiction of Japanese trade in the Southeastern Pacific.

The Army is not now prepared and will not in the future be prepared to support our western advance. The Fleet Marine Force is not sufficient to support the necessary operations alone.[20]

A month later, on November 22, Stark wrote Richardson a letter which was significant in that it conceded that the fleet at Pearl Harbor was vulnerable. "Much is being done by the Army, and by the Navy in support of the Army, to maintain security of the Panama Canal," the chief of naval operations stated. "Of at least equal importance is the security of our fleet against sudden destructive attack. And the fleet is, as usually must be the case, in a more exposed situation."

Adm. Richardson remained in his command only four months after he took issue with Roosevelt. On February 1, 1941, after only thirteen months in a post where the normal tour of duty was two years, he was relieved. His successor, Adm. Kimmel, was designated not only commander-in-chief of the United States fleet, but commander-in-chief of the Pacific fleet, a new command created with his accession.

Richardson reported in Washington to Secretary Knox on March 24, 1941. "When I saw the Secretary," he related, "I said, 'In all my experience in the Navy, I have never known of a flag officer being detached in the same manner as I, and I feel I owe it to myself to know why.' The Secretary said the President would send for me and talk the matter over."

"Did the President ever send for you?" Richardson was asked. "He did not."

"Did you seek a meeting with the President?"

"By no means."

"Did anything the Secretary say to you indicate to you why you had been detached?"

"He told me, 'The last time you were here you hurt the President's feelings.' "[21]

Adm. Richardson was not alone in the belief that the fleet at Oahu served no sensible purpose—that it could neither act as a "deterrent" to Japan, as the administration believed, nor take the offensive from its Pearl Harbor base.

Adm. Stark, said Richardson, supported him. The ousted commander said:

> It is my belief that had Adm. Stark been uninfluenced by other considerations, he'd have agreed wholeheartedly with me on that point. His letters show that in many instances. When I was given permission to return one-third of the fleet at a time to the Pacific coast for replenishment of supplies and obtaining additional men, Adm. Stark said that he gave the order "with great pleasure."[22]

Stark, when called to testify, said that he agreed with Richardson originally on the inadvisability of basing the fleet at Pearl Harbor, but by the time Kimmel was appointed commander he was inclined to believe that the fleet, at Hawaii, was a deterrent to Japan. He said that he had had one conversation with Roosevelt in which the question of withdrawing the fleet was discussed. One view, he said, was that withdrawal to the coast, followed by a return to Hawaii, would have diplomatic repercussions.

"Whenever I'm in doubt and don't know what is best," Stark quoted Roosevelt as saying, "I find it best to sit tight."[23]

Roosevelt sat tight and the fleet stayed at Pearl Harbor.

Adm. Kimmel, who inherited command from Richardson, said in his testimony before the Roberts Commission:

> I knew that the Navy Department and the administration in Washington insisted on keeping the fleet out here. I knew

of the vulnerability of the fleet here. I thought it was appreciated in the Navy Department as well as by me, but it was one of the things I felt was beyond my power to change.

I had the choice of saying I would not stay and to get another commander-in-chief, or to remain. Naturally, I wish I had taken the other course at the present time, but I did not.[24]

Adm. Leahy testified that he "was in complete disagreement" with the school of thought which contended that the fleet, in Hawaii, could exercise a restraining influence on Japan. "It was certainly not a restraining influence," Leahy said, "if it was not ready for war. I'm in complete agreement with Adm. Richardson on that."[25]

Adm. Kimmel said that, because of the depletion of fuel oil reserves, and because he possessed no air cover which would safeguard the fleet if it put to sea, he had no option except to keep his ships in harbor after dispatching his two carrier forces to Wake and Midway Islands on orders from Washington just before the Japanese surprise.* It was also necessary to keep the ships in harbor, he said, so that they could be altered in line with current war experiences.[26]

Adm. Stark, in turn, said he had no criticism of Kimmel for keeping the remainder of the fleet, including eight battleships, in harbor. There was a difference of opinion in naval circles, he said, as to whether the fleet was safer at sea or in port, where there were harbor defenses and short-range fighter planes for protection.[27] From this testimony, it is apparent that the fatal mistake was in sending the fleet to Oahu in the first place. That decision was Roosevelt's. The minority report of the Joint Congressional Committee (pp. 49-53) observed:

> The decision to base the fleet at Pearl Harbor was made by the President in March 1940, over the protest of Admiral Richardson. . . .
>
> When this decision to base the fleet at Pearl Harbor was made, certain definite facts in relation to such base must be presumed to have been fully known and appreciated by the responsible command at Washington.
>
> The base is a shallow-water base with limited base mobility, with no chance for concealment or camouflage and without

---

*The minority report of the Joint Congressional Committee (p. 54) states: "The fuel reserves were insufficient, limiting full use of the fleet at sea, required constant augmentation from the mainland, and the location of such fuel supplies was such as to make them vulnerable to any raiding attack. The fleet was required to come into the base at frequent intervals to refuel. The facilities at the base made such refueling slow. The fleet was without a sufficient supply of fast tankers to permit refueling at sea, and there was ever present the inescapable fact that a destruction of the fuel supply would necessarily immobilize the entire fleet."

enough air beaches to properly park the necessary defensive air equipment. Entrance to the base is by a narrow winding channel requiring sorties at reduced speed, and in single file, and presenting the possibility of a blockade of the base by an air or submarine attack on the entrance.

The base is surrounded by high land immediately adjacent to the city of Honolulu, thereby affording full public familiarity with installations and movements within the base at all times.

The base is located on an island where the population was heavily Japanese, and where, as was well known, Japanese espionage was rampant, and making it probable that any defensive insufficiency of any kind or nature would be open to Japanese information.

All of the fuel for the base must be transported, by tanker, from the mainland more than 2,000 miles away, thus intensifying the necessity for complete defensive equipment and supplies for the base.

The waters about Oahu are of a depth facilitating the concealed movement of submarines, and the near approach of submarines to the shore, thereby favoring such methods of hostile attack.

The approaches to Oahu cover a full circle of 360°, with open sea available on all sides.

The situation thus confronting the Pacific fleet upon reaching its Pearl Harbor base seems entirely clear. Before the base could be a safe base, it must be supplied with adequate defense facilities, which facilities must be in kind and amount in relation to the physical characteristics of the base above referred to. An absence of adequate defensive facilities directly increased the peril of the fleet. Since the decision to base the fleet at Pearl Harbor was made at Washington, the responsibility for providing proper base defense for the fleet rested primarily upon Washington. (See Stark letter, Nov. 22, 1940, Tr., Vol. 5, pp. 706 ff.). . . .

The record discloses that with full knowledge of the defense necessities inherent in the defense of the Pearl Harbor base, and with full knowledge of the dangers and peril imposed upon the fleet while based at the Pearl Harbor base, and with full knowledge of the equipment essential to a proper protection of the fleet at such base, it was decided by President Roosevelt to remove the fleet from the mainland bases and base it at Pearl Harbor. . . .

We are forced to conclude, therefore, that in view of the obligations assumed by the government in other military theaters, ... and the consequent inability of the government to properly contribute to the safety of the fleet at Pearl Harbor, that the only alternative left which might have relieved the fleet from the resultant peril would have been to have changed the original decision to base the fleet at Pearl Harbor, and *thereupon return the fleet to its several mainland bases.* It appears obvious that the safety of the fleet would have been helped by such removal. The perimeter of a defense at a mainland base would only be 180° instead of 360°, thus permitting distant patrol reconnaissance by one-half as many planes. The transportation and supply facilities to the mainland base would be immensely improved, as would all necessary communication facilities. The mobility of the fleet at a mainland base would have been improved and the concentration of the fleet in a single limited base would have been avoided. *We therefore are of the opinion that the fleet should not have been based at Pearl Harbor unless proper base defenses were assured.*

Since no such change in policy was approved, and the fleet remained based at Pearl Harbor without the necessary defense equipment to which we have referred—plus the fact that the precise status of the defense weakness must be assumed to have been open to the unusual Japanese espionage operating in Hawaii, and therefore that the Tokyo war office must be assumed to have been cognizant of the status of affairs at Pearl Harbor, we are forced to conclude that the failure to remove the fleet from Pearl Harbor to the mainland must be viewed as an important relevant factor necessarily involved in the success of the Japanese attack on Dec. 7.

When asked before the congressional committee whether he thought the fleet, at Hawaii, was a deterrent to Japanese aggression, Adm. Kimmel said the Jap attack on the fleet was a sufficient answer to this theory. "They made an attack," he said. "The facts speak for themselves."[28]

Chapter Six

BLUEPRINT FOR DEFEAT

THE FLEET suffered a crushing disaster on December 7, 1941, but the Japanese attack produced one unexpectedly advantageous result. With eight battleships knocked out, the fleet was forced to rely on carriers and fast cruisers. The change which the battleship admirals had rejected nine years before after Adm. Yarnell's simulated carrier attack on Oahu was thrust upon them by circumstances. At the time, however, few high officers viewed the matter in this light. In fact, a kind of paralysis seized the high command, and with the exception of a carrier raid by Adm. Halsey's task force in the Gilbert and Marshall Islands on January 31, 1942, the Pacific fleet saw almost no action for many months to come.

The attack on Pearl Harbor had demonstrated many flagrant errors in the traditional concepts held by the Army and Navy. Pearl Harbor in itself was valuable only as an advance fleet and air base from which American forces could sally forth to seek out an enemy and, as a collateral effect, protect the security of the mainland. Lying 2,091 miles west of San Francisco and 3,397 miles from Yokosuka naval base at Yokohama, it was strategically placed to serve as a spring-board against Japan. Aside from the thesis of President Roosevelt and the State Department that the fleet at Pearl Harbor served as a "deterrent" to the Japanese, the fleet was at Hawaii for no other reason than to be able to take the offensive immediately war was declared and to advance against the Japanese fleet and Japanese outposts in the Pacific.

It was necessary, of course, to prevent the Hawaiian Islands from falling into the hands of the enemy and especially to safeguard the fleet while it was in harbor. The division of responsibilities in achieving these purposes as outlined under the joint Army-Navy coastal frontier defense plan, which was approved April 11, 1941, was as follows:

A. Joint Task—To hold Oahu as a main outlying naval base, and to protect shipping in the coastal zone.

B. Army Task—To hold Oahu against attacks by sea, land, and air forces, against hostile sympathizers, and to support the naval forces.

C. Navy Task—To control the coastal zone and to control and protect shipping therein, and to support the Army forces.[1]

The protection of the base and of the fleet was primarily the duty of the Army, and for this purpose Oahu was garrisoned on December 7 by 40,469 men and 2,490 officers.[2] The Army operated the coast defense guns, all anti-aircraft batteries except those on naval ships, most of the pursuit aircraft on the island, an inshore air patrol extending 20 miles to sea, and the aircraft warning service. To the Navy was assigned distance reconnaissance extending from 200 to 600 miles to sea.[3]

The very fact that the fleet was in harbor increased the responsibilities of the Army, because the fleet when tied up was not in a position to support the Army forces, either by reconnaissance or by being at sea on an operational basis in the waters adjacent to the islands. When in harbor, the fleet was temporarily immobilized and at its most vulnerable.

The Army and Navy had, as they thought, made adequate provision for the protection of the base and fleet, but latent in the thoughts of the high command was the belief that Pearl Harbor was itself invulnerable. This outlook was reflected in an aide mémoire on the defense of Hawaii which Gen. Marshall delivered to President Roosevelt May 3, 1941. This memorandum stated flatly, "The island of Oahu, due to its fortification, its garrison, and physical characteristics, is believed to be the strongest fortress in the world."[4] The memorandum went on to say that any enemy force would be under constant attack from the time it approached within 750 miles of Oahu. This estimate presupposed that Hawaii had the necessary planes for long-range reconnaissance and was using them for that purpose, whereas neither fact was true.

When Adm. Kimmel took command of the Pacific fleet on February 1, 1941, he was "astounded at the then existing weakness" of the Pearl Harbor defenses.[5] He consulted on these problems with Adm. Richardson, whom he relieved as commander, and as a result a letter under Richardson's signature was forwarded on January 25, 1941, to

Secretary of the Navy Knox, who brought it to the attention of Henry L. Stimson, the Secretary of War. The most flagrant deficiencies pointed out in this letter were:

(a) The critical inadequacy of A.A. guns available for the defense of Pearl Harbor, necessitating constant manning of ship's A.A. guns while in port.

(b) The small number and obsolescent condition of land-based aircraft, necessitating constant readiness of striking groups of fleet planes and use of fleet planes for local patrols.

(c) Lack of suitable local defense vessels for the Fourteenth Naval district, etc.

(d) Lack of aircraft detection devices ashore.[6]

Although Washington promised to remedy these shortcomings, very little was done in the months leading up to the Japanese attack.

Gen. Short also repeatedly complained to Washington of deficiencies in the resources allotted him. From February 7 to December 7, 1941, he made requests to Washington for $22,953,697 to be used on projects to improve the Hawaiian defenses. He proposed to use this money for the installation of bunkers, military roads and trails, a battery for Kaneohe Bay, the construction of ten airports, the improvement of Wheeler Field, camouflaging airfields, bombproofing the air depot at Hickam Field, and for materials necessary to these projects.

Of this requested sum, he was allowed by the War Department only $350,000 for roads and trails. This grant represented only 1½ per cent of what he had asked.[7]

Other difficulties were put in the way of the Army in organizing an effective defense. This was especially demonstrated in Short's struggle to obtain appropriate sites for the location of radar stations. On March 6, 1941, Short wrote Chief of Staff Marshall begging for prompt action in supplying modern aircraft detection units. He said that the detection range of equipment then available was only 5 miles.[8] He reiterated the critical shortage of long-range detector devices in a second letter to Marshall on March 15. The chief of staff on March 28 promised delivery of radar units in April or May.[9]

Three permanent radar sets were delivered on June 3 and six mobile radar stations on August 1.[10] Five of the mobile stations were in operation December 7, but towers on which the permanent units were to be placed were still lying on the docks at Oakland, California, when Pearl Harbor was attacked, so that these three fixed sets were not operating December 7.[11] Mayor LaGuardia and Mrs. Roosevelt, running the Office of Civilian Defense, had been staging practice blackouts in New York and other cities and crying up the danger of transoceanic air raids on major American cities. One effect of this was that modern radar units were installed in New York, San Francisco, and Seattle before they were provided for the bastion of Hawaii.*[12]

Additional obstruction was encountered from Secretary Harold L. Ickes' Interior Department. The Park Service, which was a branch of this department, was more concerned with preserving the beauty of the landscape than with enabling Hawaii to defend itself. When Gen. Short proposed to place a radar station on Mount Haleakala, the National Park Service withheld approval of the request. Short protested against Interior Department delays in his letter of March 6 to Marshall, saying, "I believe that this matter is sufficiently important to be brought to the attention of the Secretary of War to see if permission cannot be obtained from the Secretary of the Interior to construct the Haleakala installation without the necessity of submitting detailed plans for consideration by the National Park Service."[13]

On March 15 Marshall wrote Short,

> It will be necessary to comply with certain fixed regulations in those cases where facilities are to be established on lands pertaining to the Department of the Interior. The National Park Service officials are willing to give us the temporary use of their lands when other lands are not suitable for the purpose, but they will not waive the requirements as to the submission of preliminary building plans showing the architecture and general appearance. They are also very definitely opposed to permitting structures of any type to be erected at such places as will be open to view and materially alter the natural appearance of the reservation.[14]

Ickes' department also got in the way of the Navy when it was endeavoring to construct a radio monitoring station at Winter Harbor, Maine, in order to intercept secret Japanese code messages. The

*Cf. minority report of Joint Congressional Committee (p. 55): "The installation of the radar in Hawaii was inexcusably delayed. It was a method of defense peculiarly essential in Hawaii. It was known that there were insufficient planes and insufficient guns to protect the base, and this made the availability of radar all the more necessary. It seems we could have priority for radar protection in New York and other mainland points, where no attack was probable, but none in Hawaii, where radar information was essential. The result was that fixed radio installations were not accomplished at all prior to the Pearl Harbor attack, and such fixed installations would have furnished the most distant services. The mobile sets available had, by reason of the delay, been operating only on a short experimental basis. There was a scarcity of trained operators. The operators were trying to learn and operate at the same time. The selected hours of operation, which proved of vast importance, were not wisely fixed. Service stopped at 7:00 A.M., the very time when the danger was acute."

Winter Harbor station was on National Park land and, as with the radar facilities in Hawaii, the Park Service would not permit trees to be cut down or the landscape to be otherwise altered. As a consequence, the Winter Harbor station was handicapped by high trees around its antenna.[15]

Five radar stations, however, were operating on Oahu the morning of December 7. Although the stations had been operating every day from 4:00 to 7:00 A.M., with continued operation of three sets for training for a large portion of the day, they were ordered to close down on December 7 at 7 o'clock. Through one of those coincidences which bulked so large in the all-around lapse of defenses on December 7, a Signal Corps second lieutenant, Grove C. White, had obtained permission from the control officer the preceding day to close down the stations at that hour.[16]

Another failure of equal concern was the absence of distance reconnaissance from Hawaii on the morning of the attack. This was a Navy task. The Army on December 7 had only six B-17's in flyable condition,[17] while one hundred eighty were required under its plans for search and attack upon the enemy. The Navy had forty-nine patrol planes in flyable condition.[18] All of these planes had arrived during the preceding four weeks. They were experiencing the shakedown difficulties of new planes. New engine sections which had cracked up required replacement. A program for the installation of leakproof tanks and armor was under way. There were no spare parts and no relief crews.

Adm. Kimmel testified before the Congressional Investigating Committee:

> To insure an island base against a surprise attack from fast carrier-based planes, it is necessary to patrol the evening before to a distance of 800 miles on a 360° arc. This requires eighty-four planes on one flight of 16 hours. Of course, the same planes and the same crews cannot make that 16-hour flight every day. For searches of this character over a protracted period, a pool of 250 planes would be required. . . .
> It is clear that I did not have a sufficient number of planes to conduct each day a 360 degree distant search from the island of Oahu. . . . A search of all sectors of approach to an island base is the only type of search that deserves the name. . . . The Secretary of the Navy in his indorsement of the record of the Naval Court of Inquiry has stated: "There were sufficient fleet patrol planes and crews, in fact, available at Oahu during the week preceding the attack to have flown, for at least several

weeks, a daily reconnaissance covering 128 degrees to a distance of about 700 miles."

This statement assumes that I could have used all the patrol force for this type of search alone without keeping any planes in reserve for emergency searches or to cover movements of ships in and out of the harbor and in the operating area. . . . If I instituted a distant search of any 128° sector around Oahu on and after November 27, within the foreseeable future I would have deprived the Pacific fleet of any efficient patrol plane force for its prescribed war missions.[19]

Kimmel emphasized that he had twice been directed to be prepared to carry out raids on the Marshall Islands under the Navy's war plan, which would become effective the moment that hostilities began, and that his patrol planes were required for extended use from advance bases under this plan. He had to decide what was the best use of the patrol planes in view of the war tasks confronting him. Had he directed their use for intensive distant reconnaissances from Oahu, he faced the peril of having them grounded when the war plan was executed. His decision was to conserve the planes in order that he might go on the offensive in compliance with his standing orders under the war plan.[20]

The Naval Court of Inquiry which investigated the Pearl Harbor disaster in 1944 submitted this estimate of the decision reached by Kimmel:

The task assigned the commander-in-chief, Pacific fleet, was to prepare his fleet for war. War was known to be imminent—how imminent he did not know. The fleet planes were constantly being used in patrolling the operating areas in which the fleet's preparations for war were being carried on. Diversion of these planes for reconnaissance or other purposes was not justified under existing circumstances and in the light of available information.

If so diverted, the state of readiness of the fleet for war would be reduced because of the enforced suspension of fleet operations. The value of the fleet patrol planes to the fleet would be reduced seriously after a few days because of the inability of planes and crews to stand up under the demands of daily long-range reconnaissance.

The omission of this reconnaissance was not due to oversight or neglect. It was the result of a military decision, reached after much deliberation and consultation with experienced officers and after weighing the information at hand and all factors involved.[21]

These were the reasons why Kimmel was not conducting distant reconnaissance on December 6-7. First, he did not have the planes to do so. Second, the planes available to him were earmarked for tasks with the fleet under a predetermined war plan. On December 7 only a few planes were up on the dawn patrol, all of them to the south and west of Oahu, in the fleet operating area.

If Kimmel had possessed the requisite number of planes, both for reconnaissance from Oahu and for patrol duty with the fleet, his task would have been simple. The danger to be expected from air attack had clearly been foreseen in at least two prophetic estimates. The first was the product of Gen. Hugh A. Drum, former commander of Army forces in Hawaii. In 1935 he submitted a memorandum to the War Department in which he warned that Pearl Harbor, with its oil and ammunition storage and air installations on the island of Oahu, was "extremely vulnerable to air attack." He further warned that "the first enemy hostile action will be attempted as a surprise."

"One Oriental power," Gen. Drum wrote, "is strong enough in surface vessels and aircraft to execute successful air attacks against these objectives unless intercepted in sufficient time and with sufficient strength to defeat the attacks."

Gen. Drum asserted that first information of approaching carriers must be obtained when they were at least 300 miles at sea to permit bombers to attack them before they could launch their planes. He recommended the establishment of air fields on the islands surrounding Oahu in order to reduce the flight time of intercepting bombers.[22]

A reply from Maj. Gen. E. T. Conley, then adjutant general of the Army, drafted in April, 1936, estimated that enemy carriers could approach within 600 to 900 miles of Oahu by dusk of the day preceding the attack, and then, after making a fast night run, launch their planes from between 275 and 330 miles of the target. Gen. Conley said that long-range search planes, not available at that time in sufficient numbers, accordingly would have to patrol an arc with a perimeter of 4,000 miles and would be faced with the difficult task of tracking the carriers at night.[23] Radar for the detection of approaching aircraft had not yet been developed.

The plan of attack which Gen. Drum outlined in 1936 was followed almost exactly by the Japs on December 7.

The second prevision of the Jap attack was produced by Maj. Gen. Frederick L. Martin and Vice-Adm. Patrick N. L. Bellinger, commanders of the Army and Navy air forces on Oahu at the time of Pearl Harbor. In an estimate drafted April 9, 1941, they said:

In the past Orange [Japan] has never preceded hostile action by a declaration of war.

A successful, sudden raid against our ships and naval installations on Oahu might prevent effective defensive action by our forces in the Western Pacific for a long period.

It appears possible that Orange submarines and/or an Orange fast raiding force might arrive in Hawaiian waters with no prior warning from our intelligence service. . . . Orange might send into this area one or more submarines, and/or one or more fast raiding forces composed of carriers supported by fast cruisers. . . . It appears that the most likely and dangerous form of attack on Oahu might be an air attack. It is believed that at present such an attack would most likely be launched from one or more carriers, which would probably approach inside of 300 miles. . . . In a dawn air attack there is a high probability that it would be delivered as a complete surprise in spite of any patrols we might be using and that it might find us in a condition of readiness under which pursuit would be slow to start.[24]

This estimate also contained the significant line, "Any single submarine attack might indicate the presence of a considerable undiscovered surface force, probably composed of fast ships accompanied by a carrier." A submarine was, in fact, detected and sunk outside of Pearl Harbor by the destroyer "Ward" a full hour before the attack, but the report of this action failed to produce a justified general alarm.

On April 14 Martin and Bellinger transmitted to Gen. Marshall their estimate of the danger from surprise air attack, which the Army Pearl Harbor Board termed "prophetic in its accuracy and uncanny in its analysis of the enemy's intention." This document stated:

The Hawaiian air force is primarily concerned with the destruction of hostile carriers in this vicinity before they approach within range of Oahu where they can launch their bombardment aircraft for a raid or attack on Oahu.

Our most likely enemy, Orange, can probably employ a maximum of six carriers against Oahu. . . .

. . . The early morning attack is, therefore, the best plan of action open to the enemy.

The most favorable plan of action open to the enemy, and the action upon which we should base our plans of operation is the early morning attack in which the enemy must make good the following time schedule:

(1) Cross circle 881 nautical miles from Oahu at dawn of the day before attack. . . .

(3) Launch his planes 233 nautical miles from Oahu at dawn the day of the attack. . . .

. . . The sole purpose of the existence of the military establishment on Oahu, ground, and air, is for the defense of Oahu as an outlying naval base.

Then, in a sharp comment on Gen. Marshall's memorandum to the President on the assumed strength of Oahu, the Martin-Bellinger report remarked,

It has been said, and it is a popular belief, that Hawaii is the strongest outlying naval base in the world and could, therefore, withstand indefinitely attacks and attempted invasions. Plans based on such convictions are inherently weak and tend to create a false sense of security, with the consequent unpreparedness for offensive action.[25]

If Martin and Bellinger had had the Japanese operations orders before them, they could not have predicted the attack more accurately. Their report proposed to forestall the enemy by employment of long-range bombardment aviation to intercept a surface fleet. This, as William Bradford Huie has pointed out in *The Case against the Admirals,* was the very act which the Baker board appointed to survey the Army Air Corps in 1934 "had proclaimed could never be performed; the very doctrine under which the general headquarters air force had struggled to develop the B-17; the very principle which the Navy command had railed against for 20 years and which they refused to accept even then in 1941."[26]

Martin and Bellinger explained,

The key to this plan is found in the provision for, first, a complete and thorough search of the Hawaiian area daily during daylight; secondly, an aerial attack force available on call to hit a known objective located as a result of the search; and thirdly, if the objective is a carrier, to hit it the day before it can steam up to a position offshore of Oahu where it could launch its planes for an attack.

The report proposed a force of 180 B-17 Flying Fortresses for both search and attack. It was said that this plane was suitable for both functions and that, with 180 B-17's all possible approaches could be swept every day up to a radius of 800 miles. The admiral and general also asked for thirty-six long-range torpedo planes to supplement this force. The report said:

Our leading tacticians and strategists here concur in the opinion that this plan will solve the defense of the Hawaiian Islands, and in our knowledge it is the best and only means that can be devised to locate enemy carriers and make attacks thereon before said carriers can come within launching distance of Oahu. We must ferret out the enemy and destroy him before he can take action to destroy us. We must be prepared for D-day at any time.

It is believed that a force of 180 four-motored aircraft with 36 long-range torpedo airplanes is a small force when compared with the importance of this outpost. This force can be provided at less cost to the government than the cost of one modern battleship.[27]

What happened to this plan in Washington? The Army Air Force indorsed it; the Navy refused even to consider it. Since 1935 the Navy had fought the Flying Fortress with every weapon it possessed. It had imposed a limitation that the Army should have no bombers capable of going more than 300 miles to sea. It had thrown the weight of the Navy lobby against every appropriation for land-based bombardment planes. The plan reached Washington at a time when the Navy was seeking huge appropriations for its new battleship program. Accordingly, the Navy sought to prevent the plan from being circulated among even the higher echelons of the War and Navy departments, let alone the responsible committeemen in Congress.

Gen. Martin was sacked after the Pearl Harbor disaster at the same time as Gen. Short and Adm. Kimmel, but when the Roberts Commission uncovered the Martin-Bellinger plan, they realized they had the wrong man for their purposes. Martin was hastily restored to duty and no further word of censure was breathed against him.

Thus, the responsibility for failure to provide the means of reconnaissance and counter-attack which would without question have saved Hawaii again comes home to Washington. Although aircraft production was lagging in 1941, there was a sufficient number of patrol planes to have assured the safety of Hawaii—if the planes had gone to Hawaii, instead of to Britain and other countries under the Roosevelt administration's policy. While the Hawaiian air commanders were clamoring for planes to safeguard the base, 1,900 patrol planes were being lend-leased to foreign countries between February 1 and December 1, 1941. Of these, 1,750, or almost ten times the number which would have rendered Oahu safe, went to Great Britain.[28]

Lend-lease was also the reason why Oahu was short of anti-aircraft weapons. Gen. Short had available 82 three-inch anti-aircraft guns on December 7, while 98 were required by defense plans. He had 20 37-mm. anti-aircraft guns, with 135 required. He had 109 .50 caliber machine guns, with 345 required. He pointed out that the .50 caliber was the most effective weapon against planes coming in low over the water. Other weapons could not be depressed sufficiently to fire effectively on low flying planes. A year after the attack, Short said, Hawaii was equipped with more than seven times the number of these weapons he possessed.[29]

Replying to requests by Short for anti-aircraft weapons, Gen. Marshall on March 15, 1941, said that 16 three-inch anti-aircraft guns were not slated for arrival in Hawaii until December, and that 115 37-mm. anti-aircraft guns would not arrive until February, 1942.[30]

Despite this shortage of weapons, the Army had 60 mobile guns and 26 fixed guns, in addition to its 37-mm. and .50 caliber anti-aircraft guns.[31] The fact is, however, that only four of the Army's 32 anti-aircraft batteries ever opened fire on the Japs, according to the Army Board, and the first of these to get into action—the detachment at Sand Island—did not fire its first shots until 20 minutes after the raid had begun. The next battery to get into action was Battery "G" at Fort Weaver, which began to fire 35 minutes after the raid started. It was followed by Battery "A" at Fort Kamehameha 39 minutes after the beginning of the raid and Battery "F" at Fort Kamehameha one hour after the raid had begun. The only battery which claimed any enemy planes was that at Sand Island, which shot down two, while with the exception of these four batteries no other was in position ready to fire until well after the departure of the last of the Japanese raiders.[32]

The principal reason for this general ineffectiveness was that ammunition had not been issued because the ordnance department objected to having it out convenient to the guns for fear that it might get dirty. Thus none of the 16 mobile guns was supplied with ammunition on December 7. It required about six hours to get the ammunition broken out and distributed. The mobile guns had to obtain their ammunition from Aliamanu Crater, 2 to 3 miles from Army headquarters at Fort Shafter. Although the fixed batteries had their ammunition in boxes adjacent to the guns, few of them got into action because they were not manned. The Army Pearl Harbor Board found that most members of the two Army divisions on Oahu were in their quarters when the attack began, and that it took them a number of hours to move out after the raid to their positions.[33]

The lack of ammunition was illuminated by the statement of Maj. Gen. Henry T. Burgin, commander of the Coast Artillery, that

> it was almost a matter of impossibility to get your ammunition out, because in the minds of every one who has preservation of ammunition at heart it goes out, gets damaged, comes back in, and has to be renovated. The same was especially true here. It was extremely difficult to get your ammunition out of the magazines. We tried the ordnance people without results. Gen. Max Murray* and myself went personally to Gen. Short. Gen. Murray pled for his ammunition for the field artillery. I asked for ammunition for the anti-aircraft. We were put off, the idea behind it being that we would have our ammunition in plenty of time, that we would have warning before any attack ever struck.[34]

In this hope Gen. Burgin was destined to be disappointed, but the ultimate responsibility for the failure to give warning in sufficient time rested with Washington, rather than with his immediate superiors. As it was, the failure to supply the guns with ammunition cannot be excused. The only utility of the guns in being in Hawaii at all was to be able to meet an attack where and when it developed. It is evident that the commanders thought if there were to be any attack, it would come in the form of an attempted landing in force, and in this event they would have sufficient time to move the guns and troops into position and to break out the ammunition. Like the Navy, the last thing the Army was looking for was an air attack.

The anti-aircraft guns of the fleet were in a better state of readiness to meet a surprise attack than were those of the Army, but there was still room for improvement. Although *Battle Report,* the Navy's semi-official account of the Pearl Harbor attack, stated that "American guns were firing before the first of the invading planes had cleared the scene of attack,"[35] this was true only of a limited number of guns. For example, the officer of the deck on the light cruiser "Helena," after sounding the general alarm, cried in the same voice, "Break out service ammunition."[36] The minimum of ready guns aboard fleet units was placed at two .50-caliber guns, and, in most instances, two 5-inch dual purpose guns.[37] Secretary Knox, in a secret report after the attack, said that it was about four minutes before the first anti-aircraft fire from the Navy began.[38]

The battleship "Nevada," which was probably more successful than any other ship in getting its guns into action quickly, had four

*Maj. Gen. Maxwell Murray commanded the 25th Infantry Division.

ready machine guns, two forward and two aft, which were able to open fire at once. They were joined shortly by the ship's 5-inch anti-aircraft and broadside batteries, and, in combination, these weapons claimed five enemy planes.[39]

While putting up a comparatively more heavy curtain of fire than most of the other warships in Pearl Harbor, the "Nevada" could not avoid taking one torpedo and six bomb hits. This damage was sustained although the "Nevada" was the only warship in harbor to move away from the docks. A naval reservist, Lieut. Comdr. Francis J. Thomas, who was the senior officer aboard, is to be credited with this attempt to save the "Nevada" by getting her to open water where she could maneuver, but in the end the heavily damaged ship grounded near floating drydock no. 2. She was moved from that position by tugs and run aground in the shallow across from Hospital Point.

As to volume of fire, the battleship "Pennsylvania" was credited with firing more than 50,000 rounds of .50-caliber ammunition during the attack, but, with this expenditure, could claim no more than two Japanese planes and four probables.[40]

In the confusion attending the attack, American anti-aircraft crews fired upon their own planes. Adm. Kimmel told of six planes from the "Enterprise" being fired on as they came into Ford Island, and Rear Adm. Robert A. Theobald said that eighteen scout bombers from the same carrier were fired upon late in the evening of December 7.[41] American planes seeking the Japanese striking force after the attack also mistakenly bombed the cruiser "Portland" which was west of Pearl Harbor, believing it to be a Jap carrier, but fortunately damage was slight.[42]

The Navy Board of Inquiry said of the general state of preparedness aboard ship, "On all ships inside Pearl Harbor a considerable portion of the anti-aircraft guns was kept manned day and night and with ammunition immediately at hand," but it qualified this finding with the statement, "The anti-aircraft batteries installed on ships in Pearl Harbor were incapable of a volume of fire at all comparable to that of the batteries of the same ships today."*[43]

The primary reason for this was that the admirals had not yet awakened to the danger of air attack, but in part the lack of weapons was the result of administration policy which diverted material from our own forces and sent it to other nations, particularly Great Britain and Russia, under lend-lease. While the Pearl Harbor commanders

*There were 780 naval anti-aircraft guns, all ship-based (Maj., p. 67).

were appealing for anti-aircraft, 1,900 anti-aircraft weapons were sent to other nations between February and December, 1941, 1,500 of them to the British.[44]

The underlying failure of the defenses on December 7 must be attributed to the fact that the Army and Navy—both the high command in Washington and the forces in the field—had still to catch up with the lessons of modern war as demonstrated in Europe after September 1, 1939. As usual, they were prepared to fight the war before last. The early success of the Japanese grew out of the fact that they, far more than our own services, had been willing to abandon obsolete concepts and fight a 1941 war in 1941.

As was observed by the Associated Press reporter, Clark Lee, "The Pearl Harbor attack was a psychological blow to many of our admirals. They had put their faith in those 'elephants,' the battleships. Stripped of their battleships they were as lost as a man suddenly deprived of his trousers in the middle of Fifth Avenue. Their instinct was to cover up, to assume the defensive rather than to seek out the enemy for a finish fight."[45]

At the time of the Pearl Harbor assault, despite a number of estimates that the principal danger to the fleet would come from surprise air attack, the Army was worried about sabotage and the Navy about training and danger from enemy submarines. Officers of both services undoubtedly felt that the fleet, behind a submarine net and with its own guns supplementing those of the base defenses, was safe.

The admirals still held that the primary function of airplanes was to serve as the eyes of the fleet and to subserve battleships, scouting for them and protecting them while their 16-inch guns destroyed the enemy. Even with the lessons of war in the Mediterranean before them, the admirals were still accustomed to say that planes could inflict no great damage to battleships and were useful only in the degree that they could serve as spotters and increase the accuracy of battleship fire.

No one in the American services had been warned of the danger of aerial torpedo attack, although the British in their assault on the Italian fleet at Taranto on November 11, 1940, had demonstrated the deadly results which could be obtained with this weapon. British torpedo planes, taking the Italian fleet by surprise, had sunk or seriously damaged two battleships, two cruisers, a destroyer, and several supply ships.

On January 24, 1941, Secretary Knox had listed an air torpedo plane attack as one of the possible forms of hostile action against

Pearl Harbor.[46] Subsequently Adm. Stark, chief of naval operations, forwarded to the Pacific fleet and Adm. Bloch, commandant of the Fourteenth Naval District, detailed technical advice which practically eliminated from consideration an air torpedo attack as a serious danger to ships moored in Pearl Harbor.

The shallowness of the water in the harbor, which was 30 feet or less, except in the channels, where it was generally 45 feet, was thought to exclude an attack of this kind. On February 15, 1941, Stark wrote Kimmel with reference to the advisability of installing anti-torpedo baffles for protection of the ships in harbor. Stark said:

> It is considered that the relatively shallow depths of water limit the need for anti-torpedo nets in Pearl Harbor. . . . A minimum depth of water of 75 feet may be assumed necessary to successfully drop torpedoes from planes. One hundred and fifty feet of water is desired. The maximum height of planes at present experimentally dropping torpedoes is 250 feet. Launching speeds are between 120 and 150 knots. The desirable height for dropping is 60 feet or less. About 200 yards of torpedo run is necessary before the exploding device is armed, but this may be altered.

In this letter Stark emphasized that the depths of water in which torpedoes were launched in the attack at Taranto were between 14 and 15 fathoms; that is, 84 to 90 feet of water.[47]

Stark expressed these opinions despite the fact that on November 22, 1940, just after the Taranto attack, he had written Adm. Richardson, "Since the Taranto incident, my concern for the safety of the fleet at Pearl Harbor, already great, has become even greater."[48]

On June 13, 1941, Stark sent another letter to Kimmel and Adm. Bloch reaffirming his belief that Pearl Harbor was safe from torpedo attack.[49] The Naval Court of Inquiry concluded that the torpedoes launched by the Japanese at Pearl Harbor constituted, in effect, a secret weapon unknown to the best professional opinion in Great Britain and the United States at the time.[50] Adm. King, war-time commander-in-chief of the fleet, said in his indorsement of the findings of the court, "It is evident in retrospect that the capabilities of Japanese aircraft torpedoes were seriously underestimated."[51]

Secretary of the Navy Forrestal noted, however, that in April, 1941, an intelligence report had been circulated in the Navy Department describing demonstrations in England in which torpedoes equipped with special wings had been launched in 42 feet of water, about the same depth as in Pearl Harbor.[52] No word of these findings ever was sent to Adm. Kimmel, nor was Adm. Stark impressed by them as he should have been.

Despite these facts, Forrestal, in overruling the findings of the Navy board and putting the blame on Kimmel, said that "a due appreciation of the possible effects of an air attack should have induced Adm. Kimmel to take all practical precautions to reduce the effectiveness of such an attack." Among the measures which Forrestal said were "reasonably" open to Kimmel was to install anti-torpedo nets to protect the larger vessels in port.[53] In other words, Forrestal wanted Kimmel to display a prescience which was not possessed either by the chief of naval operations or the Navy Department in general, and wanted him, moreover, to procure and install anti-torpedo nets or baffles which the fleet in Hawaii did not have the facilities to manufacture.

On February 15, 1941, Stark informed Kimmel that existing torpedo nets were so cumbersome that their installation at Pearl Harbor would interfere with the movement of ships and ability of the fleet to get away on short notice. He said, "There is apparently a great need for the development of a light efficient torpedo net which could be laid temporarily and quickly within protective harbors, and which can be readily removed."[54] Kimmel was later to state that if such a net was ever developed by the Navy Department, he never heard of it or received it. That neglect in taking proper precautions against torpedoes was attributable to the Navy Department, rather than to Kimmel, was admitted by Adm. King when he said in his indorsement of the Navy board's report, "The decision not to install torpedo baffles appears to have been made by the Navy Department."[55]

There was a great deal of wisdom after December 7 on the part of responsible officials in Washington, but very little before the attack. Secretary Knox, for example, in his report to President Roosevelt upon his return from an inspection trip to Pearl Harbor following the attack, said that the principal fear of the Army had been sabotage and that of the Navy submarine attack, and that neither was expecting or sufficiently prepared to defend against air attack. The only specific measure of protection against air attack taken by the Navy was to disperse the ships in harbor so as to provide a field of fire covering every approach from the air.[56]

Despite the many mistakes of omission and commission at Oahu on December 7, the main deficiency of the Pearl Harbor defense was the absence of a proper state of readiness to meet attack. These conditions of readiness in Hawaii on December 7 were known to Washington and had its tacit approval. They were not countermanded, nor were more forcible orders sent. The commanders in Hawaii had been denied access to intelligence available in Washington which, as the Army Board points out, conclusively established a condition of "known impending war." If the degree of readiness prevailing at Oahu did not satisfy the government and high command, they had recourse to a simple remedy. All they needed to do was to issue orders directing the Hawaiian commanders to institute an all-out alert. No such orders ever were sent.

Four years after Pearl Harbor this ultimate responsibility on the part of Washington was finally admitted by Gen. L. T. Gerow, chief of Army war plans in 1941. He conceded that Gen. Short was justified in assuming his defense alert number 1 had the full approval of the Army high command. This admission followed the reading to the congressional committee of excerpts from the *Staff Officers' Field Manual,* stating that the general staff is responsible for making sure its instructions to field commanders are understood and for enforcing execution of such instructions.[57]

Chapter Seven

BACK DOOR TO WAR

For years before Pearl Harbor Mr. Roosevelt had talked of peace. For months he had schemed for war. His deeds belied his words. These are some of the things he said, and some of the things he did:

At Chautauqua, New York, August 19, 1936, he said, "I hate war."[1]

At the dedication of the Chicago Outer Drive bridge on October 5, 1937, he proposed a "quarantine" of aggressors.[2]

To students of the University of North Carolina on December 5, 1938, he denied that "you and your little brothers would be sent to the bloody fields of Europe."[3]

On January 4, 1939, he urged repeal of the arms embargo and resort to methods "short of war" but "stronger than words" to deter aggressors.[4]

In the same month he told the Senate military affairs committee, "The American frontier is on the Rhine."[5]

On April 15, 1939, he said that the only excuse for war was "self-evident home defense . . . [which] does not mean defense thousands and thousands of miles away."[6]

In June, 1939, he received King George VI and Queen Elizabeth of Great Britain at the White House when they made an unprecedented visit to the United States three months before war began in Europe.

On October 26, 1939, almost two months after the start of the European war, he described as "one of the worst fakes in current history" protests against "sending the boys of American mothers to fight on the battlefields of Europe."[7]

On November 4, 1939, after his fourth appeal to Congress in a year, neutrality legislation was revised to permit "cash and carry" shipments of arms to belligerents.[8]

On June 10, 1940, when Belgium and Holland had capitulated, the British army had fled from Dunkirk, and France was collapsing, he described Italy's declaration of war as a stab in the back of France.[9]

On June 20 he enrolled the erstwhile Republicans, Frank Knox and Henry L. Stimson, in his cabinet as secretaries, respectively, of Navy and War, in order to further his third-term aspirations and suggest coalition support of his war policy.[10]

During June he stripped American arsenals to re-equip the British army, which had abandoned its arms at Dunkirk.[11]

On August 18, 1940, he executed a defense pact with Canada,[12] a belligerent, encouraging Prime Minister Churchill of Britain to observe two days later that the empire and America were "somewhat mixed up together."[13]

On August 28, Roosevelt mustered the National Guard into federal service.[14]

On September 2, 1940, by executive decree, he transferred fifty American destroyers to Britain for rights to bases in British possessions in the western hemisphere.[15]

On September 16, he signed the first peacetime conscription bill in America's history, under which 42 million men were enrolled October 16 for military duty.[16]

At Boston, October 30, 1940, campaigning for the third term, he assured parents, "I have said this before, but I shall say it again and again and again: Your boys are not going to be sent into any foreign wars."[17]

On November 8, 1940, after his re-election, he allocated half of American war production to Britain.[18] The effect of the third-term victory upon Britain was described by Adm. Stark in a letter November 12, 1940, to Adm. Hart, commander-in-chief of the Asiatic fleet. Stark reported: "Ghormley (Vice-Adm. Robert L. Ghormley, naval observer in London) tells me that the British expected us to be in the war a few days after the re-election of the President—which is merely another evidence of their slack ways of thought and of their non-realistic views of international political conditions and of our own political system."[19]

On December 17, 1940, Roosevelt proposed lend-lease to eliminate the "silly, foolish old dollar sign" in paying Britain's war bills.[20]

On December 29, 1940, he announced that the United States was to become "the arsenal of democracy," but told the people they could "nail any talk about sending armies to Europe as deliberate untruth."[21] Churchill on Feb. 9, 1941, echoed: "Give us the tools, and we will finish the job."[22]

On January 24, 1941, Roosevelt ignored protocol by hastening to Annapolis to greet Lord Halifax, the new British ambassador, who had arrived on the battleship "King George V."[23]

On March 11, 1941, he signed the lend-lease act, which made the United States, to all intents and purposes, a belligerent.[24] More than 49 billion dollars in aid was to be granted under lend-lease.[25]

On April 9, 1941, Mr. Roosevelt transferred ten Coast Guard cutters to the British and assumed a protectorate over Greenland.[26]

On May 29, 1941, he permitted British airmen to train here.[27]

On June 14, 1941, he froze German and Italian funds and, on June 16, ordered consular staffs of the two nations out of the United States.[28]

On June 22, he promised Russia support in its new war with Germany.[2]

On July 7, 1941, he ordered American Marines into Iceland to relieve the British garrison.[30]

During the same month thousands of American workers streamed into Londonderry, North Ireland, to build a great American naval base.[31]

On August 14, 1941, Roosevelt and Churchill proclaimed the Atlantic Charter after a meeting at sea off Newfoundland.[32] The Selective Service Act was extended on the same day and the previous limitation that not more than 900,000 men should be in training at one time was removed.[33]

On September 11, 1941, after torpedoes were fired at the destroyer "Greer" near Iceland, Roosevelt issued an order to the Navy to "shoot on sight" if German or Italian warships were encountered.[34]

On October 27, 1941, in his Navy Day speech, Roosevelt announced to the country that "the shooting has started" and "we Americans have cleared our decks and taken our battle stations."[35]

On November 17, 1941, Roosevelt received authority to arm merchant ships.[36]

On November 24, he sent troops to occupy Dutch Guiana, source of the bauxite for 60 per cent of America's aluminum production.[37]

These were the things he was doing and saying openly.* Here are some of the things that he was doing secretly:

On April 21, 1941, he directed units of the Atlantic fleet to "trail" German and Italian merchant and naval ships and aircraft and to broadcast their movements in plain language at four-hour intervals for the convenience of British and allied warships and planes.[38]

On May 22, 1941, he ordered Adm. Stark to prepare an expedition of 25,000 men to seize the Azores from neutral Portugal.[89] Plans to seize Martinique, French possession in the Caribbean, were laid at the same time.[40]

On August 11, 1941, at the Atlantic conference, he revived the plan to seize the Azores, which had been left in abeyance. Prime Minister Churchill agreed at the same time that Britain would seize the Canary Islands from Spain and the Cape Verde Islands from Portugal.[41]

On August 25, Roosevelt ordered the Atlantic fleet to "destroy surface raiders."[42]

On September 13, 1941, he ordered the fleet to protect ships of any nationality between American ports and Iceland, and to escort convoys in which there were no American vessels.[43]

On September 14, the crew of the Coast Guard cutter "Northland" seized a German trawler in Greenland waters and took the first prisoners of a war not yet acknowledged.[44]

On September 26, Roosevelt promulgated "Western Hemisphere Defense Plan No. 5," which, while assigning new tasks to the fleet, stated that it must be recognized that "the United States is not at war in the legal sense," and hence would have no belligerent rights under international law.[45]

On October 11, 1941, he implemented this hemisphere defense plan with an order assigning American warships to operations under British and Canadian naval command and placing sixty British Royal Navy and Royal Canadian Navy destroyers and corvettes engaged in convoying "under the strategic direction of the United States."[46]

On November 7, 1941, a month before Pearl Harbor, Adm. Stark, referring to this nondeclared war, wrote to Adm. Kimmel, "Whether the country knows it or not, we are at war."[47]

Stark told the Congressional Investigating Committee that he was thinking of the interchange of command among American, British,

*For a comprehensive and illuminating account of the foreign policy of the United States as defined for public consumption by Roosevelt, Hull, Wendell Willkie, and other politicians, see Charles A. Beard's *American Foreign Policy in the Making: 1932-1940* (New Haven: Yale University Press, 1946).

and Canadian warships and orders he had issued at the President's direction to fire on German submarines. He said his own opinion was that "the time had come for us to get in" the war.[48]

Representative Gearhart asked Stark, "It was because of action which the President was directing from day to day against the Germans and the consequent exchange of fire with German submarines that caused you to state we were at war in the Atlantic before Pearl Harbor?"[49]

"That is correct," Stark replied. "Technically, or from an international standpoint, we were not at war, inasmuch as we did not have the right of belligerents because war had not been declared. But actually, so far as the forces operating under Adm. King in certain areas, it was war against any German craft that came inside that area. They were attacking us and we were attacking them."[50] He said that American warships were considered to be enforcing the congressional will to deliver lend-lease supplies.

"And there was no limit upon their belligerent rights in so far as serving that objective, was there?" Gearhart inquired.

"It was not all-out," said Stark. "It was limited, but it was effective and it was war, to my mind. . . . When you are shooting at the other fellow and he is shooting at you, it to all intents and purposes is war, even though of a restricted nature. We were not, for example, flying planes over Germany."[51]

Citing the President's Navy Day speech, in which Roosevelt recounted that eleven members of the crew of the destroyer "Kearny" had been killed by submarine action, Gearhart said, "That shows that they were making war on us, too, doesn't it?"

"Yes it does," Stark said. "I am simply trying—"

"I know," Gearhart interrupted. "You are trying to point out the legalistic differences."

Stark conceded under further examination by Senator Ferguson that the orders for the nondeclared Atlantic war came from Roosevelt.

"Where we state, 'The President directs,' it was his directive," the admiral said. "No one but the President, I would say, could direct us to take the action indicated in those plans."[52]

"That would indicate, though," suggested Ferguson, "that congressional approval was not considered necessary for an overt act."

"I do not know that you would call an act an overt act if you considered it in self-defense or in defense of carrying out the congressional will of getting material abroad," Stark responded.

Long before Pearl Harbor other high officers were also proceeding on the assumption that we would inevitably be fighting beside the British before long. In an undated memorandum in the summer of 1941, Gen. Marshall informed Roosevelt:

"Britain is reaching the limit of usable manpower. We must supplement her forces. . . . Germany cannot be defeated by supplying munitions to friendly powers and air and naval operations alone. Large ground forces will be required."[53]

Maj. Gen. Sherman Miles, former chief of Army Intelligence, said that throughout 1941 he considered that the European war represented "a much bigger picture" than any threat from Japan.[54] His intelligence estimate for November 29, 1941, stated, "The United States is contributing powerfully to the decision in the Battle of the Atlantic by direct naval action." On December 5, two days before the Pearl Harbor attack, his estimate contended that American naval power and economic blockade "are primary deterrents against Japanese all-out entry into the war."[55]

Adm. Ingersoll agreed that in the fall of 1941 the Navy knew it was committing overt acts which could provoke Germany to declare war.[56] In that he echoed the statement of Adm. Stark, who, on October 8, 1941, in a memorandum to Secretary Hull, said that Hitler "has every excuse in the world to declare war on us now if he were of a mind to."[57]

Vice-Adm. Smith said that Washington thought that "the war was in the Atlantic."[58]

As the Atlantic war mounted, the Pacific fleet was stripped of important units and trained personnel to support the operations in the other ocean. When the Azores seizure was first planned in May, 1941, practically all of the trained and equipped Marines on the West Coast, six transports, and some other small craft, were transferred from the Pacific to the Atlantic.[59] Gen. Marshall withheld fourteen Flying Fortresses from Hawaii for the same operation.[60]

In April and May, 1941, one aircraft carrier, three battleships, four cruisers, and eighteen destroyers—approximately one-fourth of the fighting ships of the Pacific fleet—were transferred to the Atlantic. Stark described these fleet units as "the first echelon of the Battle of the Atlantic."[61] In June, 1941, when he visited Washington, Adm. Kimmel intervened personally with Roosevelt to save three more of his battleships, four cruisers, two squadrons of destroyers, and an aircraft carrier.[62]

According to Rear Adm. Inglis, the United States had 105 fighting craft in the Pacific before the transfers in May, 1941, compared to 162 in the Jap fleet.[63] On December 7, Inglis said, American fleet dispositions were as follows:

VESSEL	ATLANTIC	PACIFIC	ASIATIC
Battleships	6	9	0
Carriers	4	3	0
Heavy cruisers	5	12	1
Light cruisers	12	10	1
Destroyers	97	54	13
Submarines	58	23	29
Mine layers	0	9	0
Minesweepers	37	26	6
Patrol vessels	5	13	14
Totals	224	159	64

Although the computation of Adm. Inglis showed 159 units in the Pacific fleet, we were actually outnumbered in the major categories of surface craft, 162 to 88, on December 7.

The comparison follows:

VESSEL	U.S.	JAPAN
Battleships	9	10
Carriers	3	8
Light and heavy cruisers	22	35
Destroyers	54	109

Almost all of the naval officers who testified before the congressional committee conceded that because of transfers of fleet units and lend-lease diversions to Britain and other nations, the defenses of Pearl Harbor were seriously impaired and the fleet, in any encounter with the Japanese, would have been defeated. The minority report of the Joint Congressional Committee (Conclusion 17, pp. 49-50) says on this point:

> High authorities in Washington failed to allocate to the Hawaiian commanders the material which the latter often declared to be necessary to defense and often requested, and no requirements of defense or war in the Atlantic did or could excuse these authorities for their failures in this respect.

The first part of this conclusion calls for no special citations of authority. In reports of the President's Commission, of the Army Pearl Harbor Board, and of the Navy Court of Inquiry, three points in this respect are accepted as plain facts: (1) The ultimate power to allocate arms, ammunition, implements of war, and other supplies was vested in the President and his aide, Harry Hopkins, subject to the advice of Gen. Marshall and Adm. Stark; (2) Gen. Short and Adm. Kimmel made repeated demands upon their respective departments for additional material, which they represented as necessary to the effective defense of Pearl Harbor; and (3) Washington authorities, having full discretion in this regard, made decisions against Gen. Short and Adm. Kimmel and allocated to the Atlantic theater, where the United States was at least nominally at peace, matériel, especially bombing and reconnaissance planes, which were known to be absolutely indispensable to efficient defense of Pearl Harbor. (See Exhibits 106 and 53, request for materials.)

The second part of this conclusion may be arguable from the point of view of some high world strategy, but it is not arguable under the Constitution and laws of the United States. The President, it is true, had powers and obligations under the Lease-Lend Act of March, 1941. But his first and inescapable duty under the Constitution and laws was to care for the defense and security of the United States against a Japanese attack, which he knew was imminent; and, in the allocations of matériel, especially bombing and reconnaissance planes, he made or authorized decisions which deprived the Hawaiian commanders of indispensable matériel they could otherwise have had and thus reduced their defensive forces to a degree known to be dangerous by high officials in Washington and Hawaii.

In a secret report to Roosevelt December 15, 1941, Secretary Knox said that lack of an adequate number of fighter planes to defend Hawaii against air attack "is due to the diversion of this type before the outbreak of the war to the British, the Chinese, the Dutch, and the Russians." He said there had been a "dangerous shortage" of anti-aircraft artillery, "the next best weapon against air attack," through no fault of Gen. Short.[64] As has been seen, the United States in the ten months before Pearl Harbor lend-leased 1,900 patrol planes and 1,900 anti-aircraft guns, of which 1,750 planes and 1,500 guns went to the British.

In February, 1941, when this country was deficient 10,000 planes in its 14,000-plane program, Britain was asking America to deliver 50,000 planes in 1942. At the time this request was made, Army plans called for the dispatch of only eighty-one fighter planes to Pearl Harbor.[65]

Col. Melvin W. Maas, of the Marine Corps Reserve, former Minnesota Congressman, said that when two hundred fifty patrol bombers necessary to bring Hawaii up to required minimum strength of three hundred planes came off the production lines, Washington ordered them sent to Britain. When protests were made to Roosevelt, he referred the admirals to Harry Hopkins, in charge of allocating war materials.

"Hopkins received them as he lay in bed, nonchalantly smoking a cigaret," said Maas. "He listened to them, then told them the interview was over and that he had already made the allocation. Adm. Kimmel told me if those two hundred fifty patrol planes had been sent to Hawaii, the December 7 attack could never have succeeded, and probably would never have been attempted."[66]

Prime Minister Churchill made some acknowledgment of the effect of lend-lease in handicapping American defense when, in an address to the United States Senate December 26, 1941, he said, "If the United States has been found at a disadvantage at various points in the Pacific Ocean, we know well that it is to no small extent because of the aid which you have been giving us in munitions for the defense of the British Isles and to the Libyan campaign, and above all, because of your help in the Battle of the Atlantic."[67]

Capt. Edwin T. Layton, intelligence officer of the Pacific fleet, asserted that if the fleet had been able to spot the approaching Jap force before December 7 and had gone out to meet it, we would have been beaten. Our battleships, he said, were too slow to have brought the Jap vessels under gunfire, and the remainder of our fleet would have "suffered severe damage if not defeat by reason of the great [enemy] superiority in the air."[68]

Although Secretary of War Stimson promised to rectify Hawaii's deficiencies in patrol bombers, fighter planes, anti-aircraft guns, and aircraft warning equipment by June, 1941, Rear Adm. Bloch, Pearl Harbor base defense officer, complained four months after the Secretary's deadline had passed that "the only increment that had been made to the local defense forces during the last year, exclusive of [harbor] net vessels, was the U.S.S. "Sacramento," an old gunboat of negligible gun power and low speed."[69]

Adm. Kimmel forwarded Adm. Bloch's letter on October 17, 1941, with a complaint of his own concerning the "reluctance or inability" of the Navy Department to provide him the vessels he asked. "A fleet, tied to its base by diversions to other forces of light forces necessary to its security at sea is, in a real sense, no fleet at all," Kimmel said.[70]

Not only had the light screening units been diverted to patrol duty in the Atlantic, and fifty highly useful "over-age" destroyers given to the British by Roosevelt been lost to our fleet, but Kimmel had only eleven tankers when seventy-five were necessary to keep his fleet at sea.[71] This fact, together with Washington's failure to maintain adequate fuel deliveries for the fleet, condemned the Pacific commander to a policy of keeping a substantial part of the fleet in harbor like sitting ducks.

Thus President Roosevelt weakened the Pacific fleet and the Pearl Harbor defenses to sustain the nondeclared war into which he had plunged in the Atlantic. Although he was itching to get into the war in Europe, Hitler would not oblige him with an incident of sufficient gravity to take the nation to war.

Grand Adm. Karl Doenitz, testifying at the Nuernberg war crimes trials, told the international tribunal that Hitler was so anxious to keep the United States out of the European war that he overruled the admiral's plans to mine North Atlantic shipping lanes carrying lend-lease supplies to Britain. Doenitz said:

> A ·300 mile safety zone was even granted to America by Germany when international law called for only a three mile zone. I suggested mine fields at Halifax and around Iceland, but the Fuehrer rejected this because he wanted to avoid conflict with the United States. When American destroyers in the summer of 1941 were ordered to attack German submarines, I was forbidden to fight back. I was thus forced not to attack British destroyers for fear there would be some mistake.[72]*

The President's dilemma was frankly discussed by his sympathizers of the war party. As early as June, 1941, Joseph Alsop and Robert Kintner, a pair of columnists favored by the White House (Alsop was a relative of the President), wrote,

> In the last week, he [the President] has been repeatedly urged to order immediate action. He has been warned that to delay is to court disaster. He has been able to act, for all the preparations for meeting the Germans' threat in the Battle of the Atlantic have at last been completed.
>
> Yet he has not acted, because he hopes to drive the Germans to shoot first. . . . The problem was mentioned in this space in a recent discussion of the Atlantic patrol, in which it

---

*Doenitz received the lightest sentence of any of the twenty-two Nazi defendants at the Nuernberg war crimes trial. The International Military Tribunal imposed a term of ten years' imprisonment on him. This comparatively lenient treatment may, or may not, reflect the court's belief in the credibility of his testimony.

was pointed out that the President and the men around him privately hoped that the patrol would produce an incident. No man can doubt the German high command will do everything possible to avoid shooting first.

The writers attributed the President's hesitation to his many pledges to stay out of war. "He does not feel he can openly violate them," they said. "But he can get around them the 'smart way.'"[73] The "smart way" was to provoke an attack.

The pact of Berlin, signed September 27, 1940, suggested a method to the President. It pledged Germany, Italy, and Japan to "assist one another with all political, economic, and military means when one of the three contracting parties is attacked by a power at present not involved in the European war or the Sino-Japanese conflict." Germany was then committed to its uneasy nonaggression treaty with Russia, while Japan had specifically excepted Russia from application of the treaty. Inasmuch as the United States was the only remaining power to be reckoned with, the pact of Berlin obviously was directed against it.

The tripartite pact had, in the eyes of Roosevelt, a utility which its authors had not intended. It offered a means of entering the war in Europe by the back door, for war with Japan also meant war automatically with Germany and Italy under the terms of the pact. Thus, while the attention of the nation was almost wholly trained by official acts and utterances upon the war in Europe, the President simultaneously precipitated a crisis with Japan.

The idea of a Japanese-American conflict was not viewed unsympathetically in Berlin. The Nazis had doubts about the dependability of their Asiatic ally. They did not want to chance Japan's response under its tripartite pact commitments by initiating a war with America themselves, but if Japan could be induced to attack the United States, Hitler could hope that the natural sense of outrage in the United States would divert America's major effort to the Pacific, leaving him free to complete his unfinished business.

On July 6, 1941, shortly after Germany went to war with Russia, Ambassador Grew stated Hitler's strategy: "It is generally held that what Germany most wants Japan to do is to take steps which will tend to divert America's attention from Europe and that she is not pressing Japan to intervene in Soviet Russia."[74]

Accordingly, the Nazis began attempting to work a confidence game on their Asiatic allies. These efforts to hoodwink the Japs were continued unrelentingly up to the very moment that Japan attacked

Pearl Harbor, but they might not have been attended with success
if American diplomacy had not finally presented the Japanese with
the choice between fighting and capitulating.

On November 29 Joachim von Ribbentrop, the Nazi foreign minister, was found using all of his power of persuasion upon Maj. Gen.
Oshima, the Japanese ambassador in Berlin. Ribbentrop said,

> It is essential that Japan effect the new order in East Asia
> without losing this opportunity. There never has been and
> never will be a time when closer co-operation under the tripar-
> tite pact is so important. If Japan hesitates at this time, and
> Germany goes ahead and establishes her European new order,
> all the military might of Britain and the United States will be
> concentrated against Japan. . . . If Japan reaches a decision to
> fight Britain and the United States, I am confident that that
> will not only be in the interest of Germany and Japan jointly,
> but would bring about favorable results for Japan herself.
> "Is your excellency indicating that a state of actual war is
> to be established between Germany and the United States?"
> Oshima asked.

Ribbentrop was reluctant to promise that his country be the first
to dive off the deep end. "Roosevelt's a fanatic," he cautiously replied,
"so it is impossible to tell what he would do."[75]

The view that a wary Germany employed all possible cunning to
entice Japan into an attack upon the United States is fully supported
by the verdict of the International War Crimes Tribunal at Nuernberg.
The court found that Germany repeatedly urged Japan to attack the
British in the Far East after the Nazi attack upon Russia. It was
further stated in the verdict:

> It was clear, too, that the German policy of keeping America
> from the war if possible did not prevent Germany from promis-
> ing support to Japan even against the United States.

The court referred to Ribbentrop's representations to Oshima and
said that the Nazi foreign minister was "overjoyed" when Japan
attacked Pearl Harbor. Hitler, the court stated, expressed approval
of Japan's tactics in striking without a declaration of war.[75a]

In Rome Mussolini promised that "Italy would give every military
aid she had at her disposal" if Japan were to fight Britain and America.[76]

To stiffen Japan's resolution, Hitler worked a huge military fraud
upon the Japanese. On December 6 Berlin was heralding the imminent fall of Moscow. On December 8, the day after the Japanese

attack on Pearl Harbor, Hitler's forces were in full retreat to a predetermined winter line.[77]

The Japs were taken in, with Germany unwittingly assisting the
President in attaining his objective. Davis and Lindley wrote,

> The question perplexing many high officials was how, in
> the absence of a direct Japanese attack on the American flag,
> to summon the nation, divided as it then was on questions of
> foreign policy, to the strong action which they believed essen-
> tial. There had been considerable discussion of possible meth-
> ods. . . . It was commonly supposed that the Japanese were too
> smart to solve this problem for the President by a direct assault
> on the American flag—especially at Hawaii, which even the
> extreme isolationists recognized as a bastion of our security.

The Japanese were not smart enough.[78]

On November 29, 1941, at Warm Springs, Georgia, Roosevelt had
given intimations of war to come. "In days like these," he said, "our
Thanksgiving next year may remind us of a peaceful past; it is always
possible that our boys in the military and naval academies may be
fighting for the defense of these American institutions of ours."[79]

This was a pallid statement of the realities which he then knew
to exist. He knew for a certainty that war was not a matter of months
or a year, but of days. He knew that not only "our boys in the military and naval academies" would be called to arms, but all able-bodied
young men. And he knew that the war would start, not in the Atlantic, but in the Pacific.

Our stake in the Far East was not great. In recent years less than
3 per cent of our foreign trade had been with China, including the
British colony of Hong Kong, and trade with China amounted to less
than half of our trade with Japan, which had been America's third
best customer, taking 7.7 per cent of total American exports in 1938.
The United States, in turn, was Japan's best customer, 6.5 per cent
of our imports coming from there.[80]

The interests threatened by Japan in Asia and the Southwest Pacific
were, with the exception of China, almost wholly the interests of the
western empires, Britain, France, and Holland. None of them was
capable by the final month of 1941 of defending its colonial holdings.
It was clear to these nations long in advance of Pearl Harbor that the
United States was their one hope in resisting a Japanese rape of their
colonies.

By December 7, 1941, we had tolerated Japan's war against China
for fifty-three months. We might not like it, but the conflict was not

regarded as of sufficient concern to send America into battle. It was only when Japan began to impinge upon the prerogatives of the western imperialisms that the President began to display symptoms of the moral outrage he usually reserved for Hitler and Mussolini.

On September 22, 1940, three months after the collapse of France, the Japanese began to move in on the western empires. Japanese troops were marched into French Indo-China and the colonial authorities acceded to Japan's demands for air bases.[81] On July 21, 1941, France acquiesced when Japan demanded military control of Indo-China.[82]

This action was defended on the grounds that it was necessary to provide for Japan's military security and to assure Japan a supply of rice and other foodstuffs and raw materials. In Washington Ambassador Nomura pleaded the severity of the food situation. Japan's production of rice in 1941 was estimated at 297 million bushels, against an annual consumption of 400 million bushels.[83] Britain had embargoed the export of rice from Burma,[84] while lack of fertilizer normally obtained from Germany had cut down Japan's domestic production. As a result, Japan was compelled to look to Indo-China for its supply.

In answer to these representations, Sumner Welles, Undersecretary of State, told Nomura on July 23 that there was no basis for pursuing further the diplomatic conversations which had been in progress since March looking toward a peaceful settlement of America's differences with Japan. Welles said that the United States "must assume that the Japanese government was taking the last step before proceeding upon a policy of totalitarian expansion in the South Seas and of conquest in the South Seas through the seizure of additional territories in that region."[85]

Relations between the United States and Japan had been deteriorating for four years before the seizure of Indo-China. Afterward the process continued at an accelerated rate. The successive steps follow:

On December 12, 1937, three months after Roosevelt's "quarantine" speech, Japanese warplanes bombed and sank the American gunboat "Panay" in the Yangtze River.[86]

On July 1, 1938, after the Japanese had bombed Nanking, Canton, and other defenseless Chinese cities, the State Department asked for a "moral embargo" on sales of aircraft which might be used in attacks on civilians.[87]

On July 26, 1939, Roosevelt gave notice that the Japanese-American commercial treaty of 1911 would be abrogated as of January 26, 1940.[88]

Ambassador Grew remarked of this developing economic warfare,

"I have pointed out that once started on a policy of sanctions we must see them through and that such a policy may conceivably lead to eventual war."[89] Further American action manifested the intention of seeing them through.

On July 2, 1940, Roosevelt licensed exports of machine tools, chemicals, and nonferrous metals.[90]

On July 25 he licensed exports of oil products and scrap metal.[91]

On July 31 he licensed exports of aviation gasoline beyond the western hemisphere.[92]

On September 25, 1940, he granted China a 25 million dollar loan for currency stabilization.[93]

On September 26 he imposed an embargo, effective October 16, on all exports of scrap iron and steel except to Britain and nations of the western hemisphere.[94] Between 1933 and 1940, 10.16 million tons of scrap had been shipped from this country to Japan.[95] Japan termed the embargo an "unfriendly act"[96] and stated that further trade restrictions would make relations between the two countries "unpredictable."[97]

On October 8, 1940, American nationals were warned to leave the Far East.[98]

On November 30, 1940, an additional 100 million dollar loan was made to China.[99]

When Adm. Nomura came here as Japan's new ambassador early in 1941, he said that he doubted that Japan would extend military operations beyond their present sphere "unless the policy of increasing embargoes by this country should force his government, in the minds of those in control, to take military action."[100]

On March 11, 1941, with the enactment of lend-lease, material aid was granted the Chinese as well as the British.[101]

On April 26, 1941, the United States announced a monetary stabilization accord with China. Lauchlin Currie, the President's administrative assistant, was dispatched to China to help straighten out its finances.[102]

On July 25, 1941, four days after Japan occupied Indo-China, Roosevelt froze Japanese assets of 130 million dollars in the United States, thus ending trade relations.[103] Britain followed suit the next day.[104]

On July 26 the President nationalized the Filipino army, which became part of a new command known as the United States Army Forces in the Far East.[105]

On August 26, 1941, an American military mission under Gen. John A. Magruder was sent to China.[106]

American Army, Navy, and Marine flyers were permitted to fight for China as an "American Volunteer Group" under Brig. Gen. Chennault.[107]

American engineers were sent to reorganize traffic over the Burma Road in order to speed supplies to China.[108]

Generalissimo Chiang Kai-shek, on the President's recommendation, accepted Owen Lattimore as his political adviser.[109]

The Panama Canal was closed to Japanese shipping.[110]

This series of actions finally made it extremely doubtful that the peace could be kept. The only avenue remaining open was that of negotiation. While Secretary Hull and Ambassador Nomura were exploring the possibilities, Dr. E. Stanley Jones, a widely known missionary of long experience in the Orient, served as an unofficial mediator between the Japanese and the White House.

Dr. Jones contradicts the Roosevelt administration thesis, advanced by Hull in particular, that there never was any hope of keeping the peace. He says,

> The idea that all the Japanese officials and people were united in their approval of aggression and their plans for further conquests in the Orient, even to the point of war with the United States, is commonly held. It has been carefully nurtured by propaganda. The American citizen is supposed to believe that a united Japan undertook world-conquest, with no inhibitions and no internal opposition. But the idea is disastrously false. From the time of the attack upon China, the Japanese nation went through a deep struggle of mind and soul. . . .
>
> It was a titanic grapple between the war party and the peace party. It was touch and go as to which way the situation would swing. The struggle continued to the fall of 1941. Then the militarists triumphed. . . .
>
> Had we been wiser we would have outplanned the militarists. If we had lent aid and encouragement to the peace party in their efforts to prevent war, we could have made Japan an ally instead of an enemy. Certainly our course played into the hands of the war party.[111]

As to the American attitude, Dr. Jones says,

> I was not sure whether the highest officials in the executive branch of our government really wanted peace. From the time of the Atlantic conference between President Roosevelt and Prime Minister Churchill in August, 1941, the official attitude toward Japan had stiffened, bordering on belligerency. . . .
>
> The attitude of some of our officials seemed to be: "Well,

we have Japan by the throat by this oil embargo and we'll
strangle her. If she kicks and there is war, well, we'll send a
few planes over from Vladivostok, burn up her inflammable
cities, and it will be all over in a few weeks."

They felt that Japan was mired in China, that she was at
the end of her resources, and that this anxiety for peace on the
part of her Washington representatives was because she was
weak and helpless in our hands. As Adm. Nomura said to me
one day, "Everything I propose is suspected as weakness."

Dr. Jones found that much of the agitation for war came from
the British, the Chinese, and the Dutch. When he suggested to Dr.
Hu Shih, the Chinese ambassador, that it was one thing for America
to feel sympathy for China and to endeavor to help China, but another
thing for us to be dragged into war because of China's refusal of
mediation, Dr. Hu replied, "This is all nonsense. You are already
at war!"

Dr. Jones continued:

Great Britain was obviously trying to get us into the European war, as Mr. Churchill later openly said, and was not ad-
verse to getting us in by the back door of a Pacific war. When
I urged Lord Halifax to mediate between us and Japan and
help avert a war in the Pacific, he replied, "You will find my
views in the enclosed speech I have made." The whole tenor
of the speech was: "America must fight."

The Netherlands shared that attitude.

The real issue of the war, Dr. Jones contends, was empire.

The Japanese suspected the United States of being willing
to fight in order to preserve the white empires of the Pacific.
That was correct, as time so amply proved. We did not go to
the defense of China when she was attacked by Japan. In fact,
we continued to send Japan our scrap iron and oil. But the
moment Japan threatened Indo-China—a French possession—
we were aroused. That touched a sensitive nerve—the prerogatives of the white nations' colonial possessions in the East.

Dr. Jones's own solution was to give Japan some unexploited area
where it could dispose of its surplus population. His choice was New
Guinea, a huge island owned by the British and Dutch, who had
made no real attempt to develop it and who did not need it for emi-
grants. The island had a population of only 300,000 natives of low
culture, but with proper development, Dr. Jones thought, could sustain from 20 to 40 million people.

Dr. Jones proposed that the United States pay 100 million dollars to Holland and Australia to compensate such landowners as might be dispossessed. He found the Australian minister in Washington sympathetic. "If we don't do something now about Japan's surplus population," the minister said, "we shall have to do it within ten years." When Dr. Jones interviewed the Dutch minister, however, he was told, "No part of the Dutch empire is for sale."

On November 18, 1941, three weeks before the Pearl Harbor attack, Maxwell H. Hamilton of the State Department's Far Eastern section submitted the plan to Secretary Hull.[112] Instead of considering this face-saving method of persuading Japan to abandon the program of the militarists, Hull handed Nomura and Kurusu the President's ten-point statement of November 26, which, says Dr. Jones, "could have no other interpretation than that of an ultimatum."

Even when confronted with the American demands, Dr. Jones says that the Japanese representatives did not abandon hope that we would grant them the means of reaching a peaceful solution. Two days after the Hull ultimatum, Counselor Terasaki of the embassy, in a note transmitted to Roosevelt by Dr. Jones, pleaded, "Don't compel us to do things, but make it possible for us to do them. If you treat us in this way, we will reciprocate doubly. If you stretch out one hand, we will stretch out two. And we cannot only be friends, we can be allies."

There was no response, nor any relaxation of the pressure. As Dr. Jones says, "Our ultimatum . . . put Japan in a box. She had to knuckle under or else fight us."

In retrospect, Dr. Jones suggests that almost until the very end Japan and the United States were very close to peace. During the negotiations he was told by a member of the Senate foreign relations committee, "It has all boiled down to two air bases in North China —Japan wants to retain two air bases and we want her to get out of China." Whether we were within two air bases of peace Dr. Jones says he does not know for certain, but in one of their last conversations, Nomura told him that "it would be absurd for us to go to war over two air bases in North China. It would be very expensive for both of us."

In listing the causes of the war, Dr. Jones says a principal cause was "the pressure of a war party that surrounded the President. A Supreme Court justice said to us during the negotiations, 'We have a war party as well as Japan. They are surrounding the President and making it more and more impossible to see him.'"

If it was surrounding him, Roosevelt was also the center of it. The testimony of Sumner Welles before the congressional committee investigating Pearl Harbor showed that it was Roosevelt who was running the show. Asked whether, when the fleet was moved to Hawaii, the Navy was not being made an arm of the diplomatic negotiations with Japan, Welles replied: "It was done as an integral part of the over-all policy. You can't divorce the diplomatic field from the military field. It was a policy moving along parallel roads."

"Who made the over-all policy decisions?"

"The President, of course," Welles replied.[113]

Chapter Eight

A, B, C, D's

AMONG THE most important of the President's decisions was to consummate secret war alliances with the British and Canadians in the Atlantic and with the British and Dutch in the Pacific. News that the United States was a partner in a full-blown war alliance before a shot had been fired burst upon the American people on December 6, 1941, one day before the Pearl Harbor attack.

A *New York Times* dispatch from Melbourne, Australia, stated, "The Australian government has completed preparations, in concert with Britain, the United States, and the Netherlands Indies, for action in the event of a Pacific conflict. The four plan to match Japanese action, move by move." The report warned of "powerful American squadrons in the rear of any southward Japanese expedition."[1]

The Australian Associated Press said of the agreement, "Following eleventh-hour conversations between the ABCD powers, a declaration has been drawn up setting out their attitude to any Japanese aggression. This declaration reaffirmed the necessity for the four allies to continue to stand together. 'We are fully alive to the Japanese threat and are not afraid of it,' the statement was reported as saying."[2]

In Washington the State Department said it "did not know of any joint declaration."[3]

This secret war alliance, so casually sprung upon the American people, and denied by that people's own government, had been developing for years and had been in being for more than eight months. It had not been executed, as the Constitution provides all treaties must be, with the advice and consent of the Senate, nor had it been drafted as an executive agreement—a means of by-passing the Senate which Roosevelt on occasion was not reluctant to invoke. The President had been sufficiently prudent not even to initial it.

While Holland and China were listed among the "ABCD powers," Britain was the important partner taken under the American wing. Collaboration between the two nations in the Pacific had begun at the Washington naval conference in 1922, when Britain terminated its 1902 alliance with Japan. Disregarding Japanese opposition, nine battleships, six cruisers, thirty-four destroyers, and thirteen auxiliary units of the American fleet visited Australia and New Zealand in 1925 to signalize the new Anglo-American bonds.

This visit was the precursor to another call by four American cruisers to Australia in 1938. From there three of the cruisers proceeded to Singapore at the invitation of the British Foreign Office to attend ceremonies opening Britain's new naval base. No other foreign warships attended. The visit was obviously a demonstration of American-British solidarity for the benefit of Japan.

In March, 1938, Roosevelt suddenly rediscovered Canton and Enderbury Islands in the Phoenix group, 1,900 miles southwest of Hawaii. He asserted formal claim on the basis of century-old American discovery. Britain had taken formal possession of the islands a year before Roosevelt's proclamation of American sovereignty. In August, 1938, the islands were placed under joint Anglo-American control, and in April, 1939, the condominium was extended for fifty years. Members of Congress asserted that the supposed dispute between Roosevelt and the British was merely a screen for collusive action to intermingle the affairs of the two countries so that America would be bound to Britain in the event of an Asiatic war.

In February, 1946, Adm. Ingersoll confirmed charges in Congress at the time of the Canton-Enderbury deal that an agreement had been reached as early as 1938 looking forward toward a Pacific war alliance with the British. In December, 1937, when he was director of Navy war plans, he was called to the White House and directed by Roosevelt to go to London to explain to the British what the United States could do in a war with Japan and to determine what contribution Britain could make.[4]

A letter from Adm. Richardson to Adm. Stark on January 26, 1940, indicates that the Ingersoll conversations produced a secret understanding for joint Anglo-American use of the Singapore base against Japan:

> When the China Incident started and on every opportunity until after I left the job as assistant chief of naval operations, I used to say to Bill Leahy, "Be sure to impress on the boss that we do not want to be drawn into this business unless we have

allies so bound to us that they cannot leave us in the lurch."

There is a possibility that this constant repetition had something to do with the trip of Ingersoll.

When this understanding was reached, it had some value,
but under present conditions it has little value, as it affords us
the use of a base in exchange for an obligation to protect about
two and one-half continents."[5]

Chief of Staff Marshall, however, stated before the congressional
committee that the British first advanced the project of using Singapore as a joint fleet base in November, 1941. "The British wanted us
to base a number of vessels at Singapore," Marshall said. "They felt
that if we would base part of our Navy there it would greatly
strengthen Britain's position in the Pacific without reducing her
naval forces in the Atlantic war with Germany." The general and
Adm. Stark refused the invitation on tactical grounds. They thought
that American vessels, if moved to Singapore, would be too far removed from supply sources and would be vulnerable to air attack.[6]

Ingersoll said that his conversations in London in 1938 were rendered obsolete when, in the spring of 1941, a new understanding was
reached between the United States and Britain. The British seem to
have begun agitating for a firmer alliance in the Far East as their
troubles multiplied in the European war. Thus, Adm. Stark, writing
to Adm. Hart on Nov. 12, 1940, remarked of Britain's overtures:

> They have been talking in a large way about the defense of
> the Malay barrier, with an alliance between themselves, us, and
> the Dutch, without much thought as to what the effect would
> be in Europe. But we have no idea as to whether they would
> at once begin to fight were the Dutch alone, or were we alone,
> to be attacked by the Japanese. Then again, the copy of the
> British Far Eastern war plan . . . obtained at Singapore shows
> much evidence of their usual wishful thinking. Furthermore,
> though I believe the Dutch colonial authorities will resist an
> attempt to capture their islands, I question whether they would
> fight if only the Philippines, or only Singapore, were attacked.[7]

At length, however, Stark succumbed to British pressure and
agreed to convoke a joint staff conference in Washington.

"I did not ask the President's permission or that of Col. Knox,"
he told the congressional committee. "There was some dynamite in
the fact that we were holding conversations with the British. . . . I
informed [the President] in January, after the committee was here,
that I was going ahead with those conversations. . . . I told him that

I would prefer to be panned for being ready rather than be reproved when the time came and I was not ready, and he let it go at that."

"What did he say?"

"Well, he did not pan me. Later on all those conversations, that is, the boildown and the plans, were shown to him."[8]

The American representatives at the secret staff conversations, held from January 29 to March 27, were Maj. Gen. Stanley D. Embick, representing the joint United States–Canadian defense board; Brig. Gen. Sherman Miles, chief of intelligence for the Army general staff; Brig. Gen. Leonard T. Gerow, war plans officer, general staff; Col. Joseph T. McNarney, subsequently a member of the Roberts commission, representing Army aviation; Rear Adm. Robert M. Ghormley, American naval observer in England; Rear Adm. Richmond K. Turner, naval war plans officer; Capt. A. G. Kirk, chief of naval intelligence; and Capt. Dewitt C. Ramsey, representing the Navy Bureau of Aeronautics.

The British representatives were Rear Admirals R. M. Bellairs and V. J. Danckwerts, Maj. Gen. E. L. Morris, Air Vice-Marshal J. C. Slessor, and Capt. A. W. Clarke.[9]

"The staff conference assumes," its report said, "that when the United States becomes involved in war with Germany, it will at the same time engage in war with Italy. In these circumstances, the possibility of a state of war arising between Japan and an association of the United States, the British commonwealth, and its allies, including the Netherlands East Indies, must be taken into account."

The important word was "when." There was no "if."

"Since Germany is the predominant member of the Axis powers," the document continued, "the Atlantic and European area is considered to be the decisive theater. The principal United States effort will be exerted in that theater, and operations in other theaters will be conducted in such a manner as to facilitate that effort." The United States was to use its fleet to weaken Japanese economic power and "to support the defense of the Malay barrier by diverting Japanese strength away from Malaysia," principally by raids into the Marshall Islands.

Not only was Malaya to be protected, but the British stipulated that they did not intend to let go of any of their Asiatic holdings. "A cardinal feature of British strategic policy," this provision held, "is the retention of a position in the Far East such as will insure the cohesion and security of the British commonwealth."

The plans for a war with Japan provided that the United States should be responsible for the defense of a vast stretch of the Pacific— the ocean areas from the coast of North and South America westward to a short distance from the coast of Australia, and north of the equator to a line extending to the westward of the Marianas up to latitude 30 degrees north, where the area was extended to include the reaches of the ocean all the way to the Asiatic continent.

A second staff conference was held in Singapore April 21-27 to draft an American-British-Dutch war plan for the Pacific in conformity with the master plan for global war laid down at the Washington staff conference. The American representatives were Capt. W. R. Purnell, chief of staff of the Asiatic fleet; Col. A. C. McBride, assistant chief of staff of Gen. MacArthur's forces in the Philippines; Capt. A. M. R. Allen, naval observer at Singapore; and Lieut. Col. F. G. Brink, military observer at Singapore.

The principal British representatives were Air Chief Marshal Sir Robert Brooke-Popham, commander-in-chief, Far East, and Vice-Adm. Sir Geoffrey Layton, commander-in-chief, China. There were six Australian representatives, six Dutch delegates, three New Zealanders, and one representative from India and from the British East Indies.[10]

On the basis of the previous Washington agreement, the United States Pacific fleet was to operate against the Japanese mandated islands and Japanese sea communications. The Asiatic fleet at Manila was to employ only its submarines and its naval air and local naval defense forces in support of the American Army in its defense of Luzon, while cruisers and destroyers were to report at Singapore to operate under strategic command of Adm. Layton. Submarine tenders, destroyers, tankers, and flying boats were to be dispatched to Singapore before the commencement of hostilities. Most of Adm. Hart's cruisers and destroyers were eventually lost fighting in defense of the British and Dutch colonial empires.

The security of Luzon was termed of "subsidiary interest" to the security of Singapore and of sea communications. The Singapore plan envisioned loss of the Philippines. "Upon the ultimate defense area (which includes Corregidor and the entrance of Manila Bay) becoming untenable," the agreement said, "all remaining naval and naval air forces retaining combat value will . . . retire southward, passing under the strategic direction of the commander-in-chief, China."

Chief of Naval Operations Stark testified before the congressional committee that there was general agreement with the conclusion that the Philippines could not be held. He related that, in conversations with the Japanese ambassador, Adm. Nomura, he had predicted that the Japanese would score many early successes in a Pacific war, but that they would eventually be beaten down.

"I'm inclined to think Nomura agreed with me," Stark said.

"Did you think we would lose the Philippines?"

"I hoped we could put up a good fight, but I always conceded we would lose them."

"Did you discuss this with the President?"

"Yes, he was thoroughly familiar with the picture."[11]

The primary reason why the Philippines—and with them Guam[12] —were written off at Singapore, however, was that the Pacific was considered a secondary front. The staff conference agreed that "to insure that we are not diverted from the major object of the defeat of Germany and Italy, our main strategy in the Far East at the present time must be defensive." Clark Lee, in *They Call It Pacific,* asserts that "the dead of Bataan . . . would have still been living if the United States had not decided that the Pacific was a secondary front."[13]

The defense of the Roosevelt administration later for entering a war alliance through the Washington and Singapore staff agreements was that the commitments assumed were not binding. The Washington agreement nowhere provided for ratification by the Senate or even that notification be given Congress that any such alliance existed. The Singapore agreement, while disclaiming that any political commitment was implied, specified that the agreement was to implement the war plan previously adopted in Washington, which provided for no congressional approval.

The Washington agreement on the master war plan was approved by Secretary Knox on May 28 and by Secretary Stimson on June 2.[14] Adm. Stark appeared before the congressional committee with a prepared statement saying that the plan was approved by the two secretaries "and by the President," but deleted the reference to Roosevelt. He said he had learned to his surprise just recently that while the President had full knowledge of the military agreements, he had not ratified them.[15] Stark added, however, that the President had approved these plans, "except officially."*

Lieut. Col. Henry C. Clausen, who had taken a world-tour in 1944 to look for evidence in support of Secretary Stimson's thesis that blame for the Pearl Harbor disaster solely attached to the commanders

*See Note 17, Appendix.

on the spot, told the congressional committee that his inquiries led him to the White House, but that he was discouraged from entering.

Clausen said that the statements of Army leaders convinced him there was "an informal agreement but not a binding agreement" on the part of the United States to fight Japan if the British or Dutch were attacked.

"That may make sense to you; it didn't to me," he told the committee.

"I suggested that the inquiry would lead to the White House, but I was told that it was beyond the scope of my function to investigate there." He said that he was so informed by Col. William J. Hughes, assistant to the Army judge advocate general.[16]

However strenuously it might be denied that the intention of Roosevelt was to circumvent constitutional limitations,[17] the indisputable fact is that as soon as the staff agreements were drafted the Army and Navy drew up supplementary Pacific war plans of their own designed to carry out master strategy in concert with the British and Dutch. The joint Army and Navy basic war plan, which bore the short title "Rainbow No. 5," was approved by Stimson and Knox on the same dates upon which they approved the report on the Washington staff conversations, which bore the short title "ABC-1."[18]

On the basis of Rainbow 5, the Navy basic war plan, known as "WPL-46," was promulgated May 25. The Pacific fleet's plan to support the basic Navy plan was distributed on July 25 and approved September 9 by the chief of naval operations. It was known as "WPPac-26." The Army also drew up a plan of operations to supplement Rainbow 5. This was approved by Chief of Staff Marshall on August 19.[19]

The objectives of the joint Army-Navy plan were described by Adm. Turner, Navy war plans officer, in the following words:

> The plan contemplated a major effort on the part of both the principal associated powers against Germany initially. It was felt in the Navy Department that there might be a possibility of war with Japan without the involvement of Germany, but at some length and over a considerable period this matter was discussed and it was determined that in such a case the United States would, if possible, *initiate efforts to bring Germany into the war against us in order that we would be able to give strong support to the United Kingdom in Europe*.* We felt that it was incumbent on our side to defeat Germany, to launch our princi-

*Italics supplied.

pal efforts against Germany first, and to conduct a limited offensive in the Central Pacific, and a strictly defensive effort in the Asiatic.[20]

The statements of other high-ranking American officers were equally illuminating concerning the practical effects of the staff agreements. They suggested that the reluctance of the American people to be pulled into war was the real reason why the agreements were drafted in secret and why they were kept secret from Congress.

Thus, while asserting that America's broad military objective was the defeat of Germany, Marshall and Stark, in their instructions to American representatives at the Washington staff conference, warned that the American people desired to stay out of war.[21]* The same conclusion was voiced by Lieut. Col. George W. Bicknell, assistant to Gen. Short's G-2. In an intelligence estimate on October 17, 1941, Bicknell said that there was "no known binding agreement between the British and Americans for joint military action against Japan" because "the American public is not yet fully prepared to support such action."[22]

In questioning Short, Senator Ferguson referred to Bicknell's phrase "no known binding agreement" and asked, "What do you understand by 'binding agreement'? Do you mean by treaty?"

"To be binding, it should be approved by the Congress, as I understand it," Short replied. "He might have meant simply any agreement that had been made and approved by the President, and not made public."

"What was your understanding about that part of it that 'the American public is not yet fully prepared to support such action'?"

"I felt at that time," Short responded, "that the American public would not have been willing to have an agreement ratified that we would go to war to defend the Netherlands East Indies or Singapore."[23]

Adm. Kimmel testified that he was no better informed than Gen. Short about American commitments to the British and Dutch. He said that he had tried to find out what the United States would do if the Japanese moved toward Singapore, Thailand, or Borneo, but all the enlightenment he received was in a letter from Stark on No-

---

*The percentage of Americans favoring entry into the war from October, 1939, until May, 1941, the month that the Washington master war plan and the joint Army-Navy war plan were approved, was shown by the Gallup poll to be as follows: October, 1939, 5 per cent; June 2, 1940, 16 per cent; June 14, 1940, 19 per cent; July 6, 1940, 14 per cent; July 19, 1940, 15 per cent; October, 1940, 17 per cent; December, 1940, 15 per cent; Feb. 2, 1941, 15 per cent; March, 1941, 17 per cent; April, 1941, 13 per cent; May, 1941, 19 per cent.

vember 25, 1941, mentioning reports that the Japanese were planning aggressive moves in the Southwest Pacific. "I won't go into the pros and cons of what the United States may do," Stark said, "I will be damned if I know."[24]

Stark himself testified before the congressional committee that his "honest opinion was that no one knew the answers to such questions."[25] Under questioning of Senator Ferguson, he admitted that there was "not so much" difference between the informal war alliance with Britain in the Atlantic and the similar arrangement with the British and Dutch in the Pacific. "We did not come to Congress," he said of both. Nor did he dispute Ferguson when the Senator pointed out that "in the Atlantic, with what you call technical war, we went in without Congress."[26]

Gen. Marshall was shown a memorandum in which he and Stark advised Roosevelt on November 27, 1941, to take "military action" if Jap forces moved into western Thailand or advanced southward through the Gulf of Siam.

"Did you feel," asked Ferguson, "that a Japanese move against British territory would inevitably involve the United States in war?"

"Yes," said Marshall.[27]

In carrying out its engagements under the Singapore pact, Marshall admitted, the Army was building landing strips and accumulating bombs, gasoline, oil, and other material before December 7 at Port Moresby, New Guinea; Darwin, Australia; Rabaul, New Britain; Balikpapan, Borneo; and Singapore.[28]

Even after the drafting of ABC-1, Rainbow No. 5, WPL-46, WP-Pac-26, and the Army plan of operations for the Pacific, new joint war plans were being worked up with the British and approved by Washington almost to the very hour of the December 7 attack. On November 11, for instance, Stark advised Adm. Hart that previous joint plans were considered "dead." Hart was instructed to confer with Adm. Tom S. V. Phillips, who was coming to Singapore as commander of the British Far Eastern fleet, in drawing up a new joint naval operating plan.[29]

Hart subsequently reported that he and Phillips, after a secret conference in Manila, had made an agreement to enlarge the harbor at Manila for use as a base by British naval units. Phillips had brought out the battleship "Prince of Wales" and the battle cruiser "Repulse" —both to be sunk in a Jap air attack in the South China Sea on December 8—and Manila could not accommodate such large units. The agreement was reported by Hart on December 6 and approved by

Stark just before the attack upon Pearl Harbor the following day.

Although Hart was charged with perfecting joint war plans in the Far East, even he did not know the full extent of aid which the White House was pledging to the British. On December 7, a few hours before the attack on Oahu, Hart sent a message to Stark saying, "Learn from Singapore we have assured British armed support under three or four eventualities. Have received no corresponding instructions from you."[30]

Four years later Hart told the congressional committee that he had been informed of these undertakings by Capt. John Creighton, American naval attaché at Singapore, who had been told of them by Air Marshal Brooke-Popham. Hart said that the attack at Pearl Harbor intervened before he received any clarification from Washington.

Capt. Creighton, following Hart before the committee, produced the message which Brooke-Popham had received from London setting forth the terms for American aid. It read:

> We have now received assurance of American armed support in cases as follows:
>
> A) We are obliged to execute our plans to forestall Japanese landing Isthmus of Kra or take action in reply to Nips invasion any part of Siam.
>
> B) If Dutch are attacked and we go to their defense.
>
> C) If Japs attack us, the British therefore without reference to London put plan in action if, first, you have good info Jap expedition advancing with the apparent intention of landing in Kra; second, if the Nips violate any portion of Thailand. If N.E.I. attacked, put into action operation plans agreed upon between British and Dutch.[31]

These contingencies did not provide that American aid should be dependent upon a Japanese attack on any American possessions. The conditions had the effect of giving the British commanders at Singapore a blanket authorization to call American forces into war any time the Japanese moved against British or Dutch possessions or even against Siam. It is not known who in the British government sent word to Brooke-Popham outlining the conditions under which the United States would enter the war, but it is impossible to believe that Britain would have instructed its commander-in-chief for the entire Far East of such conditions if they had not been agreed upon.

Once the United States signed the Washington and Singapore staff agreements, the British, Australians, Dutch, and Chinese proceeded on the assumption that this country was an outright ally and increased their pressure to hasten the day when America should be formally at war. Secretary Hull described their attitude in a memorandum of a conference on November 24 with Lord Halifax, British ambassador; Richard G. Casey, Australian minister; Hu Shih, Chinese ambassador; and A. Louden, Netherlands minister. Hull noted:

> They seemed to be thinking of the advantages to be derived without any particular thought of what we should pay for them, if anything. I remarked that each of their governments was more interested in the defense of that area of the world [Southwest Pacific] than this country, but they expected this country, in the case of a Japanese outbreak, to be ready to move in a military way and take the lead in defending the entire area.[32]

Senator Ferguson asked Adm. Stark: "Isn't that exactly what happened, just what Mr. Hull prophesied would happen, that we would have to defend the whole area and we would have to have the war for the whole area?"

"We would have the major role," Stark replied.[33]

Japanese diplomatic messages show that America's role as a partner of Britain, China, and Holland in a Pacific war alliance was not lost upon the Japanese. Two messages sent by Ambassador Nomura from Washington in the last month before hostilities began demonstrate that the Japanese had suspected or somehow learned of this joint military program. On November 10 Nomura advised Tokyo:

> 1. I sent [Frederick] Moore [legal adviser to the Japanese embassy] to contact Senator [Elbert D.] Thomas [of Utah] of the Senate Military Affairs Committee and Hull. His report reads as follows:
> "The United States is not bluffing. If Japan invades again, the United States will fight with Japan. Psychologically the American people are ready. The Navy is prepared and ready for action."
> 2. Yesterday evening, Sunday, a certain Cabinet member, discarding all quibbling, began by saying to me:
> "You are indeed a dear friend of mine and I tell this to you alone." Then he continued: "The American government is receiving a number of reliable reports that Japan will be on the move soon. The American government does not believe your visit on Monday to the President or the coming of Mr. Kurusu will have any effect on the general situation."
> I took pains to explain in detail how impatient the Japanese have grown since the freezing; how they are eager for a quick understanding; how both the government and the people do not

desire a Japanese-American war; and how we will hope for peace until the end.

He replied, however: "Well, our boss, the President, believes those reports and so does the Secretary of State."[34]

Again, on December 3, Nomura notified Tokyo: "Judging from all indications, we feel that some joint military action between Great Britain and the United States, with or without a declaration of war, is a definite certainty in the event of an occupation of Thailand."[35]

Other Japanese diplomatic messages showed that the Japanese had a clear appreciation of Mr. Roosevelt's role as a protector of Britain, Holland, and China. On November 24, a message from Tokyo to Washington described the American President as "acting as a spokesman for Chiang Kai-shek."[36]

America's protective occupation of Dutch Guiana on November 24 aroused Japanese fears that Roosevelt contemplated similar action in the Dutch East Indies. On November 27 Nomura expressed belief to Tokyo that, "depending upon the atmosphere at the time the Japanese–U.S. negotiations break off, Britain and the United States may occupy the Netherlands East Indies."[37]

Foreign Minister Togo, on December 6, drew a sardonic parallel between America's occupation of Dutch Guiana and Japan's conduct in Indo-China. "Based on an agreement with France," he said, "we penetrated southern French Indo-China for joint defense. Scarcely were our tracks dry, when along comes good old nonchalant America and grabs Netherlands Guiana. If she needs any of the American countries for her own interests, hiding under the camouflage of joint defense, she will take them, as she has just proven."[38]

In two speeches after the Pearl Harbor attack had brought the United States into the war, Prime Minister Churchill made it clear that it had been his constant policy to entangle the United States in any conflict Japan might bring upon Britain, and that in this object he had the eager assistance of Roosevelt. His remarks show that the staff agreements were considered binding by both Roosevelt and himself, and that the President had fortified their effect with additional personal assurances.

On January 27, 1942, in a speech to the House of Commons, Churchill said,

It has been the policy of the cabinet at almost all cost to avoid embroilment with Japan until we were sure that the United States would also be engaged. . . . But as time has passed the mighty United States, under the leadership of Presi-

dent Roosevelt, from reasons of its own interest and safety but
also out of chivalrous regard for the cause of freedom and democracy, has drawn ever nearer to the confines of the struggle.
And now that the blow has fallen it does not fall on us alone. . . .

I have explained how very delicately we walked, and how
painful it was at times, how very careful I was every time that
we should not be exposed single-handed to this onslaught which
we were utterly incapable of meeting. . . .

On the other hand, the probability, since the Atlantic conference, at which I discussed these matters with Mr. Roosevelt,
that the United States, even if not herself attacked, would come
into the war in the Far East, and thus make final victory sure,
seemed to allay some of these anxieties. That expectation has
not been falsified by the event. . . . As time went on, one had
greater assurance that if Japan ran amok in the Pacific, we
should not fight alone. It must also be remembered that over
the whole of the Pacific brooded the great power of the United
States fleet, concentrated at Hawaii. It seemed very unlikely
that Japan would attempt the distant invasion of the Malay
Peninsula, the assault upon Singapore, and the attack upon the
Dutch East Indies, while leaving behind them in their rear this
great American fleet."[39]

Again, on February 15, Mr. Churchill crowed in Commons,

When I survey and compute the power of the United States
and its vast resources and feel that they are now in it with us,
with the British commonwealth of nations all together, however
long it lasts, till death or victory, I cannot believe that there
is any other fact in the whole world which can compare with
that. This is what I have dreamed of, aimed at, and worked
for, and now it has come to pass.[40]

The most straightforward estimate of Roosevelt's policy was provided by Capt. Oliver Lyttelton, British production minister in Churchill's cabinet. Speaking June 20, 1944, before the American Chamber
of Commerce in London, he asserted that "America provoked Japan
to such an extent that the Japanese were forced to attack Pearl Harbor. It is a travesty on history ever to say that America was forced
into war."[41]

Later he apologized for speaking the embarrassing truth that the
will to get into war came from this side of the water—from the White
House.

Chapter Nine

MEETING AT SEA

As EARLY as February, 1941, Prime Minister Churchill had begun to press Mr. Roosevelt to take the lead in deterring Japan from seizing British possessions in the Far East. He besought the President then to "instil in Japan anxiety" that any Japanese move toward Singapore would mean war with the United States.[1] To the Atlantic conference in August he brought renewed proposals that Roosevelt throw down the gauntlet to Japan. Although Britain's hand in the Orient was so weak that Churchill had been forced to shut down the Burma Road only a year before in órder to appease Japan, the Prime Minister euphemistically referred to the proposed course as "parallel action" by Britain and the United States.

More than four years after the Atlantic conference Sumner Welles told the congressional committee investigating Pearl Harbor the detailed story of the conference. Welles's notes of conversations between the two leaders on August 10 and 11 provided the fullest first-hand account of the Charter meeting yet made public.[2] Welles dealt at length with the so-called "parallel declaration" to be made by the United States, Britain, and Holland warning Japan against further aggression in the Far East.

On Sunday, August 10, Welles wrote, he accompanied Roosevelt to a conference with Churchill aboard the battleship "Prince of Wales."

> Sir Alexander Cadogan [British permanent undersecretary for foreign affairs] told me before lunch that in accordance with the conversation which was had between the President, the Prime Minister, Sir Alexander, and myself at the President's dinner last night, he had made two tentative drafts covering proposed parallel and simultaneous declarations by the United States and British governments relating to Japanese policy in

the Pacific and of a proposed joint declaration to be made by the President and the Prime Minister when their present meeting was terminated.

The draft of the "parallel declaration" to Japan read as follows:

Declaration by the United States government that:

1. Any further encroachment by Japan in the Southwestern Pacific would produce a situation in which the United States government would be compelled to take counter measures even though these might lead to war between the United States and Japan.

2. If any third power becomes the object of aggression by Japan in consequence of such counter measures or of their support of them, the President would have the intention to seek authority from Congress to give aid to such power.

Identical declarations were to be made by Great Britain and the Netherlands, with the names of those nations and appropriate references to their governments substituted for the United States and the President. A notation at the bottom of the document read, "Keep the Soviet government informed. It will be for consideration whether they should be pressed to make a parallel declaration."

Welles's memorandum continued,

As I was leaving the ship to accompany the President back to his flagship, Mr. Churchill . . . impressed upon me his belief that some declaration of the kind he had drafted with respect to Japan was in his opinion in the highest degree important, and that he did not think there was much hope left unless the United States made such a clear-cut declaration of preventing Japan from expanding further to the south, in which event the prevention of war between Great Britain and Japan appeared to be hopeless.

He said in a most emphatic manner that if war did break out between Great Britain and Japan, Japan immediately would be in a position through the use of her large number of cruisers to seize or to destroy all of the British merchant shipping in the Indian Ocean and in the Pacific and to cut the lifelines between the British dominions and the British Isles unless the United States herself entered the war. He pled with me that a declaration of this character, participated in by the United States, Great Britain, the dominions, the Netherlands, and possibly the Soviet Union, would definitely restrain Japan. If this were not done, the blow to the British government might be almost decisive.

On the following day Churchill was received by Roosevelt aboard the cruiser "Augusta." Churchill again brought up the subject of the parallel declaration. Welles noted:

The Prime Minister then said that he desired to discuss the situation in the Far East. He had with him a copy of a draft memorandum, of which he had already given the President a copy, and which suggested that the United States, British, and Dutch governments simultaneously warn Japan that further military expansion by Japan in the South Pacific would lead to the taking of counter measures by the countries named, even though such counter measures might result in hostilities between them and Japan, and, second, provided that the United States declare to Japan that should Great Britain go to the assistance of the Netherlands East Indies as a result of aggression against the latter on the part of Japan, the President would request from the Congress of the United States authority to assist the British and Dutch governments in their defense against Japanese aggression.

After further discussion of proposals submitted by Ambassador Nomura in behalf of the Japanese government to Secretary Hull—"all of which," Churchill remarked, "were particularly unacceptable" —Roosevelt said that he would ask Hull by radio to inform Nomura that he was returning to Washington the following Saturday or Sunday and that he desired to see the Japanese ambassador immediately upon his return.

The President, Welles recorded, stated that in this interview he would inform Nomura that if the Japanese would pledge themselves to keep hands off the Southwest Pacific and to withdraw the troops they then had in Indo-China, "the United States would in a friendly spirit seek to explore the possibilities inherent in the various proposals made by Japan for the reaching of a friendly understanding between the two governments."

Roosevelt, however, was unwilling to assent to Japan's proposals that, as conditions to any such pledge undertaken by Japan, the United States abandon economic and financial sanctions, take no further military measures in the Southwest Pacific in concert with the British and Dutch, and "use its good offices for the initiation of direct negotiations between the Japanese government and the Chiang Kai-shek régime for the purpose of a speedy settlement of the China incident."

The President, Welles continued, announced that he would

further state that should Japan refuse to consider this procedure and undertake further steps in the nature of military expansions, the President desired the Japanese government to know that in such event in his belief various steps would have to be taken by the United States, notwithstanding the President's realization that the taking of such further measures might result in war between the United States and Japan.

Churchill, Welles reported,

immediately declared that the procedure suggested appeared to him to cover the situation very well. He said it had in it an element of "face saving" for the Japanese and yet at the same time would constitute a flat United States warning to Japan of the consequences involved in a continuation by Japan of her present course.

Churchill's satisfaction was understandable. The position which Roosevelt announced he intended to take was that Japan must clear out of China and guarantee immunity to the British and Dutch colonial holdings without getting anything in return except a promise that the United States would continue to "explore" the possibilities of a settlement. Such terms obviously would be unacceptable to Japan. Therefore, the bite was at the finish of Roosevelt's proposed lecture to Nomura: if the Japs moved against British and Dutch territory, they would have a war with the United States on their hands.

The discussion then turned to whether the threat of American action should be broadened to cover any aggressive steps by Japan against Russia. Welles suggested that

the real issue which was involved was the continuation by Japan of its present policy of conquest by force in the entire Pacific region and regardless whether such policy was directed against China, against the Soviet Union, or against the British dominions or British colonies, or the colonies of the Netherlands in the Southern Pacific area. I said it seemed to me that the statement which the President intended to make to the Japanese government might more advantageously be based on the question of broad policy rather than be premised solely upon Japanese moves in the Southwestern Pacific area.

The President agreed to this comprehensive enlargement of the warning.

Roosevelt, in calling for the withdrawal of Japanese troops from Indo-China, proposed that that country and Thailand be neutralized by a general agreement to which Japan should be a party. He said that Japan might more readily acquiesce in this proposal if he could state that he had been informed by the British government that Great

Britain "had no aggressive intentions whatever" upon Thailand. Welles suggested the addition that "the British government had informed the United States government that it supported wholeheartedly the President's proposal for the neutralization of Indo-China and of Thailand." Churchill authorized these statements, by means of which Roosevelt undertook to carry the diplomatic ball for Britain.

"The President expressed the belief," Welles said, "that by adopting this course any further move of aggression on the part of Japan which might result in war could be held for at least thirty days." Churchill said that the procedure gave a "reasonable chance" that Japanese policy might be modified.

The thirty-day estimate is at variance with that given by Lindley and Davis, who said that Roosevelt, in endeavoring to check Churchill's impetuous desire to bring a showdown with Japan at once, had asked, "Wouldn't we be better off in three months?" Churchill agreed, but when he still professed doubt whether the respite would be forthcoming, Roosevelt was quoted as saying in an airy, offhand way, "Leave that to me. I think I can baby them [the Japs] along for three months."[3]

Whether it was one month or three, the President by either reckoning was manifesting a conviction that war was inevitable. Once he had taken that position, it is difficult to see what meaning attached to the negotiations for a peaceful settlement which were to go on in Washington for another four months between Hull and Nomura. The decisions which Roosevelt and Churchill reached at their meeting at sea virtually precluded any constructive resolution of the problems between the United States and Japan.

Having decided to warn Japan that further moves in any direction meant a war with America, the conferees indulged in a curious parley as to how much of this the Chinese should be permitted to know. Welles relates:

> I said that while I felt very definitely that every effort should be made to keep China closely informed of what was being done in her interest by Great Britain and by the United States, I wondered whether telling China of what the President intended to state to the Japanese government at this particular moment would not mean that the government at Chungking for its own interests would make public the information so received.
>
> If publicity resulted, I stated I feared the extreme militaristic element in Tokyo and that portion of the Tokyo press which

was controlled by Germany would immediately take advantage of the situation so created to inflame sentiment in Japan to such an extent as to make any possibility remote, as it might anyhow be, of achieving any satisfactory result through negotiation with Japan.

Cadogan, said Welles,

was entirely in accord and would be governed by these views. He said, of course, I realized how terribly persistent the Chinese were and that the present ambassador in London, Dr. Wellington Koo, would undoubtedly press him day in and day out to know what had transpired at the meeting between the Prime Minister and the President with regard to China. He said he felt that the best solution was for him merely to say in general terms that the two governments had agreed that every step should be taken that was practicable at this time for China and its defense and avoid going into any details.

Accordingly, the Chinese were left as completely uninformed about what went on at the Atlantic conference as the American public.

Having disposed of Japan to his satisfaction, Churchill tackled the problem of getting Roosevelt to sign an acknowledgment of Anglo-American alliance in the Atlantic which could be waved in Hitler's face. Roosevelt assented without making difficulties. The Atlantic Charter was the product.[4]

On August 17, upon his return to Washington, Roosevelt summoned Adm. Nomura to the White House and there read him what was tantamount to an ultimatum. After reviewing Japanese penetration of Indo-China and charging Japan with having "continued its military activities and its disposals of armed forces at various points in the Far East," the President said:

Such being the case, this government now finds it necessary to say to the government of Japan that if the Japanese government takes any further steps in pursuance of a policy or program of military domination by force or threat of force of neighboring countries, the government of the United States will be compelled to take immediately any and all steps which it may deem necessary toward safeguarding the legitimate rights and interests of the United States and American nationals and toward insuring the safety and security of the United States.[5]

The oral warning which the President gave Nomura followed the Churchill draft only as far as the beginning of the clause "compelled to take counter-measures even though these might lead to war." Welles said that Roosevelt's revisions constituted a "watering down" of the original statement.

"But the two instruments meant the same thing in diplomatic language?" asked Senator Ferguson.

"That is correct," said Welles.*[6]

No public announcement was made by Roosevelt of the joint action agreement, although he addressed Congress August 21 on his meeting at sea, nor was it announced that the President had submitted an ultimatum to Japan. Roosevelt reserved his confidences for Churchill alone. On the day after addressing his statement to Nomura, he advised the Prime Minister that he had warned the Japanese ambassador against further moves by Japan in the Pacific.

"I made to him," Roosevelt said, "a statement covering the position of this government with respect to the taking by Japan of further steps in the direction of military domination by force. . . . The statement made to him was no less vigorous and was substantially similar to the statement we had discussed."[7]

Under the parallel action agreement, Churchill and the Dutch government were also obligated to follow Roosevelt in addressing ultimatums to Japan, but they seem to have been content to let the United States threaten the Japanese. State Department files do not show that either Churchill or the Dutch gave warnings in the same manner or form as the President had, although Churchill approached a parallel declaration in his radio speech of August 24, when he reported on the Atlantic conference.

After reviewing Japan's military adventures and discussing the potential Japanese threat to Singapore, Siam, and the Philippines, he said, "It is certain that this has got to stop. Every effort will be made to secure a peaceful settlement. . . . But this I must say: that if these hopes should fail we shall of course range ourselves unhesitatingly at the side of the United States."[8]

On November 10 Churchill returned to this theme, stating that "it is my duty to say, that, should the United States become involved in war with Japan, the British declaration will follow within the hour."[9]

In Tokyo, Ambassador Grew was much gratified. "It does one's

*As to the effect of this warning, the minority report of the Joint Congressional Committee says, "In his statement to the Japanese ambassador on Sunday, Aug. 17, immediately following his return from the Atlantic conference, President Roosevelt warned Japan against further attempts to dominate 'neighboring countries,' not merely the possessions of the United States, and used diplomatic language which, according to long established usages, had only one meaning, namely, that such further attempts would result in a conflict with the United States" (Min., p. 15).

heart good," he remarked, "to hear such an unqualified statement by the British Prime Minister, leaving nothing to the imagination."[10]

The only evidence that Churchill ever went beyond his public speeches in taking parallel action against Japan is provided in a memorandum written November 27, 1941, by Dr. Stanley Hornbeck.[11] Hornbeck, reviewing America's relations with Japan, said: "By August of 1941 the situation had become definitely threatening. Toward the end of that month, the British government and the American government served on Japan a strong warning against further extending of her courses of aggression."

When Senator Barkley, chairman of the investigating committee, observed that "if such a protest or representation was made by Great Britain, the document itself would prove what it contained," Senator Ferguson reminded him, "Mr. Chairman, it is clear that the British papers are not subject to our examination."[12]

That the effect of the Roosevelt warning of August 17 was that of an ultimatum is attested by Welles, Capt. R. E. Schuirmann, the Navy's liaison officer on diplomatic relations, and by the Japanese themselves.

Senator Ferguson read Welles a press report from Tokyo dated August 13, while Roosevelt and Churchill were meeting at sea, stating that Japanese political sources believed America would match Japan "move for move" and that the Japanese had "no doubt what the next move would be."

"Doesn't that indicate parallel action had been taken?" asked Ferguson.

"Those would be the implications of the Atlantic Charter," Welles replied.

"Didn't the parallel declaration by Churchill and Roosevelt at the Atlantic conference commit us to 'take the lead' in the war?"

"It envisaged a possible conflict," conceded Welles. "My understanding of the document is that if Japan continued its aggression, the United States would be obliged to take the necessary steps, which would include military action."[13]

Capt. Schuirmann characterized the Roosevelt statement at a meeting on November 5, attended by Gen. Marshall, Adm. Stark, and other high-ranking officers, as "an ultimatum to Japan that it would be necessary for the United States to take action in case of further Japanese aggression."[14]

The Japanese also viewed the statement as an ultimatum. On November 28 Adm. Nomura cautioned Tokyo,

What the imperial government must, of course, consider is what Great Britain, Australia, the Netherlands, and China, egged on by the United States, will do in case the imperial forces invade Thailand. Even supposing there is no armed collision with British forces, in the oral statement of President Roosevelt on the 17th he prophesied that suitable action would be taken immediately in case Japan carries on any further penetration beyond Indo-China.[15]

The President's statement was not the first ultimatum addressed by American spokesmen to the Japanese, nor would it be the last. The first had come from Counselor Eugene Dooman of the American embassy in Tokyo, who, on February 14, 1941, had informed Chuichi Ohashi, the Japanese vice-minister for foreign affairs,

It would be absurd to suppose that the American people, while pouring munitions into Britain, would look with complacency upon the cutting of communications between Britain and the British dominions and colonies overseas. If, therefore, Japan or any other nation were to prejudice the safety of those communications, either by direct action or by placing herself in a position to menace those communications, she would have to expect to come into conflict with the United States.[16]

Ambassador Grew said he approved this statement.[17] The impression had been created in Japan, he told the congressional committee, that the United States was "isolationist, pacifistic, and too divided to fight a war." The controlled press, he said, played up anti-war speeches and strikes in the United States.

"Dooman was in the United States during the 1940 Presidential campaign," said Representative Keefe of Wisconsin. "Were his speeches played up in Japan?"

"I cannot recollect," said Grew.

"Well," said Keefe, "during that campaign there were a lot of speeches made by nonisolationists, including the President himself, indicating that we did not want to fight a foreign war."[18]

A second warning was given Japan by Adm. Turner, Navy chief of war plans. Meeting Ambassador Nomura in July, 1941, Turner told Nomura he thought "Congress would declare war" if Japan attacked the Dutch East Indies or the British in Malaya. The admiral said that his report of the conversation was relayed to Roosevelt.[19]

Welles's statement to Nomura on July 23 that Japan, by occupying Indo-China, had removed the basis for a "peaceful" settlement with the United States, had suggested that the only remaining alternative was a solution by resort to force.[20]

The striking fact is that all of these statements promised Japan war with the United States if the Japanese attacked territory not belonging to the United States. Dooman threatened war in behalf of Britain and its dominions and colonies. Turner threatened war in behalf of Dutch and British colonies. Welles ruled out prospects of a peaceful settlement because Japan moved against Indo-China, then the property of Vichy France. Roosevelt was thinking of the British empire lifeline when he gave his all-inclusive warning. And, as will be seen, Secretary Hull acted at the insistence of the Chinese when he abandoned his own device to keep the peace and submitted terms to Japan which brought on the Pearl Harbor attack and the war.

It was in this strange climate of the United States conducting its foreign relations in the interest of everybody else that diplomatic negotiations proceeded in the hope of averting a war between the United States and Japan.

Chapter Ten

THE LAST OF THE JAPANESE MODERATES

WITH PREPARATIONS for war cut and dried, and the war itself already fairly under way in the Atlantic, diplomatic negotiations supposed to preserve peace in the Pacific went on in Washington. Ambassador Grew, in a moment of optimism some two months before the Pearl Harbor attack, had given a description of the mission of diplomacy. After reviewing America's differences with Japan, he said:

> In facing these difficult and highly complicated problems, let us not forget that diplomacy is essentially our first line of national defense, while our Navy is but the second line and our Army, let us hope, the third line. If the first line, diplomacy, is successful, those other lines will never have to be brought into action, even although that first line is immeasurably strengthened by the mere presence of those other lines, the reserves behind the front. It is the first line, diplomacy, that must bear the responsibility for avoiding the necessity of ever using those reserves, and it is in that light that I look on my duties here in Japan.[1]

American diplomacy, however, did not accomplish this purpose. It failed even to delay the coming of war until the nation was prepared. The minority report of the Joint Congressional Committee (p. 3) said of American-Japanese diplomatic negotiations:

> The question of the wisdom of the foreign policy pursued by the government of the United States is excluded by the terms of the committee's instructions. In any case, to go into this issue would involve the committee in the complexities of history extending back more than 50 years and in matters of opinion

which cannot be settled by reference to anything as positive and definite as the Constitution, laws, and established administrative practices of the United States government. To understand the questions involved, however, an examination of our relations in the Far East, and of the diplomatic negotiations leading up to December 7, 1941, are part and parcel of the explanation of the responsibilities involved in this inquiry.

Diplomacy failed because diplomacy was not employed to avert war, but to make certain its coming. Grew himself has described his mission to Tokyo as a labor of peace, but as early as December 14, 1940, when, as one Groton schoolfellow to another, he addressed a "Dear Frank" letter to Mr. Roosevelt, he seems to have grown tired of the struggle. In that letter he told the President that it was a question of "when" we were to call a halt to Japan's expansion rather than "whether."

"About Japan and all her works," he said. "It seems to me increasingly clear that we are bound to have a showdown some day, and the principal question at issue is whether it is to our advantage to have that showdown sooner or to have it later." He then expressed the belief that "we are bound eventually to come to a head-on clash with Japan."[2]

Replying on January 21, 1941, Roosevelt said, "I find myself in decided agreement with your conclusions."[3] The President then spoke of American policy in the Pacific in relation to the efforts of the British in the war in Europe:

> The British need assistance along the lines of our generally established policies at many points, assistance which in the case of the Far East is certainly well within the realm of "possibility" so far as the capacity of the United States is concerned. Their defense strategy must in the nature of things be global. Our strategy of giving them assistance toward insuring our own security must envisage both sending supplies to England and helping to prevent a closing of channels of communication to and from various parts of the world, so that other important sources of supply will not be denied to the British and be added to the assets of the other side.[4]

The President then proclaimed it to be the extraordinary duty of the United States not only to support Britain in the European war, but to accept a stewardship entailing the protection of Britain's colonial empire while Britain was occupied in Europe. He said:

> The conflict [in Europe] may well be long and we must

bear in mind that when England is victorious she may not have left the strength that would be needed to bring about a rearrangement of such territorial changes in the Western and Southern Pacific as might occur during the course of the conflict if Japan is not kept within bounds.[5]

In order to preserve British imperialism in Asia and the Pacific, therefore, the United States must see to it that Japan was "kept within bounds." The subsequent course of American diplomacy in dealing with Japan may be interpreted in this light.

"Is it fair to say," Senator Ferguson inquired of Grew before the congressional committee, "that you foresaw war between the United States and Japan?"

"I was doing all in my power to avert war," Grew said. "That is the only position a diplomatic representative should take. . . . The clash need not have been military. Economic measures might have brought Japan to a position to deal with us."

"Was it your opinion that Japan would fight or that she was bluffing?"

"I never thought Japan was bluffing," the ambassador replied. "I thought they would fight under certain circumstances."[6]

In February, 1941, at a time when Grew was remarking, "The outlook for the future of the relations between Japan and the United States has never been darker,"[7] Adm. Nomura arrived in Washington as the new Japanese ambassador. Nomura, known as an admirer of the United States and Britain, had inherited a difficult job. Facing him were Americans who made no effort to conceal their skepticism of his and Japan's intentions. At his back, in Tokyo, were the jingoists of the Japanese army and navy, who did not want any mission of peace to succeed, and the agents of Hitler's Germany, spinning their intrigues to involve Japan and the United States in a war which would take America off Germany's back and tie the untrustworthy Japanese firmly to their Axis alliance.

When Nomura was sent to the United States, Grew noted that

the Germans here are doing everything possible to prevent Adm. Nomura from going to Washington and to bring about a partial or complete break in diplomatic relations with the United States, and they are also about to intensify their efforts to embroil the two countries and to propel the [Japanese] southward advance.[8]

Almost at once upon his arrival in Washington, Nomura opened negotiations looking toward a solution of Japan's difficulties with the

United States. In his first interview with the President on February 14, the admiral referred to the chauvinistic military group in Japan as being the chief obstacle to a moderate policy.[9] He also pointed out, according to a memorandum written by Secretary Hull on March 8, that the people of Japan with few exceptions were very much averse to getting into war with the United States.[10]

On April 9 an informal draft, outlining the basis of a cordial resolution of the outstanding differences between the two nations was presented to the State Department by private Japanese and American individuals.[11] It provided that the United States would request the Chiang Kai-shek government to negotiate a peace with Japan which would be based on the guaranty of an independent China, withdrawal of Japanese troops, no indemnities or territorial changes, recognition of Manchukuo, and coalescence of the Wang Ching-Wei Chinese puppet government with that of Chiang.

The Japanese were to pledge "no large-scale concentrated immigration of Japanese into Chinese territory" and the "Open Door" was to be resumed. The draft agreement stipulated that if the Chinese rejected a settlement tendered through President Roosevelt on these terms, America was to discontinue supplying aid to Chiang's government.

Japan was to undertake to limit the military grouping among nations not then involved in the European war, and would execute its commitments under the tripartite pact only if one of its partners were "aggressively attacked" by a power not then involved. In return, the United States would pledge to stay out of any "aggressive alliance" designed to assist one nation against another. Both Japan and the United States were to guarantee the independence of the Philippines.[12]

The draft of April 9 had been prepared by its private sponsors in collaboration with Ambassador Nomura. Secretary Hull, after first expressing skepticism that the time was opportune for it to be presented as a basis for negotiations, finally agreed that it could be used as a framework for beginning discussions if it were supplemented with the following points:

(1) Respect for the territorial integrity and the sovereignty of each and all nations.

(2) Support of the principle of noninterference in the internal affairs of other countries.

(3) Support of the principle of equality, including equality of commercial opportunity.

(4) Nondisturbance of the status quo in the Pacific, except as the status quo may be altered by peaceful means.[13]

On May 12 Nomura submitted an official revision of the April 9 draft to Secretary Hull, the principal changes being that the United States was to pledge to take no "aggressive measures" against any other nation, and was to acknowledge Premier Konoye's basis for a settlement in China, providing for a neighborly friendship between China and Japan, joint defense against communism, and economic co-operation not based upon any Japanese attempt to attain economic monopoly.[14]

Four days later the State Department submitted revisions of these proposals, in which the American pledge to discontinue assistance to China if Chiang refused the Japanese peace tender was rejected, the Konoye principles were not stated in the text, and the proviso that China and Japan should undertake joint defense against communism was rephrased to read "parallel measures of defense against subversive activities from external sources." Recognition of Manchukuo was left for later negotiations between China and Japan. Secretary Hull also insisted that this country should not be bound to any course of action which would limit all-out assistance to Britain in its fight with the Axis partners in Europe, and Nomura was asked to state that Japan's Axis commitments were not inconsistent with the policy of permitting America to intervene against its partners in the tripartite pact.[15]

A week later, after Foreign Minister Matsuoka had stated Japan's obligations to support Germany in the event of American entry into the war in Europe, Hull informed Nomura that there could be little progress in negotiations until Japan, in effect, agreed that we should be permitted a free hand to give aid to Britain, even if that should lead to the United States being drawn into the European war. Nomura expressed the view that Matsuoka was talking for home consumption. The ambassador said that Japan would make its own independent decision as to its Axis obligations, and that once the proposed American-Japanese agreement was signed it "would cause a weakening in the influence of the jingoes."[16]

On May 31 Hull again revised the draft basis for negotiations by inserting the provision, "Obviously, the provisions of the pact do not apply to involvement [in the European war] through acts of self-defense." The "joint defense against communism" clause now became "co-operative defense against injurious communistic activities," and was tentatively to provide for the continued presence of some Japanese troops in China.[17] Two days later Nomura informed Hull that he and his associates were in agreement with the document as it stood, except for some changes in phraseology, but Hull remained distrustful, even to the extent of questioning whether Japan sincerely desired a settlement.[18]

The negotiations now stalled on the issue of whether Japan was to permit the United States to carry intervention as far as it liked in Europe without obliging Japan to honor its commitments under the tripartite pact. On June 21 Hull handed Nomura a complete revision of the American draft,[19] and accompanied it with an oral statement that it was illusory to expect substantial results from an agreement between the two countries as long as certain Japanese leaders were committed to the support of Germany.[20]

Nomura on July 15 expressed Japan's objections to the American attitude in saying that "Japan could not give a blank check for anything that America might call self-defense."[21] Japan, however, did take measures to meet the objections Hull had stated June 21 against pro-German Japanese leaders when the Konoye cabinet was revised on July 18 and Foreign Minister Matsuoka, who had signed the tripartite pact in behalf of Japan, was dropped.[22]

On July 2 representations were made by Tadao Wikawa, an officer of the Capital Cooperative Bank of Japan, to the State Department that he had been informed by J. P. Morgan & Co. that diplomatic conversations had already been closed by the United States, and that Japanese funds in this country were soon to be frozen.[23] This intelligence, which preceded by twenty-three days the actual issuance of the freezing order, did not bring any tangible response from the State Department. On July 25 the freezing order was issued,[24] and Britain followed suit the next day. On the same day, as has been noted before, the United States also prohibited the export of petroleum, petroleum products, and scrap metal without a specific license from the administrator of export control. These measures were supposedly taken in retaliation for Japanese assumption of military control over Indo-China, which occurred July 21, but in view of Wikawa's complaint three weeks earlier about the impending freezing order, it seems clear that they had been meditated for some time.

That the Roosevelt administration embarked upon its program of economic sanctions against Japan with the clear understanding that these measures might easily precipitate war is amply documented. The question had been fully explored by Ambassador Grew in what he called his "green light" dispatch of September 12, 1940, to the State Department. After reviewing the trend of events in the Far East, the ambassador urged the United States to embark on a course of economic sanctions in order to curb Japanese military expansion.

Of this message Mr. Grew remarked in his book, *Ten Years In Japan,* "Another important event, from my point of view, was the sending to Washington in September of what I can only call my 'green light' telegram, perhaps the most significant message sent to Washington in all the eight years of my mission to Japan."[25]

Discussing the risks of adopting a policy of sanctions against Japan, Grew remarked, in his message to the State Department,

> I have expressed the opinion in previous communications that American-Japanese relations would be set on a downward curve if sanctions were applied by the United States. It is true that measures are now justified by our new program of national preparedness which need not fall within the category of outright sanctions. On the other hand, the probability must be contemplated that drastic embargoes on such important products as oil, of which a super-abundance is known to be possessed by the United States, would be interpreted by the people and government of Japan as actual sanctions and some form of retaliation might and would follow. The risks would depend not so much upon the careful calculations of the Japanese government as upon the uncalculating "do or die" temper of the army and navy should they impute to the United States the responsibility for the failure of their plans for expansion. It may be that such retaliation would take the form of counter-measures by the government but it would be more likely that it would be some sudden stroke by the navy or army without the prior authorization or knowledge of the government. These dangers constitute an imponderable element which cannot be weighed with assurance at any given moment. However, it would be shortsighted to deny their existence or to formulate policy and adopt measures without fully considering these potential risks in determining the wisdom of facing them squarely.

Grew said, however, that it was impossible to stand still when Japan and its Axis partners represented a way of life which threatened Britain and America as the "leaders of a large world-wide group of English speaking peoples." He remarked,

> In general, the uses of diplomacy are bankrupt in attempting to deal with such powers. Occasionally diplomacy may retard, but it cannot stem the tide effectively. Only by force or the display of force can these powers be prevented from attaining their objectives.

American interests in the Pacific are definitely threatened by her [Japan's] policy of southward expansion, which is a thrust at the British empire in the east. Admittedly America's security has depended in a measure upon the British fleet, which has been in turn and could only have been supported by the British empire. If the support of the British empire in this, her hour of travail, is conceived to be in our interest, and most emphatically do I so conceive it, we must strive by every means to preserve the status quo in the Pacific, at least until the war in Europe has been won or lost.[26]

Before the Congressional Investigating Committee, Senator Ferguson asked Grew, "Why did you send the 'green light' telegram?"

"Because the time had come to apply economic measures," Grew replied.[27]

That the American government and military services were well aware that the imposition of oil sanctions would force Japan into further aggressions was demonstrated at the congressional committee hearings. For example, Senator Ferguson asked Adm. Stark, "About the oil question, and your attitude toward Japan: Did you not testify before the Navy Court that after the imposition of economic sanctions upon Japan in the summer of 1941, you stated that Japan would go somewhere and take it [oil], and that if you were a Jap you would?"

"I think that is correct," Stark responded. "I stated it, and I stated in the State Department, as I recall, that if a complete shutdown was made on the Japanese, throttling her commercial life and her internal life, and her essential normal peace life by stopping her from getting oil, the natural thing for a Jap was to say, 'Well, I will go down and take it.' "[28]

Ferguson then asked whether Stark recalled a White House conference on July 24, 1941, when Roosevelt said he had told Ambassador Nomura that, should Japan attack to get oil by force, the Dutch and British would go to war against her.

When Stark said he had no recollection of this statement, Ferguson read the following transcript of the President's remarks to Nomura:

The President said that if Japan attempted to seize oil supplies by force in the Netherlands East Indies, the Dutch, without a shadow of a doubt, would resist, the British would immediately come to their assistance, war would then result between Japan, the British and the Dutch, and, in view of our own policy of assisting Britain, an exceedingly serious situation would immediately result.[29]

"Now," Ferguson said, "do you know whether or not shortly after that, in fact, in about 48 hours, the embargo did go on?"

"The embargo went on, as I recall," Stark replied, "on the 26th. This is the 24th. Yes, sir."[30]

Ferguson then read a memorandum of a conversation on July 25, 1941, between Arthur A. Ballantine, Assistant Secretary of State, and Col. Iwakuro, Japanese military attaché in Washington. Col. Iwakuro stated that, in view of the imposition of the oil embargo, Japan would have no alternative sooner or later but to go into Malaya and the Dutch East Indies for oil and other materials.

"Now, Admiral," said Ferguson, "taking the high ranking officials in our government, you said that you thought sanctions such as this oil, etc., would bring war on ultimately. Who else agreed with you?"

Stark replied that he believed the State Department, Army leaders, and practically all high officials in Washington took that position. He read from *Peace and War:*

> Practically all realistic authorities have been agreed that imposition of economic sanctions or embargoes against any strong country, unless that imposition be backed by a show of superior force, involves serious risk of war. The President and heads of the Army and Navy and Department of State were in constant consultation through this period regarding all the aspects of the diplomatic and military situation.[31]

Ferguson then produced a covering letter written by Stark July 22, 1941, to Undersecretary of State Welles, attached to which was an analysis of the expected effects of an oil embargo which had been drafted by Adm. Turner. This analysis set forth the Navy's official position on the advisability of imposing the embargo, as attested by a notation from Stark to Welles saying, "I concur in general."[32]

Turner, in his analysis, said,

> It is generally believed that shutting off the American supply of petroleum will lead promptly to the invasion of the Netherlands East Indies. While probable, this is not necessarily a sure immediate result. . . . Japan has oil stocks for about eighteen months' war operations.

Turner said, however, that an

> embargo on exports will have an immediate severe psychological reaction in Japan against the United States. It is almost certain to intensify the determination of those now in power to continue their present course. Furthermore, it seems certain that, if Japan should then take military measures against the British and

Dutch, she would also include military action against the Philippines, which would immediately involve us in a Pacific war.

In listing his conclusions, Adm. Turner said,

> An embargo would probably result in a fairly early attack by Japan on Malaya and the Netherlands East Indies, and possibly would involve the United States in early war in the Pacific. If war in the Pacific is to be accepted by the United States, actions leading up to it should, if practicable, be postponed until Japan is engaged in a war in Siberia. It may well be that Japan has decided against an early attack on the British and Dutch, but has decided to occupy Indo-China and to strengthen her position there, also to attack the Russians in Siberia. Should this prove to be the case, it seems probable that the United States could engage in war in the Atlantic, and that Japan would not intervene for the time being, even against the British.

Turner's final recommendation was "that trade with Japan not be embargoed at this time."[33]

Three days after the Navy counselled the State Department and Roosevelt against the embargo, the President imposed it.

Four days before the freezing and embargo orders, Nomura, perturbed by the turn events were taking, endeavored to see in turn Secretary Hull and Adm. Stark, but, unable to reach either, finally called on Adm. Turner. Turner's report of this conversation depicts Nomura as speaking with considerable frankness as one naval officer to another:

> Ambassador Nomura stated that for some weeks he had frequent conferences with Mr. Hull, in an endeavor to seek a formula through which the United States and Japan could remain at peace. He no longer hoped for 100 per cent agreement on all points, but would be content if a partial agreement could be reached which would prevent war between the two countries. Such an agreement would necessarily be informal, since Japan is now committed by treaty to Germany, and this treaty could not be denounced at this time. However, he noted that the decision as to when the military clauses of the treaty would come into effect lies entirely in Japan's hands, and that these would be invoked only if Germany were to be the object of aggression by another power. He stated that Japan entered the Axis solely because it seemed to be to Japan's interest to do so. Japan's future acts will be dominated solely by Japan, and not by any other power. Whatever military action Japan takes will be for her own ultimate purposes.

The ambassador also told Adm. Turner that, as a result of the United States export restrictions, Japan's economic position was bad and steadily getting worse. American and British military support to China, in contrast, was steadily increasing. Nomura informed Turner that within the next few days Japan would occupy Indo-China. He expressed himself as personally opposed to this move, and feared that the United States would take further military and economic action in reprisal. He proposed that if the United States could change its policy in regard to the Japanese embargo and aid to China, and that if it could bring itself to agree to permitting Japanese troop concentrations on the border of Inner Mongolia, whatever action was taken by the United States in the Atlantic would not be of great concern to Japan.

This was the Japanese proposal in its plainest form, and Adm. Turner inferred that it would mean Japanese troop withdrawal from the greater part of China.[34]

On July 23, however, Welles, who was acting as Secretary of State, told Nomura there was no basis for pursuing further the conversations between Japan and the United States.[35] This statement provoked such profound concern in Tokyo that the new Japanese foreign minister, Adm. Teijiro Toyoda, informed Grew on July 26 that he had "hardly slept at all during recent nights."[36] Adm. Nomura, however, left Welles after expressing the hope that no hasty conclusions would be reached and after voicing his own "belief that a friendly adjustment could still be found."[37]

President Roosevelt on July 24 proposed that if Japan would withdraw its troops from Indo-China, he would make every effort to obtain an agreement from the British, Dutch, and Chinese for the neutralization of this area. Nomura responded that withdrawal, with the attendant problem of saving face, presented difficulties that were probably insuperable.[38] The fact that Roosevelt's suggestion was not received in Tokyo until after news of the American freezing order, thus increasing Japanese resentment, made it clear to Grew that the proposal could not be favorably considered at that time.[39]

On August 6 Nomura informed Hull that Japan would pledge that "it will not further station its troops in the Southwestern Pacific areas except French Indo-China and that the Japanese troops now stationed in French Indo-China would be withdrawn forthwith on the settlement of the China Incident."

In return for these concessions, Japan asked that the United States agree that Japanese citizens in the Philippines would not be discriminated against, that the United States would suspend its military measures in the Southwest Pacific, and, on the successful conclusion of the conversations, would attempt to induce Britain and Holland to take similar steps; that normal trade relations would be restored by the United States; that both nations were to co-operate in assuring free access to the natural resources of the Southwest Pacific and East Asia, and that the United States was to "use its good offices for the initiation of direct negotiations between the Japanese government and the Chiang Kai-shek régime for the purpose of a speedy settlement of the China Incident."[40] Hull's formal reply termed these proposals "lacking in responsiveness to the suggestion made by the President."[41]

Thus, when Roosevelt went off to the Atlantic conference, where he promised Churchill that the United States would take an uncompromising position against Japan, even if it resulted in war, the negotiations in Washington were stalemated.

When the President returned from his meeting at sea to present Nomura with his warning of August 17 that America would fight, the Japanese ambassador brought up the plan for a radical solution of Japan's differences with this country. It was nothing less than that Roosevelt should hold a Pacific conference with Premier Prince Konoye, just as he had held an Atlantic conference with Churchill, and that face to face the leaders of the two countries should achieve a settlement once and for all.

Adm. Nomura told the President that Prince Konoye "feels so seriously and earnestly about preserving [peaceful] relations that he would be disposed to meet the President midway, geographically speaking, between our two countries and sit down together and talk the matter out in a peaceful spirit."[42]

This proposal was not new with the Japanese. It had first been suggested in the formal draft of April 9 presented by nonofficial Japanese and Americans to the State Department as the outline for resolution of the strained relations between the two countries. It had then been proposed that this meeting be held during May at Honolulu. Thus the idea of a Roosevelt-Konoye meeting preceded the Atlantic conference by four months.[43]

On August 8,[44] two days before Roosevelt met Churchill off Newfoundland, and again on August 16,[45] Nomura repeated his request for a meeting between the President and Konoye to Secretary Hull, but Hull gave him no encouragement. On August 17 Nomura submitted the plan directly to Roosevelt. The President made no direct reply at the time.

In Tokyo, Foreign Minister Toyoda, pressing Ambassador Grew to support such a meeting, expressed high hopes that it would solve all of the difficulties. Grew personally appealed for "very prayerful consideration" of the proposal "for the sake of avoiding the obviously growing possibility of an utterly futile war between Japan and the United States." The ambassador wrote Secretary Hull,

> Not only is the proposal unprecedented in Japanese history, but it is an indication that Japanese intransigence is not crystallized completely owing to the fact that the proposal has the approval of the Emperor and the highest authorities in the land. The good which may flow from a meeting between Prince Konoye and President Roosevelt is incalculable.[46]

The hopes of the Japanese moderates were centered on this plan.* They believed that the best hope of peace was for peace elements in Japan to establish themselves firmly in control, as against the military extremists, and to co-operate with the United States in shifting Pacific relationships onto a new basis. It was believed, however, that a certain measure of immediate agreement was a prerequisite to establishing the moderates in control, because it would form a counterweight on Japanese public opinion against the pressures of the militarists and of axis propaganda. Finally, on August 23, Roosevelt said that if such a meeting was to be held, it might be arranged for about October 15, but Nomura stressed the urgency of an earlier date.[47]

On August 27 Prime Minister Konoye sent a personal appeal to Roosevelt for a meeting "as soon as possible."[48] The President, although willing to meet Churchill, now raised difficulties about getting away for twenty-one days to go as far as Hawaii. He suggested that if the meeting were held in Juneau, Alaska, it would require only about two weeks of his time and would allow for about a three- or four-day conversation.[49] Nomura replied that Juneau was acceptable, and that Konoye would get there in about ten days by warship. He suggested the period between September 21 and 25 as most suitable for the meeting.[50]

Hull took the position that all of the decisions to be reached at the proposed meeting should be agreed to preliminary to it, and looked upon Juneau as merely a ratification meeting. He brought up the

*The majority report of the Joint Congressional Committee (p. 48) states: "That there were elements in Japan who desired peace is unquestioned. But for many years the government of that nation had been divided into two schools of thought, the one conceivably disposed to think in terms of international good will with the other dominated by the militarism of the war lords who had always ultimately resolved Japanese policy."

serious consequences to both governments if the meeting failed to reach an agreement, but he did not give equal consideration to the hazards of having no meeting at all. Nomura tried to allay his doubts, particularly as to the crucial question of Japan's commitments under the tripartite pact, by saying that this alliance would present no difficulties at the conference because "the Japanese people regarded their adherence to the Axis as merely nominal and . . . he could not conceive of his people being prepared to go to war with the United States for the sake of Germany." He asserted, however, that for the United States to demand that Japan grant America a blank check for any action against Germany "was equivalent to asking for a nullification of the tripartite pact," and that he did not think Japan's leaders were willing to go that far as long as they were subject to pressure, if not belligerent action, by a combination consisting of the United States, Britain, and Holland.[51]

On September 3 Roosevelt submitted a formal reply to Konoye's proposal for a meeting, adopting the view expressed by Hull that preliminary agreements were necessary to insure a successful outcome.[52] But, at the same time, he said that such preliminary agreements would have to be submitted to and discussed with the British, Chinese, and Dutch before he could take them up in negotiations with Konoye.[53] This proviso not only made an early meeting a practical impossibility, but reduced the possibility of arranging a conference at all. It demonstrated unmistakably that this country already had an alliance, admitted or not, with China and the western imperialisms and was conducting its diplomacy much more with the view to protecting their interests than its own.

Prince Konoye, in his memoirs, stated that on August 28 Roosevelt had summoned Nomura and told him, "I desire a meeting of about three days with Prince Konoye." But something happened, Konoye continued, and Roosevelt's enthusiasm cooled between then and September 3.[54] Although the conference project continued to be discussed, it had been rendered a dead letter by the President's attitude. The American diplomatic representatives in Tokyo noted that, almost until the very end, Konoye and the moderate element were willing to go to almost any lengths to bring off the meeting and avert war. Eugene Dooman reported on September 18 that an understanding had been reached among influential elements in Japan enabling Konoye to give Roosevelt direct oral assurance in regard to the tripartite pact which "would be entirely satisfactory to the President."[55]

On September 27, Foreign Minister Toyoda again urged a Pacific conference in describing to Ambassador Grew his concern over the growing tension in relations between Japan and America. He said that he hoped for an adjustment, not only for the sake of the two countries, but in the belief that such a step "would become the opening wedge to bringing about peace throughout the world." Toyoda said:

> Since assuming my post two months ago, I've been working on the matter of adjusting Japanese-U.S. relations even to the extent of almost forgetting to eat and sleep. It is with the same objective that Premier Konoye has expressed his willingness to act as a leader in a conference with President Roosevelt.
>
> Japan is connected to Germany and Italy by an alliance. The fact that the premier of Japan had volunteered to meet the President, in itself has given rise to much misunderstanding regarding her relations with Germany and Italy. Thus, there is proof that Japan is making a supreme sacrifice. Moreover, the history of Japan has no precedent of an instance where the premier himself has gone abroad in behalf of diplomacy. This fact in itself should clearly show the sincerity of the government of Japan in its expressed desire of adjusting the relationship between Japan and the United States, and, through that, of maintaining peace in the Pacific, and, indeed, for the world.
>
> Maintenance of peace is Japan's sole motivating power. Should there be those who believe that Japan was forced to her knees by U.S. pressure, it would indeed be a sad misconception on their part. Japan desires peace; she is not succumbing to outside pressure. Moreover, Japan is not one to yearn for peace at any price.

Toyoda said that the vessel to transport Konoye and his party to the meeting had already been selected, and the personnel of the party, including generals and admirals, had been decided upon. "We are in a position to start at any moment now," he said.[56]

Toyoda further told Grew,

> Time, as I have often said, is a vital factor from both internal and international viewpoints. The decision [whether to hold the conference] must be made as soon as possible. So I desire to ask for the most speedy and sincere consideration of the American government. I may add that, as regards the date for the meeting, October 10-15 will suit the Japanese government.
> Finally, by way of a conclusion, I should like to say that negotiations of this sort require sincerity and mutual confidence. I need not dwell on the character, the convictions, and faith of

Prince Konoye as well as his political position, all of which are well known to Your Excellency. Without Prince Konoye and the present cabinet under him, an opportunity for Japanese-American rapprochement is likely to be lost for some time to come. I wish to emphasize again the urgent necessity of having the proposed meeting at the earliest possible date.[57]

On September 29 Grew sent a strong plea to Washington in behalf of the meeting. He left no doubt of the alternative if Konoye's request were spurned.

In this message the American ambassador said that the advent of the Konoye-Toyoda régime had given American diplomacy a new lease on life. Expressing hope that "so propitious a period be not permitted to slip by," Grew said that in his opinion the time had arrived when "liberal elements in Japan might come to the top" if encouraged. He said that the United States must choose between a policy of economic strangulation or the method of constructive conciliation.

If the Konoye proposal for a conference leading to rapprochement were rejected, Grew continued, Konoye's cabinet would fall, a military dictatorship would come into power, "unbridled acts" might be expected, and a situation would result "in which it will be difficult to avoid war." Grew said Konoye, while unable to renounce the Axis alliance, would reduce Japan's adherence to "a dead letter." The Roosevelt-Konoye conference, the ambassador concluded, presented "the hope that ultimate war may be avoided in the Pacific."[58]

This forecast was prophetic. Roosevelt was being offered the chance that might have avoided war. He chose to refuse it. Events then followed their inevitable course.*

After dispatching this message, Grew commented in his journal:

> For a prime minister of Japan thus to shatter all precedent and tradition in this land of subservience to precedent and tradition, and to wish to come hat in hand, so to speak, to meet the President of the United States on American soil, is a gauge of the determination of the government to undo the vast harm

---

*President Roosevelt's responsibility in conducting diplomacy was described in the minority report of the Joint Congressional Committee (p. 12) as follows:

"The duty of conducting negotiations with foreign governments from March 4, 1933, to Dec. 7, 1941, was vested in President Franklin D. Roosevelt, under the Constitution, laws, and established practice of the United States, and he could delegate to the Secretary of State, Cordell Hull, such correspondence and communications relating thereto as he deemed fitting and proper. In respect of matters assigned to him it was the duty of Secretary Hull to keep the President informed of all transactions that were critical in nature and especially those involving the possible use of the armed forces of the United States."

already accomplished in alienating our powerful and progressively angry country.[59]

Even in the face of such representations, Secretary Hull remained obdurate and maintained that Japan's failure to make specific advance commitments was a sign of insincerity and evidenced the intention to continue a policy of aggression.[60] In Japan such unwillingness to compromise, Dooman observed, occasioned doubt whether the United States ever intended to come to an agreement.[61] Roosevelt and Hull refused to act and matters drifted along until the outside date of October 15 proposed by Toyoda for the conference had slipped by. On the following day, October 16, the Konoye cabinet resigned and Gen. Tojo and the militarists took over the government of Japan.

"Although I knew that the failure of progress in the American-Japanese negotiations would almost certainly bring about Konoye's fall sooner or later," Grew said, "I had not looked for it so soon."[62]

In an exchange of letters with Konoye the following day, Grew warmly commended the former premier for his "distinguished official service" to Japan.[63] Later Grew commented:

> The reason why I mentioned his outstanding service was the fact that he alone tried to reverse the engine, and tried hard and courageously, even risking his life and having a very close call as it was. Whatever mistakes he made directing Japan's policy, he had the sense and the courage to recognize those mistakes and to try to start his country on a new orientation of friendship with the United States.[64]

Konoye had indeed pursued his policy at the risk of his life. On August 14, Baron Hiranuma, the 75-year old vice-premier in his cabinet, had been struck by two bullets fired by a member of the Black Dragon Society who found the moderation of the government intolerable. The incident was interpreted as a warning that Konoye and the moderates who were endeavoring to avert a war with the United States must go.[65]

Konoye, facing an order from American military occupation headquarters for his arrest as a war criminal, ended his life with poison December 16, 1945. In Oscar Wilde's De Profundis, one of the last books Konoye had read, this passage was underlined: "Society as we have constituted it will have no place for me, has none to offer; but nature, whose swift rains fall on the unjust and just alike, will have clefts in the rocks where I may hide, and secret valleys in whose silence I may weep undisturbed."[66]

No one else wept for the lost peace.

Chapter Eleven

DIPLOMACY FOR D-DAY

Despite the accession of Gen. Tojo and a military government, all hope was not yet lost. Tojo started the war and has been brought to dock as a war criminal, but he was not installed as premier with the purpose of embarking upon a conflict with the United States which would end in the ruin of Japan. The danger that the conflict would materialize lay, as far as Japan was concerned, in the insensate ambitions of the military extremists.[1] The strategy of Hirohito and his advisers was, therefore, to vest in a representative of this very element responsibility for the policies and conduct of the Japanese government, in the hope that by so doing a restraining influence could be exerted over the hotheads by one of their own number.

Ambassador Grew wrote in his journal October 20,

> Despite the fact that, as anticipated, the Konoye government was succeeded not by a civilian but by a military man, indications of a willingness on the part of the Tojo government to proceed with the conversations . . . would imply that it is premature to stigmatize the Tojo government as a military dictatorship committed to the furtherance of policies which might be expected to bring about armed conflict with the United States.

Noting that Tojo, as distinguished from previous Japanese military prime ministers, was not a retired officer, but a full general in active service, Grew observed, "It would be logical, therefore, to expect that Gen. Tojo, in retaining his active rank in the army, will as a result be in a position to exercise a larger degree of control over army extremist groups."[2]

As further encouragement to hopes for preserving peace, Grew reported to the State Department that "a reliable Japanese informant" had told him that just prior to the fall of the Konoye cabinet a conference of the leading members of the privy council and of the Japanese armed forces had been summoned by the Emperor, who inquired if they would be prepared to pursue a policy which would guarantee that there would be no war with the United States. The representatives of the army and navy who attended the conference did not reply to the Emperor's question, whereupon the latter, with a reference to the progressive policy pursued by the Emperor Meiji, his grandfather, in an unprecedented action ordered the armed forces to obey his wishes.

The Emperor's definite stand necessitated the selection of a prime minister who would be in a position effectively to control the army, the ensuing resignation of Prince Konoye, and the appointment of Gen. Tojo who, while remaining in the active army list, is committed to a policy of attempting to conclude successfully the current Japanese-American conversations.[3]

There was, in fact, an active appreciation, especially on the part of the Japanese navy, that it might well be an invitation to disaster to undertake a war against the United States. Konoye, in his memoirs, asserted that Adm. Isoroku Yamamoto, the commander-in-chief of the combined imperial fleets, when asked what the chances were if a war should develop, told him, "If they say it must be done, we will run around at will for about half a year or a year, but if it stretches into two or three years, I have no confidence in a successful ending."[4]

The Roosevelt administration had already kicked over the best hope of preserving peace when it refused to strengthen the hand of Konoye, and a plain warning of the consequences, embodying an inferential criticism of the Roosevelt policy toward Japan, was dispatched by Ambassador Grew to Hull on November 3. Grew said that if efforts at conciliation were to fail,

the ambassador foresees a probable swing of the pendulum in Japan once more back to the former Japanese position or even farther. This would lead to what he has described as an all-out, do-or-die attempt, actually risking national hara-kiri, to make Japan impervious to economic embargoes abroad rather than to yield to foreign pressure. It is realized by observers who feel Japanese national temper and psychology from day to day that, beyond peradventure, this contingency not only is possible but is probable.

. . . The view that war probably would be averted, though there might be some risk of war, by progressively imposing drastic economic measures is an uncertain and dangerous hypothesis upon which to base considered United States policy and meas-

ures. War would not be averted by such a course, if it is taken.
. . . The primary point to be decided involves the question
whether war with Japan is justified by American national objectives, policies, and needs in the case of failure of the first line
of national defense, namely, diplomacy, since it would be possible
only on the basis of such a decision for the Roosevelt administration to follow a course which would be divested as much as
possible of elements of uncertainty, speculation, and opinion.
The ambassador does not doubt that such a decision, irrevocable
as it might well prove to be, already has been debated fully
and adopted, because the sands are running fast.[5]

Grew was here saying that Roosevelt and his administration had
already committed themselves to war, and that the policy of economic
strangulation and the refusal to support the Konoye government as
the one hope of peace were merely symptoms of the fundamental
decision already reached.

Grew continued,

The ambassador . . . does not at all mean to imply that
Washington is pursuing an undeliberated policy. Nor does he
intend to advocate for a single moment any "appeasement" of
Japan. . . . The ambassador's purpose is only to insure against
the United States becoming involved in war with Japan because
of any possible misconception of Japan's capacity to rush head-
long into a suicidal struggle with the United States. . . . He
points out the shortsightedness of underestimating Japan's obvious preparations to implement an alternative program in the
event the peace program fails.

He adds that similarly it would be shortsighted for American
policy to be based upon the belief that Japanese preparations
are no more than saber-rattling, merely intended to give moral
support to the high-pressure diplomacy of Japan. Action by
Japan which might render unavoidable an armed conflict with
the United States may come with dangerous and dramatic suddenness.[6]

The Japanese government, however, would make one further endeavor to reach a solution. Even before the collapse of the Konoye
cabinet, it had been determined to dispatch Saburo Kurusu, an
experienced diplomat, to Washington to assist Nomura in this final
attempt to come to an understanding.[7] Kurusu left Tokyo on his
mission November 5. With or without his knowledge—and Kurusu,
as well as Nomura, professed after the war that he had no advance
knowledge of the Pearl Harbor stroke[8]—the Tojo government had

already set a deadline for reaching an understanding with the United States. Upon his departure, Kurusu said that he refused to take a later Clipper for "technical reasons."[9] The obvious inference was that he was working within a fixed time limit. Nor were the reasons for this decision difficult to perceive.

By November the economic war initiated by the United States had already reduced Japan to a desperate pass. Not only had Japanese assets been frozen by the Americans, British, and Dutch, cutting off trade with these countries, but the Panama Canal had been closed to Japanese shipping. These actions, together with the trade stagnation incident to the Russo-German war, had cut off about 75 per cent of Japan's normal imports, causing a serious food shortage and weakening the general economy.[10] These dislocations were so severe that, according to the information given Grew November 7 by "a leading Japanese," the Tojo government had

> decided the limits to which it will be possible to go in an endeavor to meet the desires of the United States, but nevertheless should these concessions be regarded as inadequate by the government of the United States, it is of the highest importance that the Washington conversations be continued and not permitted to break down.[11]

This insistence that the conversations be continued, even if there were recognition of failure on both sides, again hints that a deadline had already been established for agreement, after which any further conversations would be merely for the purpose of deceiving the none too prescient administration in Washington and its Army and Navy command. The Japanese pretense of keeping up the conversations after November 26 was, in fact, designed to stall for time until a military plan already set in train could be executed.

When Grew complained to his informant of the bellicose tone of the Japanese press, his visitor merely remarked that "frightened dogs bark and the greater the fright the louder the bark," adding that "at present the military party in Japan are frightened by the prospects opening up before them."[12]

Even before Kurusu arrived in Washington, however, the new Tojo government had displayed a disposition to strive for an understanding by authorizing Nomura to present to Secretary Hull on November 7 a memorandum dealing with the disposition of Japanese troops on the Asiatic mainland and pledging that all troops, with the exception of garrisons in North China and Inner Mongolia, would be withdrawn from China within two years after the conclusion of a peace, and that Japanese troops would also be withdrawn from Indo-China after the conclusion of the Chinese war.[13] Three days later Nomura again endeavored to satisfy President Roosevelt's concern about Japan's commitments under the Axis pact by saying, "All I have to ask you is to 'read between the lines' and to accept the formula as satisfactory."[14]

In Tokyo Shigenori Togo, the new Japanese foreign minister, spoke grimly to Grew on November 10 of America's refusal to display what he termed "sincerity." Grew said that the minister stated:

> The population of this country is steadily and rapidly increasing; that it was now about 100 million; and it was necessary to assure raw materials necessary for their existence. It was his opinion that unless the American government realizes this fact as among the realities of the situation, successful conclusion to the conversations would be difficult. During the conversations carried on for a period of more than six months, the Japanese government had repeatedly made proposals calculated to approach the American point of view, but the American government for its part had taken a more advanced position. Those being the facts, "we in Japan are led to wonder what is the degree of sincerity of the American government in continuing with the conversations." He said that national sentiment will not tolerate further protracted delay in arriving at some conclusion.

Later in the conversation Togo asserted that "the freezing by the United States of Japanese assets had stopped supplies of many important raw materials to Japan. Economic pressure of this character is capable of menacing national existence to a greater degree than the direct use of force."

The minister also inquired of Grew why America took a holier-than-thou attitude toward Japanese military activity, voicing "his impression that the American government is now resorting, under the plea of self-defense, to measures over and beyond those that are generally recognized by international law."[15]

All of these many months the American government had considered its discussions with the Japanese merely as preliminary and exploratory conversations, but now the Japanese deemed that they had advanced sufficiently to be raised to the level of "formal and official negotiations."[16] The Japanese also pleaded for more speed in the negotiations, but were answered by Roosevelt with the statement that the six months already consumed was but a short time to deal with such important problems. He then counseled patience.[17] Foreign Minister Togo was described as "shocked" on hearing from No-mura that Hull and Roosevelt did not appreciate the urgency of the negotiations and the necessity to bring them to an early successful conclusion. Japan was so thoroughly subjected to militaristic propaganda that Togo realized, like Konoye before him, according to the statement of Grew, that he was endangering his position and even his life by opposing extremist groups and keeping the negotiations alive.[18]

On November 15, however, Secretary Hull said he would not even enter the stage of negotiations until Great Britain, China, and the Netherlands had been consulted, and that he objected to receiving "ultimatums" on the question of speeding up the discussions because, he said, the United States had been pursuing a peaceful course all the while and the Japanese government was the one which had been "violating law and order." He added that to reach an agreement while Japan's obligations to Germany remained in force would cause so much outcry in this country that he "might well be lynched."[19]

Hull now suggested a new commercial agreement providing for co-operation by the United States and Japan in reducing trade barriers generally, and restoring normal trade between the two countries, except as each might find it necessary to restrict exports for its own security and self-defense.[20] American embargo orders against Japan had not mentioned that country by name but had generally prohibited exports of certain products except to the western hemisphere and Great Britain in the interest of "self-defense," so that resort to the same phrase in Hull's new offer could be interpreted as constituting an escape clause by which this country could give Japan a promise but no tangible benefits.

Upon Kurusu's arrival in Washington November 17, Hull threw cold water on his mission at the outset by insisting on an outright Japanese disavowal of the tripartite pact before discussing anything else, and expressing the opinion that Kurusu had nothing new to offer.[21] Hull, in continuing conference sessions, displayed no more readiness to compromise, stating at a meeting November 18, "We can go so far but rather than go beyond a certain point it would be better for us to stand and take the consequences."[22] Kurusu told Hull that, while he could not say that Japan would abrogate the tripartite pact, "Japan might do something that would 'outshine' the tripartite pact."[23] Hull was not impressed. When Kurusu then asked for a State Department formula by which Japan could deal with her Axis obligations, Hull dismissed the request with the statement that "this was a matter for Japan to work out."[24] Nomura, also pressing for some means to change Japan's course, pointed out that "big ships cannot turn around too quickly, that they have to be eased around slowly and gradually."[25]

To attain this end, the Japanese on November 20 and 21 made what was to be their last offer. This was the so-called *modus vivendi* which was to serve until some further agreement could be reached. Hull asked whether the Japanese proposal was intended as a temporary step to help organize public opinion in Japan and whether the Japanese emissaries intended afterward to continue the conversations, looking to the conclusion of a comprehensive agreement. Kurusu replied in the affirmative.

According to the State Department account,

> Mr. Kurusu said that some immediate relief was necessary and that if the patient needed a thousand dollars to effect a cure, an offer of $300 would not accomplish the purpose. . . . The secretary replied that although the Japanese proposal was addressed to the American government, he had thought it advisable to see whether other countries would contribute and he found that they would like to move gradually.

This view entirely discounted Kurusu's insistence that some kind of speedy settlement, even of a stop-gap character, was necessary. "The ambassador," Hull said, "explained that Japan needed a quick settlement and that its psychological value would be great."[26] But Hull couldn't, or wouldn't, move that fast.

The Japanese proposals were as follows:

> (1) The governments of Japan and the United States undertake not to dispatch armed forces into any of the regions, excepting French Indo-China, in the Southeastern Asia and the Southern Pacific area.
>
> (2) Both governments shall co-operate with the view to securing the acquisition in the Netherlands East Indies of those goods and commodities of which the two countries are in need.
>
> (3) Both governments mutually undertake to restore commercial relations to those prevailing prior to the freezing of assets.
>
> The government of the United States shall supply Japan the required quantity of oil.
>
> (4) The government of the United States undertakes not to resort to measures and actions prejudicial to the endeavors for the restoration of general peace between Japan and China.
>
> (5) The Japanese government undertakes to withdraw

troops now stationed in French Indo-China upon either the restoration of peace between Japan and China or the establishment of an equitable peace in the Pacific area; and it is prepared to remove the Japanese troops in the southern part of French Indo-China to the northern part upon the conclusion of the present agreement.

As regards China, the Japanese government, while expressing its readiness to accept the offer of the President of the United States to act as "introducer" of peace between Japan and China as was previously suggested, asked for an undertaking on the part of the United States to do nothing prejudicial to the restoration of Sino-Japanese peace when the two parties have commenced direct negotiations.[27]

In regard to the Axis pact, Kurusu stated, Japan undertook to interpret its commitments "freely and independently." He declared that the Japanese government "would never project the people of Japan into war at the behest of any foreign power; it [would] accept warfare only as the ultimate, inescapable necessity for the maintenance of its security and the preservation of national life against active injustice."[28]

This was as far as Japan had ever gone in disavowing the war threat of the pact, but Hull noted that he "did not think this would be of any particular help and so dismissed it."[29] The Secretary also objected to the clause specifying that the United States would refrain from "actions prejudicial to the endeavors for the restoration of general peace between Japan and China." This clause apparently required suspension of American aid to Chiang, and the Secretary said that the purpose of our aid to China was the same as that of our aid to Britain[30]—implying an all-out American support of Chinese victory, regardless of its effect upon relations with Japan. On November 22 Hull further insisted that Japanese troops be withdrawn not only from southern Indo-China, but from all of that country.[31]

On November 24 Grew reported from Tokyo that Foreign Minister Togo expressed perplexity concerning the reasons of the American government for not accepting the Japanese proposal. Togo said he did not expect American aid to China to be discontinued until such time as negotiations between China and Japan were to begin, at which time he assumed hostilities would have ceased. Grew concluded from these remarks that this point in the Japanese proposal was primarily intended to save face.[32]

Long after the event, Secretary Hull would describe the Japanese proposals of November 20 and 21 as the "final Japanese proposition,

an ultimatum."[33]   On November 26 he submitted the American
counter-proposal, and it meant war. Grew noted in his diary on November 29 that when Hull's proposals became known in Japan, most
Japanese leaders, among them Togo and Prince Konoye, were "very
pessimistic."[34] On December 5 he reported having received a letter
from a prominent Japanese who said that almost all of the people
with whom he had talked believe "that Washington has delivered an
ultimatum to us."[35]

On November 30 the Japanese state of mind was reflected in a
bellicose speech delivered by Premier Gen. Tojo under the auspices
of the Imperial Rule Assistance Association and Dai Nippon East Asia
League. The Premier asserted:

> The fact that Chiang Kai-shek is dancing to the tune of
> Britain, America, and communism at the expense of able-bodied
> and promising young men in his futile resistance against Japan
> is only due to the desire of Britain and the United States to
> fish in the troubled waters of East Asia by pitting the East
> Asiatic peoples against each other and to grasp the hegemony
> of East Asia. This is a stock in trade of Britain and the United
> States.
>
> For the honor and pride of mankind, we must purge this
> sort of practice from East Asia with a vengeance.[36]

Hull's proposals of November 26 were clearly unacceptable to the
Japanese and were known to be so in advance by the Secretary. They
made it clear that the State Department had reached the end of negotiations. On the day before submitting them to Nomura and Kurusu, Hull expressed the belief at a meeting of the war council "that
there was practically no possibility of an agreement being achieved
with Japan, that in his opinion the Japanese were likely to break out
at any time with new acts of conquest by force; and that the question of safeguarding our national security was in the hands of the
Army and Navy." He also expressed his judgment "that any plan
for our military defense should include an assumption that the Japanese might make the element of surprise a central point in their
strategy and also might attack at various points simultaneously with
a view to demoralizing efforts of defense."[37] In the light of these
opinions, Hull could not have expected much to come of his proposals of the following day.

Roosevelt also had no misconceptions about what would happen when the proposals were tendered Japan. In a message to Prime
Minister Churchill on November 24, he stated, "I am not very hope-

ful and we must all be prepared for real trouble, possibly soon."[38] Again, at a meeting at the White House on noon of the 25th, the day before Hull handed the President's counter-proposals to Japan, Roosevelt "brought up the event that we were likely to be attacked, perhaps [as soon as] next Monday."[39]

Hull stated before the Congressional Investigating Committee that he conducted his diplomacy in close collaboration ,with the British, Australian, Dutch, and Chinese governments, all of which were consulted in the preparation of the November 26 note,[40] and whose views, particularly those of the Chinese, he accommodated, even though they had a profound effect upon bringing on the war.

One of his memoranda, for instance, showed that on November 25, the day before he submitted the American terms to Japan, he consulted Ambassador Halifax, who wanted the proposals to the Japanese to include removal of all Jap troops and naval and air forces from Indo-China, instead of permitting 25,000 troops to remain, as Hull had suggested. The American secretary amended his government's terms to accommodate the British ambassador's view.[41]

Halifax also wanted Hull's relaxation of economic restrictions to be amended to forbid export to Japan of all goods "of direct importance to the war potential, in particular, oil." Halifax said the British were anxious to "facilitate Hull's difficult task," but said the British empire's economic structure was so complicated that Britain considered it impracticable "to give carte blanche to diplomatic representatives."[42]

In a message to Roosevelt on November 26, Churchill acknowledged receipt from the President of a "message about Japan" informing the British government of Hull's submission of his ultimatum to the Japanese envoys on that date. Churchill told the President, "It is for you to handle this business."

"There is only one point that disquiets us," Churchill went on. "What about Chiang Kai-shek? Is he not having a very thin diet? Our anxiety is about China. If they collapse, our joint dangers would enormously increase. We are sure that the regard of the United States for the Chinese cause will govern your action. We feel that the Japanese are most unsure of themselves."[43]

Churchill could have spared himself his worries about the Chinese. They were taking care of themselves. The fact was brought out at the congressional hearings that Hull cast away the last hope of averting war by yielding to their importunities.

Before he submitted his document of November 26, which the

Army Pearl Harbor Board described as "touching the button that started the war,"[44] Hull had inclined toward the idea of submitting a *modus vivendi* of his own to effect a three months' truce with Japan. This scheme was in the forefront of his mind as late as the morning of the 25th, as attested by Secretary of War Stimson. Stimson said:

> At 9:30 Knox and I met in Hull's office for our meeting of three. Hull showed us the proposal for a three months' truce, which he was going to lay before the Japanese today or tomorrow. It adequately safeguarded all our interests, I thought as I read it, but I did not think that there was any chance of the Japanese accepting it because it was so drastic.[45] In return for the propositions which they were to do, namely, to at once evacuate and at once to stop all preparations or threats of action, and to take no aggressive action against any of her neighbors, etc., we were to give them open trade in sufficient quantities only for their civilian population. This restriction was particularly applicable to oil. We had a long talk over the general situation. We were an hour and a half with Hull, and then I went back to the department, and I got hold of Marshall.[46]

With the chief of staff, Stimson then went to the White House, where, together with Secretaries Knox and Hull and Adm. Stark, they heard the President make his prediction of a Japanese attack "perhaps next Monday."

On the following day, November 26, Stimson learned that Hull had determined to abandon the *modus vivendi*. Stimson recounted,

> Hull told me over the telephone this morning that he had about made up his mind not to make the proposition that Knox and I passed on the other day to the Japanese but to kick the whole thing over—to tell them that he has no other proposition at all. The Chinese have objected to that proposition—when he showed it to them; that is, to the proposition which he showed to Knox and me, because it involves giving to the Japanese the small modicum of oil for civilian use during the interval of the truce of three months.
>
> Chiang Kai-shek had sent a special message to the effect that that would make a terrifically bad impression in China; that it would destroy all their courage and that it would play into the hands of his, Chiang's, enemies and that the Japanese would use it. T. V. Soong had sent me this letter and has asked to see me and I had called up Hull this morning to tell him so and ask him what he wanted me to do about it. He replied as I have

just said above—that he had about made up his mind to give up
the whole thing in respect to a truce and to simply tell the
Japanese that he had no further action to propose.[47]

When Adm. Stark was examined before the congressional committee, Representative Gearhart brought up the White House conference
at noon on the 25th and asked whether Hull at that time gave any
intimation that he proposed to abandon the proposal for a three
months' truce. Stark said he could not recall, but that Hull, in a
memorandum of November 27, mentioned that as early as the 25th
he was considering abandoning the *modus vivendi* and on the 26th
did abandon it.

"Well, weren't you very, very much disturbed, and wasn't Gen.
Marshall very much disturbed by the progress of that conference in
the things that were said and the things that were being planned by
Mr. Hull?" asked Gearhart.

"We were disturbed because we thought things were heading up
so fast toward a showdown, if you will, and we wanted more time
and it began to look as though we were not going to get it," Stark
replied. "If you read the *modus vivendi,* it is nothing like so drastic
as the so-called ten-point note which he handed to the Japs on the
26th, but it is my understanding that the ten points mentioned in the
note on the 26th were the points which were going to be taken up,
perhaps one at a time, under the *modus vivendi,* and that the *modus
vivendi* would provide some weeks, or three months, to discuss these
particular points, and that then the *modus vivendi* was thrown over-
board and the points with which you are all familiar were handed to
the Japanese."

"It has been stated," Gearhart said, "that the *modus vivendi* was
abandoned because Chiang Kai-shek vigorously objected to it. Was
any mention made of Chiang Kai-shek's attitude toward the *modus
vivendi* in that meeting of the 25th?"

"I do not recall that it was," Stark replied. "I have an extremely
clear recollection of Mr. Hull telling me how he felt about the *modus
vivendi* separate from that meeting of the 25th."

"You heard the President say in the course of that meeting, in substance or in effect, that we were likely to be attacked, perhaps as soon
as next Monday?"

"Yes, I recall that."[48]

A memorandum by Secretary Hull to Roosevelt of November 26
was produced. It read:

With reference to our two proposals prepared for submission to the Japanese government:

1. A proposal in the way of a draft agreement for a broad, basic, peaceful settlement for the Pacific area which is henceforth to be made a part of the general conversations now going on, to be carried on if agreeable to both governments with a view to a general agreement on this subject.

2. The second proposal is really closely connected with the conversations looking towards a general agreement which is in the nature of a *modus vivendi* intended to make more feasible the continuance of the conversations. In view of the opposition of the Chinese government and either the half-hearted support or the actual opposition of the British, the Netherlands and Australian governments, and in view of the wide publicity of the opposition and of the additional opposition that will naturally follow through utter lack of an understanding of the vast importance and value otherwise of the *modus vivendi,* without in any way departing from my views about the wisdom and benefit of this step to all of the countries opposed to the aggressor nations who are interested in the Pacific area, I desire very earnestly to recommend that at this time I call in the Japanese ambassador and hand to him a copy of the comprehensive basic proposal for a general peaceful settlement and at the same time withhold the *modus vivendi* proposal.[49]

Commenting upon Hull's change of mind, which resulted in the abandonment of the *modus vivendi,* Stark said, "I think there was boiling in Mr. Hull's mind the message from Chiang Kai-shek and it jellied on the 26th."[50]

Stimson first heard of Hull's decision to substitute his ultimatum for the *modus vivendi* on November 27, one day after the Secretary of State's interview with the Japanese envoys. Stimson related,

The first thing in the morning I called up Hull to find out what his finale had been with the Japanese—whether he had handed them the new proposal which we passed on two or three days ago, or whether, as he suggested yesterday he would, he broke the whole matter off. He told me now that he had broken the whole matter off. As he put it, "I have washed my hands of it and it is now in the hands of you and Knox—the Army and the Navy."

I then called the President. The President gave me a little different view. He said they had ended up, but they ended up with a magnificent statement prepared by Hull. I found out afterwards that this was not a reopening of the thing but a statement of our constant and regular position.[51]

Adm. Stark said that he probably first heard on November 27 that Hull had thrown over the *modus vivendi* and had submitted his ten-point ultimatum. He said he recalled Hull's statement that "it was now up to the Army and Navy" which, to his mind, "pointed clearly to the fact that he [Hull] had no hope of reaching a satisfactory settlement in the Pacific through further negotiations."

"When I learned of it, I considered it very important, particularly as we were playing for time," Stark said.[52]

Returning to the influence exerted by the Chinese in inducing Hull to abandon the *modus vivendi,* Senator Ferguson produced the message transmitted to Secretary Stimson on November 25 by T. V. Soong, Chiang Kai-shek's brother-in-law. Stark identified it as the message which had disturbed Hull.

"Isn't it true that the Chinese government not only went to the Secretary of State but they went to other agencies and Mr. Hull was upset about it?" Ferguson asked.

"Very much upset."

Ferguson asked whether the Chinese had not put pressure even on Congress to induce Hull to abandon the truce proposal.

"That is my understanding, and confirmed, without any question, by Mr. Hull's statement to me that they were crying appeasement on the Hill, another thing which greatly perturbed him."[53]

Ferguson then produced a memorandum by Hull of a conversation he had had on November 25 with the Chinese ambassador, Dr. Hu Shih, which bore the title, "Opposition of Generalissimo Chiang Kai-shek to *Modus Vivendi."* Describing his conversation with Dr. Hu, Hull said:

> I said very recently that the Generalissimo and Mme. Chiang Kai-shek almost flooded Washington with strong and lengthy cables telling us how extremely dangerous the Japanese threat is of attack to the Burma Road, to Indo-China, and appealing loudly for aid, whereas practically the first thing this proposal of mine and the President's does is to require the Japanese troops to be taken out of Indo-China and thereby to protect the Burma Road from what Chiang Kai-shek says is an imminent danger.[54]

Stark commented on this as follows: "I remember very clearly how upset Mr. Hull was, of his telling me that even the Hill was crying appeasement, that the Chinese themselves should have supported him,

because he was doing this in their behalf, and that apparently they
didn't understand it. Also he pointed out that the British, he thought,
were only half-way supporting it."[55]

"Now, will you tell us why the *modus vivendi* was not sent?"
Ferguson asked Stark. "You were one of the top officials representing
the United States Navy, and this would be a naval war in the Pacific,
would it not?"

"Largely, yes. I always looked on it as largely a naval war."

Stark said that both he and Gen. Marshall were fighting for time,
"because the defense of the Philippines, which was an Army problem,"
required a greater state of readiness for war.[56]

Stark then referred to a memorandum of a conversation November 29 between Hull and Lord Halifax, in which Hull stated:

> The British ambassador called at his request and I soon discovered that he had no special business except to check on the
> aftermath of the conversations between the President and myself and the Japanese, with special reference to the question of
> the proposed *modus vivendi*. This caused me to remark in a
> preliminary way that the mechanics for the carrying on of diplomatic relations between the governments resisting aggressor
> nations are so complicated that it is nearly impossible to carry
> on such relations in a manner at all systematic and safe and
> sound. I referred to the fact that Chiang Kai-shek, for example,
> had sent numerous hysterical cable messages to different cabinet
> officers and high officials in this government other than the State
> Department, and sometimes even ignoring the President, intruding into a delicate and serious situation with no real idea
> of what the facts are.
>
> I added that Chiang Kai-shek had his brother-in-law, located
> here in Washington, disseminate damaging reports at times to
> the press and others, apparently with no particular purpose in
> mind; that we have correspondents from London who interview
> different officials here, which is entirely their privilege to do,
> except that at times we all move too fast without fully understanding each other's views, et cetera, et cetera. I stated that this
> was well illustrated in the case of the recent outburst by Chiang
> Kai-shek. In referring to this I remarked that it would have
> been better if, when Churchill received Chiang Kai-shek's loud
> protest about our negotiations here with Japan, instead of passing the protest on to us without objection on his part, thereby
> qualifying and virtually killing what we knew were the individual views of the British government toward these negotiations,
> he had sent a strong cable back to Chiang Kai-shek telling him

to brace up and fight with the same zeal that the Japanese and the Germans are displaying instead of weakening and telling the Chinese people that all of the friendly countries were now striving primarily to protect themselves and to force an agreement between China and Japan. Every Chinese should understand from such a procedure that the best possible course was being pursued and that this calls for resolute fighting until the undertaking is consummated by peace negotiations which Japan in due course would be obliged to enter into with China.[57]

"I felt the same way about the impropriety of flooding all of Washington in the manner in which Mr. Hull stated," Stark remarked. "I thought they should have gone to him with all of their troubles and not gone into the highways and byways."

"But after we are all through, it is apparent that Mr. Hull followed just what the Chinese wanted?" asked Senator Ferguson.

"He did. He broke off so far as the *modus vivendi* is concerned," replied Stark. "And he gives extensive reasons there for it. Perhaps he may have agreed with some of Chiang Kai-shek's thoughts that even a leak to the effect that the United States was going to let Japan have oil or other materials or ease up on the freezing might be such a blow to their morale as to make it impossible for them to continue. He talked it over, I assume, with his Chief and he came to that conclusion."

"But, Admiral," said Ferguson, "isn't this true, that when you take what Mr. Hull said about Chiang Kai-shek, it indicated that he was not going to follow that route—rather that he was going to follow what he wanted. It was a criticism of the Chinese stand, was it not?"

"I do not know if he criticized so much," Stark replied, "although he may have criticized Chinese understanding in some respects. That, I would say, could have been resolved and set straight between Mr. Hull and the ambassador. But when it was broadcast, and Mr. Hull gained the impression that even here at the capitol he was considered guilty of appeasement, that may have influenced him in the action which he took."

"Now, wait. Do I understand, then, that the opinion that Mr. Hull was appeasing Japan may have had something to do with his throwing out the *modus vivendi* and putting in the note of the 26th?"

"Whether or not that criticism which was being leveled at him in official Washington had anything to do with his final decision only Mr. Hull could answer," replied Stark. "I do know that it greatly annoyed him."[58]

This was the background when Nomura and Kurusu called at the State Department at 5:45 P.M. on November 26, to be handed the American terms. The Chinese had got under Hull's skin with their shouts about "appeasement," and the Secretary of State, with Roosevelt's blessing, responded by kicking peace out the window.[59] The proposals he submitted to Japan were as follows:

(1) The government of the United States and the government of Japan will endeavor to conclude a multilateral non-aggression pact among the British Empire, China, Japan, the Netherlands, the Soviet Union, Thailand, and the United States.

(2) Both governments will endeavor to conclude among the American, British, Chinese, Japanese, the Netherlands, and Thai governments an agreement whereunder each of the governments would pledge itself to respect the territorial integrity of French Indo-China and, in the event that there should develop a threat to the territorial integrity of Indo-China, to enter into immediate consultation with a view to taking such measures as may be deemed necessary and advisable to meet the threat in question. Such agreement would provide also that each of the governments party to the agreement would not seek or accept preferential treatment in its trade or economic relations with Indo-China and would use its influence to obtain for each of the signatories equality of treatment in trade and commerce with French Indo-China.

(3) The government of Japan will withdraw all military, naval, air, and police forces from China and from Indo-China.

(4) The government of the United States and the government of Japan will not support—militarily, politically, economically—any government or régime in China other than the national government of the Republic of China with capital temporarily at Chungking.

(5) Both governments will give up all extraterritorial rights in China, including rights and interests in and with regard to international settlements and concessions, and rights under the Boxer Protocol of 1901.

Both governments will endeavor to obtain the agreement of the British and other governments to give up extraterritorial rights in China, including rights in international settlements and in concession and under the Boxer Protocol of 1901.

(6) The government of the United States and the government of Japan will enter into negotiations for the conclusion between the United States and Japan of a trade agreement, based upon reciprocal most favored nation treatment and reduc-

tion of trade barriers by both countries, including an undertaking by the United States to bind raw silk on the free list.

(7) The government of the United States and the government of Japan will, respectively, remove the freezing restrictions on Japanese funds in the United States and on American funds in Japan.

(8) Both governments will agree upon a plan for the stabilization of the dollar-yen rate, with the allocation of funds adequate for this purpose, half to be supplied by Japan and half by the United States.

(9) Both governments will agree that no agreement which either has concluded with any third power or powers shall be interpreted by it in such a way as to conflict with the fundamental purpose of this agreement, the establishment and preservation of peace throughout the Pacific area.

(10) Both governments will use their influence to cause other governments to adhere to and to give practical application to the basic political and economic principles set forth in this agreement.[60]

Lindley and Davis candidly remark,

When the document was out of his hands, . . . Mr. Hull had a feeling that it somehow put an end to the grueling, anxious year and a half since Sedan, the period of the diplomatic defensive during which the White House and Department of State, lacking military might, had deployed the country's moral suasion and economic strength around the globe in an effort to keep war from our shores. Mr. Hull regretfully thought he might have kept the peace a little longer without sacrifice of vital interests, but the issue of war or peace had been taken out of his hands.[61]

Points 3, 4, and 9, requiring withdrawal of all Japanese troops from China and Indo-China, Japanese recognition of the Chiang Kai-shek régime, and abandonment of the Axis, were the most important of the ten demands and promises. "After the Japanese had read the documents," Assistant Secretary of State Joseph W. Ballantine recounted, "Mr. Kurusu asked whether this was our reply to their proposal for a *modus vivendi*." Hull said that it was. Kurusu said he "did not see how his government could consider paragraphs 3 and 4 of the proposed agreement and that if the United States should expect that Japan was to take off its hat to Chiang Kai-shek and propose to recognize him, Japan could not agree."

After looking over the American terms further, Kurusu said that when he and Nomura reported the American answer, their government "would be likely to throw up its hands." He suggested that it might be better if they did not refer the statement to Tokyo before discussing its contents further, but Hull said that the proposal "was as far as we would go at this time." When Hull repeatedly referred to public opinion as conditioning his actions, asserting that he "might almost be lynched if he permitted oil to go freely to Japan," Adm. Nomura remarked that "sometimes statesmen of firm conviction fail to get sympathizers among the public; that only wise men could see far ahead and sometimes suffered martyrdom; but that life's span was short and that one could only do his duty."

Kurusu said that he felt that the American response to the Japanese proposals was "tantamount to meaning the end," and asked again whether the United States were not interested in a *modus vivendi*. Hull dismissed the question by saying, "We have explored that."[62]

On the following day the two Japanese ambassadors called with Hull on President Roosevelt. They expressed disappointment about the failure of any agreement regarding a *modus vivendi*. The President refused to temper the American proposals and told the ambassadors,

> We remain convinced that Japan's own best interests will not be served by following Hitlerism and courses of aggression, and that Japan's own best interests lie along the courses which we have outlined in the current conversations. If, however, Japan should unfortunately decide to follow Hitlerism and courses of aggression, we are convinced beyond any shadow of doubt that Japan will be the ultimate loser.[63]

Replying to this, Kurusu, in an interview with Hull on December 1, "disclaimed on the part of Japan any similarity between Japan's purposes and Hitler's purposes," while Nomura

> pointed out that wars never settle anything and that war in the Pacific would be a tragedy, but he added that the Japanese people believe that the United States wants to keep Japan fighting with China and to keep Japan strangled. He said that the Japanese people feel that they were faced with the alternative of surrendering to the United States or fighting. The ambassador said that he was still trying to save the situation.[64]

Hull did not even profess still to be trying. On November 29, he told Lord Halifax that "the diplomatic part of our relations with Japan was virtually over and that the matter will now go to the officials of the Army and Navy." He said further that it would be

> a serious mistake for our country and other countries interested in the Pacific situation to make plans of resistance without including the possibility that Japan may move suddenly and with every possible element of surprise and spread out over considerable areas and capture certain positions and posts before the peaceful countries interested in the Pacific would have time to confer and formulate plans to meet these new conditions; that this would be on the theory that the Japanese recognize that their course of unlimited conquest now renewed all along the line probably is a desperate gamble and requires the utmost boldness and risk.[65]

These military moves were indeed in train. The day before Hull submitted the President's ten-point program, the Japanese fleet which would descend upon Pearl Harbor had already put to sea from Hitokappu Bay. In view of the irreconcilable attitude of both governments, it was now almost beyond the bounds of possibility that the striking force would be recalled from its mission, but even as late as December 2 Adm. Nagano again ascertained from Adm. Yamamoto that the fleet could be turned in its course if a settlement should somehow be attained.[66] Although conversations continued in Washington off and on during the ensuing ten days, they did not change the status, and the fact that war was inevitable was apparent to both sides.

On December 2, for instance, Undersecretary Welles complained of Japanese military activity in Indo-China and elsewhere, reading a statement from Roosevelt conveying implied notice that the United States would act under his warning of August 17 in the event of new Japanese aggression. Mr. Roosevelt said:

> The stationing of these increased Japanese forces in Indo-China would seem to imply the utilization of these forces by Japan for purposes of further aggression. . . . Such aggression could conceivably be against the Philippine Islands; against the many islands of the East Indies; against Burma; against Malaya, or either through coercion or through the actual use of force, for the purpose of undertaking the occupation of Thailand. Such new aggression would, of course, be additional to the acts of aggression already undertaken against China, our attitude toward which is well known, and which has been repeatedly stated to the Japanese government.[67]

To this Nomura, foreshadowing the final Japanese answer, replied,

> The Japanese people believe that economic measures are a much more effective weapon of war than military measures; . . . they believe they are being placed under severe pressure by the United States to yield to the American position; and that it is preferable to fight rather than to yield to pressure.[68]

On December 5 Adm. Nomura told Hull that the Japanese were "alarmed over increasing naval and military preparations of the ABCD powers in the Southwest Pacific area, and that an airplane of one of those countries recently had flown over Formosa. He said that our military men are very alert and enterprising and are known to believe in the principle that offense is the best defense."[69] If the ambassador was waxing sardonic, the effect was lost upon Hull. The Secretary of State remarked after some further discourse that "we were not looking for trouble but that at the same time we were not running away from menaces."[70]

The only other development preceding the outbreak of war was President Roosevelt's direct appeal to Hirohito on December 6, which, as Hull later remarked, was "for the record."[71] The message was withheld from Ambassador Grew for ten and a half hours and was finally placed in the hands of the Emperor at 3:00 A.M., Tokyo time, December 8, twenty minutes before the attack on Pearl Harbor.[72] In the course of his remarks Roosevelt stated:

> During the past weeks it has become clear to the world that Japanese military, naval, and air forces have been sent to southern Indo-China in such large numbers as to create a reasonable doubt on the part of other nations that this continuing concentration in Indo-China is not defensive in its character. . . . The people of the Philippines, of the hundreds of islands of the East Indies, of Malaya, and of Thailand itself are asking themselves whether these forces of Japan are preparing or intending to make attack in one or more of these many directions. . . . It is clear that a continuance of such a situation is unthinkable. None of the people whom I have spoken of above can sit either indefinitely or permanently on a keg of dynamite.[73]

The first response was at Pearl Harbor. The second came at 6:00 A.M., Tokyo time, December 8, when Japanese imperial headquarters announced that a state of war existed with the United States and Great Britain.[74] The third came several hours after the attack had begun when Foreign Minister Togo made an oral statement "as a reply" from the emperor to the President to the effect that establishment of peace "in the Pacific and consequently of the world has been the cherished desire of his Majesty, for the realization of which he has hitherto made the government to continue its earnest endeavors."[75]

In Washington, Adm. Nomura asked for an appointment with Secretary Hull on December 7 at 1:00 P.M. (7:30 A.M., Hawaii time), but later telephoned and asked that the appointment be postponed to 1:45, as he was not quite ready. He and Kurusu arrived at the State Department at 2:05 and were received by Hull at 2:20. The attack on Pearl Harbor had begun at 1:20 P.M., Washington time. Nomura stated that he had been instructed to deliver at 1:00 P.M. the document he handed Hull, but that decoding had prevented him from fulfilling his orders.[76] The document which was handed Hull was Japan's reply to the American statement of November 26.

Although the Japanese ambassadors did not know it, the contents of this document were fully known to leaders of the American government and the military and naval services in advance of the inter-view.* The Japanese reply was a long statement which rejected every thesis in the Hull proposals and accused the American government of adopting a course of action which "menaces the empire's existence itself and disparages its honor and prestige."

In the course of this reply, the Japanese government said,

> Whereas the American government . . . objects to Japanese attempts to settle international issues through military pressure, it is exercising in conjunction with Great Britain and other nations pressure by economic power. Recourse to such pressure as a means of dealing with international relations should be condemned, as it is at times more inhumane than military pressure.
>
> It is impossible not to reach the conclusion that the American government desires to maintain and strengthen, in coalition with Great Britain and other powers, its dominant position it has hitherto occupied not only in China but in other areas of East Asia. It is a fact of history that the countries of East Asia for the last hundred years or more have been compelled to observe the status quo under the Anglo-American policy of imperialist exploitation and to sacrifice themselves to the prosperity of the two nations. The Japanese government cannot tolerate the perpetuation of such a situation since it directly runs counter to Japan's fundamental policy to enable all nations to enjoy each its proper place in the world. . . .
>
> Obviously, it is the intention of the American government

*Cf. pp. 194, 196.

to conspire with Great Britain and other countries to obstruct Japan's effort toward the establishment of peace through the creation of a new order in East Asia, and especially to preserve Anglo-American rights and interests by keeping Japan and China at war. This intention has been revealed clearly during the course of present negotiations. Thus, the earnest hope of the Japanese government to adjust Japanese-American relations and to preserve and promote the peace of the Pacific through co-operation with the American government has finally been lost.

The Japanese government regrets to have to notify hereby the American government that in view of the attitude of the American government it cannot but consider that it is impossible to reach an agreement through further negotiations.[77]

Hull, who had word of the actual attack half an hour before he received the Japanese emissaries, expressed great indignation to them over their government's language in rejecting his terms. He told them:

I must say that in all my conversations with you during the last nine months I have never uttered one word of untruth. This is borne out absolutely by the record. In all my fifty years of public service I have never seen a document that was more crowded with infamous distortions and falsehoods; infamous distortions and falsehoods on a scale so huge that I never imagined until today that any government on this planet was capable of uttering them.[78]

The need for politeness was over. It was war.

In a statement to the press later that day, Hull stated,

Japan has made a treacherous and utterly unprovoked attack upon the United States. At the very moment when representatives of the Japanese government were discussing with representatives of this government, at the request of the former, principles and courses of peace, the armed forces of Japan were preparing and assembling at various strategic points to launch new attacks and new aggressions upon nations and peoples with which Japan was professedly at peace, including the United States. . . . It is now apparent to the whole world that Japan in its recent professions of a desire for peace has been infamously false and fraudulent.[79]

In his message to Congress December 8 requesting a declaration of war, Roosevelt used similar language, referring to December 7 as "a date which will live in infamy," stating that the Japanese had attacked "suddenly and deliberately," again describing the attack as "unprovoked and dastardly," and asserting, "Always will we remember the character of the onslaught against us." The pretense of surprise was emphasized in the statement, "While the [Japanese] reply [of December 7] stated that it seemed useless to continue the existing diplomatic negotiations, it contained no threat or hint of war or armed attack."[80]

This high-flown condemnation is customary under the circumstances, but it is hard to see how the attack at Pearl Harbor could have been regarded as a completely unprovoked and unexpected act of treachery, for both governments had resigned themselves to war, and it was just a question of time when one of them should take the step that led to open hostilities. What was not known at the time, and would not be known until almost four years later, was that Hull, Roosevelt, the Secretaries of War and Navy, and the Navy high command and Army general staff had clear and indisputable evidence long before December 7 that Japan was going to fight, and that it would open the war on the date that it did at the place that it did. All of the professions of Roosevelt and Hull, therefore, that the Japanese assault was a totally unforeseen event were, to this degree, counterfeit, while the diplomacy they had pursued had made war inevitable, as both well knew.[81]

On the night of December 7, Prime Minister Churchill later would recall, he was sitting with John G. Winant, the American ambassador, at his country residence, Chequers, listening to a news broadcast. "Quite casually," he said, "came an item that the Japanese had attacked United States shipping in the Pacific. It passed almost without our realizing it, and then suddenly we realized what had happened."

Churchill obtained a connection with the White House on the trans-Atlantic telephone.

"We are all in the same boat now," said the President.[82]

The United States was in the war—not only against Japan but "all the way," as Roosevelt triumphantly announced in his radio address to the nation on the night of December 9.[83]

Chapter Twelve

MAGIC

DIPLOMATIC NEGOTIATIONS, as often as not, serve to mask the real motives and the real intentions of the governments conducting them. On any point of issue, the governments which are parties to a dispute endeavor to conceal their real aims by invoking language which will present them in the most favorable light and emphasize their passionate dedication to justice and international morality. This generality undoubtedly applies to both the United States and Japan in their discussions in Washington between February and December, 1941.

What the Japanese government did not know all the time these conversations were in progress, and what the American people would not know until four years later, was that months before the Pearl Harbor attack the American government, by a stroke of unmatched good fortune, had been placed in possession of a priceless weapon. Our intelligence had cracked the Japanese code relating to ship movements and the Japanese ultra code used in advising its diplomatic corps throughout the world. With this knowledge in their possession, President Roosevelt, the State Department, and the Army and Navy were privy to all of Japan's plans and intentions. They knew what the Japanese were saying among themselves, what they were thinking, and what they were planning to do. Our officials could not have been better informed if they had had seats in the Japanese war council. So like a gift of the gods did our leaders consider the breaking of the Japanese code that they referred to cryptanalysis as "Magic."

The first intimation that the American government had broken the Jap code came on August 29, 1945, when President Truman released the reports of the Army and Navy boards of inquiry which had investigated the Pearl Harbor disaster. The Navy Court had reported its findings to the Secretary of the Navy on October 19, 1944, and the Army Board to the Secretary of War on October 20, 1944. At that time the nation was still at war with Germany and Japan, and, by resorting to the convenient pretext of national security, the secretaries labeled the reports "Top Secret" and suppressed them for ten months. When they were finally released, large sections were still withheld, but there were enough hints in the text made public to suggest that the United States was in possession of the code secret before Pearl Harbor.

The Army Board, for instance, significantly stated,

Information from informers, agents, and other sources as to the activities of our potential enemy and its intentions in the negotiations between the United States and Japan was in possession of the State, War, and Navy departments in November and December of 1941. Such agencies had a reasonably complete knowledge of the Japanese plans and intentions, and were in a position to know their potential moves against the United States. Therefore, Washington was in possession of essential facts as to the enemy's intentions and proposals.

This information showed clearly that war was inevitable, and late in November absolutely imminent. It clearly demonstrated the necessity for resorting to every trading act possible to defer the ultimate day of breach of relations to give the Army and Navy time to prepare for the eventualities of war.

The messages actually sent to Hawaii by the Army and Navy gave only a small fraction of this information. It would have been possible to have sent safely information ample for the purpose of orienting the commanders in Hawaii, or positive directives for an all-out alert.

Under the circumstances, where information has a vital bearing upon actions to be taken by field commanders, and cannot be disclosed to them, it would appear incumbent upon the War Department then to assume the responsibility for specific directives to such commanders.

[Gen.] Short got neither form of assistance after November 28 from the War Department, his immediate supervising agency. It is believed that the disaster of Pearl Harbor would have been lessened to the extent that its defenses were available and used on December 7 if properly alerted in time. The failure to alert these defenses in time by directive from the War Department, based upon all information available to it, is one for which it is responsible. The War Department had an abundance of vital information that indicated an immediate break with Japan. All it had to do was either get it to Short or give him a directive based upon it. Short was not fully sensitive to the real seriousness of the situation, although the War Department thought he was. It is believed that knowledge of the information available in the War Department would have made him so.

General discussion of the information herein referred to follows:

The records show almost daily information on the plans of the Japanese government. In addition to that cited above and in conjunction therewith the War Department was in possession of information late in November and early in December from which it made deduction that Japan would shortly commence an aggressive war in the South Pacific; that every effort would be made to reach an agreement with the United States government which would result in eliminating the American people as a contestant in the war to come; and that failing to reach the agreement the Japanese government would attack both Britain and the United States. This information enabled the War Department to fix the probable time of war with Japan with a degree of certainty.

In the first days of December this information grew more critical and indicative of the approaching war. Officers in relatively minor positions who were charged with the responsibility of receiving and evaluating such information were so deeply impressed with its significance and the growing tenseness of our relations with Japan, which pointed only to war and war almost immediately, that such officers approached the chief of the war plans division [Gen. Gerow] and the secretary of the general staff [Col., now Lieut. Gen., Walter Bedell Smith] for the express purpose of having sent to the department commanders a true picture of the war atmosphere which, at that time, pervaded the War Department and which was uppermost in the thinking of these officers in close contact with it. The efforts of these subordinate officers to have such information sent to the field were unsuccessful. They were told that field commanders had been sufficiently informed. The secretary to the general staff declined to discuss the matter when told of the decisions of the war plans division.

Two officers then on duty in the War Department are mentioned for their interest and aggressiveness in attempting to have something done. They are Col. R. S. Bratton and Col. Otis K. Sadtler.

The following handling of information reaching the War Department in the evening of December 6 and early Sunday morning, December 7, is cited as illustrative of the apparent lack of appreciation by those in high places in the War Department of the seriousness of this information which was so clearly outlining the trends that were hastening us into war with Japan.

At approximately 10:00 P.M. on December 6, 1941, and more than fifteen hours before the attack at Pearl Harbor, G-2 delivered to the office of the war plans division and to the office of the chief of staff of the Army information which indicated very emphatically that war with Japan was a certainty and that the beginning of such war was in the immediate future. The officers to whom this information was delivered were told of its importance and impressed with the necessity of getting it into the hands of those who could act, the chief of staff of the Army and the chief of the war plans division.

On the following morning, December 7, at about 8:30 A.M., other information reached the office of G-2, vital in its nature and indicating an almost immediate break in relations between the United States and Japan. Col. Bratton, chief, Far Eastern section, G-2, attempted to reach the chief of staff of the Army in order that he might be informed of the receipt of this message. He discovered that the general was horseback riding. Finally, and at approximately 11:25 A.M., the chief of staff reached his office and received this information. Gen. Miles, then G-2 of the War Department, appeared at about the same time. A conference was held between these two officers and Gen. Gerow of the war plans division, who himself had come to the office of the chief of staff. Those hours when Bratton was attempting to reach some one who could take action in matters of this importance and the passing of time without effective action having been taken, prevented this critical information from reaching Gen. Short in time to be of value to him.

About noon a message was hastily dispatched to overseas department commanders, including Short in the Hawaiian department. This message . . . came into Short's possession after the attack had been completed.[1]

These were matters which the Roosevelt-Truman administration did not want to have explored, for they would lead into embarrassing avenues. In March, 1945, when it had become apparent that there would be further investigation of the Pearl Harbor catastrophe after the end of the war, Senator Elbert D. Thomas of Utah, chairman of the Committee on Military Affairs, introduced Senate Bill 805 in behalf of the administration. This measure provided that the disclosure of any cryptographic information, either our own or that of any other government, allied or enemy, should be punishable by a sentence of ten years in prison or a fine of $10,000, or both. This measure went to the committee with an indorsement from Secretary of War Stimson and from H. Struve Hensel, acting Secretary of the Navy, who said that enactment of the proposed legislation "is considered essential in the interest of national defense and security." Senator Thomas, elaborating on this theme, said,

> With respect to cryptanalysis, an even greater degree of secrecy is required. Such activities, of vital importance in time of war and also essential in time of peace in order to be ready for war, require even a greater degree of security because the enemy or potential enemy has it within his absolute power to deprive us of any information from this source if he suspects we are getting it.[2]

This excuse of national security was invoked by many of the principal figures who testified before the Congressional Pearl Harbor Investigating Committee in extenuation of their failure to alert the Hawaiian commanders in accordance with the decoded information in their possession.

The Thomas bill was slipped through the Senate April 9, 1945, but, because of the vigilance of Senator Ferguson, it was recalled and modified so that "any regularly constituted committee of the Senate or House" was exempted from its provisions. Ferguson had detected at once that the purpose of the bill was to stifle any prospective investigation of the Pearl Harbor debacle. The following October, when the bill was brought up for consideration in the House, it encountered so much opposition even in its amended form that it was withdrawn.[3]

On November 6, 1945, Representative Gearhart, a member of the four-man Republican minority on the ten-member congressional committee which three weeks before had been appointed to investigate Pearl Harbor, took the floor of the House and for the first time revealed the nature and content of some of the most important Japanese secret code messages intercepted and decoded in 1941.[4] It was apparent immediately why the administration had gone to such lengths to endeavor to suppress these messages for all time.

Gearhart stated that the messages he was reading were outlined in a "Memorandum of the Judge Advocate General of the Army for the Secretary of War." The messages set forth in this document all pointed unmistakably to war—and even to the time and place of the initial attack.

The Japanese code intercepts were finally disclosed in full on November 15, 1945, the opening day of the congressional investigation. More than seven hundred of them were produced, of which more than two hundred, dating back to December 2, 1940, dealt with ship movements. The report of the decoded diplomatic messages began on July 2, 1941.[5]

In response to the American order freezing Japanese assets, Foreign Minister Toyoda radioed Ambassador Nomura in Washington July 31, 1941,

> Commercial and economic relations between Japan and third countries, led by England and the United States, are gradually becoming so horribly strained that we cannot endure it much longer. Consequently, our empire, to save its very life, must take measures to secure the raw materials of the South Seas. Our empire must immediately take steps to break asunder this ever strengthening chain of encirclement which is being woven under the guidance and with the participation of England and the United States, acting like a cunning dragon seemingly asleep. That is why we decided to obtain military bases in French Indo-China and to have our troops occupy that territory.

Toyoda continued,

> I know that the Germans are somewhat dissatisfied over our negotiations with the United States, but we wish at any cost to prevent the United States from getting into war, and we wish to settle the Chinese Incident.[6]

On August 7 Nomura reported to Tokyo,

> There is no doubt whatsoever that the United States is prepared to take drastic action depending on the way Japan moves, and thus closing the door on any possibility of settling the situation. . . . It is reported that the President, accompanied by high Army and Navy officials, is meeting with Churchill. This indicates that careful preparations are being made to counter our every move without falling back a single time.[7]

On August 16, two days after the announcement of the Roosevelt-Churchill meeting at sea, Nomura reported to Tokyo,

> I understand that the British believe that if they could only have a Japanese-American war started at the back door, there would be a good prospect of getting United States to participate in the European war.[8]

On September 27 Toyoda sent Nomura a digest of a conversation which he had had with Grew the same day in which he said that Japan's paramount policy was to keep peace with the United States. He said:

> Should the United States and Japan come to blows, the Pacific, too, would be immediately thrown into the chaos that is war. World-civilization would then come crashing down. No greater misfortune could befall mankind. . . . If, at this time, Japanese–U.S. relations were to be adjusted so as to promote friendship between them, the effects would be felt not only by the United States and Japan, but would indeed contribute greatly to a world-peace. The imperial government desires the adjustment of Japanese–U.S. relations not only for the sake of Japan and the United States, but hopes that at the same time such a step would become the opening wedge to bringing about peace throughout the world.

All through the dispatches of this period Tokyo kept expressing its hopes that the proposed conference between Roosevelt and Prime Minister Konoye would provide a solution to all problems in the Pacific. On August 26 Tokyo informed Nomura, "Now the international situation as well as our internal situation is strained in the extreme and we have reached the point where we will pin our last hopes on an interview between the Premier and the President."[10] As the Konoye government entered upon its final weeks of life, the urgency of a Pacific conference was increasingly stressed. A message to Washington on October 1 stated, "Time is now the most important element. Whether this matter materializes or not has a direct and important bearing on peace in the Pacific and even of the world."[11]

Again, on October 3, a message to Nomura informed him that the British ambassador to Japan, Sir Robert Craigie, was so impressed with the need of jogging Washington into action in order to avoid a Pacific war that he had cabled Foreign Minister Anthony Eden and Lord Halifax as follows:

> Among the difficult points in the materialization of a Japanese–United States conference, is that with Japan speed is required. . . . By pursuing a policy of stalling, the United States is arguing about every word and every phrase on the grounds that it is an essential preliminary to any kind of an agreement. It seems apparent that the United States does not comprehend the fact that by the nature of the Japanese and also on account of the domestic conditions in Japan, no delays can be counte-

nanced. It would be very regrettable indeed if the best opportunity for the settlement of the Far Eastern problems since I assumed my post here were to be lost in such a manner. Prince Konoye is sincerely desirous of avoiding the dangers which Japan may face through her connections in the tripartite pact and in the Axis, for which the prince, himself, feels responsibility. Opposition within the country to the prince's reversal of policy is fairly strong. Therefore, unless the Japanese–U.S. conversations are held in the very near future, the opportunity will probably be lost. Moreover, if by some chance, meetings fail to materialize, or if they are unduly delayed, the Konoye cabinet will be placed in a precarious position.

The British ambassador was further quoted to the effect that both Grew and he felt it would be "a foolish policy if this superb opportunity is permitted to slip by assuming an unduly suspicious attitude."[12]

The American government was thus apprised through the ambassador of a country which it already considered its ally of the critical importance of bringing about the meeting between Konoye and Roosevelt if the moderate element in Japan was to be kept in power and peace preserved. The sentiments of Ambassador Craigie, however, were as unavailing as those of the Japanese statesmen themselves in prevailing upon Roosevelt and Hull to seize this chance of keeping the peace.

On October 8, Toyoda, in a long dispatch to Nomura, reviewed the entire course of Japan's recent relations with other powers, particularly the United States. He said that while the war between Germany and Russia was reaching a deadlock, "all the while England and the United States were strengthening their net about us and we could see no means of concluding the Sino-Japanese affair." As a consequence, he said, the Japanese government decided upon diplomatic negotiations to terminate the struggle with the Chinese, and, he added, "We feel that it is necessary to open the way for a compromise in our relations with the United States."

The Japanese foreign minister further said, "The only placid expanse of water on earth is the Pacific. Under these circumstances, it is felt that it is up to both nations to probe into the causes of the trouble between their respective governments and to assure the harmony of the Pacific."[13] This message sufficiently expressed the Japanese dilemma of having got too many bears by the tail at once, so that Japan's principal interest now was to discover a means of letting go. On October 13 Tokyo advised Nomura that "circumstances do not permit even an instant's delay."[14]

On October 16, in a message to Tokyo, Nomura reported a conversation which Mr. Terasaki, the counselor of the Japanese embassy, had had the preceding evening with Adm. Turner. Terasaki at this meeting stated the Japanese position as follows:

> The United States is exceedingly idealistic concerning the Far East. Aiding China might be called a question of principle, but if I may say so, this talk of principles is a sort of hobby among the rich. If it's not a question of principle, all I can conclude is that you all are determined to make us fight with China until we are exhausted. On the other hand, you have followed a very, very realistic policy in Central America. Forgetting the history of Panama for a moment, we can find plenty of present examples proving what I say. Well, China is not an over-simplified question of principle with us Japanese. It is a question of our life. We have already fought there for four years. You went to Japan on the "Astoria." I am sure you know something of the temperament of the Japanese. Once a Japanese is in a corner, he will forget all interest in life and death and fight back with fury. I know that we are much poorer than you Americans in material things. I don't know what the result of a Japanese-American war might be, but even though we lost, I can tell you we would put up an awful fight. If we do not achieve what we are trying to do, it may come to that. Now if you Americans would only extend your hand in friendship to us a little, you could have our lasting amity; otherwise, we may turn out to be permanent enemies.[15]

From the secret dispatches, which the Japanese did not know were being read, the American government knew that the Konoye cabinet was approaching a crisis, with the probability that any successor government which would come to power in Japan would probably be far more intransigent and offer little likelihood of avoiding war. On October 16, when it was already known that the Konoye cabinet had resigned, Hull spent two hours telling Mr. Wakasugi of the embassy staff, "The United States is certainly not playing along with a policy of procrastination. I earnestly wish to see peaceful and normal political relations re-established between Japan and the United States." He knew, of course, that his best hope of attaining that end had gone with the downfall of the Konoye government, but he and the President had done nothing in months of discussions to enable Konoye to reach the settlement which he sought.

When Hull asked Wakasugi what outlook there was for the new cabinet, the Japanese representative told him,

> No matter what sort of cabinet it is, . . . it is impossible to leave Japanese-American relations in their present state. The world being in its present condition, particularly faced by the China problem, our people cannot continue undecided as they now are in the face of American opposition. They demanded a government that would take a definite stand either to the right or to the left. There is no mistake about that. If no unanimity can be discovered between our two nations, it would be hard to say in which direction the wind will blow.[16]

On the 17th Wakasugi again related Japan's position to Hull as follows:

> Japan occupies only a small corner of what is known as the Far East; moreover, she has been occupied for over four years with the China Incident. She has, therefore, a number of circumstances which are peculiar to herself. So though she may want to comply with all of what the United States suggests, it is impossible for her to immediately do so. . . . Even if we tried to comply with the basic principles advanced by the United States, we could not do so overnight. . . .[17]

In its last message to Washington, announcing its resignation, the Konoye cabinet directed Nomura,

> Regardless of the make-up of the new cabinet, negotiations with the United States shall be continued along the lines already formulated.[18]

Although Tokyo was still leaving the door open in the hope of achieving a settlement, Nomura was discouraged and apparently saw the drift to war as almost inevitable. On October 18 he attempted to resign, reporting to the new government in Tokyo that he "was not able to do anything useful," and suggesting that he be recalled because "it should be fairly clear that I, with my limited ability, shall not be able to accomplish much in the future."[19] On October 21, however, the Tojo government informed the ambassador,

> The new cabinet differs in no way from the former one in its sincere desire to adjust Japanese-United States relations on a fair basis. Our country has said practically all she can say in the way of expressing of opinions in setting forth our stands. We feel we have now reached a point where no further positive action can be taken by us except to urge the United States to

reconsider her views. We urge, therefore, that, choosing an opportune moment, either you or Wakasugi let it be known to the United States by indirection that our country is not in a position to spend much more time discussing this matter.[20]

Here was a clear indication that time was running out, and that, if a settlement could not soon be arranged, matters would pass out of the sphere of diplomacy.

At this juncture, Nomura reported to Tokyo, statements with the effect of inflaming public opinion were made by Senator Pepper and Secretary Knox, who, on October 24, according to the ambassador, said in effect that a "Japanese-American war is inevitable and the clash of the two countries is only days ahead."[21] On October 29 Wakasugi reported to Tokyo that "U.S.–Japanese relations are now fast approaching a critical crossroad," but, he added, "If we choose to good naturedly continue these talks, I am of the opinion that all is not hopeless."[22]

On November 2 the new Japanese foreign minister, Shigenori Togo, advised Nomura that the government expected "to reach a final decision" on policy relative to the United States at a meeting on the 5th. "This will be our government's last effort to improve diplomatic relations," he said. "The situation is very grave. When we resume negotiations, the situation makes it urgent that we reach a decision at once."[23]

On November 4 another message from Tokyo said,

Well, relations between Japan and the United States have reached the edge, and our people are losing confidence in the possibility of ever adjusting them. . . . Conditions both within and without our empire are so tense that no longer is procrastination possible, yet in our sincerity to maintain pacific relationships between the empire of Japan and the United States of America, we have decided . . . to gamble once more on the continuance of the parleys, but this is our last effort. Both in name and spirit this counter-proposal of ours is, indeed, the last. I want you to know that. If through it we do not reach a quick accord, I am sorry to say the talks will certainly be ruptured. Then, indeed, will relations between our two nations be on the brink of chaos. I mean that the success or failure of the pending discussions will have an immense effect on the destiny of the Empire of Japan. In fact, we gambled the fate of our land on the throw of this die.

The message referred despairingly to the long protracted negotiations, during which, it was said,

We have already gone far out of our way and yielded and yielded. . . . Bearing all kinds of humiliating things, our government has repeatedly stated its sincerity and gone far, yes, too far, in giving in to them [the Americans]. There is just one reason why we do this—to maintain peace in the Pacific. There seem to be some Americans who think we would make a one-sided deal, but our temperance, I can tell you, has not come from weakness, and naturally there is an end to our long-suffering. Nay, when it comes to a question of our existence and our honor, when the time comes we will defend them without recking the cost. . . . This time we are showing the limit of our friendship; this time we are making our last possible bargain, and I hope that we can thus settle all our troubles with the United States peaceably.[24]

The meaning of this ominous message was made doubly clear by the statement that "the cabinet has been meeting with the imperial headquarters for some days in succession." In other words, if diplomacy failed, the alternative would be military action then being worked out by the cabinet in conjunction with the Japanese army and navy.

On the same day Tokyo forwarded to Washington the terms which, with some amendment, were submitted to the American government on November 20. So certain was the Japanese government that the settlement would be given American approval that Nomura was instructed to have it drawn up as an executive agreement so that it could take effect immediately and would not require the delay of Senate ratification.[25]

It was emphasized that "it is absolutely necessary that all arrangements for the signing of this agreement be completed by the 25th of this month"[26]—that Japan was working against a deadline, the meaning of which was still obscure.

On November 4 and 6 Nomura was advised that Kurusu had been sent to assist him in the negotiations, but that he brought with him no new instructions.[27] It was emphasized that "now that we are on the last lap of these negotiations, I do hope that he can help you in unravelling this bewildering maze, and through co-operation lead to a solution, and that right soon."[28]

On November 10 Nomura visited Roosevelt and urged upon him the view that although Japan had made many concessions, the United States "has shown no willingness to respond to our compromises." He further stated that the Japanese people regarded the freezing of funds as a kind of economic blockade, adding that "there seem to be some who say that modern warfare is not limited to shooting alone." He told the President that the reports from Japan were serious and threatening and that the only solution was to come to an agreement without further delay. The President, according to Nomura, continued to temporize, but stated the necessity of discovering a *modus vivendi*, by which Nomura inferred that he meant some kind of provisional agreement.[29]

In a meeting with Hull November 12, Nomura again explained the Japanese proposals,[30] but the Secretary, as noted by Tokyo, seemed still to assume that the talks were of a preliminary nature. Nomura was asked to correct Hull's impression, and other messages intercepted by American authorities reinforced the point that the situation could not be more urgent.[31]

A message from Tokyo to Hong Kong on November 14 showed, indeed, that there would be war if the discussions led nowhere. This message stated,

> Though the imperial government hopes for great things from the Japan-American negotiations, they do not permit optimism for the future. Should the negotiations collapse, the international situation in which the empire will find herself will be one of tremendous crisis. Accompanying this, the empire's foreign policy, as it has been decided by the cabinet, is:
>
> *a*) We will completely destroy British and American power in China.
>
> *b*) We will take over all enemy concessions and enemy important rights and interests (customs and minerals, etc). in China.
>
> *c*) We will take over all rights and interests owned by enemy powers, even though they might have connections with the new Chinese government, should it become necessary.
>
> In realizing these steps in China, we will avoid, insofar as possible, exhausting our veteran troops. Thus we will cope with a world-war on a long-time scale. Should our reserves for total war and our future military strength wane, we have decided to reinforce them from the whole Far Eastern area.[32]

No one could possibly misinterpret this message. It meant that war had been decided upon if the negotiations failed, and it referred to Britain and America as "the enemy."

Although under instructions to reach an agreement by November 25, Nomura on November 14 cautioned "patience for one or two months in order to get a clear view of the world-situation." He stated,

As I told you in a number of messages, the policy of the American government in the Pacific is to stop any further moves on our part either southward or northward. With every economic weapon at their command, they have attempted to achieve their objective, and now they are contriving by every possible means to prepare for actual warfare. In short, they are making every military and every other kind of preparation to prevent us from a thrust northward or a thrust southward; they are conspiring most actively with the nations concerned and rather than yield on this fundamental political policy of theirs in which they believe so firmly, they would not hesitate, I am sure, to fight us. It is not their intention, I know, to repeat such a thing as the Munich conference which took place several years ago and which turned out to be such a failure. Already, I think, the apex of German victories has passed. Soviet resistance persists, and the possibility of a separate peace has receded, and hereafter this trend will be more and more in evidence.

Nomura spoke of the suspicion in this country that Japan was ready "to stab the United States right in the back." He said that if Japan carried out

a venture southward for the sake of our existence and our lives, it naturally follows that we will have to fight England and the United States, and chances are also that the Soviet will participate. Furthermore, among the neutral nations, those of Central America are already the puppets of the United States, and as for those of South America, whether they like it or not, they are dependent for their economic existence on the United States and must maintain a neutrality partial thereto.

It is inevitable that this war will be long, and this little victory or that little victory, or this little defeat or that little defeat, do not amount to much, and it is not hard to see that whoever can hold out till the end will be the victor.[33]

Thus, as plainly as he could, Nomura attempted to dissuade the war lords of Tokyo from embarking upon a course which would bring the might of the United States down upon them. He urged that a peaceful solution continue to be sought through the Washington conversations. "I believe that I will win out in the long run in these negotiations," he said.[34]

The following day Nomura reported that Hull was still standing pat on his demand that the tripartite pact "shall become a mere scrap of paper." Although Nomura again endeavored to persuade the Secretary that there need be no clash between a Japanese-American peace and the continued existence of the Axis pact, Hull's unyielding attitude compelled him to look ahead if relations "should unfortunately break down, that, as a consequence, we pursue an unrestricted course." He inquired if Japan had made arrangements for a neutral power to take over its interests in the United States, and whether an exchange of embassy and consular staffs was being planned. In discussing an exchange of nationals, Nomura said, "Dependence on ships of neutral register . . . would be an exceedingly precarious undertaking should war actually be declared."[35]

On November 16 an ominous note was introduced in another Tokyo message to Washington which conveyed detailed instructions for the destruction of code machines "in the event of an emergency."[36] On the same day Tokyo advised Nomura that

> the fate of our empire hangs by the slender thread of a few days, so please fight harder than you ever did before. . . . In your opinion we ought to wait and see what turn the war takes and remain patient. However, I am awfully sorry to say that the situation renders this out of the question. I set the deadline for the solution of these negotiations . . . and there will be no change.[37]

On November 17 Kurusu arrived by plane in Washington and was received by Hull and Roosevelt. When the special envoy had landed at San Francisco, he had optimistically expressed the hope of "making a touchdown" in his talks in Washington. His first statement to Roosevelt, however, emphasized that conditions in the Pacific were strained. He said:

> The situation is so tense that we cannot tell when an explosion would occur and, even if it occurred, of what benefit would such a situation be to the United States and Japan? To be sure, Japan wishes that the Japanese-American negotiations would prove to be a success. However, the time element must be taken into consideration. Delaying the solution avails Japan nothing, since, in the meantime, conditions, both militarily and economically, would become less favorable to her if she is to defend herself.

In his conversation with the President, Kurusu said that Japan's adherence to the tripartite pact, one of the principal stumbling-blocks to a settlement, meant that Japan alone would determine its obligations to go to war. The United States, he continued, "apparently interprets this to mean that Japan will wait until the United States is deeply involved in the battle on the Atlantic and then stab the United States in the back." Kurusu said that the impression was erroneous, that Japan was not Germany's tool, and that a settlement between Japan and the United States "would far outshine the tripartite pact." Hull expressed the hope that Kurusu could attack the general problem from a different angle. He said that he and Nomura "always seem to come back to a certain point and then start going around and around the same circle."[38]

In new instructions November 17, Tokyo twice emphasized to its Washington emissaries that America seemed intent on disregarding Japan's "sacrifices" during the four and one-half years of the China war.[39] The disillusion which had long since overtaken Nomura now began to creep over Kurusu. When Hull, on the 18th, spoke of the necessity of removing "the fundamental trouble," Kurusu remarked, "If something is impossible to do, it simply can't be done, regardless of what fancy words may be used to dress it up."[40] Nevertheless, the next day in a message to Tokyo, he expressed hope of achieving some settlement, and counseled against "forming a hasty conclusion."[41]

On November 19, however, Tokyo stated in terms stronger than ever before that a complete breakdown in relations was impending. In its message to Washington, it stated:

> In case of emergency (danger of cutting off our diplomatic relations), and the cutting off of international communications, the following warning will be added in the middle of the daily Japanese language short wave news broadcast:
> (1) In case of Japan–U.S. relations endangered: Higashi No Kazeame (east wind rain).
> (2) Japan–U.S.S.R. relations: Kitanokaze Kumori (north wind cloudy).
> (3) Japan–British relations: Nishi No Kaze Hare (west wind clear).[42]

In another message the same day, Tokyo advised that if diplomatic relations were becoming dangerous it would add at the beginning and end of Japan's intelligence broadcast the word "Higashi," signifying that relations with America were imperiled; "Kita," applying to a rupture of relations with Russia, and "Nishi," if relations with Britain, including Thailand, Malaya, and the Netherlands East Indies, were affected.[43]

Nomura, also reporting on November 19, said that of the three courses before the empire in relation to America—maintaining the status quo, breaking the deadlock by force of arms, or achieving a mutual nonaggression agreement—he was endeavoring to bring about the third. He said:

> After exhausting our strength by four years of the China Incident, following right upon the Manchuria Incident, the present is hardly an opportune time for venturing upon another long-drawn-out warfare on a large scale. I think it would be better to fix up a temporary "truce" now in the spirit to "give and take" and make this the prelude to greater achievements to come later.[44]

On November 22 Tokyo sent a significant message to Nomura and Kurusu urging them to work hard and try to bring about a solution and again stressing that they were working against a deadline. The dispatch said:

> It is awfully hard for us to consider changing the date we set. . . . You should know this. However, I know you are working hard. Stick to our fixed policy and do your very best. Spare no efforts and try to bring about the solution we desire. There are reasons beyond your ability to guess why we wanted to settle Japanese-American relations by the 25th, but if within the next three or four days you can finish your conversations with the Americans; if the signing can be completed by the 29th (let me write it out for you—twenty-ninth); if the pertinent notes can be exchanged; if we can get an understanding with Great Britain and the Netherlands; and in short if everything can be finished, we have decided to wait until that date. This time we mean it, that the deadline absolutely cannot be changed. *After that things are automatically going to happen.**[45]

All of these communications were known to the leaders of the American government and to the Army and Navy high command almost as soon as or sooner than they were known to the Japanese representatives in Washington. They showed how far Japan was willing to go in reaching an agreement, and the point beyond which it felt that it could not go. From the middle of November on, certain of the messages showed a new and dangerous drift. They indicated that if an agreement were not soon reached, there would be a rupture of diplomatic relations, the usual prelude to an outbreak of hostilities. Finally, they showed that an irrevocable deadline had been fixed, and that after that things were "automatically going to happen."

Responsible American officials might not be expected to guess exactly what would happen, but they had been given adequate warning

*Italics supplied.

of war in the event of a breakdown of negotiations and they knew
that some Japanese plan undoubtedly pointing to a surprise belligerent
stroke had been set in train, and that after the 29th it would be impossible for Japan to turn back. These inferences were to be drawn
from any careful and reasonably intelligent reading of the code intercepts.

The duty therefore devolved upon the men who had taken it upon
themselves to evaluate these intercepts either to reach an agreement
with Japan, or, if for moral or political reasons that were regarded as
impossible, to take all possible defensive precautions against Japanese
belligerent action, and to be on the alert against a surprise blow from
whatever quarter. The agreement could either have been in the nature of the discarded *modus vivendi,* designed to buy time until our
Pacific forces could assume a proper posture of defense, or it could
have been a settlement of the kind envisioned by Ambassador Grew
—just and equitable, entered in a spirit of conciliation, and not par-
taking of "so-called appeasement."[46]

The leaders of the American government followed neither course.
They were then left with the responsibility—even more clearly and
starkly etched by the Tokyo messages intercepted after November 22
—to serve unequivocal notice on the field commanders to stand ready
to repel attack.

Chapter Thirteen

THE WRITING ON THE WALL

ALTHOUGH DIPLOMATIC exchanges continued in Washington up to the very moment of the December 7 attack, and even beyond it, they became hopeless after Secretary Hull's submission of his proposals of November 26, and apparently were so regarded in the State Department even before that. On November 22, for instance, Ballantine asked Nomura and Kurusu the rhetorical question whether it were not the duty of every politician to "strive for peace up to the day before war is found to be unavoidable."[1]

Meanwhile, other messages between Tokyo and its diplomatic outposts throughout the world which Army and Navy intelligence continued to intercept showed that the crisis was fast approaching. The sequence of these messages, with the interpretation which military intelligence might logically have placed upon them, was as follows:

NOVEMBER 24

Tokyo advised its Washington ambassadors that the deadline previously set for reaching an agreement was in Tokyo time, November 29—November 28 in Washington.[2]

Interpretation: After the 28th things were "automatically going to happen."

NOVEMBER 25

Japanese representatives in Hanoi, Indo-China, informed Tokyo:

We are advised by the military that we are to have a reply from the United States on the 25th. If this is true, no doubt the cabinet will make a decision between peace and war within the next day or two. . . . Should . . . the negotiations not end in a success, since practically all preparations for the campaign have been completed, our forces shall be able to move within the day.[3]

186

Interpretation: Hanoi, although not advised of the extension of the deadline to November 29, reported that troops were prepared to begin military action in a matter of hours.

Another message from Bangkok, Siam, discussed the "empire's taking decisive action in a southward advance," indicating that this attack would be directed against Burma and Malaya and would involve the occupation of Thailand.[4]

Interpretation: Objectives of the Japanese attack in that quarter now known to Washington. They violate Roosevelt's warning of August 17 and require the President to give military assistance to Britain under his parallel action obligations.

NOVEMBER 26

This was the day on which Hull submitted the American terms to Japan. The Japanese envoys in Washington were sent a new word code to be used in telephone reports to Tokyo in order to save time. Roosevelt was to be designated as "Miss Kimiko" and Hull as "Miss Fumeko." "The child is born" would be interpreted as the arrival of a crisis or the decision to go to war.[5] Upon receipt of this code, Kurusu telephoned Kumaicho Yamamoto, head of the American section of the Japanese foreign office, and expressed a feeling of hopelessness concerning any successful outcome of the negotiations.[6]

Interpretation: The "child" would soon be born.

Reporting that same evening on Hull's submission of the ten points, Nomura said that he and Kurusu had been "dumbfounded" at the terms and felt they could not even report them to Tokyo. "Why," he asked, "did the United States have to propose such hard terms as these? Well, England, the Netherlands, and China doubtless put her up to it."[7]

Interpretation: Hull's terms were unacceptable. America's ABCD partners were thrusting America forward to force a showdown with Japan.

In a later message Nomura said that the American government was endeavoring to cast "the responsibility for the rupture of negotiations" upon Japan, and implied that while the negotiations were still technically in progress, Japan should not "deliberately enter into our scheduled operations."[8]

Interpretation: Matters had passed out of the realm of diplomacy, and, with military operations in the making, each country was now endeavoring to fasten "war guilt" upon the other.

November 27

Tokyo forwarded Washington a series of hidden word signals to be used if other means of communication failed.[9]

Interpretation: This step was obviously in anticipation of hostilities.

That night Kurusu used the telephone code established the previous day in a call to Yamamoto, who told him that although a crisis seemed imminent, he was not to break off negotiations. The army, Yamamoto said, "is champing at the bit."[10]

Interpretation: The Japanese military had now taken over and were impatient to start operations. Diplomacy henceforward would be useful only to mask military intentions and moves.

In a code message that night, Nomura told of having gone with Kurusu to see Roosevelt. The President told them that at the Atlantic conference he and Prime Minister Churchill had agreed that "our respective basic policies coincided."[11]

Interpretation: Under the parallel action agreement, Japan would be forced to fight both Britain and the United States.

November 28

Tokyo sent a message of the utmost importance to its emissaries in Washington. Nomura and Kurusu were told,

> Well, you two ambassadors have exerted superhuman efforts, but, in spite of this, the United States has gone ahead and presented this humiliating proposal. This was unexpected and extremely regrettable. The imperial government can by no means use it as a basis for negotiations. Therefore, with a report of the views of the imperial government on this American proposal which I will send you in two or three days, the negotiations will be *de facto* ruptured. This is inevitable. However, I do not wish you to give the impression that the negotiations are broken off. Merely to say to them that you are awaiting instructions . . . . From now on do the best you can.[12]

Interpretation: This message, intercepted and decoded ten days before the Japanese handed in their reply to Hull coincident with the Japanese attack on Pearl Harbor, showed that the Japanese government had already rejected Hull's terms. The deadline after which things were "automatically going to happen" had now passed. The ambassadors were instructed to stall from then until the finish, which would occur whenever that which was "automatically going to happen" did happen. The American government thus had a clear warning to direct its forces to go on an all-out alert in preparation for certain war.

Tokyo then began to notify its diplomatic and consular representatives in Hawaii, Indo-China, Argentina, and other countries that Hull's counter-proposal "overlooks all we stand for; therefore, of course, we disregard it," and that relations with the United States and Britain would soon be broken off. The message to Honolulu stated significantly: "Do not destroy the codes without regard to the actual situation in your locality, but retain them as long as the situation there permits and until the final stage is entered into."[13]

Interpretation: Whatever was "automatically going to happen" was approaching a "final stage," in which Hawaii would have such an important role that codes were to be retained for transmission of last-minute information until hostilities should present the danger that the codes would be confiscated.

A message from Hsinking, Manchukuo, to Tokyo discussed in detail the policy to be followed in dealing with British and American nationals in the Japanese puppet state when war came. It was reported that plans had been made to intern 81 American citizens and 339 British subjects until they could be exchanged, and that other "obnoxious characters with pro-British and American leanings are to be suitably taken care of."[14]

Interpretation: War with the United States and Britain.

NOVEMBER 29

A message from Berlin to Tokyo related a conversation between the Japanese ambassador and Von Ribbentrop, the Nazi foreign minister, in which Ribbentrop drew a highly optimistic picture of the course of the Nazi war with Russia and predicted eventual defeat of Britain, whether Germany should be compelled to land its army in England or not. Ribbentrop urged the Japanese to press for the "new order" in the Far East and pledged, "Should Japan become engaged in a war against the United States, Germany, of course, would join the war immediately."[15]

Interpretation: Hitler urges Der Tag with deceptive estimates of Germany's military situation. The three partners of the Axis would all be at war with the United States if Japan took the plunge.

NOVEMBER 30

In response, Tokyo advised its Berlin ambassador that the Washington conversations "now stand ruptured—broken." The ambassador was directed to inform Hitler and Ribbentrop that

lately England and the United States have taken a provocative attitude, both of them. Say that they are planning to move
military forces into various places in East Asia and that we will
inevitably have to counter by also moving troops. Say very secretly to them that there is extreme danger that war may suddenly break out between the Anglo-Saxon nations and Japan
through some clash of arms and add that the time of the breaking out of this war may come quicker than any one dreams.*[16]

Interpretation: Unmistakable. Negotiations were over. Military
movements would begin. War would come soon—"quicker than any
one dreams."

This reading is sustained by further remarks in a later message.
It was said that the Japanese government had decided to discontinue
negotiations with the United States because "a continuation of negotiations would inevitably be detrimental to our case." The American
proposal of November 26 was termed "insulting" in that it attempted
to obtain a disavowal from Japan of its commitment to assist Germany
and Italy if the United States intervened in the European war. American consultation with England, Australia, the Netherlands, and China
during the course of the negotiations was cited as proof of "collusion,"
and it was said that all of these powers regarded Japan, as well as
Germany and Italy, as an enemy.[17]

In a telephone conversation the same day with American Division
Chief Yamamoto, Kurusu noted that until a few days before his government had been insistent that the negotiations be brought to a conclusion, but that "now you want to stretch them out." He said that
Tokyo could help him in this undertaking if Premier Tojo and Foreign Minister Togo could be persuaded to adopt a more temperate
tone in their speeches.[18]

Interpretation: As made unmistakably clear in Tokyo's November
28 message to Nomura and Kurusu, the continuing conversations in
Washington were now play acting, intended to cover some movement
which would not take effect until after a further lapse of time. Hull,
on December 7, would complain of Japanese treachery in attacking
"at the very moment when representatives of the Japanese government
were discussing with representatives of this government . . . principles
and courses of peace." Roosevelt, in his message to Congress December 8, asking a declaration of war, would decry the Japanese attack

---

*"The President regarded this message as of such interest that he retained a copy
of it, contrary to the usual practice in handling the intercepted messages" (Min., pp.
21-22).

as coming "when the United States was at peace with that nation and . . . still in conversation with its government and its emperor looking toward the maintenance of peace in the Pacific." How could either have been sincere in such statements? They knew that after November 28 Japan continued the conversations only in an endeavor to throw dust in the eyes of the American government.

DECEMBER 1

Tokyo again advised its Washington ambassadors of the necessity of stalling. This message said:

> The date set [November 28, Washington time] . . . has come and gone, and the situation continues to be increasingly critical. However, to prevent the United States from becoming unduly suspicious, we have been advising the press and others that though there are some wide differences between Japan and the United States, the negotiations are continuing.[19]

Interpretation: As above. The deadline was past. Japan's plan had been set in motion. The stalling in Washington was to allay suspicion. Told this in so many words, Washington should have ordered American forces everywhere to exercise the utmost vigilance. But Washington manifested no suspicion, so far as its actions and orders show.

Another message to Washington the same day said that when faced with the necessity of destroying codes, the embassy should obtain chemicals for that purpose which were on hand at the office of the Japanese naval attaché.[20] Other messages that day directed London, Hong Kong, Singapore, and Manila to destroy their code machines and burn their codes.[21] Still another message to Hsingking said that "Manchuria will take the same steps toward England and America that this country will take in case war breaks out."[22]

Interpretation: War against Britain and the United States, and quickly. Code and code machine destruction was the penultimate step.

Nomura, reporting a conversation December 1 with Hull, said that the Secretary had expressed objections to new Japanese army and navy movements in Indo-China and said that as long as Japan acted in this fashion "there is absolutely no way of bringing about a settlement."[23]

Interpretation: Hull, who should have known that the game was up, was still talking as if peace could be saved if the Japanese reformed.

In response, Nomura said to Hull,

> Peace between Japan and China could not be attained

through any such terms as were contained in your most recent proposal. We hear your argument to the effect that you cannot stand by and do nothing while China dies. The converse of that argument should be even stronger. That is, that it is of the utmost importance for us to avoid standing by and watching our own respective countries die, just because of the China problem.[24]

Interpretation: Hull was directly informed that his November 26 terms could not be accepted.

DECEMBER 2

The Japanese embassy in Washington was ordered by Togo to destroy one of its two code machines and to burn most of its codes.[25] Similar instructions as to the destruction of codes and secret documents were sent to consular and diplomatic officers in the American republics, Hawaii, and Canada.[26]

Interpretation: War now very close. Washington's retention of its one remaining code machine was to receive the Japanese reply to the American November 26 proposal, which obviously would coincide with the beginning of hostilities.*

A supplementary "hidden word" code was sent to Singapore, Chile, and Brazil the same day, so that information could be communicated to Tokyo concerning the arrival of American military planes, the identity of British and American merchantmen docked in port, and similar data useful only for military purposes.[27]

Interpretation: Hostilities assumed within a short time.

Also on December 2, Canton advised Tokyo that

if hostilities are to begin, we here are all prepared. The army has completed all preparations to move immediately on Thai. Should the British resist to the bitter end, it is understood that the army is prepared to go so far as to militarily occupy the country.[28]

Interpretation: Plain. Jap forces in South China ready. Thailand to be seized in defiance of Roosevelt's warning of August 17 that the United States would be compelled to act in this event.

DECEMBER 3

The Japanese ambassadors in Washington were advised that it was "inappropriate" to renew the suggestion that a meeting take place

*"It is well known in diplomatic and military circles that destruction of codes, code machines, and secret documents is usually the last step before breaking off relations between governments. War does not necessarily have to follow, but it may follow either simultaneously or close on the heels of the destruction of codes" (Min., p. 60).

between the President and the Japanese premier. They were instructed to stand on the Japanese proposals for a settlement tendered November 20.[29]

Interpretation: Tokyo no longer interested in diplomatic solutions.

The ambassadors informed Tokyo in response that "we feel that some joint military action between Great Britain and the United States, with or without a declaration of war, is a definite certainty in the event of an occupation of Thailand."[30] Nomura strengthened this by stating, "There is no saying but what the United States government will take a bold step, depending upon how our reply is made."[31]

Interpretation: Nomura and Kurusu in a last admonition that the steps apparently contemplated by Tokyo would bring American counter-action.

A message from the Japanese ambassador in Rome depicted Mussolini on December 3 as pledging support to Japan under the tripartite pact when war came and saying he was not surprised that the Washington negotiations had failed.[32]

Interpretation: The negotiations having failed, the United States would find itself at war with all three members of the Axis.

Another message to Tokyo from Peking on December 3 referred to the "coming war" on two occasions and, on another, to the "next war," and stressed the necessity of attracting the native peoples of Southeast Asia to the Japanese cause "against the United States and Britain."[33]

Interpretation: A war of races to be proclaimed against the United States and Britain, with Japan offering leadership to all Asiatics.

December 4

The Washington embassy was given additional instructions on burning codes.[34] The same day Tokyo sent a code message to diplomatic posts in China that "when Japan enters a war, . . . Manchukuo shall treat Great Britain, the United States, and Netherlands Indies as enemy countries." It was directed, however, that in view of the existence of a neutrality treaty between Japan and Russia, Russian citizens were to be excepted and that Manchukuo was to "take every precaution so as not to provoke Soviet Russia."[35] Another message the same day to Japanese representatives in China and Manchukuo referred to attitudes to be adopted toward the Dutch government when war should ensue.[36] Still the same day a third message to Hsingking again designated England, the United States, and the Netherlands as enemies in the impending war.[37] Meanwhile, the evacuation of staff members of the Japanese embassies in London and Washington was discussed in other messages.[38]

Interpretation: War against the United States, Britain, and Holland, but peace with Russia.

DECEMBER 5

The Washington embassy reported to Tokyo: "We have completed destruction of codes, but since the U.S.–Japanese negotiations are still continuing, I request your approval of our desire to delay for a while yet the destruction of the one code machine."[39] (This was approved the following day.)[40]

Interpretation: War to be measured in hours from this date.

Peking, in a message to Tokyo, said that "concurrent with opening war with Britain and America, we have considered Holland as a semibelligerent"; and, "In case war breaks out with Holland, we will take the same steps toward that country that we have taken with Britain and America."[41] The same day Peking discussed with Shanghai the question of obtaining a neutral third power as custodian of the interests of Britain, America, and Holland in North China when war broke out.[42] The Navy later contended that it did not translate these messages until four days after the Pearl Harbor attack.

Interpretation: War against the United States, Britain, and Holland a certainty.

DECEMBER 6

Tokyo advised the ambassadors in Washington that it had drafted a very long reply to Secretary Hull's proposal of November 26 which would be transmitted in fourteen parts. The ambassadors were directed to withhold the reply from the American government pending arrival of a separate message setting the time it was to be presented.[43]

Capt. Laurance F. Safford, naval communications intelligence chief, said that Tokyo had advised its Washington emissaries between 11:00 and 12:00 A.M. on December 6 that its final reply was on the way. This "pilot" message, he said, was translated by the Navy Department before 11:50 A.M. The first thirteen parts of the final message started coming in shortly after noon and were translated and ready for delivery by 9:00 P.M. Safford said he regarded the first thirteen parts as "highly important" because of the abusive language that was employed.[44]

Interpretation: Under the Axis pattern, first set by Japan in the Russo-Japanese war, the end of diplomatic relations would coincide with the inauguration of a state of hostilities. Remember Port Arthur!

In another message December 6 Tokyo transmitted word to its Berlin ambassador that Japan did not contemplate hostilities with Russia, that it would not stop shipments of American lend-lease material to Russia if carried in Soviet merchantmen, but that "in case we start our war with the United States we will capture all American ships destined for Soviet Russia."[45] The Army says that this message was not translated until December 8.

Another dispatch directed Japanese authorities in Canton to advise the British and American consuls that the imperial army would assume control of public property of "hostile nations," consulates, and buildings.[46] The Army says that it did not translate this message until December 9.

Another message on the 6th, from Tokyo to Bankok, was of an importance which can scarcely be exaggerated. The Army, however, says that it was not translated until December 8. As submitted to the congressional committee, the message was in the following form:

The (......)[a] day (X Day) decided by the ....[b] liaison conference on the 6th (?)[c] is the 8th and the day on which the notice is to be given is the 7th (?) (Sunday). As soon as you have received this message, please reply to that effect.

The Navy listed "translator's assumptions" as follows:

  a "Proclamation" or "declaration."
  b "Ambassadorial" or "China."
  c This word is garbled and could be either the word "6th" or the word "November."[47]

The tentative translations given tended to obscure the meaning of the message. Here, if it had been admittedly recognized and decoded in time, was the Japanese statement that the opening of hostilities decreed on November 6 by Adm. Yamamoto, commander of the combined imperial fleets, would be December 8, Japan time (December 7, Hawaii time), and the day on which the Japanese reply to Hull's November 26 proposals would be submitted was Sunday, December 7, Washington time, the two dates coinciding.*

Many of the messages of the preceding ten days individually served notice upon the American officials who were reading them that war was distant only a few days at most, and all of them together could be read in no other light. The first thirteen parts of the Japanese final reply to Hull were couched in such language as to demonstrate that the hour when Japan would resort to arms was at hand.

*Cf. pp. 19, 21.

DECEMBER 7

About 5:00 A.M. on December 7 the fourteenth and final part of the Japanese message breaking off relations with the United States and heralding the advent of war was intercepted. It was decoded and available for distribution to all of the leaders of the government and of the Army and Navy top command by 9:00 A.M.[48] The language was clearly menacing:

> Obviously it is the intention of the American government to conspire with Great Britain and other countries to obstruct Japan's efforts toward the establishment of peace through the creation of a new order in East Asia, and especially to preserve Anglo-American rights and interests by keeping Japan and China at war. This intention has been revealed clearly during the course of the present negotiations. Thus, the earnest hope of the Japanese government to adjust Japanese-American relations and to preserve and promote the peace of the Pacific through co-operation with the American government has finally been lost.
>
> The Japanese government regrets to have to notify hereby the American government that in view of the attitude of the American government it cannot but consider that it is impossible to reach an agreement through further negotiations.[49]

Interpretation: The "peace of the Pacific" having "finally been lost," no other alternative except war was possible. It would be war at once.

Of such extreme importance did Tokyo consider its final reply to the American government that just as soon as it had finished sending, the Japanese Foreign Office instructed Nomura not to use a typist or any other person in copying out the note for submission to Hull. "Be most extremely cautious in preserving secrecy," the ambassador was admonished.[50]

Interpretation: This warning was unique and testified to the importance attached to the fourteen-part response by the Japanese government. In no other instance were such cautionary instructions dispatched to Washington.

Then, between 9:00 and 9:30 A.M., the key Tokyo message disclosing Japan's intentions to attack the United States at 1:00 P.M., Washington time, that day, was intercepted and translated.[51] Thus, at least three hours and fifty-five minutes before the attack on Pearl Harbor, the time for the outbreak of the war was in the hands of the American government. It was fixed in a message to Nomura, stating, "Will the ambassador please submit to the United States government (if possible, to the Secretary of State) our reply to the United States at 1:00 P.M. on the 7th, your time."[52]

Interpretation: The Japanese attack would come at that hour—dark night over East Asia, 2:00 A.M. at Manila, but 7:30 A.M., one hour and four minutes after sunrise, at Hawaii. It is a military axiom that sunrise is the most favorable hour for surprise air attack. Therefore, the attack would be on Hawaii, and no place else.

Two subsequent messages expressed thanks to Nomura and Kurusu and the members of the embassy staff for the efforts they had made during the negotiations, and regret that "matters have come to what they are now"—the situation being referred to as an "unprecedented crisis."[53] The embassy was then instructed to destroy its remaining cipher machine, all machine codes, and all secret documents.[54]

Interpretation: Everything was now over and done with. All that remained was the Jap attack that would open the war.

Subsequent messages to representatives in Japanese and Japanese occupied territory directed how "enemy subjects" and "enemy property" were to be handled.[55]

Interpretation: U.S., British, and Dutch nationals now enemy aliens.

Washington shortly reported back to Tokyo that it had embarked on the destruction of its codes and, upon the dispatch of this final message, would begin the demolition and destruction by fire of its last code machine and remaining ciphers.[56]

Interpretation: No further diplomatic business to transact. H-hour, D-day, now at hand.

This completes the record of significant intercepts. The process and products of decoding were known as "Magic." Certainly, no magic use was made of them. With a full insight into Japanese intentions—fuller, as will be seen, than the evidence already spread upon the record would indicate—the men in Washington permitted the blow to fall at Oahu.

Chapter Fourteen

EAST WIND RAIN

THE JAPANESE government had arranged on November 19 that if a secret decision should be made to go to war with the United States, its diplomatic corps throughout the world would be notified by insertion of the false weather report, "east wind rain," in the middle of the daily Japanese language short-wave news broadcast. If Japan was to make war on Britain, including Thailand, Malaya, and the Netherlands East Indies, the signal "west wind clear" would be broadcast; while if Russia were to be subjected to attack the signal would be "north wind cloudy."[1]

For four years the Roosevelt administration suppressed public knowledge that any Japanese secret messages had been intercepted and decoded. When that news finally leaked out, after the death of Roosevelt, the administration exerted every effort to prove that, no matter what other enemy messages had been intercepted, the "winds" message had no existence.

When fifty-two suppressed pages of the Army Pearl Harbor Board report were finally made public December 11, 1945, after the congressional investigation had been in progress twenty-one days, it was found that the board had stated,

> The "winds" message was one that was to be inserted in the Japanese news and weather broadcasts and repeated with a definite pattern of words, so as to indicate that war would take place either with Great Britain, Russia, or the United States, or all three.
>
> Such information was picked up by a monitoring station. This information was received and translated on December 3, 1941, and the contents distributed to the same high authority (White House, Army and Navy high commands).

The Navy received during the evening of December 3, 1941, this message, which when translated said, "War with the United States, war with Britain, including N.E.I., except peace with Russia."

This "winds execute" has now disappeared from the Navy files and cannot be found despite extensive search for it. It was last seen by Comdr. [Laurance F.] Safford when he collected the papers together with Comdr. [Alwin D.] Kramer and turned them over to the director of naval communications for use as evidence before the Roberts Commission.

There, therefore, can be no question that between the dates of December 4 and 6, the imminence of war on the following Saturday and Sunday, December 6 and 7, was clear-cut and definite.

Again referring to the disappearance of the "winds" message, the Army Board said,

This original message has now disappeared from the Navy files and cannot be found. It was in existence just after Pearl Harbor and was collected with other messages for submission to the Roberts Commission. Copies were in existence in various places but they have all disappeared.

The board further stated,

The radio station logs, showing the reception of the message, have been destroyed within the last year. Capt. Safford testified that this message, and everything else they got from November 12 on, was sent to the White House by the Navy. It was a circulated copy that circulated to the White House and to the admirals of the Navy.

It was this message which the Army witnesses testified was never received by the Army. It was a clear indication to the United States as early as December 4. The vital nature of this message can be realized.[2]

President Truman, Secretary of War Stimson, and Secretary of the Navy Forrestal, before releasing the suppressed comments on the "winds" signal, busied themselves trying to discredit the existence of this message and endeavoring to prevail upon witnesses who had previously testified to having seen it or handled it to change their stories. Stimson, after receiving the Army Board report and suppressing it in October, 1944, undertook three personal investigations to achieve this purpose.

He first commissioned Maj. Gen. Myron C. Cramer to prepare a précis of the most damaging evidence against himself and the Roose-

velt administration. He then directed Maj. Henry C. Clausen, a
lawyer in civil life, to make a trip around the world, seeking out
witnesses, even if he had to approach them in the middle of battle.
Guided by Cramer's outline, Clausen would then "refresh" their
memory and submit affidavits for them to sign, altering their previous testimony on relevant points. No small part of the beclouding of
the Pearl Harbor record is to be attributed to this mission.[3]

Clausen, later promoted to lieutenant colonel, said he was directed
by Stimson to make his inquiry because of discrepancies in evidence
before the Army Board and because the board had not taken testimony from most witnesses on code intercepts.[4] Chief of Staff Marshall, commenting on the irregularity of Clausen's activities, said he
had never known any other instance of a junior officer investigating
actions or statements of superior officers.

Senator Ferguson asked Marshall, "Do you know of any other case
where an investigation was taken away from a board of general officers and given to a major?"

"I don't recall a similar situation," Marshall said.

"Is it a custom in the War Department to have officers of equal
rank investigate other officers?"

"In the case of general officers, yes."[5]

The Clausen investigation, Marshall said, was controlled by the
"civilian side" of the War Department[6]—that is, by Stimson. Senator
Ferguson charged that Clausen drafted affidavits which set forth what
he and Stimson wanted witnesses to say, and then submitted them
for signature. One statement obtained from Gen. MacArthur while
he was preparing for the Leyte campaign misspelled the general's
name, an error which MacArthur himself could not have committed
if he had written the affidavit or even read it over carefully.[7]

Clausen's principal achievements were to change previous testimony before the Army Board concerning delivery of the first thirteen
parts of the final Jap reply to high officers of the Army on the night
of December 6, and to obscure the previously established fact that a
"winds" message had been intercepted several days before the attack.

On the strength of Clausen's report, Stimson, in a statement appended to the Army Board report when he finally released it, was
able to state that a witness, Col. R. S. Bratton, "corrected his testimony" of having delivered the Japanese thirteen-part message to
three of Marshall's principal aides on the night of December 6.[8]

Clausen also induced Col. Otis E. Sadtler, who had previously
testified that a "winds" message had been received, to recant this

statement. Two other officers who were persuaded by Clausen to deny
the existence of the "winds" message were Col. Harold Doud, in
charge of the code and cipher section of the Army Signal Corps intelligence service, and Col. Rex W. Minckler, who was in charge of the
signal intelligence service.[9] Neither of these officers was called as a
witness before the Congressional Investigating Committee. The Clausen report disputed the findings of the Army Board on other cardinal
points in addition to the "winds" message.

Gen. Cramer, in addition to briefing Clausen, made two other
reports to Stimson on Pearl Harbor.[10] His principal authority in
disputing the existence of the "winds" signal was Clausen—the tool
of Stimson and himself. On the basis of the affidavits gathered by
Clausen, Cramer came to the conclusion that the evidence failed to
show that this message was "ever received by the War Department."[11]
This finding dodged the issue, because all witnesses who had testified
to the existence of the "winds" message were in agreement that it had
been intercepted by a Navy monitoring station, translated by Navy
communications intelligence, and distributed by the same naval
agency. So, to deny that it was "ever received by the War Department" merely established a point which was disputed by no one.

A third independent Army investigation was undertaken in behalf of Gen. Marshall by Col. Carter W. Clarke, subsequently promoted to brigadier general. Not until November, 1945, when Maj.
Gen. Sherman Miles informed the Congressional Investigating Committee of Clarke's activities, was it known that there ever had been
such an inquiry.[12] Gerhard Gesell, associate counsel for the committee, then said that the Clarke report was in his hands, but that it
contained "Top Secret" information which the Army did not want
to get out.[13]

It was disclosed that during the 1944 Presidential campaign Clarke
had carried two secret letters from Gen. Marshall to Gov. Thomas E.
Dewey. Marshall had got wind of the fact that the Republican candi-
date knew that American intelligence had cracked the Japanese code
before the Pearl Harbor attack, and the general's letters appealed to
Dewey to make no use of this information during the campaign, on
the ground that the Japs would then be given knowledge that we
were in possession of their code secrets. Dewey refused to receive the
first letter, but did read the second. Throughout the campaign he
made no mention that the enemy code had been cracked and never
referred to the Pearl Harbor scandal.[14]

Although Marshall twice stated in the letter which Dewey did read that he was making his appeal without the knowledge of the President or Secretary of War Stimson, he could not have been unmindful that Pearl Harbor would have been a damaging issue against the Roosevelt administration, especially if Dewey had disclosed that no adequate warning had been sent the Hawaiian commanders despite the wealth of cryptographic information pointing to war which the Roosevelt circle possessed during the weeks before the attack.

Marshall's case for keeping secret the fact that the United States had cracked the enemy code was seriously weakened when Adm. Wilkinson asserted that the Germans knew as early as May, 1941, that the United States was breaking Japan's code and had so warned the Japanese.[15] William D. Mitchell, committee counsel, then produced eight Jap code messages of April and May, 1941, in which the Japanese discussed their suspicions that their secret material was being intercepted.[16] If the enemy had this information three years before the 1944 campaign, it is difficult to see what purpose except a political one could have been served by persuading Dewey not to raise the Pearl Harbor issue.

Upon receipt of the report of the Navy Court of Inquiry into the Pearl Harbor disaster, Secretary Forrestal initiated a private investigation. This inquiry was intrusted to Adm. H. K. Hewitt,[17] but again a junior officer, Lieut. Comdr. John Sonnett, actually ran the investigation.[18] Sonnett for years after his graduation from law school had held New Deal jobs. He was first appointed executive assistant to the United States attorney for the southern district of New York, but in the fall of 1943, apparently for special service in connection with the Pearl Harbor investigation, he went to the Navy Department on loan from Attorney General Francis Biddle to serve as special counsel to Secretary Forrestal. On January 15, 1944, when it appeared that Congress would demand a further Pearl Harbor investigation, he resigned from the Department of Justice and, at the age of 32, was commissioned a lieutenant commander. He held his commission for only about a year, during which he performed the same duties for Forrestal that Clausen performed for Stimson. His job completed, he was released to inactive duty early in 1945. He continued to serve in the Navy Department as a civilian until September of that year, and the following month was rewarded with appointment as an assistant attorney general.[19]

The key witness on the "winds" message, Capt. Safford, received special attention from Sonnett and Hewitt, but steadfastly stuck to his story that the "winds" signal had been intercepted, that he had handled it, and that he had seen that it reached his superiors. Safford charged before the congressional committee that Sonnett had acted as "counsel for the defense" for the late Secretary Knox and Adm. Stark, rather than as a legal assistant to Adm. Hewitt, the investigating officer.[20] Safford said,

> His purpose seemed to be to refute testimony before earlier investigations that was unfavorable to anyone in Washington, to beguile "hostile" witnesses into changing their stories, and to introduce an element of doubt where he could not effect a reversal of testimony. Above all, he attempted to make me reverse my testimony regarding the "winds" message and to make me believe I was suffering from hallucinations.[21]

Safford said the first attempt by Sonnett to make him change his story occurred on May 11, 1945, ten days before he was to testify at a special investigation conducted by Adm. Hewitt. Sonnett, failing on this occasion, tried again on May 18, and a third time a day or two later. Safford said that Sonnett tried hard to persuade him there was no "winds" message and that the captain's mind had been "playing him tricks." Sonnett suggested, Safford said, that he change his testimony to reconcile discrepancies.

"I distinctly recall," Safford stated, "Sonnett making the following statement to me: 'You are the only one who seems to have even seen the "winds execute" message. How could the "winds execute" message be heard on the East Coast of the United States and not at any other places nearer Japan? It is very doubtful that there ever was a "winds" message.'"

Sonnett, according to Safford, then said, "It is no reflection on your veracity to change your testimony. It is no reflection on your mentality to have your memory play you tricks after such a long period. Numerous witnesses that you have named have denied all knowledge of a 'winds execute' message. You do not have to carry a torch for Adm. Kimmel."

Adm. Hewitt sat by while his junior assistant was delivering this harangue. Later, after completing his testimony before Hewitt, Safford said he asked Hewitt off the record if there was still any doubt in the admiral's mind that the "winds" message had been sent by Japan and disseminated in the War and Navy departments.

"The admiral looked startled," Safford said. "Before he could reply, Sonnett broke in, saying: 'Of course, I am not conducting the case, and I do not know what Adm. Hewitt has decided, but to me it is very doubtful that the so-called "winds execute" message was ever sent.' "

Safford then quoted Hewitt as saying to him, "You are not entitled to my opinion, but I will answer your question. There is no evidence of a 'winds execute' message beyond your unsupported testimony. I do not doubt your sincerity, but I believe you have confused one of the other messages containing the name of a wind with the message you were expecting to receive."

"For my part," said Safford, "I do not doubt Adm. Hewitt's integrity, but I do believe that Sonnett has succeeded in pulling the wool over his eyes. I also believe that Sonnett employed similar tactics on other witnesses whose testimony had favored Adm. Kimmel."[22]

Despite all this pressure upon him, Safford, when he was called as a witness before the congressional committee on February 1, 1946, opened his statement with the flat assertion: "There was a 'winds' message. It meant war—and we knew it meant war."[23]

Safford said that the "winds" message was part of a Japanese overseas news broadcast from station J-A-P in Tokyo on Thursday, December 4, 1941, at 8:30 A.M., Washington time. It was intercepted, he said, by the big Navy radio receiving station at Cheltenham, Maryland. It was recorded on the special typewriter developed by the Navy which types Roman letters equivalent to Japanese characters. The "winds" message was forwarded to the Navy Department by teletype transmitter from the intercept receiving-room at Cheltenham to the page printer in the Navy Department communication intelligence unit under Safford's command.

"I saw the 'winds' message typed in page form on yellow teletype paper," Safford said, "with the translation written below it. I immediately forwarded this message to my commanding officer, Rear Adm. Leigh Noyes [chief of naval communications], thus fully discharging my responsibility in the matter."

Safford said that when Tokyo first informed its representatives overseas of the "winds" code, Adm. Wilkinson immediately sent word to him that the communication intelligence organization should make every effort to intercept any message sent in accordance with the "winds" code. Safford said that the November 29 deadline fixed by Tokyo indicated that the "winds" code might be used to notify overseas officials concerning "things which would automatically begin to happen," and that the previous messages setting up the code to give notification of war with the United States, Britain, or Russia indicated to him what would happen.

He then gave a technical description of the means used to prepare for interception, and his reasons for believing that the best chance of picking up the message was presented by the stations at Cheltenham and Bainbridge, Maryland.

On December 1 Safford was shown a Tokyo circular advising that London, Hong Kong, Singapore, and Manila had been ordered to destroy their code machines, but instructing Washington to retain its machine regardless of other instructions.

"The significance of the 'winds' message now became very clear to me," Safford said, "and I began to take the matter most seriously. So did Col. Sadtler, over in the War Department. The only means by which Tokyo could announce its decisions of peace or war to its overseas diplomatic representatives who had destroyed their regular codes was by means of the emergency 'winds' code. This applied to London and the Far East, but not to Washington."

Safford said that although the original Japanese notification establishing the "winds" code had indicated that this signal would be given on a voice broadcast, "there is no basis for assuming that the 'winds' message had to be sent" in that form. The Japanese government, he said, was sending out general information broadcasts as well as Domei news reports to its diplomatic and consular officials in foreign lands. This was done partly to give speedier service, partly to permit Japanese use of the Morse code and the Kata-Kana form of written Japanese, and partly to be independent of foreign communication systems in emergency. Each office had its own Japanese radio operator and its own short-wave receiving set. This was common practice, for the American government was doing the same thing itself, with a Navy radio operator serving at each post, and the Germans were following a similar method, except that they were using machine reception.

"We expected that the 'winds' message would be sent in Morse code—and it was," Safford said. "If the 'winds' message had been sent on a voice broadcast, the U. S. Navy would have missed it, unless it came on a schedule receivable at Pearl Harbor or Corregidor." This, he explained, was because of conditions of reception.

Safford said that the "winds" message as finally broadcast on the so-called European schedule of Tokyo's big broadcasting station J-A-P was intended for London. "We know," Safford explained, "that the Japanese ambassador in London had destroyed his secret codes three days previously: this was the only way that Tokyo could get news to him secretly. Reception or nonreception at other points was irrelevant. Tokyo knew full well, before the 'winds' message was sent, that it probably would not be received in Washington or in Rio. That was immaterial—the 'winds' message was intended for London."

Safford said that he saw the "winds" message a little after 8:00 A.M. on December 4. It was about two hundred words long, with the code words previously prescribed by Tokyo appearing in the middle of the message, as Tokyo in its instructions of November 19 had said would be the position of the signal. All three code phrases were used, but the expression "north wind cloudy," which would have been the signal for war with Russia, was in the negative form. Safford reported:

When I first saw the "winds" message it had already been translated by Lieut. Comdr. Kramer, in charge of the translation section of the Navy Department communication intelligence unit. Kramer had underscored all three code phrases on the original incoming teletype sheet. Below the printed message was written in pencil or colored crayon in Kramer's handwriting, the following free translations:
"War with England (including N.E.I., etc.).
"War with the U. S.
"Peace with Russia."
I am not sure of the order; but it was the same as in the broadcast and I think England appeared first. I think Kramer used "U. S." rather than "United States." It is possible that the words "No war," instead of "Peace," were used to describe Japan's intentions with regard to Russia.
"This is it!" said Kramer, as he handed me the "winds" message. This was the broadcast we had strained every nerve to intercept. This was the feather in our cap. This was the tip-off which would prevent the U.S. Pacific fleet being surprised at Pearl Harbor the way the Russians had been surprised at Port Arthur. This was what the Navy communication intelligence had been preparing for since its establishment in 1924—war with Japan!
I immediately sent the original of the "winds" message up to the director of naval communications (Rear Adm. Noyes) by one of the officers serving under me and told him to deliver this paper to Adm. Noyes in person, to track him down and not take "no" for an answer, and if he could not find him in a reasonable time to let me know. I did not explain the nature or significance of the "winds" message to this officer. In a few minutes I received a report to the effect that the message had been delivered.
It is my recollection that Kramer and I knew at the time that

Adm. Noyes had telephoned the substance of the "winds" message to the War Department, to the "Magic" distribution list in the Navy Department, and to the naval aide to the President. For that reason, no immediate distribution of the smooth translation of the "winds" message was made in the Navy Department. The six or seven copies for the Army were rushed over to the War Department as rapidly as possible: here the Navy's responsibility ended. The individual smooth translations for authorized Navy Department officials and the White House were distributed at noon on December 4, 1941, in accordance with standard operating procedure. I have no reason for believing that the Army failed to make a prompt distribution of its translations of the "winds" message.

I am thoroughly satisfied in my own mind that Adm. Noyes telephoned to everyone on his list without delay: I cannot bring myself to imagine otherwise. There is some question as to whether the admiral was understood, but this only shows the unreliability of telephone messages. Any misunderstanding of what Adm. Noyes said was of negligible effect, because written translations of the "winds'" message were distributed within two or three hours of his telephone calls. In fact, it was not until 1944 that any suggestion or criticism was offered that any official on the "Magic" distribution list—Navy, Army, State Department, or White House—had not been notified that the "winds" message had been received or that the "winds" message had been translated in any terms other than war and peace.

My final verification of the fact that the "winds" message translation was typed and distributed lies in the fact that about December 15, 1941, I saw a copy of it in the special folder of messages which were being assembled for Adm. Noyes to present to the Roberts Commission. I checked these over with Kramer for completeness as well as for the elimination of irrelevant material. Kramer told me in 1944 that he had shown Assistant Secretary Forrestal a special set of pre-Pearl Harbor messages about December 10, 1941, when Secretary Knox was making his personal investigation at Pearl Harbor, and that he discussed those messages with Mr. Forrestal for about two hours. This set of messages was apparently the basis and possibly the identical file that was given Adm. Noyes and shown to the Roberts Commission via Adm. Wilkinson. This was the last time I saw the "winds" message. I believe that the translation of the "winds" message was given the JD-1 serial number of 7001, because this number is missing and unaccounted for, and comes within the range of messages translated on December 3 and 4, 1941.

The distribution of the "winds" message was the responsibility of naval intelligence and not naval communications. I had no responsibility in the matter after forwarding the original message to Adm. Noyes and after checking Kramer's folder to see that the messages were presented in a logical and understandable order.

The action taken immediately by Adm. Noyes after the "winds" message was sent to him by Safford indicated that he had received the message and understood its import. His first response was to call Safford and say that directions ought to be sent to Guam to burn excess codes and ciphers. As a result of the "winds" message and this conversation, Safford prepared five dispatches to be sent to naval stations and bases in the Pacific, clearing four of them with Capt. Joseph R. Redman, Noyes's assistant. One of these instructed Guam and Samoa to destroy at once their existing ciphers and made a new cipher effective. This message was released by Adm. Noyes himself.

Noyes toned down another of the dispatches which Safford had prepared, instructing Guam to destroy excess cryptographic aids and other secret matter. Safford said his intention was to insure that Guam "stripped ship" before a Japanese commando raid from Saipan, 100 miles away, would result in the capture of a complete set of codes and ciphers.

These two messages, Safford said, helped establish the date the "winds" message was intercepted, as well as the time and date that a warning message was prepared by Capt. A. H. McCollum. McCollum's message, submitted for dispatch to Adm. Kimmel and other commanders in the Pacific, cited the "winds" message as proof that war was imminent, Safford said. Before the congressional committee four years later, McCollum admitted drafting a warning December 4, but said that he made no reference to the "winds" signal because he had not seen it. The warning which he prepared was killed by Adm. Wilkinson and Adm. Turner—according to McCollum, on the supposition that Kimmel already had been sufficiently warned.[24]

The Navy translations given the congressional committee of the two Japanese messages notifying diplomatic agents on November 19 of the establishment of the "winds" code translated the code signals as meaning "danger of cutting off our diplomatic relations" with the United States, Britain, or Russia, with the alternative rendering, "Our diplomatic relations are becoming dangerous" with these countries. Safford said that a dispatch from Adm. Hart dispelled any doubt as to whether a stronger translation, meaning war, was not warranted.

Hart's message contained the official British translation, furnished by Singapore, reading, "NISHI NISHI ENGLAND INCLUDING OCCUPATION OF THAI OR INVASION OF MALAY AND N.E.I."

"That means war, no matter how worded," Safford said. "No one disputed this British translation in November-December, 1941; in fact, our own translation was considered consistent with it."

Two confirmations of the British rendering came from the Netherlands East Indies government translations of the Jap messages of November 19 establishing the "winds" code for use in future to give notification of war. Col. Thorpe, senior Army intelligence officer in Java, sent a dispatch on December 3 to Gen. Miles, chief of G-2. The dispatch advised:

> Japan will notify her consuls of war decision in her foreign broadcasts as weather report at end.
> East wind rain, United States.
> North wind cloudy, Russia.
> West wind clear, England, with attack on Thailand, Malay, and Dutch East Indies.

The second confirmatory dispatch that the "winds" message was to be read as meaning war was sent on December 4, Java time (December 3, Washington time), by Consul General Foote, senior American diplomatic representative in the Netherlands East Indies. This dispatch read:

> When crisis leading to worst arises, following will be broadcast at end weather reports:
> 1. East wind rain, war with United States.
> 2. North wind cloudy, war with Russia.
> 3. West wind clear, war with Britain, including attack on Thailand or Malaya and Dutch East Indies.

Referring to the alternative Jap "winds" signal, Foote reported:

> When threat of crisis exists, following will be used five times in texts of general reports and radio broadcasts:
> 1. Higashi east, America.
> 2. Kita north, Russia.
> 3. Nishi west, Britain, with advance into Thailand and attack on Malaya and Dutch Indies.

Safford said:

> My own evaluation of the foregoing, on December 4, 1941, was about as follows:
> (A) The basic Japanese war plan was divided into three

categories or provided for three contingencies, any or all of which might be followed, namely:

(1) War with the United States.

(2) War with Russia.

(3) War with England, including the invasion of Thailand and the capture of Malaya and the Dutch East Indies.

(B) The "winds" message gave us the answer in all three cases: Affirmative for the first and third categories, and negative for the second.

(C) The "winds" message was probably a "signal of execute" of some sort.

The "signal of·execute" theory received strong confirmation from a secret message received from the Philippines in the early afternoon of December 4, 1941. This message informed us that the Japanese navy had introduced a new cipher system for its so-called "Operations Code" at 0600 GCT that date. This time was seven and a half hours before the "winds" message was broadcast. I might add that there was only one J-A-P European broadcast per day, so the times coincided as closely as possible. I would like to add also that my subordinates on Corregidor spotted and reported this change only nine hours after it was made. . . . The unusual hour and unusual date at which the Japanese navy changed its "Operations Code," combined with the "winds" message and other collateral information available in the Navy Department, made this message highly significant as the probable "signal of execute" to the Japanese navy.

The analysis leaves those who denied that the "winds" signal was ever broadcast with these facts to explain away: First, if that signal, meaning war, was not transmitted on December 4, why should both the Japanese navy and the American Navy have changed their codes on that day? Second, why should the American Navy Department have radioed instructions to isolated Pacific posts and garrisons to destroy excess codes and ciphers for fear that they might be captured directly by Japan? Third, why should the Navy's expert on Far Eastern intelligence have been so gravely disturbed on December 4 that he immediately prepared an outright war warning for transmission to the Pacific fleet commanders? It is impossible to believe that critical action in so many different directions would have been taken without motivation. The "winds" signal provides the motivation.

After receipt of the "winds" message, Capt. Safford stated, only one unknown factor remained. That was the day on which the Japanese would attack. Safford said that the Army and Navy had estimated as far back as April, 1941, that any attack would come on a week-end or national holiday.[25] The War Department, he said, over-emphasized the imminence of war as forecast by Japan's message fixing a deadline of November 29, after which things were "automatically going to happen," and predicted that the Japanese would strike during the week-end of November 29-30. The Navy Department, he said, estimated the situation more accurately. The Japanese armada which had been concentrating for an invasion of Thailand and Malaya was too far from any conceivable objective to reach it by the week-end of the 29th-30th, while Japanese covering naval forces were not yet deployed. Safford said:

> The next week-end, December 6-7, 1941, was just the reverse. The "winds" message and the change of the [Japanese] naval operations code came in the middle of the week: two days to Saturday and three days to Sunday. It was unthinkable that the Japanese would surrender their hopes of surprise by delaying until the week-end of December 13-14. This was not crystal gazing or "intuition"—it was just the plain, common sense acceptance of a self-evident proposition. Col. Sadtler saw it, and so did Capt. Joseph R. Redman, USN, according to Col. Sadtler's testimony in 1944 before the Army Board of Investigation. The Japanese were going to start the war on Saturday, December 6, 1941, or Sunday, December 7, 1941. The War and Navy departments had been given 72 hours' advance notification of the attack on Pearl Harbor by the Japanese themselves.[26]

Chapter Fifteen

"IMPRISON'D IN THE VIEWLESS WINDS"

THE CHIEF corroborating witness as to the existence of the "winds" message was, until the congressional investigation, Lieut. Comdr. (later Capt.) Alwin D. Kramer, senior language officer for Navy communication intelligence. Excerpts from Kramer's testimony before the Navy Pearl Harbor Board, which were not made public until February 5, 1946, showed that he had testified before the board in 1944 that he saw a plain language Japanese message in Capt. Safford's office December 3 or 4, 1941, containing the Japanese for "east wind rain." He told the Naval Court he recognized the phrase as the code signal the Navy had been looking for, but that Safford "carried the ball" from there.[1]

On the same day that Kramer's previous testimony was released, the congressional committee received evidence that Adm. Ingersoll had told Adm. Thomas C. Hart, who conducted a Pearl Harbor inquiry for the Navy in 1944, that he recalled seeing, on or about December 4, 1941, a copy of a "winds execute" broadcast indicating that Japan was about to attack the United States and Britain.[2]

That day the congressional committee also was given other suppressed testimony before the Naval Court of Inquiry that Adm. Turner remembered getting a telephone call "about December 6, 1941," from Adm. Noyes about the "winds" signal. Turner said Noyes told him that "the 'winds' message came in or something like that." Asked what he thought at the time that this meant, Turner told the court he interpreted it as meaning a break in relations with Japan and "probably war."[3]

The committee further learned of an affidavit that Col. Moses Pettigrew, of Army intelligence, had given on February 13, 1945, to Maj. Clausen. Pettigrew stated that about December 5, 1941, he was shown a file of records containing an intercepted message which showed that "United States-Japanese relations were in danger." He said he thought that this was an implementation of Japan's prearranged "winds" code.[4]

By the time these four officers testified before the congressional committee, they were by no means as certain as they had once been that there was a "winds" message, or that, if it existed, it had the meaning they had previously assigned to it.

Kramer's story to the congressional committee was that he saw a "winds" message on December 5 when a naval communications officer had asked him to verify the interpretation of the coded words. He said that he verified that the words coincided with the previously arranged signal of "east wind rain," but he said that he would not have translated the message to mean "war," but "strained relations."

"However," Kramer said, "the fact that the code was to be used only in the event of failure in regular communications might have resulted in a deduction that war was indicated."

Kramer then said he was "not positive" that he had written anything on the message, but that he had certainly translated it in his own mind, and to the best of his recollection only one country was involved.

"What country?" he was asked by committee counsel.

"To the best of my belief," Kramer replied, "the country was England."[5]

In his testimony the following day Kramer denied that he was badgered or otherwise subjected to pressure to change his original story given the Naval Court, which agreed in all principal points with that of Capt. Safford. He said that he was not positive whether the message he saw referred to the United States. Asked by a committee member, Representative Clark, whether the message was not of such importance as to have made an indelible impression upon his mind, he replied, "I can't make a positive statement on reconstruction." He said that, although he had told the Naval Court in 1944 that the United States was named, he now believed the message referred to Great Britain.[6]

On the third day of his testimony, Kramer indicated that his change of mind as to what country Japan had designated as its enemy in the coming war dated from 1945, when he was interviewed concerning his previous testimony to the naval board by Lieut. Comdr. Sonnett. He told also of being summoned in September, 1945, to a luncheon conference at the home of Adm. Stark to discuss Pearl Harbor.[7] Stark had just been censured by Forrestal in the Secretary's indorsement of the Naval Court's report, directing that Stark was not in future to hold any position in the Navy "which requires the exercise of superior judgment."[8] Also present at the luncheon were Rear Adm. Roscoe E. Schuirmann and Capt. A. H. McCollum.

On the fourth day of his testimony Kramer admitted that he modified his recollections concerning the "winds" message as a result of this luncheon conference. He said that while Stark did not suggest that he change his story, the meeting had "refreshed" his memory on certain details.[9]

He acknowledged once more that he had seen a "winds" message during the week preceding the Pearl Harbor attack, and that he had considered it authentic at the time, but said that his recollection was that the message was received December 5, and not on December 4, as testified by Safford. He said that the disappearance of the message from Navy files could be accounted for on the theory that the Navy may never have made any official recording of the receipt of the signal. He said that a special system had been devised for handing the warning if it were received, under which all regular recording and filing procedure normally used for Japanese intercepts was bypassed by the Navy. Under this plan, Kramer said, the message was to be taken to Adm. Noyes immediately upon its receipt, without going through the regular filing channels.

Kramer made one other significant statement. He said that it was "obvious" on the morning of December 7 that the Japanese were going to attack the British in the Far East and that simultaneous attacks on the United States could be expected. He explained that intercepted messages for weeks had indicated a Japanese move toward British possessions and that "it was believed the United States would be involved." The tipoff, he said, was the December 7 message instructing Ambassador Nomura that the Japanese final reply be submitted to Secretary Hull at 1:00 P.M.[10]

On the final day of his testimony, Kramer changed his story yet again by saying that he now considered the "winds" message a "phony."[11] While he was busy delivering this dictum, the Navy was awarding the Legion of Merit, one of its highest decorations, to the unpopular Capt. Safford, who had upset the applecart by insisting that there was a "winds" message, the existence of which everybody else in Washington wanted to forget. The citation was peculiar in that, although Safford was intercepting all of the Japanese code messages throughout 1941, the medal was given for his services during the period from March, 1942, to September, 1945. The citation said that the officer, whose testimony his own superiors and colleagues had done their utmost to discredit, "was the driving force behind the development of the perfected machines which today give the United States Navy the finest system of encipherment in the world."[12]

Meanwhile, Adm. Ingersoll took the stand before the congressional committee and said there was a "winds" message in December, 1941, but that he did not recall whether he had been told of it before or after the Pearl Harbor attack. He said he recalled that some officers came to his office with "a piece of paper" which was a message putting the Japanese weather code into effect.

"However," said Ingersoll, "inasmuch as it came in after we had sent messages to our commanders telling them the Japanese had ordered destruction of their codes, it was of no importance. It merely confirmed what we already were aware of."*

Ingersoll said that the code destruction orders pointed more to war than any message announcing a break in relations, which was the interpretation he placed on the "winds" code.[13]

The next witness to testify to the interception of the "winds" message was Col. Sadtler, who was in charge of codes and ciphers for the Army Signal Corps in 1941. Sadtler's story was that on the morning of December 5 he was notified by telephone by Adm. Noyes that the "winds" message had been intercepted and that it announced a break in Japanese-British relations.

"I knew it was very easy to get only a part of a message," Sadtler said. "I thought probably the intercepting station had missed a reference to the United States and that the message must certainly mean a break with the United States as well."

Sadtler said he went directly to Gen. Miles who asked for verification of the message. Sadtler then called Noyes, but the admiral was leaving his office and asked if Sadtler would call back later.

"In view of previous messages indicating a break was imminent and because the 'winds' message was the most important I ever received," he related, "I went to Gen. Gerow. Gerow said the overseas commands had been adequately warned.

"I then went to Col. Smith [now Lieut. Gen. Walter Bedell Smith], secretary to the general staff. When he heard that I had already talked with Gen. Miles and Gen. Gerow, he said he did not want to discuss the matter further."

Sadtler told committee members that there was Army gossip that

*Cf. p. 237

key Pearl Harbor records had been destroyed or lost. "At Fort Bragg in 1943," he said, "Gen. Isaac Spaulding told me nothing could be done about Pearl Harbor because the records had been destroyed. He said he got his information from Col. J. T. Bissell."[14] (Spaulding in 1941 was in the Army personnel section and Bissell in intelligence.)

The next witness, Rear Adm. Noyes, contended that he had no positive recollection that a true "winds" message was delivered to him, as previous witnesses had testified, but remembered only that several "false 'winds' messages" were brought to his attention during the first week in December. He said that these messages did not conform to the prearranged code because they did not use all the specified words or, in other cases, did not use them in the prescribed pattern. When challenged on his statement that he did not receive the message in the face of positive testimony from three other witnesses that it went to him, Noyes said, "I would have remembered it, and there would have been at least thirty copies made for distribution. There are no copies of it in the files."

Noyes was reminded of testimony by Safford that Army and Navy files for December, 1941, which would contain the key document had been destroyed. He asserted he never ordered any official files destroyed but explained that he left his Washington post in February, 1942. Nor did he dispute the fact that the files had been destroyed.[15]

Safford had testified that in 1943, when the Navy inquiry into the Pearl Harbor disaster was planned, he went to the Navy files in search of the "winds" note. "We searched the files of intercepts," he said. "There was not only no 'winds' message, but there were no copies of any intercepts from East Coast monitoring stations for December, 1941. The men in charge of the files didn't know these records had been destroyed, had no record of the destruction, and had been given no orders to destroy them."

Safford said that Capt. E. E. Stone, then in charge of naval communications, sought to locate the missing files, but found they had "vanished from the face of the earth." Safford then sought information on the "winds" document from Army files, but found records there on the subject were "completely gone."[16]

Safford was questioned before the congressional committee about his statement during Adm. Hewitt's inquiry that he had "third-hand" reports that all copies of the "winds" message had been destroyed by Col. Bissell on direct orders from Chief of Staff Marshall. Safford had told Hewitt that he had been told this by W. F. Friedman, chief Army cryptanalyst. Safford explained that he had given this testimony reluctantly, only because Hewitt pressed him for a lead as to what had happened to the missing messages.

Asked by Seth W. Richardson, committee counsel, whether he now believed it true that Gen. Marshall ordered the records destroyed, Safford said, "That is a question I prefer not to answer." Neither Bissell nor Friedman was ever called as a witness by the New Deal majority of the congressional committee.[17]

Safford also said that several days after the attack in 1941, orders came from Adm. Stark to section heads in the Navy Department to destroy all personal memoranda about events leading up to the attack and to make no statements about the attack until called as witnesses at formal inquiries. Safford said that this was a verbal order which was passed on to communications section heads by Adm. Noyes at a meeting in his office the morning of December 11 or 12, 1941. Noyes was quoted as saying:

> There are altogether too many rumors in the Navy Department. People are running to the papers and to radio commentators saying wrong things about Admirals Kimmel and Bloch. We've got to stop this. Above all, start no rumors. If any one wants to talk, wait to be called as a witness at a formal inquiry. Furthermore, if any one has any written memos, destroy them or they may fall into the wrong hands.

Safford said that no order was given to destroy any official files or documents.[18]

Commenting on these orders, Noyes said he did not recall any direction to communications officers to destroy their personal memoranda. "I may have issued such instructions," he said. "After the war started, it was standard procedure to have all officers in secret work destroy unofficial notes and memoranda in the interest of security."

Noyes said he agreed with Adm. Ingersoll that information more vital than the "winds" tipoff had been received on December 3, when Jap intercepts showed Tokyo had ordered its envoys abroad to destroy their codes. He said:

> That made the "winds" message less important, even if we got it, because a code destruction order was a positive indication of a trend toward war, but we were still interested in any execution of the "winds" code as a further indication of the trend, and I am certain no true "execute" came to me before December 7.[19]

Two other versions of the "winds" message were given by Adm.

Turner and Capt. McCollum. Turner said he never saw the "winds" message, but that Noyes called him on December 5 and said, "The message is in—'north wind clear,'" which would have meant war with Russia.[20] McCollum said that he, too, had not seen a message indicating that Japan had intended to attack the United States, but he said that such a message might have gone "direct to higher-ups" without passing through his hands. This would not have been unusual, he said, because, although he was charged with the duty of evaluating Japanese intentions, much relevant information was not supplied him. For instance, he said, he was never informed by the State Department about the progress of its negotiations with Japan or told what notes it was communicating to the Japanese representatives. He said that he got most of his information on American diplomacy by intercepting and decoding outgoing Japanese messages from Washington to Tokyo.

McCollum said that on December 4 or 5 a Jap weather broadcast was intercepted indicating that the "winds" code was being used by Tokyo to predict war with Russia, but that he and Capt. Kramer decided upon further study that the broadcast was actually a regular weather report.[21]

Thus, a number of witnesses agreed that there had been a "winds" message, but no two of them agreed when it was received or what meaning it had. Some who were willing to admit that the message had been intercepted were unwilling to concede that it was directed against the United States, contending that it meant war by Japan upon Britain. Others suggested that it had the meaning of war with Russia—a meaning that Tokyo could never have conveyed because Japan had no intention of fighting Russia, while it did intend to fight the United States, the British, and the Dutch.

Although at various times and before various investigating groups, Capt. Safford and Capt. Kramer, the two witnesses best qualified to testify concerning the existence of the signal and its meaning, had been in agreement that it meant war with the United States, Safford at the last was the only witness who stuck to his original story. He said that the "winds" signal had the meaning it necessarily must have possessed if it were received—that Japan intended to go to war with the three powers with which in fact it did go to war. Kramer and Adm. Ingersoll agreed with him that the message had been received, but after originally stating that the message meant war with the United States and Great Britain, both finally took the position that it applied only to war with the British.

By any rule of evidence, Safford was the most competent witness. He was the man best qualified to know the facts. Safford was the commanding officer of the division which was charged with monitoring the message, translating it, and of conveying it to Adm. Noyes. He would have handled the message directly, and he says that he did handle it. He would have had it translated, and he says that he did have it translated. He would have seen that it reached his responsible superior, and he says that he saw to that. It was not his duty to draft orders to the field once the message was received, but many of his superiors who testified concerning the "winds" message and professed to be unable to recall whether it was received, when it was received, or what it meant, did have that responsibility, and they did not discharge it. No warning based upon the "winds" intercept went to Pearl Harbor. If these men admitted the existence of the "winds" message, they knew they would be confessing their own dereliction and guilt.

Capt. Safford said that when he was unable to find the "winds" message in the Navy files of 1943, he became "suspicious of a conspiracy." Asked by committee counsel why he thought anybody would want to destroy the message, he responded, "Because it was the unheeded warning of war." Asked why anyone should fail to make use of the message the moment it came in, if it meant war, he replied, "That question has puzzled me for four years. I don't know the answer."

But, Safford observed, it is clear that no use was, in fact, made of the message, and the only logical explanation for its subsequent destruction and the administration's persistent endeavors to muddy waters that were originally clear is that these actions were intended "to cover up a mistake." That mistake, according to Safford, was "that no war warning was sent—that an attempt to send a warning was suppressed in the Navy Department December 4," when McCollum's draft was killed.[22] Whether higher authority than Admirals Turner and Wilkinson was responsible for killing this vital message which could have averted the disaster three days later—and how high that authority might have been—are questions so far unanswered. Enough has been uncovered to provide the shadowy outline of a monstrous, unbelievable conspiracy.

The only other theory advanced, except the untenable administration argument that there never was any "winds" message, is that of Capt. Kramer and Adm. Ingersoll: that the message meant war with Great Britain, but not with the United States. But, from America's commitments to the ABCD powers under the Washington and Singapore staff agreements, from Roosevelt's warning of August 17, and from the warnings addressed to Japanese officials by Turner and Counselor Dooman of the Tokyo embassy that a Jap attack upon British possessions would bring America into the war, it will be seen that a "winds" signal forecasting a Japanese war with Britain would also have meant that Japan inevitably must fight the United States. Thus, all efforts of the Roosevelt administration to get out of the draft from the "winds" collapse.

The application of the "winds" message to Roosevelt's engagements under the ABCD alliance had been convincingly emphasized in the memorandum of Maj. Gen. Cramer, giving Maj. Clausen instructions as to what he was to investigate on the world-tour he was undertaking for Stimson.

Cramer directed that Clausen, in seeking to determine the validity of the "winds" message, explore "whether Gen. Miles, Adm. Noyes, Col. Bratton, or Capt. Safford knew about the Anglo-Dutch-U.S. Joint Action Agreement, in which case they would have known that a 'war with Britain' message would necessarily have involved the United States in war."

In further study of the "winds" message, Cramer suggested that Clausen look into "whether the partial implementation 'war with Britain' was brought to Adm. Stark's or Gen. Marshall's attention, it being clear that the chief of naval operations and the chief of staff did know of the Joint Action Policy."[23]

The leads which Gen. Cramer listed indicated the belief of the Army's chief legal officer that there was a Joint Action Agreement among the United States, Britain, and Holland, that it was known to Gen. Marshall and Adm. Stark, the chief officers of the Army and Navy, and that Roosevelt was clearly aware of the provision of this agreement that the United States was bound to attack Japan if Japan attacked British or Dutch territory when, at the urging of Churchill, he delivered his ultimatum to Adm. Nomura on August 17 warning Japan against further encroachments in the Pacific.

It was on the basis of Roosevelt's commitments to Britain and Holland under the Joint Action Agreement that Gen. Cramer made the point that a "winds" signal in which Japan warned of hostilities against Britain, even if it conveyed no similar declaration of intention as regards the United States, would have obliged America to enter the war on Britain's side.

Another lead suggested by Cramer to Clausen was whether Gen.

(then Col.) Kendall J. Fielder, chief of intelligence to Gen. Short in Hawaii, "actually received the message directing him to contact Comdr. Rochefort, whether he did so, and whether there is substance to the hypothesis that he and Short were relying upon the warning they would expect to receive when the second or implementing 'winds' message would be intercepted, thus giving advance notice of hostilities."[24]

Gen. Short, during his testimony before the congressional committee, said he could shed no light on this particular question.

"I never heard of the 'winds' code until I read the Roberts report here some time in August, 1944," the general said. "That was the first time I knew there was such a thing."

"You never knew, then, that Comdr. Rochefort had known that there was intercepted a 'winds' or implementing message?" asked Senator Ferguson.

"No, sir, I never heard of it."

"So, then, you were not waiting, as a matter of fact, on an implementing 'winds' message in order that you might be given advance notice of hostilities?"

"I was not."[25]

Adm. Kimmel was also kept in the dark concerning the "winds" message. In his testimony before the congressional committee, however, he expressed his conviction that it had been intercepted, citing in proof statements in the still-secret findings of the Naval Court of Inquiry in 1944. He said:

The interception of the false weather broadcast was considered by the Navy Department to be of supreme importance. Every facility of the Navy was invoked to learn as speedily as possible when the false weather broadcast from Japan was heard and which of the significant code words were used. Extraordinary measures were established in the Navy Department to transmit the words used in the broadcast to key officers as soon as they were known. The Naval Court of Inquiry heard substantial evidence from various witnesses on the question of whether or not Japan gave the signal prescribed by the winds code. The Naval Court of Inquiry found the facts on this matter to be as follows:

"On December 4 an intercepted Japanese broadcast employing this code was received in the Navy Department. Although this notification was subject to two interpretations, either a breaking off of diplomatic relations between Japan and the United States, or war, this information was not transmitted to the commander-in-chief, Pacific fleet, or to other commanders afloat.

"It was known in the Navy Department that the com-
manders-in-chief, Pacific and Asiatic fleets, were monitoring
Japanese broadcasts for this code, and apparently there was a
mistaken impression in the Navy Department that the execute
message had also been intercepted at Pearl Harbor. No attempt
was made by the Navy Department to ascertain whether this
information had been obtained by the commander-in-chief, Pacific, and by other commanders afloat.

"Adm. Stark stated that he knew nothing about it, although
Adm. Turner stated that he himself was familiar with it and presumed that Adm. Kimmel had it. This message cannot now be
located in the Navy Department."[26]

Thus, the Army Pearl Harbor Board and the Naval Court of Inquiry both agreed that the "winds" message was intercepted, as Capt.
Safford maintained and the Army judge advocate general implied,
and that in 1944 there was substantial agreement among witnesses as
to this fact, as well as to the plain meaning of the signal.[27] The witnesses began to develop loss of memory only after the Secretary of
War and the Secretary of the Navy started bringing pressure upon
them. This campaign of intimidation, especially effective against
Army and Navy officers sensitive to prospects of promotion and status,
was launched only after tangible evidence of nonfeasance in the highest circles of the services and of the civilian government had been
adduced.

To this scandalous conduct must be added the disappearance of the
relevant intercepts from the Army and Navy secret files, the destruction of the logs of the Navy monitoring stations for the whole first
week of December, 1941, ostensibly to "make filing room,"[28] and the
attempt to jam through Congress legislation which would forever
have suppressed the code-cracking evidence under penalties so severe
as to prohibit publication or even discussion.

Chapter Sixteen

"DO-DON'T" WARNINGS

WASHINGTON, IN blaming Kimmel and Short for the disaster of December 7, contended that they had been adequately warned of the imminence of war. The first warning which was supposed to have guided the field commanders was a letter from Knox to Stimson on January 24, 1941, in which the Secretary of the Navy said, "If war eventuates with Japan, it is believed easily possible that hostilities would be initiated by a surprise attack upon the fleet or the naval base at Pearl Harbor."[1]

Although the Roberts report cited this letter against Kimmel and Short, the commission failed to state that in the ten months which intervened before the attack, neither Knox nor anyone else in Washington indicated in any warning dispatched to Hawaii that there was any likelihood of an attack upon Oahu. After the attack, the Army Board noted, none of the principal figures admitted the least suspicion that Pearl Harbor should have been the objective. The board said:

> The contrast between the written statements of many of the responsible actors prior to Pearl Harbor and after Pearl Harbor, as to their estimate of an air attack by Japan on Oahu is startling. When the Secretary of the Navy arrived in Hawaii a few days after December 7, Adm. Pye* testified his first remark was: "No one in Washington expected an attack—even Kelly Turner."†[2]

*Vice-Adm. William S. Pye on December 7, 1941, was commander, battle force (Task Force 1), of the Pacific fleet. Upon the relief of Adm. Kimmel as commander-in-chief of the fleet on December 17, 1941, he was temporarily placed in command of the fleet. On December 31, 1941, he was succeeded by Adm. Chester W. Nimitz.

†Rear Adm. Richmond Kelly Turner, chief of Navy war plans at the time of Pearl Harbor, was reckoned among the Navy's most bellicose and suspicious officers in regard to Japan.

On October 16, 1941, the first of the so-called war warnings was dispatched to Adm. Kimmel by Adm. Ingersoll. It read:

> The resignation of the Japanese cabinet has created a grave situation. If a new cabinet is formed, it will probably be strongly nationalistic and anti-American. If the Konoye cabinet remains, the effect will be that it will operate under a new mandate which will not include rapprochement with the United States. In either case, hostilities between Japan and Russia are a strong possibility. Since the United States and Britain are held responsible by Japan for her present desperate situation, there is also a possibility that Japan may attack these two powers. In view of these possibilities, you will take due precautions, including such preparatory deployments as will not disclose strategic intention nor constitute provocative actions against Japan.[3]

The conflict in this message is apparent. Hawaii was notified that if Japan embarked upon hostilities, a war with Russia was probable. This was qualified by mention of the "possibility" of an attack upon the United States and Britain. The Hawaiian commanders were to take "due precautions" and to make "preparatory deployments," but not to "disclose strategic intention" or engage in "provocative actions."

Adm. Ingersoll said that these instructions were sent both to Adm. Kimmel and to Adm. Hart, and that the order to execute a "preparatory deployment" applied to the Asiatic fleet rather than to Kimmel's Pacific fleet. He said:

> I think the preparatory deployment that would not constitute provocative action or disclose strategic intentions against Japan referred more to the withdrawal of certain units of the Asiatic fleet from the China Sea area toward the southern Philippines than to any particular deployment of the Pacific fleet, with the possible exception of sending out submarines for observation.[4]

Ingersoll, who released the order, was here in conflict with Adm. Turner, who asserted that Kimmel, under the order to execute a preparatory deployment, should have "taken his fleet to sea."[5]

Senator Ferguson pointed out the confusion arising from sending messages to two or more outposts, with certain instructions intended for one outpost and not for another.

On October 20 Short was sent the following War Department estimate of the Japanese situation: "Tension between United States and Japan remains strained but no, repeat no, abrupt change in Japanese foreign policy appears imminent."[6] Therefore, the Hawaiian commanders were told that Japan was still relying upon efforts to achieve a diplomatic settlement with the United States, and that belligerent action was not foreseen.

On November 24 Adm. Kimmel received the following message from Adm. Stark, concurred in by Gen. Marshall:

> There are very doubtful chances of a favorable outcome of negotiations with Japan. This situation, coupled with statements of Nippon government and movements of their naval and military force, indicate, in our opinion, that a surprise aggressive movement in any direction, including an attack on the Philippines or Guam, is a possibility. The chief of staff has seen this dispatch and concurs and requests action. Inform senior Army officers in respective areas. Utmost secrecy is necessary in order not to complicate the already tense situation or precipitate Japanese action.[7]

The effect of this message was to persuade Kimmel and Short that if Japan moved, it would not be toward Hawaii, but against the Philippines or Guam. They were restricted to a course of action which would maintain secrecy "in order not to complicate the already tense situation or precipitate Japanese action."

On the next day, November 25, Adm. Stark confused the directions in this message and diluted its effectiveness by sending a letter to Adm. Kimmel concluding,

> I won't go into the pros and cons of what the United States may do. I'll be damned if I know. I wish I did. The only thing I do know is that we may do most anything and that's the only thing I know to be prepared for; or we may do nothing —I think it is more likely to be "anything."[8]

On November 27 Stark sent Kimmel a "war warning" which the Pacific fleet commander showed to Short. It read:

> Consider this dispatch a war warning.* The negotiations with Japan in an effort to stabilize conditions in the Pacific have ended. Japan is expected to make an aggressive move within the next few days. An amphibious expedition against either the Philippines, or Kra Peninsula or possibly Borneo is indicated by the number and equipment of Japanese troops and the organization of their naval forces. You will execute a defensive deployment in preparation for carrying out the tasks

---

*"The use of the term 'war warning' in constant reference to this message of Nov. 27 to Adm. Kimmel creates a wrong impression. The entire message is of the utmost importance and should be read as a whole rather than adopt two words from it which when taken alone create the wrong impression." (Min., pp. 41-42.)

assigned in WPL 46. Guam, Samoa, and continental districts have been directed to take appropriate measures against sabotage. A similar warning is being sent by the War Department. Inform naval district and Army authorities. British to be informed.[9]

Whereas the message of November 24 indicated a possible attack on Guam, Washington now had decided that any Japanese movement would be directly south. Guam, and, by inference, Oahu, were to be on guard only against sabotage. While the message was termed a "war warning," it did not place in effect Navy War Plan 46, but directed only that a defensive deployment be executed in preparation for carrying out the tasks assigned to the Pacific fleet under that plan. These tasks were entirely offensive, involving raids against the Japanese mandated islands. It was indicated that later directions would be received if it became necessary to carry out this plan.

On November 27 a message was dispatched to Short under the signature of Gen. Marshall which, the Army Board said, was so ambiguous and contained so many conflicting instructions that it could only be characterized as a "Do-or-Don't" message. It read:

No. 472. Negotiations with the Japanese appear to be terminated to all practical purposes with only the barest possibilities that the Japanese government might come back and offer to continue. Japanese future action unpredictable but hostile action possible at any moment. If hostilities cannot, repeat cannot, be avoided the United States desires that Japan commit the first overt act. This policy should not, repeat not, be construed as restricting you to a course of action that might jeopardize your defense. Prior to hostile Japanese action, you are directed to undertake such reconnaissance and other measures as you deem necessary, but these measures should be carried out so as not, repeat not, to alarm the civil population or disclose intent. Report measures taken. Should hostilities occur, you will carry out the tasks assigned in Rainbow Five so far as they pertain to Japan. Limit the dissemination of this highly secret information to minimum essential officers.[10]

This message, although bearing Marshall's signature, had in fact been drafted by Secretary Stimson and Gen. Gerow with some assistance from Col. Charles W. Bundy of the general staff.[11] Marshall was in North Carolina observing Army maneuvers on November 27.[12] During the drafting of this dispatch, Stimson also consulted Secretary Knox, Adm. Stark, and Gen. William Bryden, deputy chief of staff.[13] From Stimson's own statements, it is apparent that the message was drafted primarily to guide Gen. MacArthur in the Philippines.

Describing his conference with Knox, Stark, and Gerow, the Secretary stated:

> The main question at this meeting was over the message that we shall send to MacArthur. We have already sent him a quasi-alert or the first signal for an alert; and now, on talking with the President this morning over the telephone, I suggested and he approved the idea that we should send the final alert, namely, that he should be on the *qui vive* for any attack, and telling him how the situation was. We were sending the messages to four people; not only MacArthur, but Hawaii, Panama, and Alaska.[14]

Stimson himself drafted the first sentence of the dispatch. As originally written, the first sentence read, "Negotiations with Japan have been terminated." This was softened after Stimson consulted Secretary Hull by telephone.[15] As revised, it read, "Negotiations with Japan appear to be terminated to all practical purposes with only the barest possibilities that the Japanese government might come back and offer to continue." The next sentence, "Japanese future action unpredictable but hostile action possible at any moment," was put in by Gerow or Bundy.[16]

The sentence, "If hostilities cannot, repeat cannot, be avoided, the United States desires that Japan commit the first overt act," was thus phrased because, Gerow explained, "the President had definitely stated that he wanted Japan to commit the first overt act."[17] Gen. Marshall added, "It was included on specific instructions from the President."[18] Roosevelt apparently was very mindful of his pledge not to send Americans into foreign wars "unless we are attacked."[19]

The next sentence, "This policy should not, repeat not, be construed as restricting you to a course of action that might jeopardize your defense," was inserted by Gerow or Bundy.[20] In directing Short to engage in reconnaissance, Stimson and the general staff were manifesting ignorance that distance reconnaissance was a Navy duty in Hawaii and that Short had only six planes capable of distance flights.[21]

The Army Board report remarks that the drafting of the message was "the composite work of a number of people, which may account for its confusing and conflicting tenor." The report adds,

> It is equally obvious that the November 27 message was the only message that attempted to translate the long and tempestuous course of events terminating in the counter-proposals of

the 26th of November to Japan. No other picture of the situation was given to Short except in this message. It is apparent that the message of November 27 was entirely inadequate to properly and adequately translate to Short's mind the background of events that had been taking place. While this does not excuse Short, it does necessitate an assessment of the responsibility of others.

The three principal major generals who were commanders under Short have testified that they received substantially nothing by way of information as to the international situation except what they read in the newspapers. The fact that the newspapers were urgent and belligerent in their tone was discounted by them, because they were not receiving any confirmatory information from the War Department through Short. Information that was of tremendous value both as to content and substance, which the Secretary of State, Secretary of War, chief of staff, and other high officers of the War Department had, was not transmitted to Short. The only summary of this information was the brief and conflicting tone of the message of November 27, which was but a faint echo of what had actually occurred.

It is significant that the Japanese upon the termination of negotiations by the counter-proposals of the 26th, considered by them as an ultimatum, were thereby in full possession of all the information, which our ultra-secrecy policy did not permit of full transmission to field commanders. The Japanese knew everything. The War and Navy departments transmitted to Short only so much of what they knew as they judged necessary.

It is also significant that the Secretary of War had to go and call Mr. Hull to get the information on what amounted to the practical cessation of negotiations, which was the most vital thing that had occurred in 1941.[22]

Analyzing the dispatch, the Army Board said that the first two sentences, that negotiations "appear to be terminated," with only a bare possibility that they would be resumed, and that Japan's action was "unpredictable, but hostile action possible," were inadequate and misleading. "The War Department was convinced then that war would come," the board states.[23] The statement that Japanese action was "unpredictable" did not square with the Navy warning, which Kimmel had shown to Short, that an attack, if it came, would be in the Kra Peninsula or elsewhere in the Far East.[24] In any event, Hawaii was not warned of attack.

In addition, Short was told that Japan must commit the first overt act and that he must not alarm the civilian population or disclose intent. He was told that these instructions were not to restrict his defense, but they could have no other effect.

The Army Board dismisses this "war warning" with the sharp comment:

Had a full war message, unadulterated, been dispatched or had direct orders for a full, all-out alert been sent, Hawaii could have been ready to have met the attack with what it had. What resulted was failure at both ends of the line. Responsibility lay both in Washington and in Hawaii.[25]

Gen. Short commented:

The impression conveyed to me by this message was that the avoidance of war was paramount and the greatest fear of the War Department was that some international incident might occur in Hawaii and be regarded by Japan as an overt act.[26] That this opinion was in accordance with the views of Gen. Marshall is shown by the following quotation from his testimony:

"So far as public opinion was concerned, I think the Japanese were capitalizing on the belief that it would be very difficult to bring our people into a willingness to enter the war. That, incidentally, was somewhat confirmed by the governmental policy on our part of making certain that the overt act should not be attributed to the United States, because of the state of the public mind at the time. Of course, no one anticipated that that overt act would be the crippling of the Pacific fleet."[27]

No mention was made of a probable attack on Hawaii since the alert message of June 18, 1940. An examination of the various military intelligence estimates prepared by G-2 shows that in no estimate did G-2 ever indicate the probability of an attack upon Hawaii. There was nothing in the message directing me to be prepared to meet an air raid or an all-out attack. "Hostile action at any moment" meant to me that as far as Hawaii was concerned the War Department was predicting sabotage. Sabotage is a form of hostile action.[28]

The only additional information received by Short after message No. 472 of November 27 was contained in three messages on November 27 and 28 concerning possible danger from sabotage and subversive activities. The first of these, from Gen. Miles of G-2 to Short's intelligence section, read: "Japanese negotiations have come to practical stalemate. Hostilities may ensue. Subversive activities may be expected. Inform commanding general and chief of staff only."[29]

As a warning in any real sense, this message failed. It was highly conditional: hostilities "may" ensue, subversive activities "may" be expected. Hostilities or inimical activities may be "expected" at any time. Further, the message indicated that if there were hostilities in Hawaii they would take the form of subversive activities.

Short replied as follows to the radiogram of November 27 bearing Marshall's signature: "Reurad (re your radio) four seven two 27th: Report department alerted to prevent sabotage. Liaison with the Navy."[30]

The commander of the Hawaiian department received no reply from Washington, either approving the measures he had taken or directing him to institute a higher degree of alert. He interpreted this silence as approval of the measures he had taken. His report was initialed or rubber stamped by Gen. Marshall, Secretary Stimson, and Gen. Gerow. If they were dissatisfied with his action, all they needed to do was give him an order. They did nothing.[31]

Gen. Short attributed the lack of reaction in Washington to the fact that "all who read the message believed the action was correct."[32] He cited Gen. Marshall's testimony before the Army Pearl Harbor Board in support of this thesis. Marshall testified:

> We anticipated, beyond a doubt, a Japanese movement in Indo-China and the Gulf of Siam, and against the Malay Peninsula. We anticipated also an assault on the Philippines. We did not, so far as I can recall, anticipate an attack on Hawaii; the reason being that we thought, with the addition of more modern planes, that the defenses there would be sufficient to make it extremely hazardous for the Japanese to attempt such an attack.[33]

On November 28 Short received the following message, relating entirely to sabotage and subversive activities, from the adjutant general:

> 482 28th Critical situation demands that all precautions be taken immediately against subversive activities within field of investigative responsibility of War Department. Also desired that you initiate forthwith all additional measures necessary to provide for protection of your establishments, property, and equipment against sabotage, protection of your personnel against subversive propaganda and protection of all activities against espionage. This does not, repeat not, mean that any illegal measures are authorized. Protective measures should be confined to those essential to security, avoiding unnecessary publicity and

alarm. To insure speed of transmission identical telegrams are being sent to all air stations but this does not, repeat not, affect your responsibility under existing instructions.[34]

Because of the emphasis that was again placed on protection against sabotage and subversive activities, Short was fortified in his conviction that he had instituted the kind of alert which Washington wanted. He thought the adjutant general's dispatch had been prepared after consideration had been given to his message reporting that he had alerted his command to prevent sabotage.

During his examination before the congressional committee, Short was asked by Representative Keefe, "Now, when you received that telegram of the 28th, after Washington had received your message in which you stated you were alerted against sabotage, did that tend to influence you in your thinking that the alert which you had was the proper alert, the alert that Washington wanted?"

"It did," said Short. "I thought it was an answer to my radiogram and [the adjutant general] wanted to emphasize the question of legality."[35]

Accordingly, to reassure the War Department as to the legality of his actions, Short explained in his reply to the adjutant general November 29 that his measures against subversive activities and sabotage were countenanced by the organic act of Hawaii and by an ordnance of the city and county of Honolulu.[36] He received no reply from the War Department and considered Washington's failure to comment as implying further tacit agreement that the measures he had taken were all that were intended or desired by the War Department. Short reported:

> When the War Department was informed that the Hawaiian department was alerted against sabotage, it not only did not indicate that the command should be alerted against a hostile surface, subsurface, ground, or air attack, but replied emphasizing the necessity for protection against sabotage and subversive measures. This action on the part of the War Department definitely indicated to me that it approved of my alert against sabotage. The War Department had nine more days in which to express its disapproval. The action of the War Department in sending unarmed B-17's from Hamilton Field, California, on the night of December 6 to Honolulu confirmed me in my belief that an air raid was not probable.[37]

Hawaii, Short explained, was a focal point in transporting troops, B-17's, and air crews to the Philippines. The planes were always sent

to Hawaii unarmed, but when sending them out to "the more dangerous area of the Philippines, we were to arm them."

None of the planes which left Hamilton Field December 6 was
equipped with ammunition or defensive armament. The machine
guns were cosmolined and had not been bore-sighted. Ferry crews
were skeletonized, consisting of pilot, co-pilot, navigator, engineer,
and radio operator. Such crews were incapable of manning the machine guns even if the guns had been properly prepared for combat
and supplied with ammunition. Short said:

> It cannot be imagined that the War Department wished to
> send these planes to Honolulu unarmed when they already had
> information of a pending Japanese attack. The only inference
> that can be drawn is that while the War Department had infor-
> mation of a pending attack, Gen. [H. H.] Arnold, the chief of
> air corps, who ordered these planes to Honolulu, and who I
> understand was present at Hamilton Field at the time of their
> departure, did not know of the critical situation in the relations
> between the United States and Japan.[38]

> Confirmation of my view that the War Department's silence
> and failure to reply to my report of November 27 constituted
> reasonable grounds for my belief that my action was exactly
> what the War Department desired is contained in Gen. Mar-
> shall's testimony before this joint committee on December 11,
> 1945.

Short then cited the following colloquy:

> Senator Ferguson: "Well, would this be true from an Army
> viewpoint, that when an overseas commander is ordered to take
> 'such measures as he deems necessary and to report such meas-
> ures to you,' is he correct in assuming that if his report is not the
> kind of action that you had in mind that you would thereafter
> inform him specifically of this difference?"
> Gen. Marshall: "I would assume so."[39]

On November 28 Gen. Arnold sent Gen. Martin, chief of the Army
Air Forces in Hawaii, still another message relating entirely to sabotage and subversive activities, similar in tone to the dispatch of the
same day from the adjutant general to Short. Again the Hawaiian
command was cautioned to avoid unnecessary publicity and alarm
and confine protective measures to those essential to security, and that
illegal measures were not authorized. Martin was instructed to report
his action under these orders by December 5.[40]

On December 4 Short and his air general sent a detailed report to

Arnold of measures taken by them against sabotage and subversive activities. They underlined the prevailing condition of alert in Hawaii by stating, "This entire department is now operating and will continue to operate under an alert for prevention of sabotage."[41] The Hawaiian department received no reply disagreeing in any way with the action reported.[42]

The Martin-Short report, the final message from Hawaii to Washington, was dispatched only three days before the attack. Although Washington then had an abundance of information pointing to war almost at once, it was still talking as if the principal and only danger to Hawaii was from sabotage and subversive activities, and it was accepting without comment reports from the Hawaiian command which showed a complete misapprehension as to the gravity of the situation which Washington knew to exist.

In their message of December 4, for example, Martin and Short were suggesting to Washington that their troops could be kept from threatened disaffection by educational talks on the status of the soldier as a citizen, the ideals of the founders of the Republic, and the dangers of Fascism. The report stated:

> Entire subject of protection recently received and continues to receive detailed and comprehensive attention. . . . Instructions issued to expedite overhauling of pass system, civilian and military, now in progress. . . . Secrecy discipline given all emphasis practicable through official and quasi-official agencies.
>
> With reference to counter-propaganda, the problem is educational rather than regulatory and at present is being dealt with through the medium of squadron talks. Need is felt for a War Department publication suitably arranged and worded for use of relatively inexperienced personnel, dealing with status of soldier as citizen, ideals and doctrine influencing founders of American government, structure of government, place of military establishment in structure, national objectives, both domestic and international, together with discussion of those forms of government inimical to democratic form.[43]

This, be it remembered, was the same day that Washington knew from the intercepted "east wind rain" message that war had already been decreed against the United States without a formal declaration. No message was sent to Short or Martin to correct their misapprehensions founded on ignorance of the facts known in Washington.

Meanwhile, on November 27, the day on which he received the "war warning," Adm. Kimmel received two other dispatches from

Adm. Stark which convinced him that Washington had no expectation of an attack upon Hawaii. One of these proposed that Kimmel load twenty-five army pursuit planes on each of his two aircraft carriers and send them to Wake and Midway islands. The other proposed the reinforcement of Marine defense battalions on Wake and Midway with Army troops. Two days later Gen. Short received a dispatch from the War Department which stated that the Army proposed to take over the defense of these two islands from the Marines. Thus the dispatches sent from the War and Navy departments were in disagreement on the very fundamentals of the project.[44]

Kimmel told the congressional committee that it was not feasible to exchange Army troops for Marines on the outlying bases. The Army had no artillery or anti-aircraft weapons to equip any troops which might relieve or reinforce the Marines, and if the Marines had withdrawn, leaving their equipment and arms for the Army, Kimmel had no means of re-equipping or re-arming them. In addition, the Army had nothing in its organization comparable to a Marine defense battalion, so that the Army garrisons would have required a new table of organization.

Not only would the defense of Midway and Wake have been disrupted during the period the garrisons were being changed, but at Wake there were no harbor facilities or anchorage. Material and personnel had to be landed from ships under way in an open seaway, and at times bad weather had delayed unloadings at the island for as long as twenty-eight days. It was not unusual for a ship to require a week to unload. Extensive unloading of men and material from ships at Wake, in the face of any enemy operation, would be impossible.

"I believe," said Kimmel, "that responsible authorities in Washington would not plan or propose a project for shifting garrisons under such circumstances, if they considered that enemy action against these outlying bases was imminent." Accordingly, he recommended to Stark that the Marine garrisons remain until Army troops had been adequately equipped and trained to replace them.

The admiral also said that Washington's proposal to replace Marine planes on Wake and Midway with Army pursuit planes was impracticable.* Gen. Martin stated that the Army pursuit planes could

---

*Adm. W. W. Smith testified: "He [Adm. Kimmel] had a shock, though, in the week preceding Pearl Harbor, when we had orders from the Navy Department, and Gen. Short had orders from the War Department, to prepare a plan immediately for bringing all the Marines off the outlying islands, and replacing them with soldiers and with Army planes, and, as I remember it, practically the entire week before Pearl Harbor was spent with the two staffs together. The Army was undecided whether to

not operate more than 15 miles from land, nor could they land on a carrier. Consequently, once they were landed on one of the outlying islands they would be frozen there, while their 15-mile limit of operation radically restricted their usefulness in island defense.

The Army pursuit planes which it was proposed to send to Wake and Midway from Oahu on November 27, the same day that Kimmel was being given the so-called war warning applicable to Hawaii, constituted approximately 50 per cent of the Army's pursuit strength on Oahu. Kimmel stated:

> The very fact that the War and Navy departments proposed their transfer from Hawaii indicated to me that responsible authorities in Washington did not consider an air raid on Pearl Harbor either imminent or probable. In brief, on November 27, the Navy Department suggested that I send from the immediate vicinity the carriers of the fleet which constituted the fleet's main striking defense against an air attack. On Nov. 27, the War and Navy departments suggested that we send from the island of Oahu 50 per cent of the Army's resources in pursuit planes. These proposals came to us on the very same day of the so-called "war warning." In these circumstances, no reasonable man in my position would consider that the "war warning" was intended to suggest the likelihood of an attack in the Hawaiian area.[46]

Short, under orders November 29 from the War Department, was instructed to put into effect a plan whereby the Army garrison in Hawaii would be depleted. The plan would have required him to garrison Christmas and Canton islands, and later to take over the outlying islands—Palmyra, Johnston, and Samoa. The troops he was supposed to send to these islands would be replaced by fresh troops from the mainland.[47] This testimony showed that Washington was not looking for any attack on Hawaii after sending Short the warning of November 27; otherwise it would not have directed him to reduce his garrison.

---

put P-39's or P-40's on these islands. We told them that any planes they put on Wake would remain there for the duration, in case of war, because they would have to be taken off from a carrier and could not come back, and we had no means of putting a ship in there to bring them off, and during the discussion of this with Gen. Short and his staff, the commanding general of the Army Air Force (Gen. Martin) and Adm. Pye were present, and also Adm. Wilson Brown, the war plans officer, the operations officers and I believe Adm. Bloch. Adm. Kimmel said, 'What can I expect of Army fighters on Wake?' And Gen. Martin replied, 'We do not allow them to go more than 15 miles off shore.' That was a shock to all of us and Adm. Kimmel's reply was, 'Then, they will be no damn good to me.' The exchange was never made because the war broke before-hand."[45]

On November 29 Adm. Stark sent a message to Kimmel which was in substance a quotation of the Army "war warning" of November 27 to Short. In addition, it conveyed the following direction:

WPL 52 is not applicable to the Pacific area and will not be placed in effect in that area except as now in force in Southeast Pacific subarea and Panama naval coastal frontier. Undertake no offensive action until Japan has committed an overt act. Be prepared to carry out tasks assigned in WPL 46 so far as they apply to Japan in case hostilities occur.[48]

Kimmel explained:

WPL 52 was the Navy Western Hemisphere Defense Plan No. 5. Under this plan the Atlantic fleet had shooting orders. It was charged with the task of destroying German and Italian naval, land, and air forces encountered in the area of the Western Atlantic. The Southeast Pacific subarea covered approximately 700 miles of the Pacific Ocean, off the coast of South America. Here the Southeast Pacific naval force had similar shooting orders and a similar task.

In the dispatch of November 29, the chief of naval operations informed me that WPL 52 was not applicable to the Pacific. This was to impress upon me the fact that I did not have shooting orders and that I was not to shoot until Japan had committed an overt act.[49]

On November 30 the Navy Department sent Kimmel, for information, a dispatch addressed to Adm. Hart, stating that there were indications that Japan was about to attack points on the Kra Isthmus. Hart was ordered to scout for information but to avoid the appearance of attacking.[50] On December 1 Kimmel received for information another Navy Department dispatch addressed to Hart, describing a proposed Japanese intrigue designed to draw British forces over the border of Thailand in order to give Thailand a pretext for calling upon Japan for aid. This would have facilitated the Japanese entry into Thailand as a full-fledged ally and have given Japan air bases on the Kra Peninsula in order to carry out further operations.[51]

"In short," Kimmel said, "all indications of the movements of Japanese military and naval forces which came to my attention confirmed the information in the dispatch of Nov. 27—that the Japanese were on the move against Thailand or the Kra Peninsula in Southeast Asia."[52]

On December 1 the fortnightly Navy intelligence summary issued by Stark, under the heading "The Japanese Naval Situation," informed

Kimmel, "Major capital ship strength remains in home waters, as well as the greatest portion of the carriers."[53] This estimate could not have been more disastrously wrong.

Three more messages were sent by the Navy Department to Kimmel in the days preceding the attack. The first, on December 3, stated that Japanese consular and diplomatic posts at Hong Kong, Singapore, Batavia, Manila, Washington, and London had been ordered to destroy "most of their codes and ciphers"—not all—a point noted by Kimmel and his staff at the time. "This information," Kimmel said, "seemed to fit in with the information we had received about a Japanese movement in Southeast Asia."[55]

Kimmel told the congressional committee that he did not know that warnings had been given to Japan as early as July, 1941, that Japanese moves against British and Dutch possessions in the Southwest Pacific would compel the United States to "take steps" to protect its rights. Consequently, he testified, when definite reports were received late in November that the Japanese were concentrating forces for their southward move, he was not aware that such action was in violation of specific warnings from the American government.

The only thing he knew, he said, was that his war plans called for raids against the Marshall Islands to draw the Japanese away from the Malay barrier, but only in the event of war between Japan and an association of the United States and Great Britain.[56]

Two other dispatches were received by Kimmel on December 4 and 6. Of these the Army Board remarks,

This record does not provide either a true copy or a paraphrase copy of the messages of December 4 or December 6. The information we have is no better than that contained in the Roberts report, which reads as follows:

"The message of December 4, 1941, instructed the addressee to destroy confidential documents and means of confidential communication, retaining only such as were necessary, the latter to be destroyed in event of emergency [this was sent to the commander-in-chief of the Pacific fleet for information only]; and the message of December 6, directing that in view of the tense existing situation the naval commands on the outlying Pacific islands might be authorized to destroy confidential papers then or later, under conditions of greater emergency, and that those essential to continued operations should be retained until the last moment."[57]

The dispatch of December 4 was apparently that drafted by Capt. Safford to be sent to Guam following receipt of the "winds" signal.

Gen. Short denied that he ever saw the three messages of December 3, 4, and 6.[58] The Roberts report commented,

> The foregoing messages did not create in the minds of responsible officers in the Hawaiian area apprehension as to probable imminence of air raids. On the contrary, they only served to emphasize in their minds the danger from sabotage and surprise submarine attack. The necessity for taking a state of war readiness which would have been required to avert or meet an air attack was not considered.[59]

The Army Board remarked,

"There is a serious question raised why the War Department did not give instructions to Short direct which would have put him on his guard as to the tenseness of the situation."[60]

The final message from Washington to Hawaii was drafted by Gen. Marshall at 11:58 A.M. December 7, one hour and twenty-seven minutes before the Japanese attack began on Oahu, and was dispatched to Gen. Short at 12:18 P.M., Washington time (6:48 A.M., Honolulu time), one hour and seven minutes before the first bombs and torpedoes were launched by the Japanese. The message read:

> Japanese are presenting at 1:00 P.M., Eastern Standard Time, today what amounts to an ultimatum. Also they are under orders to destroy their code machine immediately. Just what significance the hour set may have we do not know but be on alert accordingly. Inform naval authorities of this communication.[61]

This message did not carry a "priority" classification and was not marked "urgent." Early in the morning the Army radio in Hawaii had had difficulty in maintaining communication with the War Department in Washington. Because the War Department message center was dubious about getting through to Hawaii on its own set, it was decided to send this vital message by RCA commercial radio.

Marshall had on his desk a scrambler telephone—which renders conversations a hash of meaningless sounds, which are unscrambled at the receiving end—with which he could have reached Gen. Short in a matter of minutes. The chief of staff later explained that he hesitated to use this device because it was known that German agents had tapped scrambler telephone conversations between President Roosevelt and Prime Minister Churchill, and because they had also tapped communications from William Bullitt when he was serving as ambassador to France.[62] Marshall said that "there was a possibility of a leak which would embarrass the State Department" if the Japanese had tapped any warning he telephoned Short.[63] Since the Japanese intended to embarrass the whole nation with their attack upon Pearl Harbor, the explanation is curious.[64]

The chief of staff also had at his disposal the powerful Navy Department and FBI radio transmitters over which his message, if marked for priority handling, could have been sent to Hawaii in a very short period. Adm. Stark, who was with him when the last minute warning was drafted, offered Marshall the use of the Navy radio.[65] Marshall, however, did not choose to use either the Navy or FBI sets.

His message was brought to the code room of the War Department signal office by Col. Bratton. Col. French, in charge of the traffic operations branch, had it typed for clarity.* It was then encoded.[66] The message was received by RCA in Honolulu at 7:33 A.M., twenty-two minutes before the attack on Pearl Harbor. When the Jap assault began, a bicycle messenger boy was carrying it through the streets of Honolulu. It was not actually delivered to the Army signal office at Fort Shafter until 11:45 A.M., two hours after the last Jap plane had retired. Because it was not marked "priority," other messages which were so marked were decoded first at the signal office. The message was finally placed in the hands of the decoding officer at 2:40 P.M. It was decoded and delivered to Col. Dunlop, adjutant general of the Hawaiian department, at 2:58 P.M. Dunlop turned it over at 3:00 P.M. to Gen. Short's aide, Capt. Trueman, who delivered it to Short. The warning thus was in Short's hands eight hours and twelve minutes after being filed for transmission and seven hours and five minutes after the attack had begun.[67]

These were the messages which Washington called "war warnings" and which the leaders of government and of the Army and Navy high command said should have put the Hawaiian commanders on guard against a surprise attack upon Pearl Harbor. All of them sent previous to December 7 were termed by the Army Board "Do-Don't" messages, which told the commanders in Hawaii to prepare for defense but to do nothing in preparing that might precipitate trouble with the large Japanese population or excite the public. The

---

*Col. French testified (Maj., p. 225, APH Top Secret, pp. 189-205) that he had not considered using the telephone; that the telephone was never used by the signal center; that it was unsuitable for a classified message; and that, in any event, "if they wanted to use the telephone that was up to the individuals themselves, chief of staff, or whoever was the individual concerned." In other words, the decision as to whether to use the telephone was up to Gen. Marshall as the originator of the message and operating chief of the Army.

commanders were to prepare to take the offensive, but also to take the first punch: "The United States desires that Japan commit the first overt act." They were warned by Washington against sabotage and subversive activities, but were held responsible when a disaster resulted from an air attack which no one in Washington had foreseen. They were told that hostilities would begin in Southeast Asia, but were blamed when the Japs crossed up the brain trust in Washington by attacking Hawaii.

The message of December 7 might have served to convey some sense of danger if it had not been so horribly bungled in transmission, but it was scarcely less ambiguous than its predecessors. Although Marshall stated that he did not know the significance of the 1:00 P.M. deadline and other Jap actions, he nevertheless instructed the Hawaiian commanders to "be on alert accordingly." In accordance with what? He did not suggest against what they were to be on the alert.

The minority report of the Joint Congressional Committee (Conclusion 13, pp. 38-40) appraises all of these warnings as follows:

> *The messages sent to Gen. Short and Adm. Kimmel by high authorities in Washington during November were couched in such conflicting and imprecise language that they failed to convey to the commanders definite information on the state of diplomatic relations with Japan and on Japanese war designs and positive orders respecting the particular actions to be taken —orders that were beyond all reasonable doubts as to the need for an all-out alert. In this regard the said high authorities failed to discharge their full duty.*

We content ourselves with presenting the following facts in respect to the conflicting, imprecise, and insufficient character of these messages.

It should be here observed that Washington had taken unto itself such a minute direction of affairs as regards outposts that the usual discretion of outpost commanders was narrowly limited.

First of all, it is to be noted that the four reports by the Army and Navy boards created to investigate Pearl Harbor found the warning messages insufficient to put the Hawaiian commanders on a full war alert; and the President's commission on Pearl Harbor, while finding the commanders guilty of dereliction of duty, itself places neglect on the part of the War Department, in respect to such orders, as among the contributory causes of the catastrophe at Pearl Harbor, thus qualifying its own conclusions.

The President's commission, though limited by his instructions to a search for derelictions of duty and errors of judgment on the part of the Army and Navy personnel, made a point of declaring that the Secretary of State, the Secretary of War, and the Secretary of the Navy had fulfilled their obligations with regard to matters bearing on the situation at Pearl Harbor and that the chief of staff and the chief of naval operations had fulfilled their command responsibilities in issuing warning messages to the two commanders.

But the commission includes among the grounds for charging Gen. Short and Adm. Kimmel with dereliction of duty their failure "to consult and confer" with each other *respecting the meaning and intent of the warnings."* Thus the commission in effect concedes that the war warning messages were couched in language so imprecise that the commanders would have to consult and confer in order to discover what the messages meant.

Having made this statement, the commission goes on to lay some of the blame for the Pearl Harbor catastrophe on the War Department and the Navy Department (that is, upon Secretary Stimson, Secretary Knox, and/or Gen. Marshall and Adm. Stark, whom the commission had earlier in its report exculpated). The commission declared that among the—

"causes contributory to the success of the Japanese attack were: Emphasis in the warning messages on the probability of aggressive Japanese action in the Far East and on antisabotage measures. Failure of the War Department to reply to the message relating to the antisabotage measures instituted by the commanding general, Hawaiian department."

Had the commission been in a mind to do so, it might have added: Failure of the War and Navy Departments to mention in these messages the probability of an attack on Pearl Harbor.

Finally, it is to be noted that the commission also places among the "contributory causes" the "nonreceipt by the interested parties, prior to the attack, of the warning message of Dec. 7, 1941." As a matter of fact the "nonreceipt" of this warning message was due to inexcusable delays of high authorities in Washington.

Hence, it appears that the President's commission, by direct statements and by implication, admits definitely that the war-warning messages to Gen. Short and Adm. Kimmel were imprecise, indefinite, and constituted no sufficient warning for an all-out alert, particularly the messages to Gen. Short, whose primary duty it was to defend Pearl Harbor and protect the fleet while in the harbor.

The Army Pearl Harbor Board, after a careful examination

and comparison of the war-warning messages, concluded that
the messages of Nov. 27 were "conflicting" and that the statements in the message to Gen. Short were "inadequate" and
"misleading." The Army Board also criticized the War Department for failure to send "specific directives" to outpost commanders.

Despite its conclusion that Gen. Short had displayed lack of
judgment, the Army Board laid against him no charge of dereliction of duty and made no recommendations in that respect.
The Navy Court of Inquiry likewise criticized the war-warning
messages for lack of directives as to actions at Pearl Harbor
and concluded that "no offenses have been committed nor serious blame incurred on the part of any person or persons in the
naval service." It recommended no further proceedings be had
in the matter.

In the testimony and other evidence presented to this committee there is no proof that warrants traversing the judgment
reached by the President's commission, the Army Pearl Harbor
Board, or the Navy Pearl Harbor Court to the effect that the
war-warning messages were not in fact clear and unmistakable
directives for an all-out alert against a probable Japanese attack
on Pearl Harbor.

Again (Conclusion 18, p. 59), the minority report states:

*Whatever errors of judgment the commanders at Hawaii
committed and whatever mismanagement they displayed in preparing for a Japanese attack, attention to chain of responsibility
in the civil and military administration requires taking note of
the fact that they were designated for their posts by high authorities in Washington—all of whom were under obligation to
have a care for competence in the selection of subordinates for
particular positions of responsibility in the armed forces of the
United States.*

This conclusion is self-evident, especially in view of all that
goes before, and needs no comment.

Chapter Seventeen

"KNOWN IMPENDING WAR"

THE UTILITY of the warnings sent to Hawaii may be judged in the light of how the Hawaiian commanders reacted. Short thought he was being warned against sabotage and subversion. He prepared his defenses against them. Kimmel thought he was being warned to get ready for offensive action against the Marshall Islands under the Navy war plan. He prepared himself for his mission, conserving his long-range reconnaissance planes and their crews for the tasks ahead. Neither commander was given to understand that there would be an attack anywhere except in Southeast Asia or the Southwest Pacific—certainly not against Hawaii.

The effectiveness of the messages may also be judged in the light of what Washington knew. The Army Board stated that "the messages actually sent to Hawaii gave only a small fraction"[1] of the information Washington possessed. Adm. Kimmel called the dispatches he received "a pale reflection of actual events."[2] The report of the Navy Court of Inquiry commented upon the need in Hawaii for "information indicating that an attack was to be expected within narrow limits of time,"[3] paraphrasing this again to say that defense plans were "ineffective because they necessarily were drawn on the premise that there would be advance knowledge that an attack was to be expected within narrow limits of time, which was not the case on that morning."[4]

Washington had knowledge of the narrow limits of time within which the attack was to be expected. After November 26 the only possible description of the situation was, in the phrase of the Army Board, "known impending war."[5] That the time and place of the attack were revealed in the fourteen-part Japanese reply of December 6-7 and the 1:00 P.M. pilot message of December 7 is attested by the

243

statement of the Naval Court, "In the early forenoon of December 7, Washington time, the War and Navy Departments had information which appeared to indicate that a break in diplomatic relations was imminent and, by inference and deduction, that an attack in the Hawaiian area could be expected soon."[6]

None of this knowledge possessed by Washington was imparted to Kimmel and Short. They were denied three principal categories of intelligence:

1. Knowledge of the conduct of America's side of the diplomatic negotiations, showing that Japan had been put in a box where it must knuckle under or fight.

2. Knowledge of hundreds of significant Japanese diplomatic code intercepts informing Roosevelt and his circle not only that Japan would fight, but when war was coming.

3. Knowledge of messages to and from Tokyo and its corps of spies in Hawaii, pointing precisely to Pearl Harbor as the target for attack.[7]

That the various so-called war warnings transmitted to Hawaii constituted any sort of real warning was bitterly disputed by Kimmel and Short. Kimmel, in his defense before the congressional committee, said that he realized that information about America's relations with Japan and the plans of the Japanese government were of supreme importance to him. "The Pacific fleet," he said, "was dependent upon the Navy Department in Washington for information derived from intercepted Japanese diplomatic messages."

In February, 1941, soon after he took command of the Pacific fleet, he was told by Vice-Adm. Wilson Brown, just then arrived in Hawaii from Washington, that there was confusion in the Navy Department as to whether he was to be furnished secret information by naval operations or by naval intelligence. On February 19 Kimmel wrote to Adm. Stark, calling his attention to the situation and asking, "Will you kindly fix that responsibility so that there will be no misunderstanding?"[8] Stark replied March 22 that "ONI is fully aware of its responsibility of keeping you adequately informed."[9]

On May 26 Kimmel returned to the subject, saying that he was in a very difficult position, "far removed from the seat of government, in a complex and rapidly changing situation." Without full information from Washington, he said, he would be left in a state of uncertainty, unable to evaluate the situation confronting him. He suggested that it be made a cardinal principle that he "be immediately informed of all important developments as they occur and by the quickest secure means available." He took this letter with him to Washington in June and handed it to Stark, receiving an assurance that he would be given all information.[10]

In July Kimmel received from Stark at least seven dispatches quoting intercepted Japanese diplomatic messages. The Jap messages were referred to by numbers assigned them in Tokyo and the dispatches gave the verbatim text.[11] By such means Washington won Kimmel's confidence. He felt that he was receiving all of the code intercepts which had any bearing on his course of action. Washington did not disabuse him.

As late as the week preceding the Pearl Harbor attack Washington was still giving the appearance of relaying everything to the admiral. On December 1 Stark sent him a dispatch quoting the Japanese ambassador in Thailand on contemplated activities against the British.[12] On December 3 Kimmel received another dispatch quoting by number Tokyo's "circular 2,444" to diplomatic agents. On the same day still another dispatch was forwarded apprising Kimmel of instructions sent to Jap diplomatic and consular posts.[13] True, these intercepts had no bearing on his own situation at Pearl Harbor, but they encouraged him to believe that Washington was, if anything, overzealous in keeping him abreast of all developments. Not until after the sudden Japanese blow against the Pacific fleet did he finally learn how completely he had been deceived. Kimmel said:

> The Navy Department thus engaged in a course of conduct calculated to give me the impression that intelligence from important intercepted Japanese messages was being furnished to me. Under these circumstances a failure to send me important information of this character was not merely a withholding of intelligence. It partook of the nature of an affirmative misrepresentation. I had asked for all vital information. I had been assured that I would have it. I appeared to be receiving it. My current estimate of the situation was formed on this basis. Yet, in fact, the most vital information from the intercepted Japanese messages was not sent to me. This failure not only deprived me of essential facts. It misled me.[15]

Kimmel said that throughout 1941 he received dispatches and letters from Adm. Stark which might be broadly described as "war warnings." These hazarded many guesses as to where Japan might strike, but the only one which mentioned Pearl Harbor was a quotation from the message which Ambassador Grew telegraphed the State Department on January 27, 1941, almost eleven months before

Japan attacked. Grew reported that the Peruvian minister had informed a member of his staff that he "has heard from many sources, including a Japanese source, that in the event of trouble breaking out between the United States and Japan, the Japanese intend to make a surprise attack against Pearl Harbor with all of their strength and employing all of their equipment."[16] Grew said that the Peruvian minister himself considered the rumors fantastic, but felt that he should convey them to Grew's staff.

In relaying this report to Kimmel, Stark said, "The division of naval intelligence places no credence in these rumors. Furthermore, based on known data regarding the present disposition and employment of Japanese army and naval forces, no move against Pearl Harbor appears imminent or planned for in the foreseeable future." Kimmel observed that this estimate as to the improbability of a move against Pearl Harbor was never withdrawn.[17]

The commander of the Pacific fleet stated that when the War and Navy departments wished to put the forces in Hawaii on alert against attack, they could and did use appropriate language to that end. In evidence, he cited the dispatch of June 17, 1940, from Chief of Staff Marshall to Gen. Herron which directed, "Immediately alert complete defensive organization to deal with possible trans-Pacific raid."[18]

This alert in 1940 lasted six weeks. It was then suspended, but was later reinstated for a further period. It was an all-out alert in which troops occupied field positions with full equipment and ammunition. Gen. Herron said that it occasioned no disturbance of the civilian population. This alert was invoked when Gen. Marshall was chief of staff under conditions which in no degree were comparable to the known existing danger in November and December of 1941, when Marshall was still chief of staff. He could have issued his orders then in language equally clear if convinced that Hawaii was in immediate peril.*

Kimmel said:

It is one thing to warn commanders at a particular base of the probable outbreak of war in theaters thousands of miles away, knowing and expecting that they will continue their assigned tasks and missions after the receipt of such warning, and that the very nature of the warning emphasizes to them the necessity for continuing such tasks and missions.

*The minority report of the Joint Congressional Committee (p. 43) points out that in contrast to the "war warnings" of November, 1941, the language of the Herron alert was "crystal clear."

It is quite another thing to warn commanders at a particular base of an attack to be expected in their own locality. In 1941, we of the Pacific fleet had a plethora of premonitions, of generalized warnings, and forebodings that Japan might embark on aggressive action in the Far East at any one of the variously predicted dates. After receipt of such warnings, we were expected to continue with renewed intensity and zeal our own training program and preparations for war rather than to go on an all-out local alert against attack. . . .

Throughout 1941, the Navy Department had several courses open. It could furnish me directly with the best evidence of Japanese intentions and plans—the intercepted Japanese military and diplomatic messages. This would have given me an opportunity to judge for myself the gravity and intensity of the crisis as December 7, 1941, approached, and the probability of a Japanese attack on Hawaii. The Navy Department failed to do this. The Navy Department did not permit me to evaluate for myself the intercepted Japanese military and diplomatic messages.

Another course of action then remained. That was to issue an order which would have directed dispositions of the fleet to guard against an attack in Hawaii. The message of June 17, 1940, "Be on the alert against hostile overseas raids," was such an order. It would have had the same effect in December of 1941 as it had in June of 1940. Such an order was not given.

It then remained for the War and Navy departments to order Short and himself to execute their joint coastal frontier defense plan, or to order the fleet and Army to mobilize under the Pacific war plan, which would have placed the fleet on a war basis without authorizing acts of war. Neither of these was done.[19]

Discussing the so-called "war warning" of November 27, Kimmel said,

The phrase "war warning" cannot be made a catch-all for all the contingencies hindsight may suggest. . . . The statement . . . that ·negotiations had ceased on November 27 was a pale reflection of actual events; so partial a statement as to be misleading. The parties had not merely stopped talking. They were at swordspoints. So far as Japan was concerned, the talking that went on after November 26 was play-acting. It was a Japanese stratagem to conceal a blow which Japan was preparing to deliver. The stratagem did not fool the Navy Department. The Navy Department knew the scheme. The Pacific fleet was exposed to this Japanese stratagem because the Navy Department did not pass on its knowledge of the Japanese trick.[20]

In six separate dispatches, on November 5, 11, 15, 16, 22, and 24, Japan specifically established a deadline of November 25, later advanced to November 28, Washington time, by which its ambassadors in Washington were to have concluded an agreement with the United States for a settlement of Pacific problems. On November 22 Tokyo advised the ambassadors that if no such agreement were reached by the time of the deadline, "things are automatically going to happen." Messages from November 28 on, which were intercepted and decoded, informed the American government that Hull's proposal of November 26 was completely unsatisfactory to Japan and that an actual rupture of negotiations would occur upon receipt of the Japanese reply. The dispatches showed that Japan attached great importance to the continuance of negotiations to conceal from the United States whatever plan automatically took effect on November 28.

As time went on after November 28, Japanese insistence that the ambassadors keep up the pretense of negotiating to divert the suspicion of the United States constituted evidence that the operation which Japan had put into effect on November 28 would require a substantial time interval before its results became apparent to the American government, and that in its initial phases the Japanese evidently believed that it could be effectively concealed.

There was another category of intelligence available in Washington which would have pointed directly to Pearl Harbor as the objective of this mysterious plan.* These were the spy messages between Tokyo and Hawaii. No word of them was sent to Kimmel or Short.

On September 24 the Japanese government instructed Consul General Nagoa Kita in Honolulu to divide the waters of Pearl Harbor into five sub-areas in reporting on warships at anchor or tied up at wharves, docks, or buoys. Area "A" was the term prescribed to delineate the waters between Ford Island and the arsenal; "B" the waters south and west of Ford Island; "C," East Loch; "D," Middle Loch; and "E," West Loch and communicating water routes.

"With regard to warships and aircraft carriers," the consul was instructed, "we would like to have you report on those at anchor (these are not so important), tied up at wharves, buoys, and in docks. (Designate types and classes briefly. If possible we would like to have

---

*"In the days immediately preceding Pearl Harbor, Japan made no effort to conceal the movements or presence of her naval forces in South East Asia (Tr., Vol. 3, p. 453). The movements of her troops in Indo-China at that time were the subject of diplomatic exchanges between the United States and Japan (For. Rel. II, p. 779). Yet the intercepts showed that some Japanese plan went into effect automatically on Nov. 29, from which Japan hoped to divert American suspicion by a pretext of continued negotiations" (Min., p. 26).

you make mention of the fact when there are two or more vessels alongside the same wharf.)"[21]

On September 29 Kita replied to this dispatch by listing a detailed system of symbols to be used thereafter in designating the location of vessels in Pearl Harbor.[22] On November 15 Tokyo sent the following dispatch to Honolulu, "As relations between Japan and the United States are most critical, make your 'ships in harbor report' irregular but at the rate of twice a week. Although you already are no doubt aware, please take extra care to maintain secrecy."[23] On November 18 another Tokyo message directed Honolulu: "Please report on the following areas as to vessels anchored therein: Area N, Pearl Harbor, Mamala Bay (Honolulu), and the areas adjacent thereto. (Make your investigation with great secrecy.)"[24]

On November 18 the Japanese consul general in Honolulu reported in detail to Tokyo the ships in harbor and the course and speed of vessels entering the harbor, and their distances apart.[25] On November 20 Tokyo instructed Honolulu to make a comprehensive investigation of fleet bases in the neighborhood of the Hawaiian military reservation.[26]

The most significant of these instructions to Honolulu agents concerning the berthing of the fleet was sent on November 29. It said, "We have been receiving reports from you on ship movements, but in future will you also *report even when there are no movements.*"*[27] The date of this dispatch was the same as that on which Tokyo had stated that "things are automatically going to happen." What was happening was that the Japanese fleet was bearing down on Pearl Harbor for the attack, and Tokyo wanted assurance that the warships of the Pacific fleet would be found where they were expected to be —set up as stationary targets at their harbor moorings.

On December 2 the spies in Hawaii were informed:

In view of the present situation, the presence in port of warships, airplane carriers, and cruisers is of the utmost importance. Hereafter, to the utmost of your ability, let me know day by day. Wire in each case whether or not there are any observation balloons above Pearl Harbor or if there are any indications that any will be sent up. Also advise me whether or not the warships are provided with anti-mine nets.[28]

At 7:22 P.M., December 6, the night before the Japanese carrier assault on Pearl Harbor, American intelligence intercepted this report by the spies to Tokyo:

*Italics supplied.

The following ships were observed at anchor: nine battle-ships, three light cruisers, three submarine tenders, seventeen destroyers, and in addition there were four light cruisers and two destroyers lying at the docks. The heavy cruisers and air-plane carriers have all left. It appears that no air reconnaissance is being conducted by the fleet air arm.[29]

At 12:42 A.M., December 7, American intelligence intercepted an-other message from Kita which was a clear give-away. After dis-cussing the lack of balloon barrage defense, the consul at Honolulu reported as follows to Tokyo:

However, even though they have actually made preparations, because they must control the air over the water and land run-ways of the airports in the vicinity of Pearl Harbor, Hickam, Ford and Ewa, there are limits to the balloon defense of Pearl Harbor. I imagine that in all probability there is considerable opportunity left to take advantage for a surprise attack against these places.[30]

On December 4, Washington intercepted the "east winds rain" code report that apprised Roosevelt that Japan had determined upon a state of war with the United States, omitting a formal declaration. After the decoding of the long series of messages from the Jap spies telling of the fleet disposition in Pearl Harbor, there could be no ques-tion where the attack would come. The spy message of December 6 set up our warships in harbor for the attack of the following day. Yet no word of warning went from Washington to Kimmel and Short until too late.

Washington's excuse is that the last two messages were not decoded until December 8.[31] They were intercepted by the Army monitoring station at San Francisco and copies were mailed to Washington. When the Army signal intelligence service heard they were on the way, San Francisco was ordered to put them on a teletype which had been installed that very day. Army translators were called back on duty in Washington that night, but spent their time decoding Jap diplomatic messages.

Although the information in the messages had been requested by Tokyo in a message intercepted at Hawaii on December 2, the request for this intelligence was forwarded to Washington by air mail for decoding and did not arrive there until December 23. Army intelli-gence thus was deprived of the tipoff that the responses from Hono-lulu would point to Japanese intentions to attack the fleet and base.[32]

A third message of similar purport was translated in the rough at Washington by 1:00 P.M. on Saturday, the 6th. This message was sent from Honolulu on December 3 by Consul General Kita. The message arranged light signals to be shown in windows at night which could only have served to guide an enemy offshore attacking force. Testimony was given by Army cryptographers that they were instructed to hold up distribution of the translation until they achieved a "smooth translation."[33]

"If you could have had that information," Senator Ferguson asked Gen. Short, "it would have indicated an attack on Hawaii, would it not?"

"Yes, sir," Short agreed.

Referring to the message of December 6 stating that there were no barrage balloons up and that there was opportunity for a surprise attack, Ferguson asked Short, "If that had been decoded and sent to you, or the information from it, would that have meant anything to you?"

"That would practically have meant a surprise attack was in store for us or was a certainty," Short said.

"And would that alone have alerted you?"

"Very decidedly."[34]

Adm. Kimmel testified before the congressional committee that in the volume of intercepted Japanese dispatches eliciting and obtaining information about American military installations and naval movements, the dispatches concerning Pearl Harbor, on and after September 24, stand out, apart from all others. He said:

> No other harbor or base in American territory or possessions was divided into sub-areas by Japan. In no other area was the Japanese government seeking information as to whether two or more vessels were alongside the same wharf. . . . With the dispatch of September 24 and those which followed, there was a significant and ominous change in the character of the information which the Japanese government sought and obtained. The espionage then directed was of an unusual character and outside the realm of reasonable suspicion. It was no longer merely directed to ascertaining the general whereabouts of ships of the fleet. It was directed to the presence of particular ships and particular areas; to such minute detail as what ships were double-docked at the same wharf.
>
> In the period immediately preceding the attack, the Jap consul general in Hawaii was directed by Tokyo to report even when there were no movements of ships in and out of Pearl Harbor. These Japanese instructions and reports pointed to an

attack by Japan upon the ships in Pearl Harbor. The information sought and obtained, with such painstaking detail, had no other conceivable usefulness from a military viewpoint. Its utility was in planning and executing an attack upon the ships in port. Its effective value was lost completely when the ships left their reported berthings in Pearl Harbor.

No one had a more direct and immediate interest in the security of the fleet in Pearl Harbor than its commander-in-chief. No one had a greater right than I to know that Japan had carved up Pearl Harbor into sub-areas and was seeking and receiving reports as to the precise berthings in that harbor of ships of the fleet. I had been sent Mr. Grew's report earlier in the year with positive advice from the Navy Department that no credence was to be placed in the rumored Japanese plans for an attack on Pearl Harbor. I was told then that no Japanese move against Pearl Harbor appeared "imminent or planned for in the foreseeable future." Certainly I was entitled to know when information in the Navy Department completely altered the information and advice previously given to me.[35]

The irony of Kimmel's predicament was that the information which the Roosevelt administration denied the commander-in-chief of the United States fleet was being freely given to the British all through 1941. Gen. Miles testified that the secret American process for decoding Japanese communications was given to Britain as early as January.[36]

Kimmel told the congressional committee that he, as commander-in-chief of the fleet, was just "as entitled to receive copies of intercepted Japanese communications as the British Admiralty."[37] Knowledge of these dispatches, the admiral said, would have radically changed his estimate of the situation in the Pacific and would even have afforded an opportunity to "ambush the Japanese striking force as it ventured to Hawaii."

Gen. Short protested against receiving the same kind of treatment.

While the War Department G-2 may not have felt bound to let me know about the routine operations of the Japanese in keeping track of our naval ships, they should certainly have let me know that the Japanese were getting reports of the exact location of the ships in Pearl Harbor, which might indicate more than just keeping track, because such details would be useful only for sabotage, or for air and submarine attack, in Hawaii. As early as October 9, G-2 in Washington knew of this Japanese espionage. This message, analyzed critically, is really a bombing plan for Pearl Harbor.[38]

The Hawaiian commanders, as has been seen, were also denied knowledge of the final Jap diplomatic note of December 6-7, followed by the pilot message directing that the statement be handed in to Hull at 1:00 P.M. The Army Board has shown that there could have been no misconception as to the meaning to be read into these dispatches. "It was well known," the report states,

> that Japan's entry into all wars of the past has been character-
> ized by the first overt act of war coming simultaneously with
> the declaration. The services, both Army and Navy, were well
> aware of this Japanese characteristic. It was, therefore, to be
> expected that an unexpected attack would be made by Japan as
> the first indication of a breach of relations.[39]

The breach of relations would come at 1:00 P.M., Washington time. Therefore, that was the hour for war and the first overt act. Kimmel asserted:

> All this information was denied to Gen. Short and me. Had
> we not been denied this many things would have been different.
> Had we been furnished this information as little as two or three
> hours before the attack, which was easily feasible and possible,
> much could have been done.[40]

What Kimmel could have done in those crucial two hours has been told by Adm. Wilkinson. He testified that Kimmel could have sent his major fleet units out of Pearl Harbor and into the open sea at ten-minute intervals, with destroyers and other smaller craft leaving si-multaneously. In two hours Kimmel could have got twelve major ships and as many as twelve to fourteen smaller vessels out of the confined harbor, where they were trapped by the Jap torpedo and bombing planes.[41]

Gen. Short's testimony showed how helpless the fleet was, moored to its berthings in harbor. He said that the Japs' low-flying torpedo planes probably would have been able to get through our anti-aircraft barrage even if the harbor defenses had been on a full alert, because our anti-aircraft was ineffective against low-flying aircraft.[42]

If the ships had left harbor, however, the story, Adm. Kimmel says, would have been different. In the open sea they would have been dispersed, they would have been able to maneuver against at-tack, they would have been expecting attack, and they would have been on a full alert, with battle stations manned and all guns firing. A good number of the planes based on Hawaiian fields would have been in the air to meet the oncoming attack force. Kimmel said:

I surely was entitled to know of the hour fixed by Japan for the probable outbreak of war against the United States. I cannot understand now—I have never understood—I may never understand—why I was deprived of the information available in the Navy Department in Washington on Saturday night and Sunday morning. . . . The Pacific fleet deserved a fighting chance. It was entitled to receive from the Navy Department the best information available. Such information had been urgently requested. I had been assured that it would be furnished me. We faced our problems in the Pacific confident that such assurance would be faithfully carried out. . . .

If this investigation succeeds in preserving for the future the pertinent facts about Pearl Harbor, I shall be content. History, with the perspective of the long tomorrow, will enter the final directive in my case. I am confident of that verdict.[43]

Gen. Short faced the congressional committee with a similarly resolute spirit. He said:

As a matter of the interests of the country and as a loyal soldier, I maintained a steadfast silence for four years and I bore the load of public censure during this time and I would have continued to bear it so long as I thought the question of national security was involved. However, the war is now ended.[44]

Short was especially severe in his criticism of Washington for failing to correct his anti-sabotage alert and then blaming him for not having instituted a higher degree of readiness:

When any department of the Army has issued an order on any matter of importance, it has performed only one-half of its function. The follow-up to see that the order has been carried out as desired is at least as important as issuing the order. The War Department had nine days in which to check up on the alert status in Hawaii and to make sure that the measures taken by me were what was desired, which it did not do. The check-up would have required no more than a reading of my report of measures taken.

I felt, and still feel, that if the chief of staff wanted an all-out alert in Hawaii, he would have ordered it himself and not expected me to make the decision, knowing as he did how relatively limited was my information as compared to that available to him.[45]

Marshall himself, when examined before the congressional committee, inferentially conceded the justice of this complaint. He was questioned by Representative Keefe as follows:

KEEFE: When you issued the alert on the 17th of June, 1940, you used the language, "To deal with possible trans-Pacific raid."

MARSHALL: That is correct, sir.

KEEFE: Yes. Well, now, then, let us put it this way without splitting words: Gen. Marshall, on the morning of the 28th of November you had tremendously more information as to the possibility of an attack by the Japanese than you had in June, 1940?

MARSHALL: That is correct, sir.

KEEFE: If you had information in June, 1940, as to the possibilities of a trans-Pacific raid, you had a mountain of evidence on the 27th of November, did you not, to the same effect?

MARSHALL: That is correct.[46]

Marshall was interrogated by Keefe as follows concerning his responsibility to check up on the measures taken by Short and reported by him in response to War Department message No. 472:

KEEFE: So we get down to the simple fact that here is a message from your commanding general in the bastion of defense in the Pacific to which all of our defenses, as you have testified, were tied, in which he tells you that he is alerted to prevent sabotage; liaison with Navy. Now in all fairness, Gen. Marshall, in the exercise of ordinary care as chief of staff ought you not to have proceeded to investigate further and give further orders to Gen. Short when it appeared that he was only alerted against sabotage?

MARSHALL: As I stated earlier, that was my opportunity to intervene and I did not do it.

KEEFE: Well, now, you say that was your opportunity. That was your responsibility, was it not?

MARSHALL: You can put it that way, sir.

KEEFE: Well, I don't want to put it that way. I am asking you. You used the words "that was your opportunity," I do not want an opportunity to arise in the future discussion of this matter to have a conflict of words and not to be able to understand just what you meant. Do I understand that your use of the word "opportunity" is synonymous with responsibility?

MARSHALL: Mr. Keefe, I had an immense number of papers going over my desk every day informing me what was happening anywhere in the world. . . . I noted them and initialed them; those that I thought the Secretary of War ought specifically to see I put them out for him to see, to be sure that he would see it in case by any chance he did not see the same message.

I was not passing the responsibility on to the Secretary of War. I merely wanted him to know.

Now the same thing related to these orders of the War Department. I was responsible. I was responsible for the actions of the general staff throughout on large matters and on the small matters. I was responsible for those, but I am not a bookkeeping machine and it is extremely difficult, it is an extremely difficult thing for me to take each thing in its turn and give it exactly the attention that it had merited.

Now in this particular case a very tragic thing occurred, there is no question about that, there is no question in regard to my responsibility as chief of staff. I am not attempting to evade that at all, but I do not think it is quite characterized in the manner that you have expressed yourself.

KEEFE: Well, now, let me put it in another way. You have now stated it was your responsibility as chief of staff to see to it that Gen. Short out there in Hawaii, which you have described as being your bastion of defense, to see that he was alerted, and if he misinterpreted your order to see that that order was carried out.

MARSHALL: That is my responsibility, sir.

KEEFE: Now, I have stated it correctly, haven't I?

MARSHALL: Yes, sir, you have.[47]

Gen. Gerow admitted that there had been a failure to follow up the warning sent to Short November 27. "If there was any responsibility to be attached to the War Department for failure to send an inquiry to Gen. Short," he said, "the responsibility must rest on war plans divisions, and I accept that responsibility as chief of war plans division."[48]

When Representative Keefe asked Marshall about Gerow's assumption of responsibility, the chief of staff stated, "He had a direct responsibility and I had the full responsibility."[49]

"The War Department," commented Short, "had four years to admit that a follow-up should have been made on the November 27 message and on my report of the same date, but no such admission of responsibility was made public until Gen. Gerow and Gen. Marshall testified before this committee."[50]

As to his conclusion that sabotage was the principal danger, Short said that 37 per cent of the population of Hawaii (about 161,000 persons) was of Japanese descent. Of these 40,000 were aliens. Many lived in close proximity to air fields and defense installations.[51] Marshall himself on May 3, 1941, had described sabotage as the primary danger in Hawaii. In an aide mémoire to President Roosevelt, the chief of staff said: "In point of sequence, sabotage is first to be expected and may, within a very limited time, cause great damage. On this account, and in order to assure strong control, it would be highly desirable to set up a military control of the islands prior to the likelihood of our involvement in the Far East."[52]

Marshall, writing Short on February 7, 1941, just after the general had assumed command in Hawaii, said, "The risk of sabotage and the risk involved in a surprise raid by air and by submarine constitute the real perils of the situation."[53]

Short said:

> I felt that I had a right to expect the War Department to inform me by the most rapid means possible if a real crisis arose in Japanese relations. I did not expect that when the crisis arose the message would remain in the hands of Gen. Miles and Col. Bratton without action from 9:00 A.M. till 11:25 A.M., and that when action was finally taken the desire for secrecy would be considered more important than the element of time. Had the message in regard to the Japanese ultimatum and the burning of their code machines been given me by telephone as an urgent message in the clear without loss of time for encoding and decoding, delivery, etc., or if I had been directed by telephone to go on an all-out alert for a dawn trans-Pacific raid, without being told the reason, I would have had approximately four hours to make detailed preparations to meet an immediate attack.

In that time, Short said, he could have warmed up his planes and got them into the air, just as Kimmel could have put to sea with his ships. Short continued:

> My decision to put the Hawaiian Department on an alert to prevent sabotage was based upon a belief that sabotage was our gravest danger and that air attack was not imminent. I realize that my decision was wrong. I had every reason to believe, however, that my estimate of the situation coincided with that of the War Department general staff, which had the signal advantage of superior sources of intelligence as to enemy intentions.
>
> I know it is hindsight, but if I had been furnished the information which the War Department had, I do not believe that I would have made a mistaken estimate of the situation. To make my meaning clear, I want to add that I do not believe that my estimate was due to any carelessness on my part or on

the part of the senior Army and Navy officers with whom I consulted. Nor do I believe that my error was a substantial factor in causing the damage which our Pacific fleet suffered during the attack.[54]

Senator Ferguson contrasted the hampering restrictions laid by the November 27 warning upon the Pacific fleet and Hawaii garrison with the original Roosevelt administration theory that the fleet, at Pearl Harbor, would constitute a "deterrent" to Japan.

Ferguson asked Short how he could have committed an "overt act" against Japan. The general said that he could have committed it only by sending out his long-range bombers, with a subsequent attack by them upon a Japanese ship or submarine, or by arresting consular agents or Japanese nationals and thus occasioning offense to Tokyo.

Short said that the "overt act" restriction in the November 27 warning "meant to me simply that the War Department was extremely anxious to avoid war, and they did not want any international incident to happen in Hawaii that might provoke war or might give the Japanese an opportunity to claim that we had started the war."

Senator Ferguson recalled that "we had put the fleet in Hawaii in order that we might show Japan our strength, and we were backing up our diplomacy by the fleet being out there." He asked why, then, with a strong army in Hawaii, the United States should have instructed it to act as if "we were weak and afraid."

Emphasizing the contradiction, Ferguson said to Short,

> In one case, we put the Navy in there as a symbol of strength, and in the other case—in your case—we tried to conceal the fact that you had a strong army and you were ready for anything that might happen.
> Now, would it have been possible that if we had a full mobilization of the Army—some 40,000 men in Hawaii—if we had shown that we were on the alert for anything that might come, we would never have had an attack at Pearl Harbor?

Short replied:

> I think it quite probable that if that had been reported to the Japanese, they would have turned back the attacking force.

Ferguson asked Short if the warning of November 27 had omitted the restrictions against alarming the public or disclosing intent, and if Short had then fully alerted his command, with the soldiers under arms, the machine guns manned, the radar working twenty-four hours a day, "then would you have come to the conclusion, in your opinion as an Army general, that they would have turned back?"

"There would have been a very excellent chance that they would have turned back," said Short. "That would have been the tendency, because they would have felt, or they would be sure, that they would take heavy losses. Surprise was the only opportunity they had to succeed."[55]

Ferguson then asked Short to assess the blame for having given the Japanese the inestimable advantage of surprise. The Senator recalled that Short had said, "I do not feel that I have been treated fairly or with justice by the War Department. I was singled out as an example, as the scapegoat for the disaster."

"You are covering very broad ground when you use the words 'War Department,'" said Ferguson. "I wish you would be specific and tell me who you had in mind."

"I had in mind the general staff in particular," Short replied, "because they were primarily responsible for the policies pursued by the War Department."

"And the general staff was headed by whom?"

"Gen. Marshall."

"And who else would be in there?"

"Gen. Gerow as head of the war plans division had the direct responsibility of keeping me informed. Gen. Miles, the head of G-2, had a very direct responsibility."

"What about the Secretary of War?" asked Ferguson. "Is he included there in the words 'War Department?'"

"As far as technical things went, I would not have expected him to be as fully aware of the significance of technical things. I would expect him to be fully aware of any policy."

"So, as far as the policy was concerned, he would be included in that?"

"Yes, sir."[56]

It is time to consider the policy-makers.

Chapter Eighteen

THE LIGHT THAT FAILED

THE ARMY Operations Manual in use on December 7, 1941, makes the following pertinent observation:

> From adequate and timely military intelligence the commander is able to draw logical conclusions concerning enemy lines of action. Military intelligence is thus an essential factor in the estimate of the situation and in the conduct of operations.[1]

In his statement to the congressional committee, Gen. Short said,

> There was a vast amount of highly significant information available in the War Department which no responsible military man could exclude from consideration in forming an estimate of the situation. The War Department was aware of the fact that I did not have this information and had already decided that I should not get this information. It was therefore their duty not only to make the estimate of the situation but to make the decision as to what military action it required, and to give me orders to go on an all-out alert instead of permitting my sabotage alert to stand. This was in line with their centralized peacetime control system.[2]

That Washington withheld the vital intelligence in its possession from the Hawaiian commanders was admitted by Gen. Miles. "It was not considered necessary that the commanding generals know the day-to-day diplomatic developments," he said, "but only information which might call for military action on their part."[3]

Discussing the information denied Kimmel and himself, Short said,

> If this information is connected up with the knowledge gained of the definite Japanese intention to expand southward,

it is clear that the War and Navy departments must have known that war was a certainty, and that they, with this exclusive intelligence, wanted to make the estimate and decision as to American military defensive action. This explains their care in ordering me not to disclose intent, alarm the population, or do anything which Japan could use as propaganda that the United States had provoked war.[4]

This policy permitted a small circle in Washington to restrict the "Magic" intelligence to themselves, to interpret it, and to issue directives to the field in the light of their evaluation. The evidence was abundant and its meaning clear. Jap spying was extensive and effective, but in the competition for information American intelligence had a great edge over the Japs. Our intelligence failure was not in acquiring the information; it was in evaluating it, and, most of all, in transmitting orders based on the known situation to the commanders who would be forced to meet the coming assault. This failure was in Washington.

The tragedy of December 7 is the measure of Washington's failure. That failure was confessed when the Manual of Army Field Regulations was revised June 29, 1942. A section of this manual which was not in effect on December 7 reads:

> In time of strained relations, the War Department must exhaust every possible source of information to keep itself and commanders of field forces advised of air, military, and naval dispositions and movements of potential enemies and of the trend of diplomatic relations.

This section, taking further cognizance of the Pearl Harbor defeat, added that field commanders must keep informed of the "possibility of a surprise attack" prior to a war declaration, and "must dispose their forces so that a sudden attack will be defeated."[5]

Who was responsible for the failure? Gen. Miles has supplied the answer. He told the congressional committee that the Japanese code intercepts went to only nine persons: President Roosevelt, Secretary of War Stimson, Secretary of the Navy Knox, Secretary of State Hull, Chief of Staff Marshall, Chief of Naval Operations Stark, Gen. Gerow, Col. R. S. Bratton, and Miles himself.[6]

To these Capt. Alwin Kramer, the Navy's custodian of secret material in trips to the White House, added Harry Hopkins, the President's confidant. Kramer testified[7] that although Hopkins was not on the official list of recipients, he regularly saw the decoded messages.

Kramer's instructions to show "Magic" to Hopkins came from Chief of Naval Operations Stark. The captain said that he even made two special trips to the naval hospital at Bethesda to deliver files of intercepts to Hopkins while the latter was a patient.

Not even the existence of the messages, Miles said, was known to Gen. Short and Adm. Kimmel in Hawaii. Miles said that Gen. Marshall's policy was to confine knowledge that the United States was decoding Japanese communications to a very few persons in order to conceal a "military secret of incalculable value."

"Who made the decision that these messages should not be·sent to Hawaii as they were intercepted and translated, as far as the Army is concerned?" Miles was asked.

"That followed from the general policy laid down by the chief of staff that these messages and the fact of the· existence· of these messages or our ability to decode them should be confined to the least possible number of persons; no distribution should be made outside of Washington."[8]

The emphasis given by Miles was to secrecy for secrecy's sake. It was considered more important to preserve the secret that the messages were being intercepted and decoded than to make intelligent use of the information thus provided. A similar admission was made by Marshall in explaining his failure to telephone the warning of December 7 to Hawaii. As Gen. Short remarked, "There was a feeling still at that time that secrecy was more important than the time element in getting the information to us as rapidly as possible."[9]

Miles made the astonishing statement to the congressional committee that the Army and Navy top command attached no particular significance to the intercepted messages pointing to an attack on Pearl Harbor. It was a regrettable error, he confessed, in view of what happened, but it was "perfectly normal" for the Japs to be seeking and acquiring such information at the time. Only "hindsight," he remarked, gave the decoded messages their significance as preparations for a surprise attack.[10]

The naval communications intelligence division and the signal intelligence unit of the Army intercepted, decoded, and translated the messages, Miles said, and then delivered them to G-2. Col. Bratton supervised the transmission of the texts to those on the distribution list.

Gen. Miles said that the intercepts were conveyed in locked pouches to the nine persons intrusted with their contents, the copies for President Roosevelt being delivered to Maj. Gen. Edwin M. Watson, Presidential aide. After being read, the copies were returned to Army intelligence and burned, one file copy being retained.

Elaborating on his explanation of the necessity for strict secrecy in handling the code intercepts, Miles said that he was aware that in July, 1941, the Navy stopped sending summaries of the intercepts to Adm. Kimmel.

"I remember clearly," Miles said, "that in that summer a joint policy was developed of closing in on the secret."[11]

Kimmel and Short were not advised of the policy, Miles said. It restricted circulation of the significant intercepted messages to a handful of high officials.

Here is conclusive evidence that Mr. Roosevelt and the little circle of Washington insiders had decreed that no one except themselves should have access to the crucial information which was coming into their hands, unknown to the Japs and to our own field commanders. In reaching that decision they could not escape the responsibility that went with it. It was their duty, and theirs alone, to evaluate the intelligence they were getting, to come to proper decisions on the basis of it, to adopt a reasonable program to defend the country and its outposts against the hostile action that was explicit in the decoded messages, and, above all, to transmit to the responsible field commanders who would be compelled to meet the coming attack such information and orders as it was absolutely essential for them to have if they were to discharge their duties.

In assuming these responsibilities, the White House circle relieved Adm. Kimmel and Gen. Short of the duty of making their own decisions. They had no information on which to do so. The commanders were as much in the dark as the public as to what was going on. They depended upon Washington for guidance and they didn't get it.

The completeness of the failure in Washington to discharge the duties imposed by accepting "Magic" responsibility was forcibly pointed out to the congressional committee by two witnesses, Adm. Smith, chief of staff to Adm. Kimmel, and Capt. E. M. Zacharias, Navy expert on Japan. Smith said:

> There was entirely too much secrecy before Pearl Harbor in all branches of government connected with national defense. I can see no reason for breaking ciphers in Washington unless some use is going to be made of the contents. Adm. Kimmel never saw those messages. I never learned of them until this committee started its inquiry. We should certainly have had this information.

I think it was generally conceded that not all the Navy's brains were in Washington at that time. Adm. Kimmel had a competent staff, and he and his subordinates were concerned with what was happening, or what might happen, in the Pacific.[12]

Senator Ferguson, in examining Capt. Zacharias, pointed out that decoded copies of intercepted Japanese communications had been furnished "in the raw" to President Roosevelt and other high officials charged with determining the national policy, that is, without evaluation by intelligence officers. Zacharias observed that this procedure "took the responsibility away from intelligence officers."[13] The corollary was that Roosevelt and his amateur associates, in taking the responsibility away from specialists trained to make a proper evaluation of enemy intelligence, assumed that responsibility themselves.[14] This was made clear by Zacharias in saying that the system "resulted in evaluation by persons not knowing the background of Japanese history, philosophy, and intentions."[15]

These men could not read the Japanese intercepts with an undivided mind. They were preoccupied with procurement, training, and the hundred and one details of getting ready for the war into which they were rushing the country. They did not stop to take stock of the effects of their policy.

A bald judgment on the stupidity of the evaluation given the code intercepts was delivered by Maj. Gen. Cramer in one of his three secret reports to Secretary Stimson.

> The most that can be said relative to the Top Secret information available in Washington is that a keener and more incisive analysis by the intelligence sections of either service of the over-all picture presented by these intercepts . . . might have led to an anticipation of the possibility, at least, of an attack on Pearl Harbor at or about the time it actually occurred.[16]

Gen. Cramer was especially severe in discussing the shortcomings of Gen. Gerow, who was responsible for keeping Short informed. Referring to the Army Board's criticism of Gerow, Cramer said:

> But since we know in retrospect that Short was not, apparently, fully alive to an imminent outside threat and since the war plans division had received substantial information from the intelligence section, G-2, the [Army] Board argues that had this additional information been transmitted to Short it might have convinced him not only that war was imminent but that there was a real possibility of a surprise air attack on Hawaii.

In retrospect it is difficult to preceive any substantial reason for not sending Short this additional information or, in the alternative, checking to see whether Short was sufficiently alive to the danger. Gen. Gerow did neither. In my opinion Gen. Gerow showed a lack of imagination in failing to realize that had the Top Secret information been sent to Short it could not have had any other than a beneficial effect.

Gen. Gerow also showed lack of imagination in failing to make the proper deductions from the Japanese intercepts. For instance, the message of September 24 from Tokyo to Honolulu requesting reports on vessels in Pearl Harbor and dividing Pearl Harbor into various subdivisions for that purpose, coupled with the message of November 15 to Honolulu to make "the ships in harbor report" irregular, and the further message of November 29 to Honolulu asking for reports even when there were no ship movements, might readily have suggested to an imaginative person a possible Jap design on Pearl Harbor.

Failure to appreciate the significance of such messages shows a lack of the type of skill in anticipating and preparing against eventualities which we have a right to expect in an officer at the head of the war plans division. If this criticism seems harsh, it only illustrates the advisability of Gen. Gerow transmitting the Top Secret information to Short.[17]

Despite this castigation, coming on top of the Army Board's finding that Gerow was guilty of signal failure in the discharge of his duties as war plans officer,[18] Gerow was rewarded after Pearl Harbor with appointment as commander of the 15th Army and later was named commandant of the command and general staff school at Fort Leavenworth, the Army's postgraduate school.

Senator Ferguson asked Gen. Short whether intelligence was not to be used for two functions: First, to determine when war might come; second, to determine where war might come. Gen. Short said that these were the duties of intelligence, but that he would add a third duty—to determine the strength that the prospective enemy might bring to bear on its adversary at the point of attack.

Ferguson then asked Short whether the five so-called warning messages which he received from the Army high command before December 7 told him when war was coming. Short replied that the message of November 27 indicated that war would be coming reasonably soon, although it left open a possibility that hostilities would be avoided.

"Did they tell you where war was coming?"

"At no time after July 8 did a War Department message directed to me ever point in any direction," Short replied.

"Would you say that the alert of June 17, 1940, told Gen. Herron where war was coming?"

"It told him definitely that they were afraid of a trans-Pacific raid on the island of Oahu," Short responded.

"And that was definite information?"

"Absolutely."

"Not the date, but definite information as to where?"

"Yes, sir."

"Did you have any such warning?" Ferguson asked.

"I did not."[19]

Of all the high officials in Washington who knew the course of the Japanese-American diplomatic negotiations and were able to interpret it in the light of "Magic," Secretary Hull alone showed some dim discernment of the outcome. On November 7 he told a cabinet meeting that relations with Japan were extremely critical and that there was "imminent possibility" that Japan might at any moment start a new military movement of conquest by force.[20] Again, at a meeting of the war cabinet on November 21, Hull told the President, Stimson, and Knox to be on guard lest the Japanese "stampede the hell out of our scattered forces in the Pacific."[21] As D-day grew closer, however, Mr. Hull's clairvoyance diminished in proportion, so that finally, on December 7, when the intelligence of the last few days had left no question of what was coming, he professed to be shocked.[22]

It is now known that it was clear to President Roosevelt on the night of December 6 that war was at hand. The story of the President's response to the first thirteen parts of the Japanese reply to Hull's counter-proposals of November 26 was finally told to the congressional committee on February 15, 1946, by Comdr. L. R. Schulz, assistant naval aide at the White House in the closing months of 1941.

For four years, through successive investigations, no one had ever sought out Schulz or tried to learn what went on in the White House the night before the Pearl Harbor attack. On February 12, 1946, Senator Ferguson succeeded in having Schulz called as a witness before the congressional committee. The commander was then serving on the battleship "Indiana," which put into San Francisco and landed him in response to the congressional subpoena. Schulz boarded a plane and arrived in Washington a few hours before giving his testimony.

It developed that Capt. Kramer delivered the thirteen parts to

Schulz at the White House about 9:30 P.M. on December 6. Schulz took the pouch containing the Japanese note to Roosevelt's second-floor study, where he unlocked it with a key given him by Capt. John R. Beardall, the President's naval aide, who had gone off duty that afternoon after telling Schulz an important message was coming from the Navy Department that Roosevelt should see at once.

The President read the message at his desk while his confidential adviser, Harry Hopkins, paced the floor. Roosevelt handed the message to Hopkins, who also read it. The President then exclaimed, "This means war!"

Hopkins agreed with Roosevelt's statement. The President's confidant then said, "Since war is to come at the convenience of the Japs, it is too bad we can't strike the first blow and avert a Japanese surprise attack."

The President nodded and said, "No, we can't do that. We are a democracy. We are a peaceful people. We have a good record."[23]

The situation had been so managed that now America was to be attacked and perforce would be in the war. Roosevelt would then be absolved of his promises that Americans were not to be sent into foreign wars.

From Schulz's account, it is known that Roosevelt reached for the telephone and attempted to get Adm. Stark. He was informed that the chief of operations was at the National Theater, where "The Student Prince" was playing. He decided not to have Stark paged, lest the action alarm the public. He stated that he would get the admiral later. Comdr. Schulz then left.

What went on at the White House and among the officials of the government and of the Army and Navy high command that night is a mystery which still awaits solution. The night of December 6 was the most important in the lives of the President and the men who were charged with the defense of America. It is almost inconceivable that the witnesses still alive can have forgotten what happened, but Gen. Marshall and Adm. Stark repeatedly testified under oath that they cannot remember.

These men, with everyone else who had a pipe line into Tokyo's thinking, had absolute knowledge that war was at hand.* Yet, aware

---

*"The evidence indicated that the first thirteen parts were read on the evening of Dec. 6 by, particularly, the President, Mr. Harry Hopkins, Secretary Knox, Adm. Ingersoll, Adm. Turner, Adm. Wilkinson, Adm. Beardall, Gen. Miles, Capt. Kramer, and Col. Bratton.

"Owing to the practice of making decisions by war cabinets, councils, joint committees, and individuals, official responsibility of each man was so blurred that each man became indifferent to his own individual responsibility. A good example of this as they were that they were living in an hour of crisis, they professed not to be able to recall where they were, what they did, and whom they saw.

What Comdr. Schulz had overheard suggested that Roosevelt had the intention of calling a war conference later that night. Did he eventually bring Stark, perhaps Gen. Marshall, Hull, Secretary Knox, and Secretary Stimson to the White House?

Stark and Marshall deny it. Stark, after being informed of Schulz's evidence that he was at the theater, professed still to be uncertain about how he had spent the evening. When he read a newspaper account of a party given by the Canadian minister the afternoon of the 6th which listed Adm. and Mrs. Stark as guests, he denied that either he or his wife had attended. He could not remember a single thing.[24] This crucial day in his life was a blank.

More than three months after concluding its hearings, the congressional committee reopened the record to take testimony that Stark, after returning from the theater, had received a telephone call from Roosevelt. The admiral's recollection was refreshed to this extent by Capt. Harold D. Krick, who had been with him that night.

Krick, who was Stark's flag lieutenant, said that when Stark returned to his quarters, he was informed that there had been a call from the White House during his absence. The admiral went to his upstairs study, where he stayed five or ten minutes.

"What, if anything, did he say to you when he came down?" Krick was asked.

"Only that conditions in the Pacific were serious—that connections with Japan were in a serious state," Krick replied. "That was the substance of it."

The captain said that while he did not recall Stark telling him that he had talked with Roosevelt, he had "a distinct impression" that the admiral's conversation was with the President. He left the Stark home at 11:30 P.M.

Stark could add nothing to Krick's information. He said he had talked frequently with Roosevelt in the days of crisis, and that there would have been nothing unusual in a conversation with the President that night. He said he could only assume that Roosevelt mentioned something to him about the Japanese note.

"I thought it was nothing that required any action from me," he

is Adm. Turner's assumption that so long as Adm. Wilkinson, Adm. Ingersoll, and Secretary Knox had seen the thirteen-part message, 'I did not believe it was my function to take any action.' No one took action that night; all waited for the next day" (Min., p. 34).

said, "and I took none. If he had said anything about the imminence of war, or anything requiring action, it would have stirred me into action."

Stark said that he had searched his memory in an attempt to remember the conversation, but added, "I can only repeat I do not recall it."[25]

At 9:00 A.M. on December 7, Capt. Kramer delivered the complete fourteen-part Jap message to Stark at his office. After reading it, the admiral is supposed to have cried, "My God! This means war. I must get word to Kimmel at once."[26] He did not do so. He spent two and a half hours attempting to reach Gen. Marshall, and it was not until 11:58 A.M. that they drafted the message to be sent to Short. Stark himself made no effort to communicate with Kimmel. Thus the original mystery of what he did the night of the 6th yields to the larger mystery of his inertia on the 7th.

The committee ran into the same kind of stone wall when it questioned Gen. Marshall about the night of December 6. The general said he had no recollection of having left his quarters at Fort Myer, Virginia. Mrs. Marshall, he stated, was convalescing after an illness, which, he said, made him doubly certain he had not left home.[27] At an earlier hearing of the committee, he said that he, or an orderly, was at home during the entire evening.[28] If only an orderly was there part of the time, Marshall himself was absent some of the time. In all of his accounts, however, he insisted that the first thirteen parts of Japan's final reply were not brought to his attention on December 6.[29]

If Marshall did not get this vital information, it was because of the strange apathy displayed by Col. (now Lieut. Gen.) Walter Bedell Smith as secretary of the general staff.

The Army Board of Inquiry which investigated Pearl Harbor makes clear in its report that Gen. Smith was indifferent or derelict in the handling of the thirteen-part Jap message the night of the 6th. Smith's behavior was the more incomprehensible, the board emphasized, because it was utterly clear to all responsible officers of government and the services by December 6 that war was close at hand. The report states:

> The record shows that from informers and other sources the War Department had complete and detailed information of Japanese intentions. Information of the evident Japanese intention to go to war in the very near future was well known to the Secretary of State, the Secretary of War, the chief of staff of the

Army, the Secretary of the Navy, and the chief of naval operations. It was not a question of fact; it was only a question of
time. The next few days would see the end of peace and the
beginning of war.

When decoded Jap messages indicating immediate hostilities
"reached G-2 of the War Department not later than 9 o'clock the
evening of Dec. 6," the report further states, it was Smith in whose
hands they were placed. This intercepted information was transmitted
at once to Smith by Col. Bratton with a warning as to its extreme
importance. What did Smith do? He did nothing.

"Whatever was the reason of Col. Smith for not conveying this
message to Gen. Marshall on the night of Dec. 6, it was unfortunate,"
the report wryly remarks. "This information could have been sent
to Gen. Short on the afternoon (Honolulu time) of Dec. 6." Had
that been done, Short and Kimmel, would have had clear warning of
the probability of impending attack from twelve to eighteen hours in
advance of the Jap carrier assault. They would have been able to go
on a full alert and to make every possible preparation for defense.
Instead, they were left in the dark.

The Army Board is unequivocal on this point. Its report states:

> Action [by the War Department], would .iave been sufficient
> to have alerted the Hawaiian Department. It was in possession
> of the information which was the last clear chance to use the
> means available to meet an attack. It had the background of the
> full development of the Japanese preparation for war and its
> probable date.[30]

But nothing was done.

In the light of this disastrous failure, Gen. Smith's remarks before
the British Royal Service Institution on October 10, 1945, are of more
than passing curiosity. Smith said that American headquarters were
"a bit short on planning" and declared that if he were organizing
another headquarters again he would get "my intelligence officers and
my planners from the British War Office, if they would let me have
them."[31] The Army report concurred in by three general officers had
kind words for the intelligence section which Smith disparaged in his
speech.

"Within the scope of its activities," the report said, "this division
performed well. It gathered much valuable and vital data."[32]

Four years later Smith is found to have been installed in one of
the top jobs of the Army as Gen. Eisenhower's chief of staff, and

given the further distinction of being assigned to a diplomatic post requiring the highest degree of judgment, tact, and ability—ambassador to Russia. Col. Bratton and a colleague, Col. Otis T. Sadtler, also on duty in the War Department in December, 1941, who displayed the same ability as Bratton to distinguish a hawk from a handsaw in those crucial days, still are colonels in minor posts despite the fact that the Army Board singled them out for "interest and aggressiveness in attempting to have something done."[33] Their conduct stands in marked contrast to that of Smith, but he has been given the promotions while they were consigned to oblivion.

There are mysteries here which shout for clarification. Was Smith promoted because he withheld the warning until the blow had fallen? The war hawks of the Roosevelt administration wanted a Pearl Harbor or something very much like it to push this country into war. "It was desired," said they, "that the Japanese be permitted to commit the first overt act." Smith's conduct almost automatically insured the commission of the act.

Why were Colonels Bratton and Sadtler denied advancement when they had so faithfully and intelligently recognized their responsibilities and attempted to execute their duties? Were they on the outside, while Smith and the others later so greatly favored were the insiders in a calculated plan to invite the attack that meant war?

The tender questioning of Secretary Hull before the congressional committee failed to dispel the murk that overhung the events of the night of December 6. Testimony was incontrovertible that the thirteen-part Jap message was delivered that evening to the duty officer of the State Department, and it is inconceivable that the contents would not have been communicated to Hull at once. It was established by Capt. Kramer that the thirteen parts were delivered the night of the 6th to Secretary Knox, who "made a phone call or two, presumably including one to Secretary Hull,"[34] and then told Kramer to bring the Japanese note to the State Department at 10:00 A.M. the next day.

Knox is dead and Stimson, after standing up to the routine of office for five years, suddenly discovered himself ill when the congressional committee began its hearings. Not a single spoken question was addressed to him, although he was without doubt one of the most important living witnesses.

The most tantalizing suggestion of what might have gone on the night of December 6 is supplied by witnesses who talked to Knox shortly after the attack upon Pearl Harbor. Adm. Kimmel related that when Knox arrived in Hawaii the week after the attack, the first question he asked was whether Kimmel had received "our" dispatch the night before the attack.

Kimmel told Knox he had not. He then quoted Knox as saying, "Well, we sent you one—I'm sure we sent one to the commander of the Asiatic fleet [Adm. Hart]." Kimmel said he checked his files but found no record of any dispatch from Knox the night of December 6.

"If such a message ever was originated, it must have bogged down in the Navy Department," Kimmel suggested.[35]

Adm. Smith corroborated the story that Knox had inquired of Kimmel and his chief subordinates whether they had received the message on the night of the 6th. When told that no such message was received, Knox said, according to Smith, "That's strange. I know the message went to Adm. Hart and I thought it was sent to Hawaii." Smith said that he had since learned that no such warning was received by Adm. Hart.[36]

The committee subsequently questioned Rear Adm. Frank M. Beatty, naval aide to Knox in 1941, and Maj. John H. Dillon, confidential civilian assistant to Knox in 1941, and later Marine Corps aide to the Secretary. Beatty said that he had the "impression" in late December, 1941, that there was a "midnight warning" on December 6, but that he may have confused it with the belated warning sent to Hawaii at noon the following day by Chief of Staff Marshall. Dillon gave similar testimony about the "lost" message.[37]

The best evidence would seem to be that of Knox himself. When his recollection of events was fresh just after the attack, he made a report on Pearl Harbor to President Roosevelt on December 15, 1941. In this report Knox twice mentioned the "midnight warning" of the 6th,[38] but whereas he had implied to Kimmel and Smith that it had been transmitted by the Navy, he stated in the report that it was a "message of warning sent from the War Department on Saturday night at midnight, before the attack," and that it had been directed to Gen. Short. There is no evidence that Roosevelt disputed that there was such a message.

If the warning were sent on December 6, it was undoubtedly drafted and dispatched after consultation among all of the leaders of the administration and the Army and Navy high command—Roosevelt, Hull, Stimson, Knox, Stark, and Marshall—but none still available as a witness will admit it ever existed. So little light, after three months of investigation, was the congressional committee able to shed on one of the prime mysteries of Pearl Harbor.

So events drifted toward doomsday. The next morning in Washington there still was time to have dispatched a clear warning to Hawaii. At 9 o'clock on December 7, Col. Bratton, apparently despairing of getting any action from Col. Smith, attempted himself to reach Gen. Marshall and inform him of the all-important intercepted Jap message, now complete in all fourteen parts, announcing that relations between Japan and the United States were terminated.[39] "It was well known that Japan's entry into all wars of the past had been characterized by the first overt act of war coming simultaneously with the declaration."[40]

The minority report of the Joint Congressional Committee reinforces this view:

> *Judging by the military and naval history of Japan, high authorities in Washington and the commanders in Hawaii had good grounds for expecting that in starting war the Japanese government would make a surprise attack on the United States.*
>
> There is no evidence in the record before the committee that President Roosevelt, Secretary Hull, Secretary Stimson, and/or Secretary Knox expected at any time prior to Dec. 7 a formal declaration of war on the United States by Japan in case the diplomatic negotiations came to a break. Indeed, all the evidence bearing on expectations in Washington as to Japan's probable methods of making war point to the belief of the administration that Japan would begin with a surprise attack.
>
> For example, Secretary Hull on Nov. 25 and Nov. 28 at a meeting of "high officials," when he stated that the matter of safeguarding our national security was in the hands of the Army and Navy, "expressed his judgment that any plans for our military defense would include the assumption that the Japanese might make the element of surprise a central point in their strategy, and also might attack at various points simultaneously with a view to demoralizing efforts of defense and of coordination for purposes thereof" (Peace and War, 1943, p. 144).
>
> Speaking to Ambassador Halifax on Nov. 29, Secretary Hull said that it would be a—
> "serious mistake . . . to make plans of resistance without including the possibility that Japan may move suddenly and with every possible element of surprise . . . that the Japanese recognize that their course of unlimited conquest . . . is a desperate gamble and requires the utmost boldness and risk." (*Peace and War*, 1943, pp. 144-145).
>
> Ambassador Grew reported to Hull on Nov. 3—
> "Japan may resort with dangerous and dramatic suddenness

to measures which might make inevitable war with the United States" (*Peace and War*, p. 775).[41]

But the commanders in Hawaii did not have the information that war was at hand. Washington did. The duty of Washington to warn the Pacific outposts was therefore clear and immediate.

When Hull, Stimson, and Knox gathered at 10:30 in the office of the Secretary of State, they had the complete message.[42] They knew what it meant. Stimson later admitted he was "not surprised" that the beginning of hostilities should accompany the break of relations.[43] But none of the three secretaries did anything.

Stimson, on December 7, noted in his diary that "everything in 'Magic' indicated that they [the Japanese] had been keeping the time back until now in order to accomplish something hanging in the air." What was hanging in the air was the Japanese assault upon Oahu. "Hull," said Stimson, "is very certain that the Japs are planning some deviltry and we are all wondering where the blow will strike."

There is good reason to believe that Stimson knew not only that war was coming, but that he knew that it would break out at Pearl Harbor. Preparing for the State Department meeting on the morning of the 7th, he ordered on the night of the 6th that he be supplied at the conference with the following information: "Compilation of men-of-war in Far East: British, American, Japanese, Dutch, Russian; *also compilation of American men-of-war in Pacific fleet, with locations*, with a list of American men-of-war in the Atlantic without locations."*[44]

Admirals Stark and Ingersoll and Secretary Knox were consulted about this request. Knox directed that the information be compiled and delivered before 10 o'clock Sunday, December 7.[45] This was done. The compilation showed that practically all the major units of the Pacific fleet were in Pearl Harbor.

Representative Keefe observed:[46]

> At this time the information available in Washington showed that war was only hours away. Yet the two secretaries and the high command made no effort to direct any change in the dispositions of the fleet as shown in the Navy Department summary. They took no steps to furnish Adm. Kimmel the information which they possessed as to the imminence of war. Consequently they deprived him of any chance to alter his dispositions in the light of that information. I conclude that Secretaries Stimson and Knox and the high command in Wash-

*Italics inserted.

ington knew that the major units of the fleet were in Pearl Harbor on December 6-7, 1941, and were satisfied with that situation.

Why were they satisfied? Because they knew that an attack upon the fleet would at last produce the long-sought overt act?

Roosevelt also knew that a break in relations meant the opening act of war. The night before, with all but one part of the final Japanese note before him, he had said, "This means war!" Now, on the morning of December 7, at 10:00 A.M., the final section was delivered to him in his bedroom by Adm. Beardall. The President looked up and said, "It looks as if the Japanese are going to break off relations."[47] The message plainly told the President that Japan was announcing the break. The President knew that that meant a simultaneous act of war. Indeed, when Beardall delivered intercepted messages to him on December 4 and 5, the President had turned to him and asked:

"When do you think it will happen?"

"Most any time," Beardall replied.[48]

Col. Bratton, with the fourteen-part message now complete, also knew. He frantically called Gen. Marshall at his home, only to learn from an orderly that the chief of staff had picked that morning of all mornings to vanish on a leisurely two and a half-hour horseback ride.

Between 9:00 and 9:30, the "pilot" message instructing Nomura and Kurusu to hand in the fourteen-part note to Hull at 1:00 P.M., was delivered to Bratton.

"When I saw the message," he told the congressional committee, "I dropped everything, as it meant to me that Japan planned to attack the United States at some point at or near 1 o'clock that day."[49]

Marshall did not reach his office until 11:25. The pilot message lay in the War Department for two hours and a half before any warning was dispatched to Hawaii—a warning so delayed that it might just as well have never been sent.

Two Navy officers at least partially apprehended the Japanese intention even before seeing the pilot message. They were Adm. Wilkinson and Capt. McCollum. Together they went, at about 9:15, to the office of Adm. Stark with the complete fourteen-part note.

"I pointed out to Adm. Stark the seriousness of the language," Wilkinson related, "and advised that the Pacific fleet be notified."

Stark tried to reach Marshall, Wilkinson said, but the general was still out on his canter, so Stark did nothing. Wilkinson left Stark's office, returning between 10:30 and 10:40. By this time the 1:00 P.M. message was in Stark's hands. Wilkinson said that it "indicated that the Japs planned action sooner than we expected."[50] McCollum said that Capt. Kramer had prepared a chart showing the relative times in each overseas area, in comparison to Tokyo and Washington times, and that he gave it to the chief of operations.[51] A general discussion of the time factor followed, but Stark still did nothing.

A report made to Secretary Stimson on November 25, 1944, by Maj. Gen. Cramer asserted that Kramer had been even more explicit. The report stated:

> Capt. Safford testified that Comdr. Kramer told him in 1943 that when he submitted . . . the message to the Jap ambassadors to present the Japanese reply at 1:00 P.M. to Secretary Knox, he sent along with it a note saying in effect, "This means a surprise attack at Pearl Harbor today and possibly a midnight attack on Manila."[52]

Kramer's report supposedly was in the hands of Knox at approximately 10:00 A.M., but the Secretary of the Navy failed to act, although in his secret report to President Roosevelt on December 15, 1941, he stated that the meaning of the 1 o'clock deadline was clearly known to the leaders of the administration. Knox said in this report:

> Neither Short nor Kimmel, at the time of the attack, had any knowledge of the plain intimations of some surprise move, made clear in Washington, through the interception of Japanese instructions to Nomura, in which a surprise move of some kind was clearly indicated by the insistence upon the precise time of Nomura's reply to Hull, at 1 o'clock on Sunday.[53]

Although Knox immediately after the attack thus confessed that the meaning of the 1:00 P.M. delivery was clear, Kramer himself later denied that he had ever pointed out the significance of the time to Knox. He told the congressional committee that the only comment he made on the meaning of the 1:00 P.M. message was in telling Capt. McCollum and a State Department secretary that the message indicated a move toward Thailand and the Malay Peninsula.[54] It developed, however, that extraordinary pressure had been put on Kramer by the Navy Department to induce him to deny that the original estimate credited to him was ever submitted to Knox.[55]

At 11:25 A.M., when Marshall finally wandered into his office, everyone in Washington who had knowledge of "Magic" was sitting around waiting for an attack known to be coming in two more hours, but not a soul was doing anything about it.[56] Roosevelt and Harry Hopkins were shortly to closet themselves in the oval study of the

White House, with all incoming telephone calls shut off. The tableau could not have been more innocent—Roosevelt with his stamp collection laid out before him, Hopkins lounging in sweater and slacks on a couch, toying with Fala, the White House Scottie.

Marshall's blunder in transmitting his last-minute warning to Hawaii by only one medium, and that the slowest available, by a round-about route, and without even assigning it a priority, was assayed by Gen. Short as follows:

> It is standard staff procedure and doctrine that all important or emergency messages should be sent by all available means of communication, which in this case would have included the scrambler telephones which had been frequently used between the War Department and Fort Shafter. Col. Phillips [Short's chief of staff] and Gen. Marshall did confer by scrambler phone later in the day on December 7. If security would be violated by sending the information by phone, then the War Department should have issued the necessary alert orders which they would have known that I would have issued at once if I had the information which they possessed.[57]

Short then cited the War Department field manual on signal communication in support of his position:

> Choice of the means employed in each instance depends on the situation. Exclusive reliance upon any one means is unwise because special and unforeseen circumstances may render that means inoperative when most needed. Plans of all commanders will make advance provision for prompt employment of effective and reliable alternate means; and the simultaneous operation of several means will minimize the ill effects of complete interruption in any one.[58]

The Army Board criticized Marshall severely for his handling of the December 7 message. Despite Marshall's excuse that he feared "a leak" if he used the scrambler phone to reach Short, messages by scrambler phone were made frequently between Hawaii and Washington later in the day. Col. Fielder, Short's G-2, twice talked to Washington by this means, and himself received a call from Washington on the same phone.[59] Col. Phillips, as mentioned, communicated with Marshall by scrambler phone while the attack was in progress.

The Army Board said:

> It is important to observe that only one means of communication was selected by Washington. That decision violated all

rules requiring the use of multiple means of communication in emergency. In addition to the War Department telephone, there also existed the FBI radio, which was assigned a special frequency between Washington and Hawaii and over which it took 20 minutes to send a coded message from Hawaii to Washington or vice versa. . . . We find no justification for a failure to send this message by multiple secret means either through the Navy radio or FBI radio or the scrambler telephone or all three.[60]

Senator Ferguson developed in examining Short that the War Department was guilty of the same laxity that characterized the handling of its December 7 warning to Hawaii in alerting American forces at the Panama Canal. If the Canal, instead of Pearl Harbor, had been the objective of the Jap attack, the results might have been equally disastrous.

On December 5 Gen. Miles drafted a message to Gen. Frank M. Andrews, commander of the Panama defenses, which stated, "U.S.–Japanese relations strained. Will inform you if and when severance of diplomatic relations imminent." Miles failed to mark the message with a priority, so that in the normal handling of Army communications it was transmitted after all priority or urgent messages had been sent. This dispatch actually left Washington two days later, on December 7, after the fourteen-part Jap note and the 1:00 P.M. pilot message left no question of strained relations.[61] In the Japanese note it was plainly stated relations were broken off, and the pilot message set the hour for the first shot of the war.

Not until December 9, the Tuesday following the Sunday of the Oahu attack, did the War Department seek to ascertain why Marshall's December 7 warning went astray. When it finally acted, it provided a fine example of locking up the stable after the horse had been stolen. Whereas the vital December 7 message was not even stamped "Priority," the check-up dispatch was marked "Extra Urgent."[62]

Marshall's explanation that he refrained from using the scrambler telephone for fear of causing "a leak that would embarrass the State Department" is illogical for at least two reasons. The first is that if the Japs had overheard him talking to Short, they would have been left with the same two alternatives they already had in the absence of such a conversation; either to carry through the attack as planned, or to abandon it. The second is that, despite Roosevelt's caution against committing any overt act, the War Department on November

27 had issued orders which, if carried out before December 7, would almost certainly have led to hostilities.

Intelligence had heard reports of a considerable concentration of Japanese warships at Jaluit in the Marshall Islands. These ships and submarines were, in fact, part of Adm. Shimizu's advance expeditionary force which was to support the Pearl Harbor attack. Adm. Hart had suggested a reconnaissance over Jaluit to verify the reports that there was a Jap concentration there.[63] Gen. Arnold presented orders for the flight, which Secretary Stimson promptly approved.[64] Short was notified by radiogram of the project. He said,

> The War Department had ordered me to equip two B-24 airplanes for a special photographic reconnaissance mission over Truk and Jaluit, with particular attention to the location of naval vessels, submarines, airfields, airplanes, barracks, and camps. If attacked, the crews were directed to use all means in their power for self-preservation. These planes were to be sent to Honolulu unarmed, but I was directed to insure that both were "fully equipped with gun ammunition upon departure." The first of these two planes did not arrive in Hawaii until December 5. Presumably, had the War Department in the meantime decided that Hawaii was a zone of danger, they would have armed the plane before sending it to me. Gen. Martin wired back a request that the second B-24 bring necessary equipment other than the guns and ammunition which we could supply.[65]

"How could the use of a telephone be considered an overt act in comparison with this flight?" Senator Ferguson asked Marshall.

"It was a matter of judgment," Marshall replied.[66]

Gen. Short was asked by Representative Keefe how long it took to get a message through normally from Honolulu to Washington by scrambler telephone.

"The times I used it," Short said, "I would say ten or fifteen minutes. On the morning of the attack, along about 8:15, I directed Col. Phillips to call Gen. Marshall because I was going to my field command post. I believe that he got the connection at 8:22. I think it took seven minutes."

By way of emphasizing that seven minutes is somewhat quicker than seven hours, Keefe asked, "Do I understand that that morning, right while the attack was going on, Col. Phillips called Gen. Marshall on the scrambler telephone and got a connection in about seven minutes?"

"And told him," Short asserted, "if he would listen, he could hear the bombs."

Keefe also observed that he had been advised by J. Edgar Hoover that Robert L. Shivers, the FBI agent in charge at Hawaii, reached him in New York by direct telephone connection in just a few minutes while the attack was going on. Hoover, Keefe said, told him the connection was so clear that over the telephone he could hear the explosion of bombs.

"Well, if you could get the telephone message while this attack was going on, in just a few minutes," Keefe said, "there wouldn't be any reason why the line was not clear so a message could come from the other way, from Washington to Honolulu?"

"There wouldn't appear to be," Short said.

Keefe then questioned Short about other means of communication between Washington and Hawaii. Short said that in addition to the Army 10-kilowatt station, the Navy had a 25-kilowatt station, the FBI had a station of about equal power, and there were also commercial radio and commercial cable. He said that the Army station was not functioning well on the morning of the attack.

"Well, do you know about the Navy or the FBI?"

"I am sure that they could have gotten through."

Keefe then recalled that in the conference in Marshall's office preceding the dispatch of the warning to Short, Adm. Stark offered the use of the Navy radio, but that it was refused. Short said:

> The War Department, if not conscious at that time that more than one means of communication could be used, became fully conscious at the time they issued the order to relieve me. I got that order three different ways within thirty to forty minutes. I received a radiogram first. Ten or fifteen minutes later Gen. Emmons got off of a plane with a printed order. Fifteen or twenty minutes later the secretary of the general staff called Col. Phillips to ask if I had received the order.

Keefe said, "So you got it in—"

"Three different ways," Short interjected.

"—in three different ways?"

"Yes."

"To make sure that you got it?"

"Yes, sir."[67]

Keefe then brought up the hypothetical question of whether, if Short had been warned by Washington some time before the attack, he would have been awakened in order to act on the information.

Short responded that he could have been reached within a minute or two.

"Well," Keefe said, "the story has gone around the country that you were all drunk out there that night; that you were drunk and that Kimmel was drunk and everybody else was drunk, and that everybody was asleep out there at Pearl Harbor, sleeping off a jag. That is the way it has been told out around the country. Now, is there any truth in that, Gen. Short?"

"There is absolutely no truth in it."[68]

Short told Keefe that better radar equipment and proper interpretation of the showing on the radar screen that a large flight of planes was approaching would have made little difference in the outcome of the attack. "What we needed," he said, "was information from Washington giving us time to go into an alert."

"You could have done a pretty good job with the stuff you had out there if you had been on the alert and had been expecting an attack?" Keefe inquired.

"Yes, sir."

"And the slow torpedo planes that came in there and did most of the damage to the battleships in the harbor were pretty easy targets for your fast fighters, were they not?"

"If you knew where they were coming from, they would have been very easy."

"Now," continued Keefe, "all during this war the element of surprise has been a thing that has been involved in almost everything that has been done on both sides out there in the Pacific, isn't that true?"

"All over the world," Short agreed. "It is always the most important element."

"It is always the attempt on the part of a commander to involve his adversary in surprise, isn't that true?"

"That is correct."

"And as far as an air attack itself is concerned," Keefe went on, "our experience has been that regardless of the fact whether an attack is known or not, a lot of these planes—some of them, at least—get through and cause damage, isn't that true?"

"That is correct."

"That was true at Okinawa, was it not?"

"Yes, sir."

"Now, when we think of the exploits at Midway and the magnificent job that our Navy did in sinking the Jap navy, it was possible because of intelligence, was it not, and the fact that our Navy was informed and had the facts and knew what to do?"

"That is correct."

"And when they shot down Adm. Yamamoto, that was possible because they got an intercept which put them on notice and gave them some information?"

"That is correct. Gen. Marshall and Adm. Wilkinson have pointed out that the security of our cryptanalytic ability was risked for the slight, temporary exultation of shooting down Yamamoto's plane. Surely, then, supplying the data to me and to Adm. Kimmel would not have been inconceivably risky."

"I refer to these two incidents," said Keefe, "because it correctly illustrates the idea that intelligence is necessary and fundamental, is it not?"

"Yes, sir."

"And when intelligence fails, you are likely to have serious results?"

"Yes, sir."

"Now, your position in this case is that intelligence, so far as Washington was concerned, failed?"

"A hundred per cent."

"And thus Pearl Harbor occurred. Is that your defense?"

"Yes, sir."[69]

Chapter Nineteen

JAPAN SOLVES THE DILEMMA

IN THE complex of events from November 25 through December 7, 1941, Japanese policy shaped itself in conformity with the desires of President Roosevelt. The President wanted to get in the war.* Primarily he wanted to fight Germany, but when Hitler would not accommodate him with the pretext for asking a declaration of war, he turned to the Pacific and to Japan to achieve a back-door entry into the war in Europe, knowing that the tripartite pact made it certain that if we went to war with one of the three Axis partners, we should be at war with all of them.

Hitler, suspicious of the reliability of the Japs, did not want to fight the United States as long as the chance remained that Japan might leave him in the lurch. An attack by Japan upon the United States, however, would serve his purposes. The Japs would then be fully committed, and Hitler could hope that American power would be tied up in the Pacific until he had cleared the board in Europe.

Mr. Roosevelt seems long to have doubted, despite the overwhelming weight of evidence to the contrary, that Japan would be sufficiently foolhardy to make a direct attack upon the American flag. Accordingly, he followed an alternative plan on the assumption that Japan might fail to fulfil the prediction he had made long ago to Adm. Richardson that the Japanese "could not always avoid making mistakes and that, as the war continued and the area of operations expanded, sooner or later they would make a mistake and we would enter the war."

*At any time after 1936 it was evident that a European war would not be unwelcome to the administration at Washington; largely as a means of diverting public attention from its flock of uncouth economic chickens on their way home to roost, but chiefly as a means of strengthening its malign grasp upon the country's political and economic machinery."—Albert Jay Nock, *Memoirs of a Superfluous Man*, p. 248.

First, the President tightened the screw. Japan was reduced to desperation by embargoes and the freezing of its foreign assets. Then it was deprived of hope that any solution could be achieved through the diplomatic negotiations in Washington. Finally, the President threw over the scheme to obtain a breathing spell of from three to six months by means of a *modus vivendi* which would have provided some stopgap solution. He told Secretary Hull to go ahead and present the ten counter-proposals of November 26. The Japanese were ordered to abandon all their ill-gotten gains and become a probationary "peace-loving" nation. To a people so addicted to "face," the confession of error implicit in any such retreat would have been even more galling than the surrender of the tangible acquisitions of conquest.

Roosevelt knew that Japan would fight. The only question was whether Japan would fight the United States. If the Japanese limited the attack to the colonial empires of Britain and Holland, an excruciating dilemma would be posed to the administration. On the one hand, the President was bound by his secret commitments under the Washington and Singapore staff agreements, and by his secret engagements to Prime Minister Churchill, to go to war if British or Dutch territory were attacked. On the other, he was restricted by his repeated pledges that Americans were not going to be sent into foreign wars "except in case of attack."* In his "again and again and again" speech at Boston, he had not even made that reservation. It was because of these promises that the President kept insisting that Japan commit the first overt act.

In casting about for means to extricate himself from this quandary, Roosevelt hit upon a desperate expedient. This was nothing less than to execute a "Pearl Harbor" in reverse—to attack Japan without waiting for Japan to strike. Before acting, however, the President felt it necessary to prepare public opinion. The personal message he dispatched on December 6 to Hirohito, although eventually sent as an appeal to history for moral justification, had originally been intended as part of this conditioning. An address to Congress, and perhaps a speech to the nation, were to follow. Events moved so fast that this program could not be carried out; but they moved to the President's liking, for they saved him from a constitutional crisis.

In pursuing his war policy, Roosevelt forced a two-front war upon an unready nation over the objections of his high command. On

---

*Speech at Teamsters Union convention, Washington, Sept. 11, 1940; speech at Philadelphia, Oct. 23, 1940.

November 5, and again on November 27, Gen. Marshall and Adm. Stark addressed joint memoranda to the President appealing for delay. In the earlier memorandum they urged that "no ultimatum be delivered to Japan."[1] They said that American naval forces in the Pacific were inferior to the Japanese fleet and could not undertake an unlimited offensive; that the Philippines were only then being reinforced, and that not until March, 1942, would air and submarine strength in the Western Pacific constitute a "positive threat."

Referring to this memorandum, Senator Ferguson asked Marshall, "Were we in a position at that time to back up any additional warnings to Japan with military force?"

"We were not," said the chief of staff.[2]

The plea of November 27 came too late, Hull having given the Japanese his unacceptable conditions the day before. The Army Board observes:

> This is the memorandum asking the President not to precipitate an ultimatum with the Japanese and to give the Army and Navy more time within which to prepare; but it was too late, as the die had been cast by the Secretary of State in handing the ten-points counter-proposals to the Japanese on the previous day, which was, as the Secretary of State remarked, "washing his hands of the matter."[3]

Again, the board stated,

> Undoubtedly the Secretary of State had been frequently advised during the meetings of the war council of the inadequate status of the defenses of the United States. Our Army and Navy were not ready for war, and undoubtedly the Secretary of State had been advised of that fact. . . .
>
> This memorandum was addressed directly to the President, according to the testimony of Gen. Marshall. It contained two things: first, a statement that the most essential thing from the United States viewpoint was to gain time and to avoid precipitating military action so long as this could be done consistent with the national policy, because of the fact that the Army and Navy were not ready for war; and, second, attention was called to the desirability of counter-military action against Japan in event she engaged in specific acts of aggression. The memorandum recommended among other things that "steps be taken at once to consummate agreements with the British and Dutch for the issuance of warnings to the Japanese against taking such aggressive action."[4]

The memorandum and the question of the need for further time

were discussed on the 27th at a conference among Secretary of War
Stimson, Secretary of the Navy Knox, Adm. Stark, and Gen. Gerow.
Marshall had left the preceding afternoon for maneuvers in North
Carolina.[5] During the congressional investigation, Representative
Gearhart suggested that Marshall and Stark drafted the memorandum
the afternoon of November 25, before the departure of the chief of
staff, after it became apparent to them from discussion at a meeting
of the war cabinet in the White House at noon that the President was
crowding the country toward war. There were three telephone calls
between the general and the admiral that afternoon, but Stark professed inability to recall whether the appeal had been drafted before
Hull's terms were tendered and then withheld until it could serve no
purpose.[6]

Hull, with the assent of the President, went ahead, "kicking the
whole thing over," as he said, and stating to Stimson, "I have washed
my hands of it, and it is now in the hands of you and Knox, the
Army and the Navy."[7] The Army Board censured Hull for this conduct. Said the board:

> The action of the Secretary of State in delivering the counter-
> proposals of November 26, 1941, was used by the Japanese as
> the signal to begin the war by the attack on Pearl Harbor. To
> the extent that it hastened such attack, it was in conflict with
> the efforts of the War and Navy departments to gain time for
> preparations for war. However, war with Japan was inevitable
> and imminent because of irreconcilable disagreements between
> the Japanese empire and the American government.[8]

The inevitable and imminent war, however, was the product of
American diplomacy so managed that war could neither be averted
nor delayed until the Army and Navy were ready.* As late as November 6 Roosevelt favored a *modus vivendi* that would delay hostilities. Secretary Stimson, who kept a contemporaneous record of
events, relates that on that day he discussed the Far Eastern situation
for an hour with the President. He states:

> The thing uppermost in his mind was how we could gain
> more time. I quote from my notes: "The President outlined

*"An 'incident' can always be arranged or manufactured or better yet, provoked,
as we have often seen; and then the fat is in the fire. In recent years, as far as I can
remember, every pretext for war has been carefully hand-tailored. . . . As for the present war, the Principality of Monaco, the Grand Duchy of Luxemburg, would have
taken up arms against the United States on receipt of such a note as the State Department sent the Japanese government on the eve of Pearl Harbor."—Albert Jay Nock,
Memoirs of a Superfluous Man, p. 249.

what he thought he might say.† He was trying to think of something that would give us further time. He suggested he might propose a truce in which there would be no movement or armament for six months and then if the Japanese and Chinese had not settled their arrangement in that meanwhile, we could go on on the same basis."⁹

On November 25, one day before he tendered the Japanese the demands which they found unacceptable, Hull was still considering what Stimson called "the proposal for a three months' truce." Overnight, however, he and the President changed their minds. On the 26th Hull told Stimson that the Chinese had objected strenuously to the *modus vivendi* and that he "had about made up his mind to give up the whole thing in respect to a truce and to simply tell the Japanese that he had no further action to propose."¹⁰ That same day Hull not only "gave up the whole thing" but handed Nomura and Kurusu the conditions which he and the President knew they were certain to reject.

Stimson had been unsympathetic to the truce proposal when the President was considering it. He was still unsympathetic when he discussed the belated appeal for delay of Marshall and Stark on November 27 with Stark, Knox, and Gerow. "There was a tendency, not unnatural, on the part of Stark and Gerow to seek for more time," he wrote in his diary. "I said that I was glad to have time but I didn't want it at any cost of humility on the part of the United States or of reopening the thing, which would show a weakness on our part."¹¹

A memorandum of this conversation prepared for Gen. Marshall by Gerow stated that Stimson "wanted to be sure that the memorandum would not be construed as a recommendation to the President that he request Japan to reopen the conversations. He was reassured on that point." Later the memorandum was submitted to Stimson, who made some changes.¹²

Thus the Secretary of War, seeing that the United States was heading toward an inevitable conflict with Japan, issued orders to forestall any possibility that war would be headed off by conciliatory action on the part of the Roosevelt government. He issued these orders although fully aware of the unpreparedness of the Army and Navy to go to war, and this is among the many responsibilities which must be charged to him.

So far as the record shows, Roosevelt and Secretary Hull aban-

†To Kurusu, who was coming from Japan.

doned the *modus vivendi* because of the cries of "appeasement" which were coming from the Chinese and British. Beyond that, it seems clear that both were ready for war, even if the Army and Navy were not. Significantly, their momentous decision to submit the counter-proposals of November 26 does not appear to have been influenced by new Japanese troop movements which might have served as a convenient pretext.

On the afternoon of the 25th intelligence reports to Stimson showed five Japanese divisions moving southward by transport from Shantung and Shansi toward Indo-China. Stimson communicated the news to Hull and sent a copy of the intelligence summary to the President.[13] The following day Hull told Stimson of the decision to submit the ten points to Japan. He mentioned Chinese pressure in explaining his intention, but did not refer to the Japanese troop movement.[14]

Roosevelt, who had already approved the Secretary of State's decision to "kick over" the *modus vivendi,* had not received Stimson's report of the movement of the transports southward when Stimson telephoned him shortly after talking to Hull. The President reacted violently to the news. Stimson relates:

> He fairly blew up—jumped up into the air, so to speak, and said he hadn't seen it [the report] and that that changed the whole situation, because it was an evidence of bad faith on the part of the Japanese that while they were negotiating for an entire truce—an entire withdrawal [from China]—they should be sending this expedition down there to Indo-China.[15]

But the Hull proposals had already "changed the whole situation." Both the President and the Secretary of State knew it. Hull conceded that the following day when he told Stimson that the effect of his terms was to put matters "in the hands of you and Knox—the Army and the Navy."[16]

After November 26 and the submission of the Hull ultimatum, the attention of the Roosevelt administration was focused upon the movement of the Japanese expedition steaming southward. It now was apparent that the time was fast approaching when the President would have to honor the secret commitments which he had assumed at the Atlantic conference and which his staff officers had undertaken at the Washington and Singapore conferences.[17] The Roosevelt administration knew that once it met Japan in head-on collision, the nation would be in a global war. Its policy had been predicated upon this very knowledge.

This consideration was manifest in a statement given by Adm. Ingersoll when he was examined during the course of an independent investigation conducted by Adm. Hart for the Navy Department. Hart asked Ingersoll what meaning the Navy Department attached to the "war warning" dispatched to Kimmel November 27. "Was consideration given to the thought that mention of Western Pacific objectives only might tend to reduce the vigilance of the Pacific fleet in the Hawaiian area?" Hart inquired. Ingersoll answered:

> I am sure that the drafting of the dispatch was not meant to give such an impression. The impression it was intended to give was that events were moving in such a fashion in the Far East that the United States would become involved in war in a few days and that consequently the United States forces elsewhere in the Pacific *and also in the Atlantic would find themselves at war with the Axis when the clash actually took place in the Asiatic waters.*[*18]

The feeling in Washington was that the United States must fight even if there were no attack upon this country and Japanese belligerent action were confined to British, Dutch, or even neutral territory. This view was reflected in the intense preoccupation of the administration leaders and the high command with the idea that if Japan crossed a certain line in the Pacific, the United States would be bound by its secret undertakings to go to war. Again and again this concept entered the thinking of the principals.

The deadline was first mentioned by Lindley and Davis in their description of the Atlantic conference:

> The crisis in the Far East claimed first attention, resulting, as we have seen, in Churchill's agreement to the President's policy of delaying hostilities without invoking a "deadline." That agreement represented a unifying of English-speaking policy in the Pacific. In the discussions about a deadline, it was generally held that the geographical limit should be set at the south of Cam Ranh Bay. . . .[19]

The Singapore staff conference, in its secret report of April 27, 1941, stated:

> It is agreed that any of the following actions by Japan would create a position in which our failure to take active military counter-action would place us at such military disadvantage, should Japan subsequently attack, that we should then advise our respective governments to authorize such action:

*Italics supplied.

(*a*) A direct act of war by Japanese armed forces against the territory or mandated territory of any of the associated powers. It is not possible to define accurately what would constitute "a direct act of war." It is possible for a minor incident to occur which, although technically an act of war, could be resolved by diplomatic action. It is recognized that the decision as to whether such an incident is an act of war must lie with the government concerned.

(*b*) The movement of the Japanese forces into any part of Thailand to the west of 100 degrees east or to the south of 10 degrees north.

(*c*) The movement of a large number of Japanese warships, or of a convoy of merchant ships escorted by Japanese warships, which from its position and course was clearly directed upon the Philippine Islands, the east coast of the Isthmus of Kra or the east coast of Malaya, or had crossed the parallel of 6 degrees north between Malaya and the Philippines, a line from the Gulf of Davao to Waigeo Island, or the equator east of Waigeo.

(*d*) The movement of Japanese forces into Portuguese Timor.

(*e*) The movement of Japanese forces into New Caledonia or the Loyalty Islands.[20]

In his secret warning to Ambassador Nomura August 17, Roosevelt had served notice that any move by Japan anywhere in the Pacific would compel the United States "to take immediately any and all steps which it may deem necessary toward safeguarding the legitimate rights and interests of the United States and American nationals and toward insuring the safety and security of the United States."[21] As Undersecretary of State Welles said, this warning, in diplomatic language, meant the same thing as a promise to go to war.

Senator Claude Pepper of Florida, frequently an administration spokesman, also gave notice of the existence of a deadline when, in an interview at Boston on November 24, 1941, he said that the United States was not far from a shooting war with Japan and that "we are only waiting for Japan to cross a line before we start shooting."

"I don't know exactly where that line is," Pepper said, "and I'm not sure the President knows exactly where it is, but when they cross it we'll start shooting." Pepper added that "actual declaration of war is a legal technicality, and such technicalities are being held in abeyance as long as those brigands [the Japanese] continue in force."[22]

Chief of Staff Marshall conceded that war was known to be imminent at least eleven days before Pearl Harbor when Army intelligence

reported five Jap divisions in thirty to forty transports moving south
from Shanghai. This information, Marshall said, clearly indicated
that Japan was moving "to cross the line" which, in his opinion,
would have pulled us into war, regardless of Pearl Harbor, in order
to protect the Philippines.[23]

Secretary of the Navy Knox, in a memorandum the morning of
December 7, stated:

> I think the Japanese should be told that any movement in a
> direction that threatens the United States will be met by force.
> The President will want to reserve to himself just how to define
> this. The following are suggestions to shoot at: Any movement
> into Thailand; or any movement into Thailand west of 100 de-
> grees east and south of 10 degrees north—this in accordance
> with the recommendations of the British and Dutch and United
> States military authorities in the Far East; or any movement
> against British, Dutch, United States, Free French, or Portu-
> guese territory in the Pacific area.[24]

Secretary Stimson, in a written statement to the congressional committee, said,

> Our military advisers had given the President their formal
> advice that, if Japan attacked British Malaya or the Dutch East
> Indies or moved her forces west of a certain line in Indo-China,
> we would have to fight for the sake of our security.[25]

Again, he said,

> The opinion of our top military and naval advisers was that
> delay was very desirable, but that nevertheless we must take
> military action if Japan attacked American, or British, or Dutch
> territory or moved her forces in Indo-China west of 100 degrees
> east or south of 10 degrees north.[26]

Describing a meeting November 28 of the war cabinet, Stimson
relates in his diary that the probable objectives of the Japanese expedition moving south along the China coast were discussed. He says:

> It was now the opinion of everyone that if this expedition
> was allowed to get around the southern point of Indo-China
> and to go off and land in the Gulf of Siam, either at Bangkok
> or further west, it would be a terrific blow at all of the three
> powers, Britain at Singapore, the Netherlands, and ourselves in
> the Philippines.
>
> It was the consensus of everybody that this must not be
> allowed. Then we discussed how to prevent it. It was agreed
> that if the Japanese got into the Isthmus of Kra, the British

would fight. It was also agreed that if the British fought, we would have to fight. And it now seems clear that if this expedition was allowed to round the southern point of Indo-China, this whole chain of disastrous events would be set on foot of going.

It further became a consensus of views that rather than strike at the force as it went by without any warning on the one hand, which we didn't think we could do; or sitting still and allowing it to go on, on the other, which we didn't think we could do; that the only thing for us to do was address it a warning that if it reached a certain place, or a certain line, or a certain point, we should have to fight.[27]

In his statement to the congressional committee, Stimson said,

If war did come, it was important, both from the point of view of unified support of our own people as well as for the record of history, that we should not be placed in the position of firing the first shot, if this could be done without sacrificing our safety, but that Japan should appear in her true role as the real aggressor.[28]

Referring to the "war warning" to Short on November 27, Stimson says,

If there was to be war, moreover, we wanted the Japanese to commit the first overt act. . . . In Hawaii, because of the large numbers of Japanese inhabitants, it was felt desirable to issue a special warning so that nothing would be done, unless necessary to the defense, to alarm the civil population and thus possibly precipitate an incident and give the Japanese an excuse to go to war and the chance to say that we had committed the first overt act.[29]

Thus, the defense of the Hawaiian commanders was circumscribed in the interest of making good Roosevelt's campaign pledges.

In his diary entry of November 25, thirteen days before the Pearl Harbor attack, Stimson expressed the dilemma in its baldest terms. Describing the war cabinet meeting in the White House, he stated:

There the President . . . brought up entirely the relations with the Japanese. He brought up the event that we were likely to be attacked, perhaps [as soon as] next Monday, for the Japanese are notorious for making an attack without warning and the question was what we should do. *The question was how we should maneuver them into the position of firing the first shot without allowing too much danger to ourselves.*[*30]

*Italics supplied.

Gen. Marshall later made the illuminating comment: "Of course, no one anticipated that that overt act would be the crippling of the Pacific fleet."[31] In other words, Roosevelt and his associates wanted a little surprise; they were not looking for a major disaster.

The minority report of the Joint Congressional Committee says of the administration's intention:

> In the diplomatic documents, exhibits, and testimony before the committee there is a wealth of evidence which underwrites the statement that the tactics of maneuvering the Japanese into "the position of firing the first shot" were followed by high authorities in Washington after Nov. 25, 1941. Examples of such tactics are afforded by—
>
> (a) Secretary Hull's decision, with the approval of President Roosevelt, to discard the proposal for a temporary agreement with Japan without notifying the Secretary of War or the British and Australian representatives in Washington who had collaborated in working out a draft of a memorandum with a view to reaching such an agreement if possible.
>
> (b) The substitution for the proposed *modus vivendi* of the note of Nov. 26 to Japan, which, as Secretary Hull knew and said at the moment, practically put an end to negotiations with Japan and passed over to the Army and Navy the burden of safeguarding the security of the United States. . . .
>
> (c) The rejection of appeals made to President Roosevelt by Gen. Marshall and Adm. Stark on Nov. 5 and also later on Nov. 27, 1941, for a delay in bringing about a breach with Japan —appeals based on their belief that the Army and Navy were not then ready for war with Japan.
>
> (d) The orders of the Secretary of War to the effect that Gen. Marshall and Adm. Stark *should not* put into their memorandum appealing for delay, signed Nov. 27, anything that could be "construed as a recommendation to the President that he request Japan to reopen the conversations" (Tr., Vol. 20, p. 3325).

According to Secretary Hull, the tactics of waiting for the Japanese to fire the first shot was, in a measure, forced upon the administration by the attachment of a large part of the American people to neutrality as expressed in the neutrality legislation of Congress and by their opposition to involvement in war in the Far East as well as elsewhere.

This view Secretary Hull expressed in his statement to the committee (Tr., Vol. 7, pp. 1096 ff.) and it is set forth more fully by other documents before the committee, particularly the

State Department's publication: *Peace and War: United States Foreign Policy 1931–41,* especially chapter 1.

In this chapter the State Department explains that the President and Secretary Hull were hampered in the pursuit of the foreign policy they had "clearly" decided upon—at a date not fixed by the Secretary —on account of the opposition by "much of public opinion" in the United States. In this chapter the State Department also explains that—

"Our foreign policy during the decade under consideration (1931–41) necessarily had to move within the framework of a gradual evolution of public opinion in the United States away from the idea of isolation expressed in 'neutrality' legislation. . . . The pages (in the volume) which follow show the slow march of the United States from an attitude of illusory aloofness toward world-wide forces endangering America to a position in the forefront of the United Nations that are now (1943) making common cause against an attempt at world conquest unparalleled alike in boldness of conception and in brutality of operation."

It is a serious question whether the President and his advisers were justified in making the conclusions that the country would support them for war; and whether actions taken by them upon their own opinion without placing the matter before Congress was in violation of their responsibilities under the Constitution and laws of the land.[32]

The problem, as viewed by the President and his war council, was to discover "the basis on which this country's position could be most clearly explained to our own people and to the world."[33] Roosevelt's first attempt to reconcile his pledges to the British, the Dutch, and the Chinese with his promises to the American people was made at the weekly cabinet meeting on November 7. Stimson relates:

> The President at the meeting undertook to take an informal vote of the cabinet as to whether it was thought the American people would back us up if it became necessary to strike at Japan, in case she should attack England in Malaya or the Dutch in the East Indies. The cabinet was unanimous in the feeling that the country would support such a move.[34]

Roosevelt, with a jocular reference to a vote taken at one of Lincoln's cabinet meetings, remarked, "This time the vote IS unanimous. I feel the same way."[35]

At the meeting of the war cabinet on November 25, Stimson undertook to persuade Roosevelt that the President's warning of August 17 to Ambassador Nomura constituted sufficient warrant for him to order military action if Japan so much as crossed into neutral Thailand. He said:

> I pointed out to the President that he had already taken the first steps toward an ultimatum in notifying Japan way back last summer that if she crossed the border into Thailand she was violating our safety and that therefore he had only to point out [to Japan] that to follow any such expedition [to the south] was a violation of a warning we had already given.[36]

Three days later the President made up his mind. Stimson described the radical solution proposed as follows:

> The first thing in the morning of the next day—Friday, November 28—I received information from G-2 of such a formidable character with regard to the movements of the Japanese forces along the Asiatic coast that I decided to take it to the President before he got up.
>
> I saw him while he was still in bed, and we discussed the situation. He suggested that there were three alternatives, as my notes show: First, to do nothing; second, to make something in the nature of an ultimatum, stating a point beyond which we would fight; or, third, to fight at once.
>
> I said that I felt to do nothing was out of the question and the President agreed with me. As to the other two alternatives, the desirable thing to do from the point of view of our own tactics and safety was to take the initiative and attack without further warning. It is axiomatic that the best defense is offense. It is always dangerous to wait and let the enemy make the first move. I was inclined to feel that the warning given in August by the President against further moves by the Japanese toward Thailand justified an attack without further warning, particularly as their new movement southward indicated that they were about to violate that warning. On the other hand, I realized that the situation could be made more clear cut if a further warning were given.[37]

At the war cabinet meeting that noon, the mechanics of preparing the country to accept war were decided upon. Stimson says:

> We decided, therefore, that we could not just sit still and do nothing. On the other hand, we also decided that we could not attack without a further warning to Japan, and we discussed what form that warning should take. The President suggested a special telegram from himself to the emperor of Japan. After some discussion it was decided that he would send such a letter

to the emperor, which would not be made public, and that at the same time he would deliver a special message to Congress reporting on the danger and reporting what we would have to do if the danger happened.[38]

Stimson's report of the decision in his diary reads,

> I pointed out . . . that he had better send his letter to the emperor separate as one thing and a secret thing, and then make his speech to the Congress as a separate and more understandable thing to the people of the United States. This was the final decision at that time and the President asked Hull and Knox and myself to try to draft such papers.[39]

After the meeting Roosevelt left for Warm Springs. "The rest of the weekend," said Stimson, "was largely taken up with preparing a suggested draft of a message for the President to deliver to Congress, in which Secretary Knox and I co-operated with Mr. Hull and his associates in the State Department."[40] Hull completed the draft by noon on November 29,[41] but events moved with such speed that it was unnecessary for the President to deliver the message.

Stimson later said that the President at this time was "undoubtedly considering" an attack on Jap forces threatening Southeast Asia.[42] His position, however, was that Roosevelt, by ordering a message to "condition" Congress, showed that he was not presuming to usurp the war-making power.

A strange light is cast upon this explanation by a covering note sent to Roosevelt by Hull with the draft message to Congress. In his memorandum, Hull said, "I think we agree that you will not send message to Congress until the last stage of our relations, relating to actual hostilities."[43] Thus, only after war was an accomplished fact —only after events had passed beyond recall—was Congress to be called upon to ratify the actual existence of hostilities by jumping through the administration's hoop with a declaration of war.

On November 29 Roosevelt cut short his holiday at Warm Springs after a telephone summons from Hull. He returned to Washington December 1. The following day Stimson saw him and was encouraged to believe that he would go full speed ahead with the program to prepare the country to enter the war even if there were no attack by Japan on the United States. Stimson said:

> The President went step by step over the situation and I think has made up his mind to go ahead. He has asked the Japanese through Sumner Welles what they intend by this new

occupation of southern Indo-China—just what they are going to do—and has demanded a quick reply. The President is still deliberating the possibility of a message to the Emperor, although all the rest of us are rather against it, but in addition to that he is quite settled, I think, that he will make a message to the Congress and will perhaps back that up with a speech to the country. He said that he was going to take the matters right up when he left us.[44]

After this there was only one more mention of the President's program to condition public opinion against American entry into the war in the event that Japan withheld a direct attack upon the United States. It was disclosed that on the afternoon of December 6 Roosevelt had informed the Australian government of the steps he intended to take if Japan had not taken belligerent action by the following Wednesday, December 10.

Information regarding Roosevelt's maneuvers was supplied the Joint Congressional Committee May 26, 1946, by the Australian legation in Washington. The letter to the committee from the legation referred to a telegram from the Australian minister for external affairs in Canberra to the British secretary of state for dominion affairs in London. The legation said of this telegram:

The telegram contains the substance of a message which the Australian minister for external affairs had received from the Australian minister at Washington. This message was dispatched from Washington at 9:30 P.M. on Dec. 6, 1941. *The information contained therein regarding the procedure to be followed by the President had come orally from the President late in the afternoon of December 6.*[45]

The paraphrase of the Australian minister for external affairs' telegram is as follows:

Subject to conditions that President gives prior approval to text of warning as drafted and also gives signal for actual delivery of warning, we concur in draft as a joint communication from all His Majesty's governments. I point out that message from Australian minister at Washington just received notes that,

1. President has decided to send message to Emperor.
2. President's subsequent procedure is that if no answer is received by him from the Emperor by Monday evening,
(*a*) he will issue his warning on Tuesday afternoon or evening,
(*b*) warning or equivalent by British or others will not fol-

low until Wednesday morning, i. e., after his own warning has been delivered repeatedly to Tokyo and Washington.[46]

It is only curious that as late in the day as this Roosevelt should still have been worrying lest the Japanese fail to provide the necessary incident.

By December 1 it was clear to the President that his fears were groundless that Japan might begin hostilities against Britain and Holland without shooting at the United States. Decoded Japanese intercepts told Roosevelt what he wanted to know. Japan's Washington envoys were advised that the November 28 deadline for a diplomatic solution had come and gone. From now on things were "automatically going to happen." The ambassadors were instructed to keep talking in order to lull American suspicions. Assurances were given to Germany and Italy that, "quicker than any one dreams," Japan would be fighting the United States. Assurances were given in turn by Germany and Italy that they would fight at Japan's side.

No one could have misread these messages, nor did Roosevelt misread them. On the night of December 7, when he summoned cabinet members and congressional leaders to the White House to tell them of the Pearl Harbor attack, he said, "We have reason to believe that the Germans have told the Japanese that if Japan declares war, they will too. In other words, a declaration of war by Japan automatically brings. . . ."

The President was interrupted at that point, but he had said enough to show that he had read the Japanese code intercepts and that he knew what they meant.[47] A long report from the Japanese ambassador in Berlin on November 29 and a shorter dispatch from Tokyo to Berlin on November 30, both of which were translated December 1, had told Roosevelt that Germany would join Japan in war with the United States.

So, while Nomura and Kurusu kept up their sham conversations with Hull, Roosevelt and the leaders of the administration were busy practicing the same sort of deception on their countrymen.

Stimson, in his statement to the congressional committee, said,

From some of the comments quoted in the public press, one would get the impression that the imminent threat of war in October and November, 1941, was a deep secret, known only to the authorities in Washington, who kept it mysteriously to themselves. Nothing could be further from the truth."[48]

He then cited speeches by Knox, Welles, and Roosevelt, none delivered after November 11, as proof that the people and Congress had been adequately warned of "the imminence of war with Japan."

Nowhere did Stimson say that not a whisper of Roosevelt's August 17 ultimatum ever reached Congress or the people, that instead it had been hidden under the smoke screen of the Atlantic Charter; that in none of these speeches was there an inkling that the United States had been committed to war if Japan moved against anybody anywhere in the Pacific; that the true nature and course of the American-Japanese conversations were not disclosed until after the war was in progress; that the last of the so-called warning speeches was made more than two weeks before the definite, final crisis of November 26; and that afterward that crisis was concealed until the attack on Oahu struck the people as a monstrous, shocking surprise.

This surprise was carefully prepared by the devious statements and actions of the men in Washington who knew that war was at hand. At Warm Springs on November 29 Roosevelt suggested the possibility that "next year . . . our boys of the military and naval academies may be fighting." He knew that all of America would be at war within days. At his press conference December 2 he referred to Japan as "a friendly power with which the United States is at peace"[49] when he knew from "Magic" of Japan's announced intention to fight the United States.

Secretary Hull December 3 emphasized that diplomatic negotiations with Japan were still in progress. He called Nomura and Kurusu his "friends" and said insistently that the conversations he was having with them were "exploratory" and tentative.[50] He knew that Japan considered them final and formal, that Japan's decoded messages showed them "ruptured and broken" as a consequence of his proposals of November 26, that the conversations were being continued only to mask developing military action, and that Japan had told its diplomatic representatives and its Axis partners that it would soon be fighting the United States.

On December 4, the very day that Japan announced through the "winds" signal that a state of war had already been secretly decreed against the United States, Britain, and Holland, Stimson abandoned his post of duty and flew up to New York to see his dentist.[51] No one would have gathered from this behavior that any tasks confronted the military establishment. Nor did Stimson at a press conference December 5 offer more enlightenment. He stated, "with some humor," that he had been out of touch with the news, because, having assurance that "the conversations with Japan were still in progress," he had spent the preceding day at his dentist's in New York.[52]

A curious sidelight on the professed ignorance of Stimson and the Washington insiders that war was coming was provided before the congressional committee by Lieut. Col. Clausen. The knowledge that was supposed to be lacking in Washington was possessed in comparatively obscure quarters elsewhere, Clausen discovered.

While in Honolulu, he said, he saw a copy of a cable from Col. G. H. Wilkinson, a secret British agent in Manila, to the commercial firm in Honolulu which Wilkinson represented. Wilkinson on December 3 cabled John E. Russell, president of Theodore H. Davies & Co., Ltd., a British sugar firm in Honolulu, stating his intelligence indicated the Japanese were rushing the building of railroads and air fields in Indo-China. The cable went on to say: "Our considered opinion concludes that Japan envisages early hostilities with Britain and the United States. Japan does not intend to attack Russia at present, but will act in south."

Clausen said that Wilkinson's message bore all the earmarks of having been prompted by independent interception of the Japanese "winds" message.[53]

Clausen also obtained an affidavit from Maj. Gen. C. J. Willoughby, intelligence officer for Gen. MacArthur in the Philippines, stating that Wilkinson had approached MacArthur's headquarters with a request that he be attached as liaison officer representing Britain. Gen. Willoughby said that the British agent represented himself as having the backing of Prime Minister Churchill. Willoughby said that Wilkinson "combined the status of a respected business man with that of a secret agent."

Describing Wilkinson and others of his type, Willoughby said, "This net of potential spies is world-wide. I find them loyal to no one but themselves and the empire."[54]

If the nation were warned of war, as Stimson says, why did the Senate, on the afternoon of December 4, adjourn on the motion of Senator Lucas of Illinois* until December 8, the day after the attack on Oahu? Why, on December 5, should the House have adjourned until December 8 after a protracted session in which not one word was uttered about war at any moment with Japan?[55]

There was one flaw in the general picture of Washington's unawareness. On December 4 Maxwell Hamilton of the State Depart-

---

*Appointed four years later as a New Deal majority member of the Joint Congressional Committee to investigate Pearl Harbor.

ment's Far Eastern section was busy discussing plans with the British embassy to arrange with the Japanese for the exchange of civilian nationals when war came.[56]

Stimson says that the "people had been slow to recognize the danger."[57] The man who, having been given repeated notice of war, responded by going off to his dentist, also condemns Gen. Short. He contends that his message of November 27 gave Short the precise situation.[58] However well or badly Short was informed of the situation on the 27th, that situation changed, by Stimson's own statement, on November 28 and December 1, 2, and 6. Short, however, was left uninformed for the last ten days before the attack.

The President, Stimson, and the war cabinet had determined on November 28 that if the Japanese expedition steaming down the China Coast entered the Gulf of Siam, the United States would be at war with Japan. On December 1 there were reports that the expedition was landing near Saigon, Indo-China, instead of continuing into the gulf. "This appeared to give us a little respite," Stimson says.[59] Roosevelt, believing the report of the landing was valid, demanded of the Japanese on December 2 what "they intended by this new occupation of southern Indo-China."[60]

If Japan was not going to force a war, the President was quite willing to do so. Adm. Ingersoll told the congressional committee that this same day Roosevelt ordered three small vessels dispatched into the Gulf of Siam as a "defensive information patrol." A dispatch sent by the chief of naval operations to Adm. Hart commenced with this unusual statement: "President directs that the following be done as soon as possible and within two days if possible after receipt this dispatch."[61]

Rep. Keefe said of this project:

The President's directions were that the commander-in-chief of the Asiatic fleet was to charter three small vessels to form a "defensive information patrol." The minimum requirements to establish these ships as United States men of war would suffice in manning them. These requirements were: command by a naval officer and the mounting of a small gun and one machine gun. The employment of Filipino crews with the minimum number naval ratings was authorized. The ships were to observe and report by radio Japanese movement in the West China Sea and Gulf of Siam. The President prescribed the point at which each vessel was to be stationed. One vessel was to be stationed between Hainan and Hue; one between Camranh Bay and Cape St. Jaques; one off Pointe De Camau (Ex. 37, p. 39).

All these points were clearly in the path of the Japanese advance
down the coast of Indo-China, and towards the Gulf of Siam.
The Navy Department did not originate this plan (Tr., 11351).
The Navy Department would not have directed it to be done
unless the President had specifically ordered it (Tr., 11351).
Adm. Hart was already conducting reconnaissance off that coast
by planes from Manila (Tr., p. 11350). So far as the Navy Department was concerned, sufficient information was being received from this air reconnaissance (Tr., p. 11351). Had the
Japanese fired upon any one of these three small vessels, it
would have constituted an overt act on the part of Japan (Tr.,
p. 11352).[62]

This was only one of the long series of attempts by Roosevelt to
create an "incident" which would plunge the United States into war.
Representative Keefe submits the following comment on the program:[63]

The concept of an "incident" as a factor which would unify
public opinion behind an all-out war effort either in the Atlantic or Pacific had influenced the thinking of officials in Washington for a long time. Many plans which might have produced
an incident were from time to time discussed and considered.
As early as Oct. 10, 1940, Secretary Knox had advised Adm.
Richardson, then commander-in-chief of the Pacific fleet, of a
plan the President was considering to shut off all trade between
Japan and North and South America. This would be accomplished by means of a patrol of American ships in two lines
extending from Hawaii westward to the Philippines, and from
Samoa toward the Dutch East Indies (Tr., p. 792). This plan
was to be instituted in the event Japan retaliated against Great
Britain upon the reopening of the Burma Road scheduled for
Oct. 17, 1940 (Tr., p. 792). Adm. Richardson was amazed at this
proposal and stated that the fleet was not prepared to put such
a plan into effect, nor for the war which would certainly result
from such a course of action (Tr., p. 793).

On Feb. 11, 1941, the chief of naval operations in a memorandum for the President, described the President as considering a plan to send a detachment of vessels to the Far East and
perhaps to permit a "leak" that they were going out there (Ex.
106). He quoted the President in the same memorandum as
stating that he would not mind losing one or two cruisers, but
that he did not want to take a chance on losing five or six.
Again, in a letter of April 19, 1941, the chief of naval operations
quoted the President as saying to him:

"Betty, just as soon as those ships come back from Australia and New Zealand, or perhaps a little before, I want to send some more out. I just want to keep them popping up here and there and keep the Japs guessing" (Ex. 106).

On May 24, 1941, Adm. Stark wrote Adm. Kimmel—

"Day before yesterday the President gave me an overall limit of 30 days to prepare and have ready an expedition of 25,000 men to sail for and to take the Azores. Whether or not there would be opposition I do not know but we have to be fully prepared for strenuous opposition" (Ex. 106).

On July 25, 1941, the chief of naval operations wrote Adm. Kimmel to the effect that he might be called upon to send a carrier-load of planes to Russia via one of the Asiatic Russian ports (Ex. 106). "I don't know that you will, but the President has told me to be prepared for it, and I want you to have the thought." Adm. Kimmel replied to this suggestion as follows:

"I entertain no doubt that such an operation, if discovered (as is highly probable), will be tantamount to initiation of a Japanese-American war. If we are going to take the initiative in commencing such a war, I can think of more effective ways for gaining initial advantage. In short, it is my earnest conviction that use of a carrier to deliver aircraft to Asiatic Russian ports in the present period of strained relations is to invite war. If we have decided upon war it would be far better to take direct offensive action. If for reasons of political expediency, it has been determined to force Japan to fire the first shot, let us choose a method which will be more advantageous to ourselves" (Ex. 106).

On July 31, 1941, Adm. Stark sent Adm. Kimmel a copy of a letter to Capt. Charles M. Cooke as follows:

"Within 48 hours after the Russian situation broke I went to the President, with the Secretary's approval, and stated that on the assumption that the country's decision is not to let England fall, we should immediately seize the psychological opportunity presented by the Russian-German clash and announce and start escorting immediately, and protecting the Western Atlantic on a large scale; that such a declaration, followed by immediate action on our part, would almost certainly involve us in the war and that I considered every day of delay in our getting into the war as dangerous and that much more delay might be fatal to Britain's survival. I reminded him that I had been asking this for months in the State Department and elsewhere, etc., etc., etc. I have been maintaining that only a war psychology could or would speed things up the way they should be speeded up; that strive as we would it just is not in the nature of things to get the results in peace that we would, were we at war.

"The Iceland situation may produce an 'incident.' You are as familiar with that and the President's statements and answers at press conferences as I am. Whether or not we will get an 'incident' because of the protection we are giving Iceland and the shipping which we must send in support of Iceland and our troops, I do not know—only Hitler can answer" (Ex. 106).

Reverting to the Japanese troop convoy steaming down the coast of Indo-China, Roosevelt and his colleagues in Washington learned definitely on December 6 that the report of the landing near Saigon was in error and that the Japanese expedition had in fact crossed the line which the administration had determined would pull the United States into war. That information came in two messages from Ambassador John Winant in London. The first reached Roosevelt and Hull at 10:40 a.m., December 6, almost twenty-seven hours before the Japs struck Hawaii. This message, marked "Triple priority and most urgent" and "Personal and secret to the Secretary and the President," stated:

British Admiralty reports that at 3:00 a.m., London time, this morning two parties seen off Cambodia Point, sailing slowly westward toward Kra, 14 hours distant in time. First party 25 transports, 6 cruisers, 10 destroyers. Second party 10 transports, 2 cruisers, 10 destroyers.[64]

This dispatch, read in the light of the unanimous decision of the war cabinet on November 28 that the United States would fight if and when Japan entered the Gulf of Siam, meant to Roosevelt, Hull, Stimson, Knox, Marshall, and Stark that the United States was at war as of 10:40 a.m. that day. The actual Japanese attack on Thailand, the Isthmus of Kra, and Malaya would come in fourteen hours.

During cross-examination of Gen. Marshall, Senator Ferguson referred to the joint memorandum of November 27 in which Stark and Marshall recommended "military action" if Jap forces moved into western Thailand or advanced southward through the Gulf of Siam.

"According to your memorandum to the President," Ferguson said, "a Jap advance into Kra called for military action by us. So Winant's message meant war with Japan, didn't it?"

"It meant an attack by Japan in a military sense," Marshall lamely replied, "but the question of going to war was up to the two governments [the United States and Japan]."[65]

Winant's second dispatch of December 6, again marked "Triple priority and most urgent" and "Personal and secret for the Secretary," reached Hull at 3:05 p.m. This message read in part:

Again from Cadogan. Admiralty conference on information just forwarded, Cadogan attending. They were uncertain as to whether destination of parties is Kra or Bangkok. Latter would not be reached before Monday.

Note a discrepancy in time reported by me and time reported in our naval dispatch, latter stating 3:00 A.M. Greenwich time, by dispatch as given me 3:00 A.M. London time. Believe former correct.

British feel pressed for time in relation to guaranteeing support Thailand fearing Japan might force them to invite invasion on pretext protection before British have opportunity to guarantee support but wanting to carry out President's wishes in message transmitted by Welles to Halifax. . . .

I am having lunch with the Prime Minister tomorrow at his usual place in the country and will be constantly in contact with the embassy over private wires in case you wish to communicate with me.[66]

Efforts were made at the congressional hearings to learn from Welles the nature of the "President's wishes" as conveyed to Lord Halifax. Welles said that there was no written record of the message. He was unable to achieve any satisfactory recall.[67] Another of Roosevelt's maneuvers thus is concealed.

The dispatches from American representatives in the Southwest Pacific which came into Washington following Winant's messages show clearly, however, that the British and Dutch now considered the United States bound to come to their assistance. Adm. Hart radioed for confirmation of the British assertion at Singapore that America had assured armed support if Japan landed in the Kra Isthmus, violated any part of Thailand, or attacked the Dutch East Indies.*

The paraphrase of a second secret message from Hart, received at the War Department at 4:29 P.M. December 6, stated,

[Lieut. Col. F. G.] Brink [American military observer at Singapore] advises that at one o'clock in the afternoon, following a course due west, were seen a battleship, five cruisers, seven destroyers, and twenty-five merchant ships; these were seen at 106 degrees 8 minutes east, 8 degrees north; this was the first report.

The second report was that ten merchant ships, two cruisers, and ten destroyers were seen following the same course at 106 degrees 20 minutes east, 7 degrees 35 minutes north.

Both of the above reports came from patrols of the Royal Air Force.[68]

*See Chap. VIII.

These movements were in violation of paragraphs (*b*) and (*c*) of the deadline provisions of the Singapore conference, and the British were bringing them to American attention because they automatically required action by us.

When Adm. Stark was examined by Senator Ferguson about this message, he candidly admitted, "The presumption which we instilled into the dispatch was war."[69]

On December 6 Adm. Hart was already acting under the ABCD pact. Adm. Sir Tom Phillips, who had arrived at Singapore December 2 with the battleship "Prince of Wales" and the battle cruiser "Repulse," conferred in Manila with Hart on the 6th. Phillips had brought with him only four destroyers and utterly lacked carrier air cover for his big units. Hart agreed at this conference the day before the Pearl Harbor attack to assign Phillips four American and six Dutch destroyers to supplement his covering force, but before they could be sent to his assistance the Japanese caught and sank the "Prince of Wales" and "Repulse" December 10 in a combined bombing and aerial torpedo attack off Kuantan on the east coast of Malaya.[70]

The Australian government on December 6 held up still another message in which Col. Merle-Smith, American military attaché at Melbourne, sought to address a reminder from Dutch authorities in the East Indies that the United States was now committed to come to their assistance. Merle-Smith's message, addressed to the War Department and to Gen. Short, was dated December 6, but did not arrive in Washington until 7:58 P.M. December 7, twelve hours after the attack on Pearl Harbor, having been held up for seventeen hours by the Australians.

Merle-Smith said Dutch intelligence had reported that a Jap fleet was moving toward Ambon or Menado in the Dutch Indies, which would carry it across the Davao-Waigeo line established at the Singapore staff conference, and that, as a result, the Dutch high command in the Pacific had ordered the execution of "Plan A-2." This was the Dutch portion of Rainbow No. 5, the master war plan, calling for joint American-British-Dutch deployment against Japan.

Col. Merle-Smith's assistant, Lieut. Robert H. O'Dell, said that he and his superior were summoned to a conference the afternoon of December 5 with Air Chief Marshal Sir Charles S. Burnett, commander of the Australian air force, and Comdr. Saom, Dutch liaison officer at Melbourne. There they were told of the Jap fleet movement and of Dutch action. Merle-Smith prepared a radiogram that night to warn Hawaii and Washington of the developments, but Burnett asked Merle-Smith to "wait twenty-four hours" before sending it, and Merle-Smith "reluctantly agreed."

O'Dell further related that the Dutch action in executing their portion of the war plan "called for joint operations by the Australians, Dutch, and our navy, if nothing else."[71]

Upon first sighting the approach of this fleet, the Dutch had consulted Secretary Hull as to the advisability of addressing a warning to Japan. Hull asked the advice of Stark, who said that if the Dutch wanted to give the Japs a warning, it should be in the form of a declaration that Japanese naval vessels or expeditionary forces crossing a line running between Davao and Waigeo would be considered hostile and would be attacked.[72] Asked if he had drawn up the memorandum without informing Roosevelt, Stark responded, "I don't think I would have without consulting the President."[73]

The Dutch had ordered a comprehensive mobilization of forces in the East Indies on December 1, and the same day British troops at Singapore were also alerted for war. The eyes of the partners in the secret ABCD alliance were turned upon the United States. On December 6, in Melbourne, the four powers issued a statement in which it was promised that they would match Japan, "move by move." The State Department in Washington promptly denied that American adherence to any such manifesto was authorized.[74]

During the week Prime Minister Churchill had been importuning Roosevelt to convey a stiff warning to Japan. The President agreed to send a message to Hirohito, and, if no reply came from the emperor by Monday evening, December 8, to "issue his warning on Tuesday afternoon or evening." This was to be followed by a warning on Wednesday from the British and possibly the Dutch. A British draft of the warning, sent by Churchill December 7 to Roosevelt "for comment," warned Japan against invading Thailand.[75]

"Should hostilities unfortunately result," it read, "the responsibility will rest with Japan."[76]

As "Magic" had shown, this strategy was superfluous, for the Jap attack was certain to intervene. The administration, with war only a few hours away, with the intercepts and the Japanese spy messages pointing to an attack upon Pearl Harbor, suddenly began protesting a passion for peace.

Roosevelt, for the record alone, sent his message to Hirohito the night of the 6th, when he knew it was much too late to avoid war. Now that it no longer mattered, he did not insist that a settlement be based on Hull's ten points of the memorandum of November 26, which had served as the final goad in bringing Japan to war. He did not even mention the November 26 conditions. He knew that they were no longer relevant, just as he knew that his whole message was without meaning. It was released for publication to Monday morning papers, the day after the attack, and in the confusion of the hour seemed to confirm the administration's aggrieved cries about the duplicity of the Japs. With what is now known about Roosevelt's diplomacy, the appeal to Hirohito becomes merely the act of a politician pulling the wool over the eyes of his own countrymen.

On Sunday, December 7, when the complete fourteen-part final Japanese reply to Hull and the pilot message instructing that it be handed in at 1:00 P.M. had announced that the hour was about to strike, the pretense of innocence was maintained to the last. Roosevelt and Hopkins arranged the tableau in the White House study. Hull, Stimson, and Knox gathered in the morning in the State Department, where Stimson muttered that "something" was hanging in the air and Hull voiced the obvious conclusion that the Japs were up to "some deviltry." Stimson wrote in his diary,

> The main thing is to hold the main people who are interested in the Far East together—the British, ourselves, the Dutch, the Australians, the Chinese. Knox also had his views as to the importance of showing immediately how these different nations must stand together.[77]

The prudent Stimson had Hull and Knox dictate their views on the spot[78]—more contributions for the record, to be produced at an opportune time, as they were produced when the congressional committee at length began nosing around. Stimson states:

> The messages we were receiving now indicated that the Japanese force was continuing on in the Gulf of Siam, and again we discussed whether we would not have to fight if Malaya or the Netherlands were attacked and the British or Dutch fought. We all three thought that we must fight if those nations fought.[79]

At 2 o'clock, while he was at lunch, Stimson was telephoned the news by the President that the Japs were bombing Hawaii. Stimson's description of his reception of this news was significant. He confided to his diary, "We three [Hull, Knox, and Stimson] all thought that we must fight if the British fought. *But now the Japs have solved the whole thing by attacking us directly in Hawaii.*"*[80]

*Italics supplied.

Japan had obligingly provided the solution for President Roosevelt's dilemma.

Stimson expressed his reaction to the Jap attack which was costing 3,000 American lives with the utmost frankness. He wrote in his diary:

> When the news first came that Japan had attacked us my first feeling was of relief that the indecision was over and that a crisis had come in a way which would unite all our people. This continued to be my dominant feeling in spite of the news of catastrophes which quickly developed. For I feel that this country united has practically nothing to fear; while the apathy and divisions stirred up by unpatriotic men had been hitherto very discouraging.[81]

In other words, Stimson's view was that it was patriotic to go to war for the British and Dutch empires, and unpatriotic to try to stay at peace.

That night, at the White House meeting of cabinet members and congressional leaders, Roosevelt wonderingly observed again and again that now the nation was at war, and that war had come from an overt act on the part of Japan.

"Well," he said, "we were attacked. There is no question about that."[82]

Again, he said, "The fact is that a shooting war is going on today in the Pacific. We are in it."[83]

It was almost as if he couldn't quite believe it.

The Roosevelt policy which took the United States to war has been aptly described as resembling a river which occasionally disappears underground only to emerge nearer the sea—in this instance, the sea of total war. The Japanese attack upon Pearl Harbor averted a serious constitutional crisis in the United States. This crisis was precipitated by Roosevelt's policy of using his "commander-in-chief" powers to push through action in the field of foreign affairs which had its full intended effect before Congress could be consulted.[84]

Chapter Twenty

WHO WAS GUILTY?

THE ATTACK by Japan upon Pearl Harbor provided the long-sought incident that put the United States into the World War. The Japanese, however, had exceeded the Roosevelt administration's specifications that, in firing the first shot, they should not "allow too much danger to ourselves." Pearl Harbor was more than a mere token act of hostilities. The Japanese had kept on firing until 2,326 Americans were dead and the Pacific fleet was a wreck. Other disasters were accumulating and were foreseeable. The isolated garrisons of Wake, Guam, and Luzon were soon sacrificed to the Washington war plan.

A catastrophe of such dimensions, if admitted, might have an effect other than rallying a divided country to fight a hard and costly war which more than 80 per cent of the people hadn't wanted. If admitted, it might have diminished the willingness of the people to forget the provocative course by which the President had by-passed Congress in inviting hostilities. There might have been an attitude of serious questioning toward the acts and the wisdom of Mr. Roosevelt and the men around him. That was the last thing the "commander-in-chief" wanted or could afford.

Soon the administration strategy was clarified. The tremendous defeat at Hawaii was first ascribed to treacherous Japan, launching an attack at the very time that the American government was trying to lead the erring war lords of Nippon into the ways of peace. The administration conveniently forgot to remind the American people of the part played in bringing about the result of December 7 by its campaign of economic warfare, its secret diplomacy, its covert military alliances, the submission of demands which Japan found "humiliating," and its own complete abandonment of neutrality in favor of nondeclared war.

When it became apparent, a few days after Pearl Harbor, that the manifest failures which contributed to the crushing defeat at Oahu could not be blamed solely on the Japanese, Roosevelt and his associates in the civilian government and high command invented some new villains to divert the guilt from themselves. For the defeat at Pearl Harbor the blame—all of the blame, not part of it—was apportioned between Adm. Kimmel and Gen. Short. Secretary Knox said they were not on the alert. Roosevelt dismissed them from their commands. The Presidential commission headed by Justice Roberts confirmed the sentence by finding them guilty of dereliction of duty. They were retired. It was announced that some time in the future they would be court martialed. Under such charges, they had no recourse except to keep silent.

So the matter stood for almost four years. With all of the apparatus of wartime censorship and propaganda to support them, the administration leaders felt safe. In 1944, when the clamor for a fair investigation of Pearl Harbor forced Secretary Knox and Secretary Stimson to convoke a Navy Court and an Army Board of Inquiry, the administration's thesis that Kimmel and Short alone were to blame was badly shaken.

The findings of the Army Board reached into the President's cabinet and the high command in assessing the blame. It charged offenses to Secretary of State Hull, Chief of Staff Marshall, and Chief of War Plans Gerow, in addition to Short.[1] President Truman and Secretary Stimson, now that suspicion was beginning to be directed toward Roosevelt's official circle and the administration's service pets, felt constrained to overrule the Army Board. Stimson termed the criticism of Hull "uncalled for" and that of Marshall "entirely unjustified."[2] Truman endeavored to court martial the American people.

"The country," he said, "was not ready for preparedness. . . . I think the country is as much to blame as any individual in this final situation that developed in Pearl Harbor."[3]

The Navy Court's report was as distasteful to the administration as had been the Army Board's. The court refused to adopt the postulate that Kimmel was guilty of anything. "Based upon the facts established," the report stated, "the court is of the opinion that no offenses have been committed nor serious blame incurred on the part of any person or persons in the naval service."[4]

Adm. King, commander-in-chief of the fleet, and Secretary of the Navy Forrestal could not let that stand. They appended supplemental statements of their own to the court's report which had the effect of overruling their own investigators. They decreed that Adm. Kimmel was not to hold any post in the Navy "which requires the exercise of superior judgment." In order not to make too glaring a demonstration of prejudice, they threw Adm. Stark to the wolves, returning the same specification against him.[5]

Finally, Congress stepped into the Pearl Harbor controversy. An investigation could not be forestalled, so the administration decided the prudent thing was to make the inquiry its own. The majority party initiated the investigation, decreed its conditions, and controlled its course. Public hearings could not be avoided, nor could Kimmel and Short be bound to their four-year silence. For the first time testimony was taken in the open, and for the first time the Hawaiian commanders were able to submit a defense to the public.

Adm. Kimmel, tracing the involutions of previous investigations, said of the Roberts inquiry, "I had no way of knowing what evidence had been given the commission other than my own testimony. It was more than two years after the commission concluded its proceedings before I was permitted to know what evidence had been presented to the commission." When he did read the record, Kimmel said, he found substantial inaccuracies and misrepresentations.[6]

Of the proceedings of the Navy Court the admiral said:

> I was present at all hearings, was represented by counsel, introduced evidence, examined, and cross-examined witnesses. This proceeding was the only one of the secret investigations of Pearl Harbor in which these basic American rights were accorded to me.
>
> The Naval Court of Inquiry found unanimously that there was no ground for criticism of my decisions or actions. The findings of the Naval Court were not made public, however, until August 28, 1945. When they appeared in the press, I learned for the first time that the Naval Court of Inquiry had found that I was not guilty of any dereliction of duty or errors of judgment.
>
> On February 6, 1945, I wrote to the Secretary of the Navy requesting permission to read the findings of fact, opinions, and recommendations of the Naval Court. On February 13, 1945, the Secretary of the Navy denied my request.
>
> In May of 1945, long after the Naval Court of Inquiry had filed its report, the Secretary of the Navy detailed Adm. Hewitt to conduct a further secret investigation into Pearl Harbor. I learned from the public press that the investigation had begun. On May 8, 1945, I wrote to the Secretary requesting permission

to be present at the hearings before Adm. Hewitt, to introduce evidence, to confront and cross-examine witnesses. The Secretary of the Navy denied my request in a letter of May 14, 1945.

On May 24, 1945, I wrote again to the Secretary requesting that he reconsider his decision to exclude me from the Hewitt investigation. The Secretary of the Navy never replied. The Hewitt investigation went ahead in secret.

On the basis of this secret investigation, the Secretary, in effect, set aside the verdict of the Naval Court of Inquiry.[7]

The even more devious history of the endeavor of Secretary Stimson to make charges stick against Gen. Short was traced during the congressional hearings by Senator Ferguson and Representative Keefe.

The War Department bureau of public relations on February 28, 1942, issued a press release entitled "Retirement of Gen. Short Approved." This release read:

> The Secretary of War announced today the acceptance, effective February 28, 1942, of the application for retirement of Maj. Gen. Walter C. Short "without condonation of any offense or prejudice to any future disciplinary action."
>
> The Secretary of War announced at the same time that, based upon the findings of the report of the Roberts Commission, he had directed the preparation of charges for the trial by court martial of Gen. Short, alleging dereliction of duty. The Secretary of War made it clear, however, that the trial upon these charges would not be held until such time as the public interest and safety would permit."[8]

"I understand, then, from that, that the Secretary of War indicated that upon the basis of the Roberts report you would be court martialed at some time?" Senator Ferguson said to Short.

"He at least stated that he had directed this to be drawn," Short replied.

"Now, did you ever do anything in any way to prevent that court martial—the charges being filed?"

"I did not," Short responded. "In fact, I signed a waiver that I would agree to a court martial within six months after termination of hostilities."

"Now, have you ever made any direct request for a court martial trial?"

"I have not."

"And you have done nothing, as I understand it, to prevent such a trial?"

"I have not."

"You are prepared, then, to defend any trial that the government may start? Is that the way it stands?"

"That is the way it stands."[9]

Ferguson then developed that on April 20, 1942, the judge advocate general's office, acting on instructions from Secretary Stimson, prepared court martial charges against Short alleging violation of the 96th Article of War, with eleven specifications. A memorandum dated November 27, 1944, which was attached to the judge advocate's specifications of two and a half years before, stated, "The above charges were merely tentative and possible charges and were never approved by the judge advocate or transmitted to the Secretary of War. Of course, they were never made public."[10]

This indicated that Stimson had done his best to hang something on Short, but that the Army's chief legal officer considered the case so weak that he did not even bring it to the attention of the Secretary, let alone to public trial. Senator Ferguson then read the specifications to Short and asked him to plead them. Short pleaded not guilty to each of them in turn.[11]

Ferguson asked Short whether he had any knowledge or opinions as to why independent investigations were undertaken for Secretary Stimson by Maj. Gen. Cramer, Maj. Clausen, and Col. Clarke.

As to the Clausen inquiry, Short said, "I think that there is an explanation of that. You have to read between the lines."[12] The general, as an aid to interlinear reading, referred to a memorandum relating to the findings of the Army Pearl Harbor Board which Judge Advocate General Cramer sent to Stimson November 25, 1944.

Cramer suggested to Stimson that the board report had raised certain questions which "might advantageously be pursued." He continued, "I do not mean to suggest that the board should be reconvened for this purpose; the work could be done by an individual officer familiar with the matter."[13]

Short remarked that Gen. Marshall had testified that in all of his service he had never heard of a reviewing officer, if he were dissatisfied with the findings of a court martial or a board, taking such action as Cramer had here recommended. Marshall had said that the normal action was to refer the proceedings back to the board and direct that additional evidence be taken, if that were desired, or to direct that a review of their findings be made by the board, after which the review would then be returned to the reviewing officer. Short remarked:

In this case the judge advocate general goes out of his way to state he does not want it referred back to the board, but suggests an officer who had been on duty with the board. . . . Lieut. Col. Clausen, who was a major at the time, was assistant recorder of the board. Unquestionably Gen. Cramer had in his mind the recommending of Col. Clausen at the time he made that recommendation, which would have taken the further investigation out of the hands of the Army Board and placed it in the hands of a selected individual.

"Now, in your experience in the Army, did you ever know of that [happening]?" Senator Ferguson asked.

"I have never known of it."

"Now, as I understand it, before a real review of these findings was made, they sent Maj. Clausen out?"

"I think the review had been made, but it was not what they wanted."

"Oh. Now, that is what you are reading between the lines, that when they read this report they were not satisfied and they used the words 'certain personnel' in there?"

"And they apparently did not believe they could get what they wanted out of the Army Board," Short said.[14]

Short said that even after Clausen had done his service in attempting to tear down the Army Board report, the judge advocate general was still constrained to inform Secretary Stimson that he could not prove any offense against Short.[15] This opinion had been held by the judge advocate general's office ever since January 27, 1942, three days after the Roberts Commission had accused Short of dereliction of duty. In a memorandum of that date, the judge advocate general informed Stimson:

> Gen. Short's nonfeasance or omissions were based on an estimate of the situation which, although proved faulty by subsequent events, was, insofar as I am able to ascertain from the report of the commission, made or concurred in by all those officers in Hawaii best qualified to form a sound military opinion. That estimate was that an attack by air was in the highest degree improbable.[16]

On November 25, 1944, two days after Clausen had submitted his special report, Judge Advocate General Cramer again admitted that nothing had been turned up which would incriminate Short. He informed Stimson,

> I suggest, therefore, that a public statement be made by you giving a brief review of the board's proceedings and pointing out that Gen. Short was guilty of errors of judgment for which

he was properly removed from command, and that this consti-
tutes a sufficient disposition of the matter at this time. In the
event further investigation should disclose a different situation,
the matter could later be re-examined in the light of such additional evidence.[17]

Ferguson developed that, the Clausen investigation having proved
a flop from the viewpoint of Secretary Stimson and the administration,
they tried again—this time by dispatching Col. Carter Clarke to conduct still another inquiry. Clarke had been of previous service as a
go-between to Governor Dewey when Gen. Marshall, by crying up
"national security," had steered Dewey off the subject of Pearl Harbor
during the 1944 Presidential campaign.

"How do you account for that investigation by Carter Clarke after
Clausen got through?" the Senator asked Short.

"It is pretty difficult to say just what they were attempting to do,"
Short responded. "They were apparently wanting to find out exactly
what every man holding an important position in G-2 would say about
their estimates, and so forth, and it was a very difficult report to get
ahold of."

"And do you know whether or not it indicated in any way that
there had been an investigation by G-2 for the President and that there
had been some changes made in it by Gen. Marshall?"

"Somewhere—I have forgotten whether it was in that report or not,
but somewhere—I have run across something of that kind."

At this point Representative Murphy of Pennsylvania interjected,
"Isn't it fair to say that after reading it, there is a man named Friedman and several other witnesses and a Gen. Spalding and others who
had some kind of a rumor going about that Marshall was supposed
to have destroyed papers, and that was unequivocally, absolutely, and
positively contradicted?"

"But there is also more in it," Ferguson rejoined. "I think at some
time Carter Clarke should appear and give us the reason for it."[18]

Clarke was never summoned as a witness to explain what he knew
about the charge that Marshall had tampered with evidence relating
to the Pearl Harbor disaster.

Short rendered an oblique judgment on the process by which Stimson and high officers in the War Department had endeavored to
fasten all of the blame for the Pearl Harbor attack upon him when
he remarked, "I would like to say that I would never at any time try
to pass the buck to any single subordinate. My decision was made on
the information that the War Department had furnished me, and I

had no desire and absolutely never took any steps to pass the buck to some individual man below me."[19]

Ferguson, referring to the opinion Cramer had submitted to Stimson, read the following passage,

> There is also in cases like this the historic precedent of President Lincoln's refusal to rebuke Secretary of War Simon Cameron for a gross error of judgment. I am therefore forced to conclude that if Gen. Short is tried and if such trial should result in his conviction, there is considerable likelihood the court would adjudge his sentence less than dismissal and might well adjudge nothing beyond a reprimand.

"Would that lead us to believe, then," Ferguson inquired, "that he was of the opinion that he was concerned with the sentence, and they were concerned with that alone?"

"I would say they were greatly concerned with the effect on public opinion," Short responded, "and that they wanted to be very careful and not try me on something where they would fail and the effect would bounce back on them."[20]

Gen. Cramer, in a memorandum to the chief of staff and Secretary of War on the advisability of court martial proceedings, stated, "As to whether Gen. Short should be tried at any time, a factor to be considered is what sentence, in the event of conviction, the court would adjudge."

"Why," asked Ferguson, "would the judge advocate be concerned in advance and before he had filed the charges as to what the court would give as a penalty?"

"It would look like he was thinking of the possible effect on public opinion," Short replied. "If I were tried and found not guilty, or given a very mild sentence, the public would tend to feel that there had been no justification. That is the only conclusion I can draw."

Cramer's memorandum went on,

> As I have already indicated, upon any charge of neglect of duty, or of his various duties, Gen. Short would have the formidable defense that he responded to the request to report measures he had taken with a message, incomplete and ambiguous as it may be, but which should have prompted doubt as to the sufficiency of the action taken.
>
> My experience with courts martial leads me to the belief that a court would be reluctant to adjudge a severe sentence in a case of this kind where the general picture would be clouded by a claim that others were guilty of contributory causes.

Senator Ferguson said, "I want to ask you this question in relation to that: Couldn't that have been cured by trying all that were guilty of contributory causes?"

"Yes, sir," Short agreed.

"Do you know whether or not the War Department has ever considered the question of trying all that were guilty of contributory causes, or causes, of the disaster at Pearl Harbor?"

"I am quite sure," Short responded, "they have never made a public statement to that effect."[21]

The Joint Congressional Committee, after conducting hearings for seventy days and compiling a record of 10 million words, finally was ready to render judgment. The majority party, naturally, wrote the majority report. It rehearsed the familiar theme that Kimmel and Short were to blame, but conceded that "the errors of the Hawaiian commands were errors of judgment and not derelictions of duty." The War Plans Division of the War Department and the Intelligence and War Plans Divisions of both the War and Navy Departments were criticized incidentally, with no individuals named.[23] Inasmuch as the majority party showed every desire to continue soaring to election victories on Roosevelt's magic carpet, the late commander-in-chief was dealt with tenderly.[24]

The minority report of Senators Ferguson and Brewster, dismissing the majority report as "illogical and unsupported by the preponderance of the evidence," named some new names. For the first time in any investigation, Roosevelt, Knox, and Stimson were flatly accused of responsibility, and Secretary Hull was inferentially accused. The report concluded:

Having examined the whole record made before the Joint Committee and having analyzed the same in the foregoing conclusions of fact and responsibility, we find the evidence supports the following final and ultimate conclusion:

The failure of Pearl Harbor to be fully alerted and prepared for defense rested upon the proper discharge of two sets of *interdependent* responsibilities: (1) the responsibilities of high authorities in Washington; and (2) the responsibilities of the commanders in the field in charge of the fleet and of the naval base.

The evidence clearly shows that these two areas of responsibilities were inseparably essential to each other in the defense of Hawaii. The commanders in the field could not have prepared or been ready successfully to meet hostile attack at Hawaii without indispensable information, matériel, trained manpower and clear orders from Washington. Washington could not be certain that Hawaii was in readiness without the alert and active cooperation of the commanders on the spot.

The failure to perform the responsibilities indispensably essential to the defense of Pearl Harbor rests upon the following civil and military authorities:

FRANKLIN D. ROOSEVELT—President of the United States and Commander-in-Chief of the Army and Navy.

HENRY L. STIMSON—Secretary of War.

FRANK KNOX—Secretary of the Navy.

GEORGE C. MARSHALL—General, Chief of Staff of the Army.

HAROLD R. STARK—Admiral, Chief of Naval Operations.

LEONARD T. GEROW—Major General, Assistant Chief of Staff of War Plans Division.

The failure to perform the responsibilities in Hawaii rests upon the military commanders:

WALTER C. SHORT—Major General, Commanding General, Hawaiian Department.

HUSBAND E. KIMMEL—Rear Admiral, Commander in Chief of the Pacific Fleet.

Both in Washington and in Hawaii there were numerous and serious failures of men in the lower civil and military echelons to perform their duties and discharge their responsibilities. These are too numerous to be treated in detail and individually named.

Secretary of State, CORDELL HULL, who was at the center of Japanese-American negotiations, bears a grave responsibility for the diplomatic conditions leading up to the eventuality of Pearl Harbor but he had no duties as a relevant link in the military chain of responsibility stemming from the commander-in-chief to the commanders at Hawaii for the defense at Pearl Harbor. For this reason and because the diplomatic phase was not completely explored we offer no conclusions in his case.[25]

In support of these conclusions, the minority report[26] submitted a classic statement of the responsibilities of Roosevelt in the exercise of his duties, charging him not only with failure in discharging those duties as they bore on the events of December 7, but emphasizing that his responsibility encompassed the acts of his subordinates. The report stated:

The President of the United States was responsible for the failure to enforce continuous, efficient, and appropriate co-operation among the Secretary of War, the Secretary of the Navy, the chief of staff, and the chief of naval operations, in evaluating information and dispatching clear and positive orders to the Hawaiian commanders as events indicated the growing immi-

nence of war; for the Constitution and laws of the United States vested in the President full power, as Chief Executive and Commander-in-Chief, to compel such co-operation and vested this power in him alone with a view to establishing his responsibility to the people of the United States.

As to the power, and therefore of necessity, the responsibility of the President in relation to the chain of events leading to the catastrophe at Pearl Harbor, there can be no doubt. The terms of the Constitution and the laws in this respect are clear beyond all cavil.

The Constitution vests in the President the whole and indivisible executive power subject to provisions for the approval of appointments and treaties by the Senate.

The President, by and with the advice and consent of the Senate, appoints high officers, civil and military.

He is chief magistrate in all civil affairs, including those related to the maintenance and operation of the military and naval establishments.

Under the law he conducts all diplomatic negotiations on behalf of the United States, assigning to his appointee, the Secretary of State, such duties connected therewith as he sees fit, always subject to his own instructions and authorizations.

Under the Constitution the President is Commander-in-Chief of the armed forces of the United States, and with the approval of the Senate he appoints all high military and naval officers. He assigns them to their duties in his discretion except in the case of the chief of staff and chief of naval operations—these appointments must be approved by the Senate.

And why did the framers of the Constitution vest these immense powers in one magistrate—not in a directory or a single official checked by a council, as was proposed in the Convention of 1787?

The answer to this question is to be found in No. 70 of *The Federalist*. The purpose of establishing a single rather than a plural Executive was to assure "energy in the executive," "a due dependence on the people," and "a due responsibility." A plural executive, it is there argued, "tends to deprive the people of the two greatest securities they can have for the faithful exercise of any delegated power, *first*, the restraints of public opinion . . . ; and, *secondly*, the opportunity of discovering with facility and clearness the misconduct of persons they trust . . . ."

The acts of Congress providing for the organization, operations, powers, and duties of the military establishments under the President particularized the powers and duties of the President in relation to them; in brief, they empowered him to issue orders and instructions to the civil secretaries and also directly to the chief of staff and the chief of naval operations.

Such are the terms of the Constitution and the laws relative to the chief executive.

From March 4, 1933, to December 7, 1941, Franklin D. Roosevelt was President and Commander-in-Chief of the armed forces of the United States and in him were vested all executive powers under the Constitution and the laws.

He appointed Cordell Hull as Secretary of State in 1933 and retained him in that office during this period.

He appointed all the Secretaries of War and of the Navy during this period.

He selected, or approved the choice of, all chiefs of staff and chiefs of naval operations during this period.

He selected, or approved the choice of, all the men who served as military and naval commanders in charge of the Hawaiian area and he assigned them to their posts of duty.

In support of the doctrine that the President is entrusted with supreme executive responsibility and cannot divest himself of it, we have more recent authority. Speaking at a press conference on December 20, 1940, on a subject of administrative actions, President Roosevelt said: "There were two or three cardinal principles; and one of them is the fact that you cannot, under the Constitution, set up a second President of the United States. In other words, the Constitution states one man is responsible. Now that man can delegate, surely, but in the delegation he does not delegate away any part of the responsibility from the ultimate responsibility that rests on him" (*Papers,* 1940, p. 623).

. . .

Although there were two departments for the administration of military and naval affairs during this period, they were both under the supreme direction of the President as chief executive and Commander-in-Chief in all matters relative to separate and joint planning for defense and war, to disposition of forces and matériel, to preparedness for operation in case of an attack. In respect of the President's power, the two departments were one agency for over-all planning and operational purposes.

The President had power to issue directions and orders to the Secretary of War and the Secretary of the Navy and also directly and indirectly to the Chief of Staff and the Chief of Naval Operations and on occasions used this power.

Furthermore, under the Reorganization Act of 1939, President Roosevelt had enjoyed the power, by grant of Congress, to reorganize the Department of War and the Department of the Navy if he deemed it necessary in the interest of efficiency and more effective cooperation between the departments. Since he did not reorganize the two departments under that act, he must have deemed them properly constructed as they were.

By virtue of the powers vested in him the President had, during this period, the responsibility for determining the reciprocal relations of diplomatic decisions and war plans.

In fine, Secretary Hull, Secretary Stimson, Secretary Knox, General Marshall, Admiral Stark, General Short, and Admiral Kimmel were all men of President Roosevelt's own choice—not hang-over appointees from another administration to which incompetence may be ascribed—and the President had ample power to direct them, coordinate their activities, and bring about a concentration of their talents and energies in the defense of the United States.

Thus endowed with power and in full charge of diplomatic negotiations, the President decided long before December 7, at least as early as the Atlantic Conference in August, that war with Japan was a matter of a few weeks or months, was so highly probable and so imminent as to warrant a dedication of his abilities to preparation for that war. Having decided against an appeal to Congress for a declaration of war and having resolved that he would avoid even the appearance of an overt act against Japan, the President chose the alternative of waiting for an overt act by Japan—an attack on territory of the United States. Possessing full power to prepare for meeting attack and for countering it with the armed forces under his command, he had supreme responsibility for making sure that the measures, plans, orders, and dispositions necessary to that end were taken.

During the weeks and days preceding the Japanese attack on December 7, 1941, the President and his chief subordinates held many meetings, discussed the practical certainty of an attack, and, jointly or severally, made decisions and plans in relation to the coming of that attack—or overt act. Yet when the Japanese attack came at Pearl Harbor the armed forces of the United States failed to cope with the attack effectively.

In view of all the evidence cited in support of the preceding conclusions and more of the same kind that could be cited, this failure cannot all be ascribed to General Short and Admiral Kimmel, nor to their immediate superiors, civil and military. Those authorities had their powers and corresponding responsibilities but the ultimate power and responsibility under the Constitution and the laws were vested in the President of the United States.

Specifically, the report said of the culpability of Roosevelt and his associates in failing to place American forces in Hawaii on an all-out alert when war was known to be at hand:

> *The decision of the President, in view of the Constitution, to await the Japanese attack rather than ask for a declaration of war by Congress increased the responsibility of high authorities in Washington to use the utmost care in putting the com- manders at Pearl Harbor on a full alert for defensive actions before the Japanese attack on December 7, 1941.*
>
> The difficulty of coping effectively with the menace of Japa- nese hostilities by the method of maneuvering and waiting for an attack or attacks was recognized by the President and his immediate subordinates. They knew that the power to declare war was vested in Congress alone by the Constitution. Prime Minister Churchill, who had referred to this matter at the At- lantic Conference, again suggested to President Roosevelt, on November 30, 1941, that the President inform the Japanese that further aggression on their part would compel him "to place the gravest issues before Congress" (Tr., Vol. 8, p. 1253). President Roosevelt must have given serious thought to the constitutional difficulty during the several days prior to December 7, while he was considering plans for a special message to Congress.
>
> After it was decided, therefore, that no message be sent to Congress it then became all the more incumbent upon the Presi- dent and the Secretary of War, the Secretary of the Navy, the Chief of Staff, and the Chief of Naval Operations to make doubly certain that war warning messages to General Short and Admiral Kimmel be so clearly formulated as to mean to them an all-out alert of the forces under their command.[27]

Having decided to abide Japanese action to open the war, the re- port continues, "the appropriate high authorities in Washington . . . had every opportunity to make sure that identical and precise instruc- tions warranted by the imminence of war went to the Hawaiian commanders." The report states:[28]

> For the purpose of taking concerted actions in fulfillment of the duties imposed upon them, authorities in Washington formed two groups or organizations with a view to co-ordinat- ing the operations of the civil and military branches of the executive department. If these groups were so loosely consti- tuted as not to deserve the name of organizations, this was due to a failure on the part of the members to make them effective bodies for the discharge of their co-ordinating responsibilities. The first of these two groups consisted of the Secretary of

State, Secretary of War, Secretary of the Navy, the chief of staff, and the chief of naval operations. Sometimes it was called colloquially the "War Council."

The second group included the President, Secretary of State, Secretary of War, Secretary of Navy, usually the chief of staff and the chief of naval operations, and occasionally commanding general of Air Force, General Arnold. This group was sometimes colloquially called the "War Cabinet."

The use of these terms—"War Council" and "War Cabinet" —while the country was still at peace seems to indicate that high civil and military authorities in Washington were thinking in terms of war and should have been more alert to the probable events of war such as an attack upon our most important outpost and fleet in the Pacific.

Each of these groups or organizations— "was a sort of clearinghouse for information, a gathering place for discussion of policies, so that each of the independent actors in the scene *would know what was going on and would have information to guide him in making his own decisions* that were more or less independent, but at the same time somewhat dependent on the action of other members of the group." (Italics supplied.)

If it be argued that these groups were loosely constituted and met irregularly and informally and hence were not organizations in the strict sense of the term [they met once a week at least and had other irregular and additional meetings], it remains a fact that they existed for the purposes described. Furthermore, if, owing to their loose constitution, they did not discharge their duties efficiently, it also remains a fact that the President had the power, and the corresponding duty, to transform either or both of these groups into positive organizations with positive obligations in respect of exchanging information, making decisions, co-ordinating the civil and military branches of the executive department, and framing orders to outpost commanders.

At all events, these groups had every opportunity to make sure that identical and precise instructions warranted by the imminence of war went out to the Hawaiian commanders and the President had the power and duty to see that this was done directly or through the agency of these groups, especially the second—the "War Cabinet."

For this nonco-operation and mismanagement, high authorities in Washington were fully responsible. . . .

These conclusions are underlined by the following:[29]

These instances of failure on the part of high authorities in Washington to perform acts of duty and judgment required by their respective offices, and many others that could be cited, merely point to the greatest failure of all, namely, the failure of those authorities to organize for the war they regarded as immediately imminent. Here the conclusions reached by the Army Pearl Harbor Board as to the War Department apply to the whole executive department of which it was a part:

"A few men, without organization in a true sense, were attempting to conduct large enterprises, take multiple actions, and give directions that should have been the result of carefully directed commands, instead of actions taken by conference. We were preparing for war by the conference method. We were directing such preparations by the conference method; we were even writing vital messages by the conference method, and arriving at their content by compromise instead of by command. . . ."

To this comment, the Army Pearl Harbor Board should have added that powerful individuals among these authorities were reaching decisions on their own motion and taking actions of a dangerous nature on their own motion, despite all the conferring, talking, and compromising, were proceeding as if there was no organization in the government of the United States that was charged with preparing for and waging war.

Nor is this confusion and pulling at cross-purposes to be explained away by any such vague assertion as the Army Pearl Harbor Board offered: "that it was a product of the time and conditions due to the transition from peace to war in a democracy." Failures to perform duties commensurate with the powers vested in officials by the Constitution and the law cannot be justified by appeals to any overriding requirements of democracy. Provisions for organizing the executive department and the supreme command of the armed forces of the United States were incorporated in the Constitution and the law, and adequate powers *to organize and unify for operating purposes* all subsidiary agencies were vested in the President of the United States.

As to President Truman's attempt to saddle the blame for Pearl Harbor upon the American people, Senators Ferguson and Brewster observe:[30]

The contention coming from so high an authority as President Truman on August 3, 1945, that the "country is as much to blame as any individual in this final situation that developed in Pearl Harbor," cannot be sustained because the American

people had no intimation whatever of the policies and opera-
tions that were being undertaken. . . .

How could the American people be held responsible for the
secret diplomacy of Washington authorities? They were never
advised of the many secret undertakings by Washington authorities. Indeed, the high authorities in Washington seemed to be
acting upon some long-range plan which was never disclosed
to Congress or to the American people.

A nation in mortal danger is entitled to know the truth
about its peril. If foreign policy and diplomatic representations
are treated as the exclusive secret information of the President
and his advisers, public opinion will not be enlightened. A
people left in the dark by their leaders cannot be held responsible for the consequences of their leader's actions.

On December 1, 1941, it was known to the Secretary of War
and to the President and his close advisers that Japan had informed Hitler on December 1 that war was imminent. . . .

The Secretary of War, the President and his advisers also
were fully aware that Japanese military movements were under
way and that these movements would involve the United States
in war.

Notwithstanding his intimate knowledge of the imminence
of war, the Secretary of War told the American people as late
as December 5 that the negotiations with Japan were still in
progress. Also, despite the extreme gravity of the situation,
known fully to the "War Cabinet," the President permitted the
Senate and House of Representatives to adjourn on December
4 and 5 respectively until noon of December 8 without having
informed them of the impending danger to the country. This
seems to follow consistently the understanding observed by Mr.
Hull when he gave to the President a proposed draft of a message to Congress which was never used. Mr. Hull said: "I think
we agree that you will not send message to Congress until the
last stage of our relations, relating to actual hostilities." (JCC,
Ex. 19).

How could the American people be responsible for the war-
like operations conducted from Washington over which the
people had no control and about which they were never informed?

In the future the people and their Congress must know how
close American diplomacy is moving to war so that they may
check its advance if imprudent and support its position if sound.
A diplomacy which relies upon the enemy's first overt act to
insure effective popular support for the nation's final war deci-

sion is both outmoded and dangerous in the atomic age. To prevent any future Pearl Harbor more tragic and damaging than that of December 7, 1941, there must be constant close co-ordination between American public opinion and American diplomacy.

Eternal vigilance is still the price of liberty even in the atomic era. Whether or not the Pearl Harbor tragedy could have been avoided by diplomatic means is a most appropriate matter for consideration by all concerned with the 3,000 American boys who lost their lives. . . .

In our opinion, the evidence before this committee indicates that the tragedy at Pearl Harbor was primarily a failure of men and not of laws or powers to do the necessary things, and carry out the vested responsibilities. No legislation could have cured such defects of official judgment, management, co-operation, and action as were displayed by authorities and agents of the United States in connection with the events that culminated in the catastrophe at Pearl Harbor on December 7, 1941.*

Certainly the United States was neither informed nor alerted when Roosevelt and the men whose intentions coincided with his (because their fortunes rode with him) were warping the nation into war in 1941. The motives of these men are to this day obscure. They are even more obscure in the light of the default of all promises concerning the objectives of World War II.

Failure of the administration's domestic policy can account for the desire to go to war. Roosevelt's personal ambition and his urge to win a place in world-history can account for it. The opportunities afforded by wartime regimentation to tighten a political hold upon the country can account for it. Subservience to foreign interests can account for it.

Desire for glory and enhanced status could have contributed to it. Men in the regular establishments of the Army and Navy who saw the vision of spectacular commands and stars upon their shoulders after years of humdrum duty in offices, posts, and barracks would hardly oppose the politicians, whatever their motives. All of them were enlisted, long before Pearl Harbor, in Roosevelt's conspiracy to fight an unacknowledged and unconstitutional war in the Atlantic. All of them were parties, before December 7, 1941, in his secret war alliance with the British and Dutch in the Pacific.

*The 21 conclusions of the minority in building an integrated case against those whom it held responsible for the catastrophe at Pearl Harbor will be found in the Appendix.[31]

But, given the benefit of every doubt, credited with a sincere belief that the United States was in deadly peril and that it must fight if it were to stand, all of these men still must answer for much. With absolute knowledge of war, they refused to communicate that knowledge, clearly, unequivocally, and in time, to the men in the field upon whom the blow would fall. The silence in Washington can yield to no other explanation than a desire to do nothing that would deter or forestall the attack which would produce the overt act so long and so fervently sought. When the price of silence proved to be 2,326 lives, it was necessary to add two more victims to the list—Adm. Kimmel and Gen. Short.

In the course of the years, however, there was a significant change in assaying responsibility for the disaster of December 7. It became apparent that the attempt to explain away Pearl Harbor as the consequence of purely local command failures would not succeed. National policy, as directed by the Roosevelt administration in its program of steering the country into war, came under searching scrutiny. It became increasingly clear that this policy was neither open nor honest, and that the commanders in Hawaii were hoodwinked no more and no less than the American people had been—that they were ignored, as Congress was ignored, until they were presented with the consequences of that policy on December 7 and the attempt was then made to render them accountable for it.

By subtle gradations, however, the men who had most confidently asserted the guilt of the Hawaiian commanders were driven at length into the defense of themselves. The accusers became the accused. Finally, in an unsolicited "Summary of My Views as to the Responsibility of Members of the Army," submitted to the congressional committee, Stimson is found querulously apologizing for Mr. Roosevelt, himself, and the rest of the war-makers. He states:

Many of the discussions on this subject indicate a failure to grasp the fundamental difference between the duties of an outpost commander and those of the commander-in-chief of an army or nation and his military advisers. The outpost commander is like a sentinel on duty in the face of the enemy. His fundamental duties are clear and precise. He must assume that the enemy will attack at his particular post; and that the enemy will attack at the time and in the way in which it will be most difficult to defeat him. It is not the duty of the outpost commander to speculate or rely on the possibilities of the enemy attacking at some other outpost instead of his own. It is his duty to meet him at his post at any time and to make the best possible fight that can be made against him with the weapons with which he has been supplied.

On the other hand, the commander-in-chief of the nation (and his advisers)—particularly of a nation which has been as habitually neglectful of the possibility of war as our own—has much more difficult and complex duties to fulfill. Unlike the outpost commander, he must constantly watch, study, and estimate where the principal or most dangerous attack is most likely to come, in order that he may most effectively distribute his insufficient forces and munitions to meet it. He knows that his outposts are not all equally supplied or fortified and that they are not all equally capable of defense. He knows also that from time to time they are of greatly varying importance to the grand strategy of the war.

For all these reasons he is compelled to give account and close attention to the reports from all his intelligence agencies in order that he may satisfactorily solve the innumerable problems which are constantly arising in the performance of the foregoing duties.[32]

Stimson's intention is plain enough. He is still trying to persuade the American people that Pearl Harbor is purely a matter of military responsibility. But no amount of excuses will palliate the conduct of President Roosevelt and his advisers. The offense of which they stand convicted is not failure to discharge their responsibilities, but calculated refusal to do so.

They failed—with calculation—to keep the United States out of war and to avoid a clash with Japan. They reckoned with cold detachment the risk of manipulating a delegated enemy into firing the first shot, and they forced 3,000 unsuspecting men at Pearl Harbor to accept that risk. The "warnings" they sent to Hawaii failed—and were so phrased and so handled as to insure failure.

Pearl Harbor provided the American war party with the means of escaping dependence on a hesitant Congress in taking a reluctant people into war. Then the very scale of the disaster gave Roosevelt and his advisers the opportunity to distract attention from the policy which had produced the disaster. By cleverly leading the people to regard December 7 as a purely military calamity and by inciting the public to fix the blame for it upon the field commanders, Roosevelt and his administration hoped that the policy of which Pearl Harbor was the inevitable product would never be questioned.

Pearl Harbor was the first action of the acknowledged war, and the last battle of a secret war upon which the administration had long since embarked. The secret war was waged against nations which the leadership of this country had chosen as enemies months before they became formal enemies by a declaration of war. It was waged also, by psychological means, by propaganda, and deception, against the American people, who were thought by their leaders to be laggard in embracing war. The people were told that acts which were equivalent to war were intended to keep the nation out of war. Constitutional processes existed only to be circumvented, until finally the war-making power of Congress was reduced to the act of ratifying an accomplished fact.

APPENDIX

APPENDIX

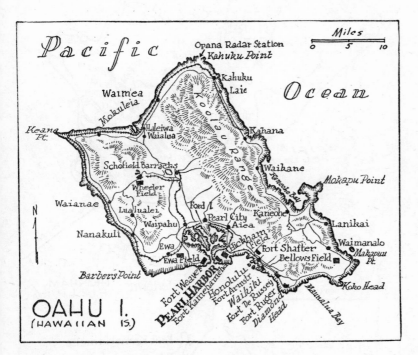

The island of Oahu, Territory of Hawaii, showing objectives of the Japanese attack of December 7, 1941, which brought the United States into World War II. [This and succeeding maps were drawn by GARY SHEAHAN.]

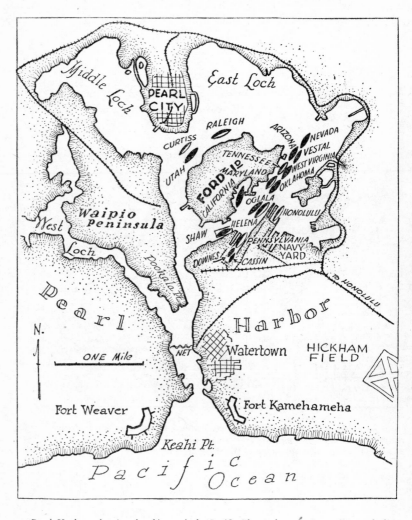

Pearl Harbor, showing berthings of the Pacific Fleet when the Japanese attacked on December 7, 1941. Warships indicated in black were sunk; those in black and white damaged but afloat.

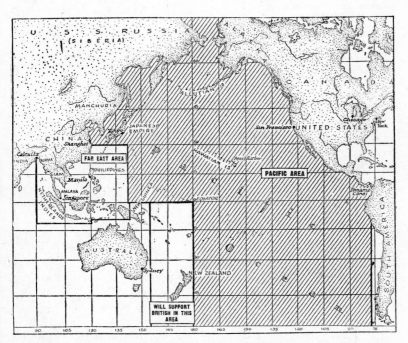

Under the Washington conference agreement, the United States was made solely responsible for the defense of a huge stretch of the Pacific Ocean (shaded area). American naval forces were to support British forces and operate under British strategic direction in the Southwest Pacific east of Australia. Britain was to exercise strategic direction in the Far East area.

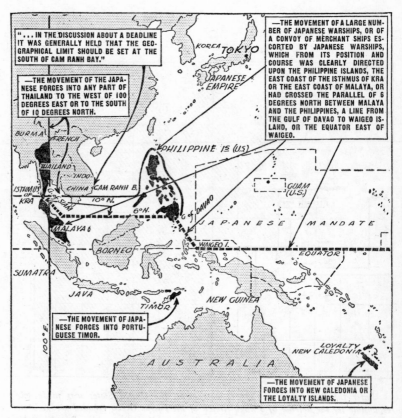

This map depicts various "deadlines" established by agreement of the United States, Britain, and Holland to contain Japanese expansion. Any movement of Japanese forces beyond these prescribed limits would compel joint resistance by the associated powers. These plans for joint action were approved by President Roosevelt months before Pearl Harbor, "except officially."

WITNESSES APPEARING BEFORE THE JOINT CONGRESSIONAL COMMITTEE TO INVESTIGATE THE ATTACK ON PEARL HARBOR AND THEIR ASSIGNMENTS AS OF DECEMBER 7, 1941

Beardall, John R., Rear Adm., naval aide to President Roosevelt.

Beatty, Frank E., Rear Adm., aide to Secretary of the Navy Frank Knox.

Bellinger, P. N. L., Vice-Adm., commander Hawaiian naval base air force (commander, patrol wing 2).

Bicknell, George W., Col., assistant chief, military intelligence service, Hawaiian Department.

Bratton, Rufus S., Col., chief, Far Eastern section, military intelligence service, War Department.

Clausen, Henry C., Lieut. Col.,[1] judge advocate general's office, assisting army Pearl Harbor board and conducting supplemental investigation for secretary of war.

Creighton, John M., Capt., USN, naval observer, Singapore.

Dillon, John H., Maj., USMC, aide to Secretary Knox.

Elliott, George E., Sergt., operator at Opana radar detector station, Oahu, T. H.

Gerow, Leonard T., Maj. Gen., chief, war plans division, army general staff, War Department.

Grew, Joseph C., United States ambassador to Japan.

Hart, Thomas C., Adm., commander-in-chief, Asiatic fleet.

Hull, Cordell, Secretary of State.

Ingersoll, Royal E., Adm., assistant chief of naval operations, Navy Department.

Inglis, R. B., Rear Adm.,[1] presented to committee Navy summary of Pearl Harbor attack.

Kimmel, Husband E., Rear Adm., commander-in-chief, United States fleet; commander-in-chief, Pacific fleet.

Kramer, A. D., Comdr., section chief, division of naval communications, handling translations and recovery of intercepted Japanese codes.

Krick, Harold D., Capt., USN, former flag secretary to Adm. Stark.

Leahy, William D., Adm., chief of staff to the President.

Layton, Edwin T., Capt., USN, fleet intelligence officer, Pacific fleet.

---

[1]Denotes witness whose connection with this investigation relates to his assignment after Dec. 7, 1941.

Marshall, George C., Gen., chief of staff, United States army, War Department.

McCollum, Arthur N., Capt., USN, chief, Far Eastern section, office of naval intelligence, Navy Department.

Miles, Sherman, Maj. Gen., chief, military intelligence service, Army general staff, War Department.

Noyes, Leigh, Rear Adm., chief, office of naval communications, Navy Department.

Phillips, Walter C., Col., chief of staff to Gen. Short.

Richardson, J. O., Adm., former commander-in-chief, United States fleet and Pacific fleet.

Roberts, Owen J., Mr. Justice, chairman, Roberts Commission.

Rochefort, Joseph John, Capt., USN, communications intelligence officer, Pacific fleet.

Sadtler, Otis K., Col., chief, military branch, Army Signal Corps, War Department.

Safford, L. F., Capt., USN, chief, radio intelligence unit, office of naval communications, Navy Department.

Schukraft, Robert E., Col., chief, radio intercept unit, Army Signal Corps, War Department.

Schulz, Lester Robert, Comdr., assistant to Adm. Beardall.

Short, Walter C., Maj. Gen., commanding general, Hawaiian Department.

Smith, William W., Rear Adm., chief of staff to Adm. Kimmel.

Sonnett, John F., Lieut. Comdr.,[1] special assistant to the Secretary of the Navy, and assistant to Adm. H. K. Hewitt in his inquiry.

Stark, Harold R., Adm., chief of naval operations, Navy Department.

Stimson, Henry L., Secretary of War (sworn statement and sworn replies to interrogatories only).

Thielen, Bernard, Col.,[1] presented to committee Army summary of Pearl Harbor attack.

Turner, Richmond K., Rear Adm., chief, war plans division, Navy Department.

Welles, Sumner, Undersecretary of State.

Wilkinson, T. S., Rear Adm., chief, office of naval intelligence, Navy Department.

Zacharias, Ellis M., Capt., USN, commanding officer, USS *Salt Lake City,* Pacific fleet.

OTHERS REFERRED TO IN THIS BOOK

Allen, A. M. R., Capt., USN, naval observer at Singapore and American delegate to the Singapore staff conference.

Alsop, Joseph, newspaper columnist.

Andrews, Frank M., Lieut. Gen., head of United States Caribbean defense command.

Arnold, H. H., Gen., commanding general, Army Air Forces.

Ballantine, Arthur A., Assistant Secretary of State.

Barkley, Alben M., United States Senator, chairman of the Joint Congressional Committee to investigate the attack on Pearl Harbor.

Bellairs, R. M., Rear Adm., RN, British representative at the Washington staff conference.

Bennion, Mervyn S., Capt., USN, commander of U.S.S. "West Virginia."

Biddle, Francis J., attorney general of the United States.

Bissell, John T., Col., executive officer, counter-intelligence group, military intelligence division, War Department.

Bloch, Claude C., Adm., commandant of 14th Naval District, Pearl Harbor base defense officer.

Brewster, Owen, United States Senator, minority member of the Joint Congressional Committee to investigate the attack on Pearl Harbor.

Brink, F. G., Lieut. Col., American military observer at Singapore, American representative at the Singapore staff conference.

Brooke-Popham, Sir Robert, Air Chief Marshal, British commander-in-chief, Far East; British representative at Singapore staff conference.

Brown, Wilson, Rear Adm., commander, Task Force 3, Pacific fleet.

Bryden, William, Maj. Gen., deputy chief of staff, War Department.

Bullitt, William B., American ambassador to France.

Bundy, Charles W., Col., War Department general staff.

Burgin, Henry T., Maj. Gen., commanding Hawaii coast artillery command.

Cadogan, Sir Alexander, British permanent undersecretary for foreign affairs.

Chamberlain, Neville, prime minister of Great Britain.

Chiang Kai-shek, Generalissimo, head of the Kuomintang government of China.

Churchill, Winston, prime minister of Great Britain.

Clark, J. Bayard, Rep., congressman from North Carolina, member of the Joint Congressional Committtee to investigate the Pearl Harbor attack.

Clarke, A. W., Capt., British representative at Washington staff conference.

Clarke, Carter, Brig. Gen., appointed by Gen. George C. Marshall to make a special investigation of the Pearl Harbor attack.

Conley, E. T., Maj. Gen., adjutant general of the army.

Cooke, Capt. Charles M., USN, former member of Adm. Stark's staff; in July, 1941, commander of U.S.S. Pennsylvania; later vice admiral commanding 7th Fleet.

Cooper, Jere, Rep., congressman from Tennessee, vice-chairman of the Joint Congressional Committee to investigate Pearl Harbor.

Craigie, Sir Robert, British ambassador to Japan.

Cramer, Myron C., Maj. Gen., judge advocate general of the Army.

Danckwerts, V. J., Rear Adm., RN, British representative at Washington staff conference.

Davis, Forrest, author.

Dewey, Thomas E., governor of New York.

Doenitz, Karl, Grand Adm., German navy.

Dooman, Eugene, Counselor of the American embassy in Tokyo.

Doud, Harold, Col., chief of the code and cipher section of the Army Signal Corps intelligence service.

Drum, Hugh A., Lieut. Gen., former commander, Hawaiian department, United States Army.

Duncan, James, civilian student pilot in Honolulu.

Embick, Stanley D., Maj. Gen., American representative at Washington staff conference.

Ferguson, Homer, United States Senator from Michigan, minority member of the Joint Congressional Committee.

Fielder, Kendall J., Col., chief of the military intelligence division, Hawaiian Department.

Foote, Walter A., American consul general in Batavia, Java.

Forrestal, James V., Secretary of the Navy.

Fort, Cornelia, civilian flying instructor in Honolulu.

French, Edward F., Col., in charge of the traffic division and signal center, Signal Corps, War Department.

Friedman, William F., principal cryptanalyst, signal intelligence service, Signal Corps, War Department.

Fuchida, Mitsue, Capt., flight group commander, 1st Japanese air fleet.

Gearhart, Bertrand W., Rep., congressman from California, minority member of the Joint Congressional Committee.

George, Walter F., United States Senator from Georgia, member of the Joint Congressional Committee.

Gesell, Gerhard, associate counsel, Joint Congressional Committee.

Ghormley, Robert L., Vice-Adm., American naval observer in London.

Goepner, O. W., Lieut. (j.g.), USNR, deck officer of the U.S.S. "Ward."

Gonzalez, Manuel, Ens., USNR, pilot on U.S.S. "Enterprise."

Halifax, Lord, British ambassador to United States.

Halsey, William F., Adm., commander of aircraft battle force (task force 2), Pacific fleet.

Hamilton, Maxwell M., chief of the division of Far Eastern affairs, State Department.

Hensel, H. Struve, Assistant Secretary of the Navy.

Herron, Charles D., Maj. Gen., former commanding general, Hawaiian Department.

Hewitt, H. Kent, Adm., appointed by Secretary of the Navy Forrestal to conduct a special investigation into Pearl Harbor.

Hiranuma, Baron Kiichiro, vice-premier of Japan.

Hirohito, emperor of Japan.

Hitler, Adolf, chancellor of Germany.

Hoover, J. Edgar, director of the Federal Bureau of Investigation.

Hopkins, Harry, confidant of President Roosevelt, head of the lend-lease program in 1941.

Hornbeck, Stanley K., adviser on foreign relations, State Department.

Hu Shih, Dr., Chinese ambassador to United States.

Hughes, William J., Col., assistant judge advocate general.

Ickes, Harold L., Secretary of the Interior.

Imamura, Ryonosuke, Capt., secretary of Japanese naval ministry.

Iwakuro, Takeo, Col., Japanese military attaché in Washington.

Jones, E. Stanley, Dr., missionary and unofficial mediator in Japanese-American diplomatic discussions.

Keefe, Frank B., Rep., congressman from Wisconsin and minority member of the Joint Congressional Committee to investigate Pearl Harbor.

King, Ernest J., Adm., commander-in-chief, United States fleet.

Kintner, Robert, newspaper columnist.

Kirk, A. G., Capt., USN, chief of naval intelligence during part of 1941, American representative at Washington staff conference.

Kita, Nagoa, Japanese consul general in Honolulu.

Knox, Frank, Secretary of the Navy.

Konoye, Prince Fumimaro, prime minister of Japan.

Koo, Wellington, Chinese ambassador to Great Britain.

Murphy, Vincent R., Comdr., USN, aide to Adm. J. O. Richardson.

Murray, Maxwell, Maj. Gen., commander, 25th Infantry Division.

Mussolini, Benito, dictator of Italy.

Nagano, Osami, Adm., chief of Japanese naval general staff.

Nagumo, Chuichi, Vice-Adm., commander, 1st Japanese air fleet.

Newton, John Henry, Vice-Adm., commander, cruisers scouting force, Pacific fleet.

Nimitz, Chester W., Adm., commander-in-chief, Pacific fleet.

Nomura, Kichisaburo, Adm., Japanese ambassador to the United States.

O'Dell, Robert H., Lieut., assistant military attaché, American legation, Melbourne, Australia.

Ohashi, Chuichi, Japanese vice-minister for foreign affairs.

Onishi, Takijiro, Rear Adm., chief of staff, Japanese 11th air fleet.

Oshima, Hiroshi, Maj. Gen., Japanese ambassador to Germany.

Outerbridge, William W., Lieut., USN, commander, U.S.S. "Ward."

Pepper, Claude, United States Senator from Florida.

Pettigrew, Moses W., Col., executive officer, intelligence group, military intelligence division, War Department.

Phillips, Sir Tom S. V., Adm., RN, commander, British Far Eastern fleet.

Phillips, Walter C., Col., chief of staff to Gen. Walter C. Short.

Pius XII, Pope.

Pomerlin, Thomas, commercial pilot in Hawaii.

Puleston, W. D., Capt., USN, naval writer.

Purnell, W. R., Capt., USN, chief of staff, Asiatic fleet; American representative at Singapore staff conference.

Pye, William S., Vice-Adm., commander, battle force (task force 1), Pacific fleet; temporary commander, Pacific fleet.

Ramsey, Dewitt C., Capt., USN, American representative at Washington staff conference.

Rankin, Jeanette, Rep., member of Congress from Montana.

Redman, Joseph R., Rear Adm., assistant director, office of naval communications, Navy Department.

Reeves, Joseph M., Adm., USN (retired), former commander-in-chief, United States fleet; member of Roberts Commission to investigate Pearl Harbor.

Ribbentrop, Joachim von, German foreign minister.

Richardson, Seth W., chief counsel of Joint Congressional Committee to investigate Pearl Harbor, succeeding William D. Mitchell.

Ricker, George W., Lieut. Col., War Department general staff.

Roosevelt, Franklin D., President of the United States.

Sakamaki, Kazuo, Sub-Lieut., commander of Japanese midget submarine.

Schuirmann, R. E., Rear Adm., Navy liaison officer with State Department.

Shidehara, Baron Kijuro, prime minister of Japan, 1945.

Shimizu, Mitsumi, Adm., commander, Japanese 6th fleet.

Shivers, Robert L., agent in charge, FBI, Honolulu.

Slessor, J. C., Air Vice-Marshal, RAF, British representative at Washington staff conference.

Smith, Walter Bedell, Lieut. Gen., secretary of War Department general staff, American ambassador to Russia.

Soong, T. V., brother-in-law of Chiang Kai-shek, named Chinese foreign minister while in Washington.

Spalding, Isaac, Gen., attached to personnel section, War Department.

Spruance, Raymond A., Adm., USN, commander-in-chief, Pacific fleet.

Standley, William H., Adm., USN, member of Roberts Commission to investigate Pearl Harbor.

Starck, Vice-Adm., commander of Russian Port Arthur fleet in Russo-Japanese war.

Stimson, Henry L., Secretary of War.

Stone, E. E., Capt., USN, in charge of naval communications in 1941.

Strong, George V., Maj. Gen., chief of Army war plans in 1940.

Taylor, Kenneth M., Second Lieut., Army fighter pilot.

Terasaki, Hindenari, counselor, Japanese embassy, Washington.

Theobald, Robert A., Rear Adm., USN.

Thomas, Elbert D., United States Senator from Utah, chairman of Senate military affairs committee.

Thomas, Francis J., Lieut. Comdr., USNR.

Thorpe, C. A., Col., senior Army intelligence officer in Java.

Togo, Heihachiro, Adm., commander of Japanese naval forces in attack upon Port Arthur, 1904.

Togo, Shigenori, Japanese foreign minister.

Tojo, Hideki, Gen., Japanese prime minister.

Toyoda, Teijiro, Adm., Japanese foreign minister.

Trueman, Capt., aide to Gen. Walter C. Short.

Truman, Harry S., President of the United States.

Tunnell, James A., United States Senator from Delaware.

Tyler, Kermit A., Lieut. Col., in charge of the radar center, Oahu, on Dec. 7, 1941.

Vitousek, Roy, civilian pilot in Honolulu.

Vogt, John H. L. Jr., Ens., USN, pilot aboard U.S.S. "Enterprise."

Wallace, Henry A., secretary of commerce.

Watson, Edwin M., Maj. Gen., aide to President Roosevelt.

Welch, George S., Second Lieut., Army fighter pilot.

White, Grove C., Second Lieut., signal corps.

Wikawa, Tadao, officer of the Capital Cooperative Bank of Japan.

Wilkinson, G. H., Col., British secret agent in Manila.

Willoughby, C. A., Maj. Gen., chief of the military intelligence division on Gen. MacArthur's staff.

Wilson, Woodrow, President of the United States.

Winant, John G., American ambassador to Great Britain.

Yamamoto, Isoroku, Adm., commander-in-chief, Japanese combined imperial fleets.

Yamamoto, Kumaicho, head of the American section, Japanese foreign office.

Yarnell, Harry E., Adm., USN.

NOTES

This book was completed before publication by the Government Printing Office of the official proceedings of the Joint Congressional Committee to investigate the attack upon Pearl Harbor. Where the transcript of committee proceedings was available, citations of testimony are referred to the transcript; otherwise, references are to the specific dates of hearings on which testimony was given. These may be checked against the daily hearings as published by the Government Printing Office.

Other sources, with abbreviations employed in the Appendix, are as follows:

AP—Associated Press

APH—Army Pearl Harbor Board: Text as printed in extra number of the *United States News*, Sept. 1, 1945.

Atlantic—Battle Report: The Atlantic War, by Comdr. Walter Karig, USNR; Lieut. Earl Burton, USNR, and Lieut. Stephen L. Freeland, USNR (Farrar and Rinehart, Inc., New York, 1946).

BR—Battle Report: Pearl Harbor to Coral Sea, by Comdr. Walter Karig, USNR, and Lieut. Wellbourn Kelley, USNR (Farrar and Rinehart, New York, 1944).

Chron.—Events Leading Up to World War II: Chronological History, 1931-1944 (House Document No. 541, United States Government Printing Office, Washington, 1944).

CR—Congressional Record

CT—The Chicago Tribune

Fed. Reg.—Federal Register

For. Rel. I and II—Papers Pertaining to Foreign Relations of the United States: Japan, 1931-1941. Two volumes (House Document No. 339, United States Government Printing Office, Washington, 1943).

Grew—Ten Years in Japan, by Joseph C. Grew (Simon and Schuster, New York, 1944). Submitted before the Joint Congressional Committee on the Investigation of the Pearl Harbor Attack as Exhibit 30.

Hart Report—Investigation of the Pearl Harbor Attack by Adm. Thomas C. Hart, USN, retired.

How War Came—How War Came, by Forrest Davis and Ernest K. Lindley (Simon and Schuster, New York, 1942).

Huie—The Case against the Admirals, by William Bradford Huie (E. P. Dutton, New York, 1946).

Intercepts—Pearl Harbor: Intercepted Japanese Diplomatic Messages, Joint Congressional Committee, Exhibit 1.

JCC—Joint Congressional Committee on the Investigation of the Pearl Harbor Attack: daily hearings.

Kimmel—Statement of Rear Adm. Husband E. Kimmel, USN, retired, to Joint Congressional Committee, Jan. 15, 1946; 108 pages (mimeograph).

Maj.—Majority Report of the Joint Congressional Committee (United States Government Printing Office, Washington, 1946).

Min.—Minority Report of the Joint Congressional Committee (United States Government Printing Office, Washington, 1946).

NCI—Report of the Naval Court of Inquiry which investigated the Pearl Harbor attack: Text as printed in extra number of the United States News, Sept. 1, 1945.

NYT—The New York Times

Papers—Public Papers and Addresses of Franklin D. Roosevelt: 1936 Volume, Random House, New York; 1937-1940 Volumes, Macmillan, New York.

Peace—Peace and War: United States Foreign Policy, 1931-1941 (United States Government Printing Office, Washington, 1943).

Puleston—The Armed Forces of the Pacific, by Capt. W. D. Puleston, USN (Yale University Press, New Haven, 1941).

R.—Report of the Presidential Commission to Investigate Pearl Harbor, headed by Associate Justice Owen J. Roberts.

Safford—Statement of Capt. L. F. Safford, USN, to Joint Congressional Committee, Feb. 1, 1946 (22 pages, mimeograph). Incorporated in transcript of the committee, pp. 9622-54.

Stimson—Statement of former Secretary of War Henry L. Stimson to Joint Congressional Committee, March 21, 1946 (68 pages, mimeograph). Incorporated in volume 70 of the committee transcript.

Tr.—Report of Proceedings before the Joint Committee on the Investigation of the Pearl Harbor Attack (Ward and Paul, Washington, official reporters).

NOTES ON FOREWORD

1. Brittanica Book of the Year, 1938-1942, p. 1511.
2. Tr., p. 8693.
3. The Army Pearl Harbor Board was appointed pursuant to the provisions of Public Law 339, Seventy-eighth Congress, approved June 13, 1944, and by order dated July 8, 1944, of the adjutant general, War Department. The board was directed "to ascertain and report the facts relating to the attack made by Japanese armed forces upon the Territory of Hawaii on Dec. 7, 1941, and to make such recommendations as it may deem proper." The board held sessions beginning July 20, 1944, and concluded its investigation on Oct. 20, 1944. Its record and exhibits cover 3,357 printed pages. Members of the board were Lieut. Gen. George Grunert, president; Maj. Gen. Henry D. Russell, and Maj. Gen. Walter A. Frank.
4. The Navy Court of Inquiry was appointed pursuant to the provisions of Public Law 339, Seventy-eighth Congress, approved June 13, 1944, and by order dated July 13, 1944, of the Secretary of the Navy James Forrestal. The court was ordered to "inquire into the attack made by Japanese armed forces on Pearl Harbor, Territory of Hawaii, on 7 December 1941 . . . and will include in its findings a full statement of the facts it may deem to be established. The court will further give its opinion as to whether any offenses have been committed or serious blame incurred on the part of any person or persons in the naval service, and in case its opinion be that offenses have been committed or serious blame incurred, will specifically recommend what further proceedings should be had." The court held sessions beginning July 24, 1944, and concluded its inquiry on October 19, 1944. The record of its proceedings and exhibits covers 1,397 printed pages. Members of the court were Adm. Orin G. Murfin, retired, president; Adm. Edward C. Kalbfus, retired, and Vice Adm. Adolphus Andrews, retired.
5. The inquiry conducted by Adm. Thomas C. Hart, United States Navy, retired, was initiated by precept dated Feb. 12, 1944, from Secretary of the Navy Frank Knox to Adm. Hart "For an Examination of Witnesses and the Taking of Testimony Pertinent to the Japanese Attack on Pearl Harbor, Territory of Hawaii."

The precept stated ". . . Whereas certain members of the naval forces, who have knowledge pertinent to the foregoing matters, are now or soon may be on dangerous assignments at great distances from the United States . . . it is now deemed necessary, in order to prevent evidence being lost by death or unavoidable absence of those certain members of the naval forces, that their testimony, pertinent to the aforesaid Japanese attack, be recorded and preserved, . . ." This inquiry was commenced on Feb. 12, 1944, and was concluded on June 15, 1944. The record of its proceedings and exhibits covers 565 printed pages.

6. Tr., Vol. 1, p. 8.
7. CR, p. 8480, Sept. 6, 1945.
8. The majority report of the committee stated, "An effort was made to elicit all facts having an immediate or remote bearing on the tragedy of Dec. 7, 1941. It is believed the committee has succeeded through its record in preserving for posterity the material facts concerning the disaster" (Maj., p. XIV).

The minority report differed. "When all the testimony, papers, documents, exhibits, and other evidence duly laid before the committee are reviewed," it said, "it becomes apparent that the record is far from complete" (Min., p. 3).

The difficulties under which the committee prosecuted its investigation are outlined as follows in the minority report:

"The committee did not have an opportunity to cross-examine any of the high civil executive principals in the Pearl Harbor affair. President Roosevelt and Secretary Knox had died before the committee was created. Harry Hopkins, who was intimately and officially associated with President Roosevelt, died shortly after the committee began its work. The ill health of Secretary of War Stimson and Secretary of State Hull prevented the committee from getting the full benefit of their knowledge, except for the information they voluntarily furnished. . . .

"These difficulties were supplemented by even greater ones stemming from Presidential restraints on the committee and from the partisan character of the committee itself.

"Even before the committee commenced its work, it was confronted with an order issued on Aug. 28, 1945, and signed by President Truman, which severely limited the power of the committee to gain access to the full facts. The order is as follows (Tr., Vol. 1, p. 26):

'AUGUST 28, 1945.

'Memorandum for—The Secretary of State.
        The Secretary of War.
        The Secretary of the Navy.
        The Attorney General.
        The Joint Chiefs of Staff.
        The Director of the Budget.
        The Director of the Office of War Information.

'Appropriate departments of the government and the joint chiefs of staff are hereby directed to take such steps as are necessary to prevent release to the public, except with the specific approval of the President in each case, of—

'Information regarding the past or present status, technique or procedures, degree of success attained, or any specific results of any cryptanalytic unit acting under the authority of the United States government or any department thereof.

HARRY S. TRUMAN."

'Restricted.

"It was not until Oct. 23, 1945, that President Truman made the order less stringent by a new order. The modification left much to be desired.

"The application of the new order was limited to the State, War, and Navy Departments. It relaxed the secrecy of records only so far as 'the Joint Committee' was concerned, while it continued to prevent 'individual' members of the committee from searching records as responsible members of Congress either alone, in groups, or even when accompanied by committee counsel. By one way or another, control over papers, records, and other information remained in the hands of the majority party members.

"The President's October order also contained the unfortunate phrase 'any information in their possession *material to the investigation,*' which provided a cloak for those reluctant to yield information requested by members of the committee. It was always possible to confront individual members with the view that the papers, data, and information desired was not 'material to the investigation.' Decisions were made by the majority ruling out evidence as 'not material to the investigation' without members of the committee ever seeing the material about which the decision was made.

"No subsequent modifying orders wholly removed these restrictions. In an order of Nov. 7, 1945, President Truman relaxed restraints on executives of the government in order that they may speak freely to *individual members* of the committee, but the order closed with the direction: 'This does not include any files or written material.'

"In this fashion every facility and concession afforded to members of the joint committee was hedged about with troublesome qualifications and restraints. The relaxation of restraints was often publicized while the continuing qualifications were but little discussed. The effect was to restrict individual members of the committee in practice while the appearance of their freedom of operations was held out to the public. In justice to committee counsel and to individual majority members of the committee, efforts made by them to overcome these restrictions should be recognized. It is a great tribute to their fairness that the committee did not break up over this issue but continued to work despite the handicaps which were never wholly removed.

"The plain fact that an investigation could not be an investigation if committee members remained mere spectators, persuaded some members that restraints on their freedom were not justified. The flimsiness of the argument for restrictions became even more evident when permission to search files and other records was denied by majority vote to individual members *even when accompanied by committee counsel.* Rightly or wrongly it was inferred from this that there was a deliberate design to block the search for the truth.

"Such a view was supported by the knowledge that restrictions on individual members of congressional investigatory bodies were contrary to the best practices in other investigations. Some celebrated instances were recalled. Speaking in the Senate on Nov. 9, 1945, during one of the discussions on committee powers, the Senator from Montana (Mr. Burton K. Wheeler) observed:

" 'I concur in what the Senator from Illinois has said with reference to the authorizing of a single member of the committee to hold hearings. I have served on a good many investigations since I have been a member of the Senate, and some very important ones. I assisted to quite an extent in the Teapot Dome investigation carried on by my colleague, Senator Walsh, of Montana, and likewise I carried on the investigation of the Department of Justice. I was a minority member of the committee.

" 'In all my experience with any investigating committee, I have never known of any one member of a committee not being permitted to go and look over the files in any department of the government of the United States. This is the first time I have ever known anything of that kind being questioned. . . .

" '. . . I call attention to the fact that in the Daugherty investigation I sent for files myself, I asked for files from the attorney general of the United States, Mr. Daugherty. He refused to give them to me. I have forgotten the ground he stated, but at any rate he refused to give them to me. When he did so, the President of the United States, Mr. Coolidge, called him in and asked for his resignation, and Mr. Daugherty was eliminated from the office of attorney general. After that time, when the new attorney general was appointed, every single file I ever asked for, as a minority member of the committee, was furnished to me.

" '. . . As I have stated, my colleague, Senator Walsh, of Montana, was a minority member of the committee investigating the Teapot Dome situation. I know of my own personal knowledge that he got from the department, and from officials in the department, information which he afterward used, and if he had not been permitted to do that, and if I had not been permitted to do it, I am sure there would have been a complete failure of the investigation of the Department of Justice. (Congressional Record, Vol. 91, No. 198, November 9, 1945, p. 10755.)'

"Another instance is the more recent one in which President Truman himself is well versed. As Senator, Mr. Truman headed a distinguished committee bearing the popular designation 'The Truman Committee' (now the Mead Committee). The cardinal principle of the Truman Committee in the four years during which it won the respect and confidence of the American people, rested on the proposition that every individual member of the committee was wholly free to search for any information deemed by him to be relevant wherever and whenever he thought it could be found. Never once did the chairman or the majority of the committee refuse to recognize that right and that responsibility of each individual member.

"Untrammeled freedom of individual committee members in these instances did not produce chaos or disorder as was argued would be the case in the Pearl Harbor inquiry. On the contrary, the procedure and results in each case did honor to the committees concerned and proved salutary for the nation. Complete concurrence with the most admirable outline of the purposes and scope of the investigation of the events leading up to Pearl Harbor and our entry into the World War as presented to the Senate by the author of the resolution at the time of its introduction and hearty approval of much that has been done by the committee must not blind us to the extent to which the investigation lived up to its advance billing by its distinguished sponsor.

"At the very inception the tested practices in investigations of this character that had demonstrated such extraordinary success in the entire history of the Truman Committee were very definitely rejected and neither of the two members of the committee who had received rather extended training under the then Senator Truman was allowed to follow the course in the investigation of Pearl Harbor that had repeatedly produced most gratifying results in his earlier experience.

"This firm refusal by the committee majority, consisting of six Democrats as against four Republicans, at the very outset to allow the scope to individual members even with every safeguard proposed against the alleged danger of abuse was both unfortunate and disquieting.

"Everything that has since developed must be viewed in the light of this iron curtain that was thus imposed.

"Permission was asked to conduct exploration for certain missing records. Vigorous and public denial was made—presumably on executive authority—that any records were missing. Subsequently it developed that several records were missing and most inadequate explanations were supplied. How any public interest could possibly have been prejudiced by affording any opportunity to examine the manner of keeping records of this character has never been satisfactorily explained.

"These incidents revealed a disquieting determination to keep entire control of the investigation in the hands of the committee majority who were thus put in the unusual position of arrogating to themselves the capacity to conduct an impartial and adequate investigation of their own administration. The history of human conduct furnishes few precedents to justify such confidence.

"Some of the effects of majority decision as well as gaps in the data and testimony due to other causes illustrate the great difficulty surrounding the work of the committee.

"Secretary Stimson declined to appear on the ground that his health did not permit him to undergo strain. Access to his diary was denied by majority vote.

"To accommodate Secretary Stimson because of his illness, Senator Ferguson on March 6, 1946, submitted 176 questions as part of the official record for Secretary Stimson to answer as if propounded in open hearing of the committee (Tr., Vol. 70, pp. 14437 ff.).

"Secretary Stimson did not answer any of these questions, and the committee made no effort to insist upon his answering these questions, which were highly pertinent to the inquiry.

"Later, Senator Ferguson submitted a supplementary list of 61 questions to be answered in the same manner (Tr., Vol. 70, p. 14476). Secretary Stimson answered these questions in writing, and his answers are part of the record. These answers did not, however, make up for the deficiencies in the failure to answer the earlier list of 176 questions.

"Secretary Hull made three appearances, in the course of which he gave his official version of the matters before the committee and was briefly examined by the counsel, but minority members of the committee were not permitted to cross-examine him. When his answers to written interrogatories from committee members proved unresponsive, there was no way to secure further information from him.

"The diary of former Ambassador Joseph C. Grew was likewise denied to the committee. The assertion of its confidential character was somewhat belied by its submission for examination to certain individuals with a view to its commercial publication.

"The denial to the committee of the Stimson and Grew diaries was particularly obstructive because these principles placed excerpts of the diaries in the record and withheld the rest. This was contrary to the prime rule in American law that if part of a document is put into the record by a witness in his own behalf, the court is entitled to demand the whole of the document. Concerning each of these diaries the committee, by majority vote, refused to issue subpenas for their production.

"Many messages, probably several hundreds, between Winston Churchill and President Franklin D. Roosevelt received prior to Dec. 7, 1941, were not available to the committee, although there is good reason to believe that they bore on the gathering crisis. Other messages between Mr. Churchill and the British embassy and American authorities were made available to the committee, but our government replies or action taken were not so available.

"The former Prime Minister of Great Britain was in this country not on official business while hearings of this committee were going on. His intimate knowledge of affairs leading up to Pearl Harbor would have cleared up many gaps in the evidence. By majority vote, a request for the appearance of Mr. Churchill was refused.

"President Roosevelt's secretary, Miss Grace Tully, was permitted to determine for herself and the committee and the country what portions of the official correspondence of the late President had any relevancy to Pearl Harbor. This could hardly be a satisfactory substitute for the responsibility placed upon this committee.

"One of the very important questions concerning the defense of Hawaii dealt with the delays in building airfields and the failure to install radar and other warning devices. Members of the committee sought to inquire into the performance of one Col. Theodore Wyman in this connection, but the committee decided against it.

"The whole question of whether or not it would have been possible to avoid war by proper diplomatic action and thus avert the Pearl Harbor tragedy was left largely unexplored.

"We are permitted only occasional glimpses into this realm but these are fascinating. . . .

"In short, the committee labored under great difficulties and was not in possession of the full historical record pertinent to the case before it. Nevertheless an investigation was made and an amazing amount of material was developed in the limited time allowed to cover such a vast field. It is the duty of the committee to render a report, regardless of the inadequacies of evidence, if sufficient facts are at hand to pass on the issues of responsibility for the catastrophe at Pearl Harbor. A careful review of the evidence is convincing enough that these issues can be decided now" (Min., pp. 3-8).

Representative Keefe, in a statement of "additional views" appended to the majority report, said:

"This investigation has not brought to light all the facts about Pearl Harbor. We have been denied much vital information. Mr. Stimson did not answer certain important interrogations which, in consideration of the state of his health, were submitted to him in writing. He has also denied to the committee his diary entries for the days Dec. 2 to Dec. 6, 1941. These were significantly omitted from his written statement. Mr. Hull's health permitted only a brief appearance before us and no examination by the minority members of the committee. Written interrogatories were submitted as to when he first saw or obtained information as to the contents of certain vital intercepted messages, including the 1:00 P.M. message. Mr. Hull answered: 'I do not recall the exact times that I first saw or learned of the contents of the messages you cite' (Tr., 14316). 'I do not recall' was an answer frequently received from other important witnesses. Messrs. Maxwell Hamilton, Eugene Dooman and Stanley Hornbeck, State Department officials who played important roles in 1941 in our Far Eastern diplomacy, have not testified. We have been denied Ambassador Grew's diary. In December, 1941, Gen. Bedell Smith was secretary to the general staff of the Army. He did not testify. His possible knowledge of the distribution of intercepted messages to Gen. Marshall on Saturday evening, Dec. 6, was not investigated. Adm. (then Capt.) Glover was the duty officer in the office of the chief of naval operations on Dec. 6, 1941. His log for that night contained the vital information about Mr. Stimson's interest in precise locations of the ships of the Pacific fleet. Adm. Glover sent the committee a telegram but did not testify. Mr. Welles's memoranda of Atlantic Charter conferences was obtained from State Department only after his oral testimony before us had been completed" (Maj., pp. 266 S and T).

9. CT, Nov. 21, 1945, 2:6.

10. Senate Document No. 244.

11. In his statement of additional views, Representative Keefe said (Maj., p. 266-A):

"Throughout the long and arduous sessions of the committee in the preparation of the committee report, I continuously insisted that whatever 'yardstick' was agreed upon as a basis for determining responsibilities in Hawaii should be applied to the high command at Washington. This indicates in a general way my fundamental objection to the committee report. I feel that facts have been marshaled, perhaps unintentionally, with the idea of conferring blame upon Hawaii and minimizing the blame that should properly be assessed at Washington.

"A careful reading of the committee report would indicate that the analysis of orders and dispatches is so made as to permit criticism of our commands in Hawaii while at the same time proposing a construction which would minimize the possibility of criticism of those in charge at Washington.

"I think that the facts in this record clearly demonstrate that Hawaii was always the No. 1 point of danger and that both Washington and Hawaii should have known it at all times and acted accordingly. Consequently I agree that the high command in Hawaii was subject to criticism for concluding that Hawaii was not in danger. However, I must insist that the same criticism with the same force and scope should apply to the high command in Washington. It is in this respect that I think the tenor of the committee report may be subject to some criticism.

"I fully agree with the doctrine relating to the placing of responsibility on military officers in the field and their resulting duty under such responsibilities. I agree that they must properly sustain this burden in line with the high and peculiar abilities which originally gave them their assignments.

"In the execution of their vitally important duties, however, the officers at the front in the field are fairly entitled to all aids and help and all information which can reasonably be sent to them from the all-powerful high staff command in Washington. If both commands are in error, both should be blamed for what each should have done and what each failed to do respectively. The committee report, I feel, does not with exactitude apply the same yardstick in measuring responsibilities at Washington as has been applied to the Hawaiian commanders. I cannot suppress the feeling that the committee report endeavors to throw as soft a light as possible on the Washington scene."

12. The Joint Congressional Committee conducted hearings on 70 days between Nov. 15, 1945, and May 31, 1946, receiving 183 exhibits and taking 15,000 pages of testimony from 43 witnesses. Testimony and exhibits of seven previous investigations were available to the committee: the inquiries of the Roberts Commission, Adm. Hart, the Army Pearl Harbor Board, the Navy Court of Inquiry, Col. Clarke, Maj. Clausen, and Adm. Hewitt. The records of these investigations total 9,754 printed pages of testimony from 318 witnesses, and 469 exhibits were filed with them. The records of these proceedings have been incorporated in the record of the Joint Congressional Committee, which encompasses approximately 10 million words (Maj., p. XIV).

NOTES ON CHAPTER I: *WAR*

1. Neville Chamberlain, Sept. 30, 1938.
2. See testimony of Baron Constantin von Neurath, former German foreign minister, at Nuernberg war crimes trials, reported in AP dispatch, June 24, 1946. Neurath asserted that signers of the Munich pact could have halted Hitler's aggressions even after the absorption of Czechoslovakia.
3. Poland No. 1, 1945: His Majesty's Stationery Office, Cmd. 6616, p. 4.
4. Ambrose Bierce, *The Devil's Dictionary* (Tower Books Edition), p. 22.
5. AP dispatch from Tokyo, Dec. 19, 1945. (Konoye memoirs introduced as JCC Ex. 173.)
6. See dispatch of L.S.B. Shapiro, NYT, March 19, 1946, 10:4. Mr. Shapiro reported: "The key to Russia's expansion program in Europe and the Near East has fallen into the hands of the State Department in Washington. Captured German documents detailing the final conversations between Russian Foreign Minister Vyacheslav Molotov and German Foreign Minister Joachim Ribbentrop in the spring of 1941 have been collated and compared with the reports of American envoys and military attachés in European capitals at that time, with the result that Washington now possesses exact pictures of the aims and desires that lie behind the current Soviet troop movements and diplomatic pressures.

"A few weeks before Germany attacked Russia in June, 1941, Mr. Molotov traveled to Berlin in a final effort to divert the Wehrmacht spearheads, which were then clearly gathering for a thrust to the east. The transcript of these last conversations between Mr. Molotov and Ribbentrop became, in 1945, the chief objective of intelligence teams of every victorious nation scouring the ruins of the Third Reich.

"This correspondent has learned, on reliable authority, that the prized transcript was in a batch of captured German documents that were dispatched to Washington during the winter. From sources in an undisputable position to know the facts, I have learned that the salient points of the transcript are as follows:

"Mr. Molotov was coldly received by Ribbentrop, who interrupted the conversations abruptly at frequent points to consult with Hitler. The latter arranged his affairs to make himself quickly available to Ribbentrop at all stages of the conversations.

"The Soviet emissary arrived with authorization from the Kremlin to offer to Germany full military alliance in return for certain territorial concessions after victory, which were permanent possession of all Polish territory then occupied by Soviet forces; incorporation of Lithuania, Estonia, Latvia, and the Karelian Isthmus, Bessarabia and Bukovina into the Soviet Union; complete control of the Dardanelles, a free hand in Iraq and Iran, and enough of Saudi Arabia to give the Soviets control of the Persian Gulf and the Gulf of Aden guarding the approaches to the Red Sea.

"Ribbentrop questioned Mr. Molotov closely on whether he would interpret the terms of a full military alliance as necessarily meaning joining the war in the west. Russia would guarantee Germany's eastern and southeastern flanks, and her own military program in the Near East would constitute military aid of an important nature.

"After numerous conferences with Hitler, Ribbentrop arrived at certain private conclusions. The first was that Russia's territorial demands were too great for acceptance. Secondly, Ribbentrop felt that even if these were suitable, he could not accept Russia's friendly assurances at face value and that Germany would still require a huge force on her eastern frontiers to watch Russia's every move.

"These decisions were put to Mr. Molotov in an extremely stormy final session and the conference broke up shortly thereafter.

"In the light of current Russian moves, this transcript has now assumed importance. American diplomats have known for several months that the apparently confusing Russian pressure all over the globe would be consolidated finally in a push toward the Persian Gulf."

7. JCC, Jan. 3, 1946.
8. *Ibid.*, Jan. 4, 1946.
9. CT, Dec. 7, 1941, 13:2.
10. Papers, 1939 vol., pp. 201-5.
11. Address to Reichstag, April 28, 1939.
12. Grew, p. 493.
13. Brittanica Book of the Year, 1938-1942, p. 1385.
14. Capt. A. H. McCollum testified before the Joint Congressional Committee (Tr., p. 9260) that "I had . . . for many years felt that in the event of an outbreak of hostilities between the United States and Japan that the Japanese would make a very definite attempt to strike the fleet at or near the commencement time of those hostilities."

   The following committee examination of Capt. McCollum (Tr., pp. 9275-6) develops the same theme:
   Question: "And you always felt that if the Japs were going to strike with her fleets the place to start was by attacking our fleet?"
   Captain McCollum: "That is correct."
   Question: "The place they would start would be by attacking the fleet."
   Captain McCollum: "They not only would do that, but that there was historical precedent, if the Japanese wished to start a war with us. Their war with China in 1895 was started that way; their war with Russia in 1907 was started that way; their war against Germany in Tsingtao in 1914 was started in that way. . . . Attacking their fleet and timing a declaration of war on presentation of the final notes."

15. *How War Came,* p. 4.
16. NYT, Dec. 7, 1941, 1:4.
17. *How War Came,* p. 5.

NOTES ON CHAPTER II: *MOUNT NIITAKA*

1. Most of this chapter is based upon the testimony of Adm. T. B. Inglis before the Joint Congressional Committee Nov. 17, 1945. See Tr., pp. 430 ff.
2. Official American and Japanese estimates on the number of planes in the attacking force disagree. The American Navy estimates navy targets at Pearl Harbor were attacked by 105 Jap planes (testimony of Adm. Inglis, Tr., p. 145). The United States Army estimates that 105 enemy planes also attacked army targets on Oahu (testimony of Col. Bernard Thielen, Tr., p. 145). The total of enemy planes thus would be 210. From Japanese sources, Adm. Inglis testified that the attacking force consisted of 361 planes, supplemented by a combat patrol of 18 fighters launched before the takeoff of the attacking force (Tr., pp. 453-4). Three Zero type float planes were assigned to pre-dawn reconnaissance, according to Japanese accounts (Tr., p. 454). Capt. Mitsue Fuchida, commander of the flight groups in the attack, stated (AP dispatch from Tokyo, Oct. 16, 1945) that 350 planes participated.
3. Richard E. Lauterbach, "Secret Jap War Plans," *Life Magazine* (March 4, 1946), p. 18.
4. Edwin Mueller, "Inside Story of Pearl Harbor," *Reader's Digest,* (April, 1944), pp. 25-27.
5. AP dispatch from Tokyo, Oct. 25, 1945.
6. *Ibid.*
7. AP dispatch from Tokyo, Oct. 16, 1945.
8. Tr., p. 457.
9. AP dispatch from Tokyo, Sept. 8, 1945.
10. NYT, Dec. 6, 1942, 1:1.
11. JCC, Jan. 24, 1946.
12. AP dispatch from Tokyo, Oct. 25, 1945.
13. JCC, Dec. 12, 1945.
14. William Bradford Huie, *The Case against the Admirals* (E. P. Dutton, 1946), pp. 153-54.
15. JCC, Jan. 19, 1946.
16. *Ibid.,* Jan. 21, 1946.
17. *Ibid.,* Feb. 1, 1946.
18. AP dispatch from Pearl Harbor, Dec. 6, 1945.

NOTES ON CHAPTER III: *THE RISING SUN*

1. BR, p. 11.
2. JCC, Dec. 15, 1945.
3. *Ibid.,* Feb. 1, 1945.
4. *Ibid.*
5. Tr., pp. 83-84.
6. BR, pp. 12-17; Tr., pp. 83-86.
7. *Ibid.,* pp. 39-41.
8. APH, p. 45.
9. BR, pp. 17-18. Capture of the sampan was disputed by Adm. Inglis (Tr., p. 86) on the ground that no entry concerning the matter appeared in the "Ward's" administrative log. No direct testimony was taken from the commander or crew of the destroyer.
10. BR, p. 15.
11. JCC, Feb. 20, 1946.
12. Radar operations at Oahu are reported extensively in Tr., pp. 75-82, and APH, pp. 33, 38-40, 44.
13. APH, p. 33.
14. Tr., p. 81; JCC, Jan. 26, 1946; Tr., p. 230.

15. APH, p. 33.
16. *Ibid.*, p. 17.
17. NCI, p. 64.
18. APH, pp. 44-45.
19. BR, pp. 23-26; APH, p. 35.
20. APH, p. 35.
21. Tr., pp. 233-36.
22. BR, p. 26.
23. APH, p. 197; BR, pp. 27 and 36.
24. JCC, Jan. 24, 1946.
25. JCC, Ex. 100. It still is not clear whether Sakamaki reconnoitered the harbor before his submarine came to grief.
26. Tr., p. 456; APH, p. 45.
27. Tr., p. 50.
28. BR, pp. 28-29.
29. Adm. Inglis (Tr., p. 90) estimates that the first attack was at Ewa, at 7:53 A.M.
30. BR, p. 42. Also see pp. 18-19 and 38.
31. Estimates on American plane losses vary. Adm. Inglis (Tr., p. 460) gives Navy losses at 102 aircraft, and Col. Thielin (*ibid.*) Army losses at 96.
32. APH, p. 43.
33. JCC, Nov. 15, 1945, Navy ex., item 9.
34. Tr., p. 87; BR, p. 30.
35. Tr., p. 91; NCI, p. 67; BR, p. 32.
36. Tr., p. 98; BR, pp. 36, 57, 73.
37. Tr., pp. 130-31.
38. The following tabulation of damage to the fleet is based upon Navy ex., item 15, introduced before JCC, Nov. 15, 1945:

"Arizona," 33,100 tons: sank at her berth after being hit by one or more aircraft torpedoes and about eight heavy bombs. One bomb, estimated at 2,000 pounds, exploded the forward magazines. The ship was considered to be a total wreck except for material which could be salvaged.

"California," 32,600 tons: sank at her berth as a result of two aircraft torpedo hits and one or more near-bomb misses. Also hit on starboard upper deck by a large bomb which caused a powder fire. Resting on bottom after attack with quarterdeck under 12 feet of water and port side of forecastle under three feet of water.

"West Virginia," 31,800 tons: sank at her berth after four or five aircraft torpedo hits and at least two bomb hits. Rested on bottom with all spaces flooded up to two or three feet below main deck.

"Oklahoma," 29,000 tons: capsized at her berth within eight to eleven minutes after receiving four aircraft torpedo hits. The hull was 20 to 30 degrees from being upside down, with a considerable portion of the bottom and starboard side above water.

"Nevada," 29,000 tons: ran aground and was subsequently beached after being struck by one or more aircraft torpedoes and eight bombs. Two other bombs were near misses, causing rupturing of the hull on the port and starboard bows, respectively. Superstructure wrecked.

"Utah," 19,800 tons: capsized at berth after being struck by two, and possibly three, aerial torpedoes. Ship was within a few degrees of being exactly upside down.

"Cassin," 1,500 tons: struck by one bomb, while a second exploding aft between her and the "Downes" knocked her partly off the drydock blocking and caused her to capsize against the "Downes" in a crazy mass of twisted metal. This resulted in a serious structural failure amidships. Fires swept the ship; the hull, besides showing more than 200 holes, was wrinkled by extreme heat.

"Downes," 1,500 tons: struck by two bombs and left ablaze from stem to stern, the resultant heat causing oil in her bunkers to reach the flash point and explode. Torpedo warheads in the starboard tube were set off and blew out the main deck and starboard side of the vessel in that area, damaging boilers and engines. A serious oil fire following the explosion caused extensive damage to both the "Downes" and "Cassin." The hull of the "Downes" was riddled with more than 400 holes.

"Shaw," 1,500 tons: hit by one bomb while docked in floating drydock number 2 and by many fragments from another bomb which struck the drydock. Fire followed, resulting in blowing up of forward magazine and breaking of the ship's back just ahead of the number 1 stack. When the drydock settled at a 15-degree list, the "Shaw's" upper works were still above the surface.

"Vestal," 9,435 tons: struck by two bombs. One hit forward and caused no great damage. The other struck aft and exploded in the hold, causing a large number of fragment holes through the shell. Flooding aft caused the after part of the vessel to submerge to the main deck. The "Vestal" was beached to prevent further sinkage.

"Oglala," 6,000 tons: sunk by one aircraft torpedo which passed under the ship and exploded against the starboard side of the "Helena." Vessel sank slowly and capsized against 10-10 dock about an hour and a half later.

Floating drydock number 2: this large drydock took five bomb hits. It was set afire and its watertight compartments holed by more than 150 fragments. It settled with one side of the drydock still above water.

"Pennsylvania," 33,100 tons: one bomb hit near the starboard side 5-inch gun. Damage from the explosion was considerable but did not extend below the second deck. One gun was put out of commission.

"Maryland," 31,500 tons: two bomb hits in the forecastle. One of these bombs passed through the port side of the ship about 12 feet under water and exploded, wrecking flats and bulkheads in that area.

"Tennessee," 32,300 tons: two 15-inch shells fitted with fins for use as aerial bombs struck numbers 2 and 3 turrets. Flames spreading from the oil fire on the nearby "Arizona" caused serious damage aft.

"Helena," 10,000 tons: hit on starboard side by aircraft torpedo, causing flooding of numbers 1 and 2 firerooms and forward engine room. The starboard engine was seriously damaged.

"Honolulu," 10,000 tons: damaged by large bomb which passed through deck and exploded 15 or 20 feet from the port side, causing considerable damage to the hull and resulting in flooding of storerooms and magazines.

"Raleigh," 7,050 tons: hit by one aircraft torpedo amidships on port side, flooding the forward half of the machinery plant. Also hit by one bomb which passed through three decks and out the ship's side, exploding about 50 feet away. Serious flooding occurred on the port side aft.

"Curtiss," 13,880 tons: struck on starboard crane by Japanese airplane out of control. This resulted in some wreckage and fire damage. One bomb struck the forward end of the port side hangar, exploding on the second deck. The explosion and resulting fire caused a great amount of wreckage and loss of material.

39. Tr., pp. 458-59.

NOTES ON CHAPTER IV: *THE SCAPEGOATS*

1. AP dispatch from Tokyo, Dec. 12, 1945.
2. *Ibid.,* Oct. 25, 1945.
3. CR, vol. 87, part 9, 77th congress, 1st session, pp. 9506, 9536-37.
4. CT, Dec. 8, 1941, 1:7.
5. NYT, Dec. 12, 1941, 4:1.
6. CR, vol. 87, part 9, 77th congress, 1st session, pp. 9652-53, 9665-67.

7. Peace, pp. 848-49.
8. CT, Dec. 9, 1941, 4:2.
9. *Ibid.,* 4:3.
10. *United States News,* April 19, 1946, p. 24-B.
11. *How War Came,* p. 4.
12. NYT, Dec. 16, 1941, 1:7.
13. BR, pp. 81-82.
14. Tr., pp. 6221-48, especially pp. 6223 and 6237. In his "Summary and Recommendations," Knox made no accusation against Kimmel or Short.
15. JCC, Jan. 5, 1946.
16. NYT, Dec. 18, 1941, 1:1.
17. *Ibid.,* Dec. 17, 1941, 9:1.
18. See address made by Roberts as chairman of mass meeting of Council for Democracy in Madison Square Garden Aug. 19, 1941: NYT, Aug. 20, 1941, 1:7.
19. CT, Jan. 25, 1942, 1:6.
20. Maj., p. 269.
21. JCC, Dec. 19, 1945.
22. *Ibid.,* Jan. 19, 1946.
23. *Ibid.,* Jan. 25, 1946.
24. *Ibid.,* Jan. 16, 1946.
25. Tr., Vol. 42, pp. 8007-8.
26. *Ibid.,* pp. 8544-45.

NOTES ON CHAPTER V: *THE BASING OF THE FLEET*

1. Papers, 1940, pp. 193-94.
2. Puleston, pp. 214-15.
3. JCC, Dec. 19, 1945.
4. That simple logic dictated an attack upon the fleet at Pearl Harbor is attested by the minority report of the Joint Congressional Committee (pp. 28-30):

"The fleet was stationed at Pearl Harbor in a large measure, if not entirely, for the purpose of exercising a deterring effect on the aggressive propensities of the Japanese government during the diplomatic negotiations and of making the government more likely to yield to the diplomatic representations of the United States in matters of policy. This was done contrary to the advice of the commander-in-chief of the U. S. Fleet, Adm. Richardson (who was removed because of protest on that issue), and with which Adm. William D. Leahy, former chief of naval operations agreed (Tr., Vol. 6, p. 916). The fleet could produce this effect only as an instrument of war that constituted a potential threat to the Japanese; that is, a powerful instrument which could be used effectively to strike Japanese armed forces if they moved too far southward in the direction of British, Dutch, and/or American possessions in that region.

"Having determined to move far southward and having moved far on the way early in December toward that region, the Japanese were warned by every principle of sound naval strategy to destroy, if possible, the American fleet at Hawaii on their left flank.

"High authorities in Washington definitely knew from a message received from Ambassador Winant in London at 10:40 A.M. Dec. 6, 1941 (Washington time) that two large Japanese forces had been seen sailing toward the Kra Peninsula and were distant only fourteen hours in time (Ex. 21). Washington authorities should have known, therefore, that this would bring the strategic principle of what to do about Hawaii into immediate military calculations. They took no steps to alert Hawaii.

"The Japanese were fully aware of this strategic principle in December, 1941, as their attack on Pearl Harbor demonstrated. . . .

"Judging by the testimony and documents before the committee, most of the high authorities in Washington, especially after the Atlantic conference in August,

1941, so concentrated their attention on American-British-Australian-Dutch plans for combined actions against the Japanese in Southeastern Asia that they failed to give sufficient, if any, careful consideration to the strategic principle which enjoined the Japanese to destroy, if they could, the American fleet at Hawaii on their left flank before advancing too deeply into southeastern waters. . . .

"The whole raison d'etre of the powerful naval and military installations in Hawaii, as publicly announced, was *defense against a Japanese attack*. Preparations for defense against attack necessarily implied the possibility of an attack. . . .

"Witnesses before the committee, it may be noted, in extenuation of their lack of emphasis on the probability of an attack on Pearl Harbor, called attention to the fact that Japanese agents were also reporting on the military and naval installations of the United States at Panama, the Philippines, the West Coast, and other points. But to men, competent, careful, and watchful, men alert on their all-around and indivisible responsibility, this fact provided no excuse whatever for minimizing the probability of an attack on Pearl Harbor any more than at any other American outpost. Nor does it excuse the failure of Washington authorities to note that far greater detail was being asked for by the Japanese about Hawaii at a time when Japanese movements in the Southwestern Pacific had to contend with the strategic position of Hawaii where the real American striking force, the fleet, rested.

"A full review of the testimony and documents before the committee confirms the conclusion reached by the Army Pearl Harbor Board after its survey of relevant facts: 'We must therefore conclude that the responsible authorities, the Secretary of the Navy and the Chief of Staff in Washington, down to the generals and admirals in Hawaii, *all expected an air attack before Pearl Harbor* (that is Dec. 7, 1941).' As a general statement, when testifying *after* the Pearl Harbor attack, they did not expect it. Apparently the only person who was not surprised was the Secretary of War, Mr. Stimson, who testified: 'Well, I was not surprised!' "

5. JCC, Jan. 30, 1946.
6. *Ibid.*, Nov. 19-20, 1945.
7. JCC, Ex. 9, Stark to Richardson, May 7, 1940.
8. *Ibid.*, Richardson to Stark, May 13, 1940.
9. JCC, Nov. 20, 1945.
10. *Ibid.*, Jan. 4, 1946.
11. *Ibid.*, Nov. 19, 1945.
12. Papers, 1940, p. 517.
13. JCC, Nov. 20, 1945.
14. *Ibid.*
15. *Ibid.*, Jan. 5, 1946.
16. *Ibid.*
17. *Ibid.*, Nov. 23, 1945.
18. *Ibid.*, Nov. 26, 1945.
19. *Ibid.*, Nov. 20, 1945.
20. *Ibid.*, Ex. 9, Richardson to Stark, Oct. 22, 1940.
21. JCC, Nov. 21, 1945.
22. *Ibid.*, Nov. 20, 1945.
23. *Ibid.*, Jan. 2, 1946.
24. Secret testimony before Roberts Commission, submitted to JCC Jan. 10, 1946.
25. JCC, Nov. 21, 1945.
26. *Ibid.*, Jan. 15, 1946.
27. *Ibid.*, Jan. 5, 1946.
28. *Ibid.*, Jan. 21, 1946.

NOTES ON CHAPTER VI: *BLUEPRINT FOR DEFEAT*

1. APH, 12.
2. JCC, Nov. 15, 1945, Army Exhibit I, p. 5.
3. APH, pp. 18, 19, 20.

4. JCC, Dec. 6, 1945.
5. APH, p. 12.
6. APH, p. 13.
7. Tr., p. 7905.
8. APH, p. 15.
9. JCC, Dec. 6, 1945.
10. APH, p. 39.
11. JCC, Jan. 24, 1946; APH, p. 38.
12. JCC, Jan. 24, 1946.
13. APH, p. 15.
14. *Ibid.*
15. JCC, Feb. 2, 1946.
16. Tr., p. 7976.
17. *Ibid.,* p. 8004.
18. Kimmel, Jan. 15, 1946, p. 65.
19. *Ibid.,* pp. 66-68.
20. *Ibid.,* p. 69.
21. *Ibid.,* p. 71.
22. JCC, Dec. 3, 1945.
23. *Ibid.*
24. APH, p. 22.
25. *Ibid.,* p. 23.
26. Huie, pp. 93-94.
27. JCC, Ex. 13.
28. JCC, Feb. 18, 1946. On March 20, 1946, a month after the regular daily hearings
of the committee were concluded, the facts on this subject were confused by admission of committee exhibit 172, a War Department memorandum to committee
counsel. The representations made in this document were seized by the committee
majority in its report (pp. 164-65) in order to advance the argument that lend-
lease did not affect the state of the Hawaii defenses. The majority report states:

"In the case of 210 B-17's and B-24's, Army heavy bombers adaptable for distant reconnaissance, delivered between Feb. 1 and Nov. 30, 1941, none were shipped
under lend-lease and a total of 113 were sold for cash to foreign countries; 12
B-17's were shipped to Hawaii and 35 to the Philippines.

"With respect to Navy planes, there were no lend-lease transfers of long-range
patrol bombers or scout bombers during the same period. Of a total of 835 Navy
planes of all types delivered during this period, Feb. 1 to Nov. 30, 582 were delivered to the Navy and 253 to foreign countries (Britain, Canada, Australia, the
Netherlands, and Norway) under cash transactions. Of the 582 planes delivered
to the Navy, 218 were sent to the Hawaiian area, 146 of the planes being assigned
to carriers.

"It appears that of 3,128 Army and Navy planes of various types delivered between Feb. 1 and Nov. 30, 1941, only 177 were shipped under lend-lease to foreign
countries and none of these were capable of performing distant reconnaissance.
The record is clear, therefore, that the chief of staff and the chief of naval operations
did not prejudice our own defenses in approving excessive allocations to foreign
governments."

The minority report (pp. 50-55) arrives at entirely different conclusions:

"It becomes important, therefore, to consider what defensive equipment was
essential to protect the Pearl Harbor base, whether such defensive equipment was
supplied, and, if not, the reasons for such failure.

"The character of the defensive equipment necessary for the defense of the
Pearl Harbor base is not seriously in dispute. The base most essential, being located on an island, approachable from all directions, the first protective equipment
necessary was a sufficient number of long-distance patrol planes to permit proper
distance reconnaissance covering a 360° perimeter. The evidence indicates that to

supply such a reconnaissance program would require approximately 200 patrol planes, with a sufficient supply of spare parts to keep the planes in operation, and a sufficient number of available crews to permit a continuous patrol.

"Base defense also required sufficient fighter planes to meet any attack which might be considered possible. This would require approximately 175 planes.

"The second class of essential defense equipment was a suitable number of anti-aircraft batteries with suitable and sufficient ammunition and sufficient experienced crews for ready operation.

"The third class of defense equipment were torpedo nets and baffles. It would be necessary for a considerable portion of the fleet to be in Pearl Harbor at all times, fueling and relaxation of men together with ship repairs requiring the ships in the fleet to have constant recourse to the base at more or less regular intervals. The mobility of the Pearl Harbor base was limited, and ships using the base were in a more or less defenseless situation except for the defense power of their own ship batteries. . . .

"Approximately four-fifths of the damage to the fleet upon the attack was the result of torpedoes fired by torpedo-bombing planes attacking the base at low altitudes. Against such an attack, anti-torpedo baffles and nets would have been of extraordinary value. . . .

"The fourth class of defense equipment for the base lay in the newly discovered device known as radar, which before Dec. 7 had been sufficiently perfected to permit the discovery of approaching planes more than 100 miles away. . . .

"The record discloses that from the time the fleet arrived at Pearl Harbor until the attack on Dec. 7, the high command at Hawaii, both in the Army and the Navy, frequently advised the military authorities at Washington of the particular defense equipment needs at the Pearl Harbor base (Exhibits 53 and 106). Nowhere in the record does any dissent appear as to the reasonableness, or the propriety, of the requests for defense equipment made by the high command in Hawaii. On the contrary, the necessity for such equipment was expressly recognized and the only explanation given for a failure to provide the equipment was that by reason of unavoidable shortages, the requested defense equipment at Hawaii could not be supplied.

"It was asserted that more equipment had been provided for Hawaii than for any other base, and this is probably correct. The trouble with such an explanation is that Hawaii was the only nonmainland base charged with the defense of a major part of our Pacific fleet, and the equipment supplied to Hawaii was admittedly insufficient. The Philippines received much equipment which might well have gone to Hawaii, because Hawaii could have been defended, whereas no one expected the Philippines to be able to stand a direct Japanese onslaught. Gen. Marshall reported to the President in March, 1941 (Exhibit 59), that 'Oahu was believed to be the strongest fortress in the world' and practically invulnerable to attack and that *sabotage* was considered the first danger and might cause great damage.

"The government made the Atlantic theater the primary theater and the Pacific theater a secondary and a defense theater. We raise no issue as to the propriety of such decision, but we cannot fail to point out that such decision resulted in the failure of the military authorities in Washington to supply the Pearl Harbor base with military defense equipment which everyone agreed was essential and necessary for the defense of the base and the fleet while in the base. As we have said, such a more or less defenseless condition imposed increased peril upon the Pacific fleet, so long as it was based at Pearl Harbor. . . .

"The record discloses that the Army and Navy had available, between Feb. 1 and Dec. 1, 1941, an abundance of long distance patrol planes suitable for reconnaissance purposes. Exhibit 172 shows that the Army received between Feb. 1 and Dec. 1, 1941, approximately 600 long distance bombers capable of flying loaded missions of 1,250 miles or more. Of these 12 went to Hawaii and 35 went to the Philippines. During the same period the Navy received approximately 560 similar long distance bombers, of which approximately 175 were assigned to carriers in the Pacific. During the same period the Army received approximately 5,500 anti-aircraft guns, of which 7 went to Hawaii and 100 to the Philippines. If it be true that it was found necessary to send this equipment elsewhere, as we assume, still it would seem that Hawaii instead of having high priority, occupied a subordinate position. . . .

"The fleet itself had been depleted by assignments to the Atlantic theater, and the man supply for plane service had likewise been used as a reservoir from which to supply reserve demands for that theater. . . .

"The lack of material does not appear to be the fault of a failure of appropriations by Congress to the Army and Navy. . . .

"The fatal error of Washington authorities in this matter was to undertake a world campaign and world responsibilities without first making provision for the security of the United States, which was their prime constitutional obligation."

The record of Congress in providing for the nation's defense between the advent of President Roosevelt and Pearl Harbor is described by Representative Keefe in his statement of additional views appended to the majority report of the Joint Congressional Committee (pp. 266-U and V):

"The record clearly demonstrates how the Army and Navy get the funds needed for national defense. The Army and Navy are required to submit their respective estimates each year to the Bureau of the Budget. This bureau acting for the President conducts hearings and finally makes recommendations to the President as to the amounts to be recommended to the Congress for appropriation. The Congress is in effect the people of America. The record discloses that in the fiscal years 1934 to 1941, inclusive, the Army and Navy jointly asked for $26,580,145,093. This is the combined total of Army and Navy requests made to the Bureau of the Budget. In the same period the President recommended to the Congress that it appropriate to the combined services $23,818,319,897. The Congress actually made available to the Army and Navy in this period $24,943,987,823. Thus it is apparent that the President himself recommended to the Congress in the fiscal years 1934 to 1941, inclusive, that it appropriate for the Army and Navy $2,761,826,033 less than had been requested by the Army and Navy. The people's representatives in the Congress gave to the Army and Navy in the form of appropriations and authorizations for expenditure $1,256,667,926 more than the President had recommended in his budget messages to the Congress.

"The mere recital of these undisputed figures should dispose of the contention that 'the country is as much to blame as any individual in this final situation that developed in Pearl Harbor.' "

Representative Keefe submitted for ready reference a complete statement:

	Asked	Budget	Congress
1934	$320,900,513	$280,746,841	$280,066,381
1935	305,271,321	288,960,155	283,862,094
1936	361,351,154	331,799,277	363,224,957
1937	467,022,915	391,065,510	401,914,645
1938	468,204,851	436,495,336	439,872,423
1939	630,803,130	598,016,016	611,848,391
1940	1,019,342,730	995,442,760	970,822,098
1941	13,612,977,763	13,067,553,812	13,487,184,058
Total	17,185,874,377	16,390,079,707	16,828,795,047
Total both services	17,185,874,377	16,390,079,707	16,828,795,047
	9,394,271,553	7,428,240,190	8,115,192,776
	26,580,145,930	23,818,319,897	24,943,987,823

Roosevelt cut: $2,761,826,033.
Congress restored: $1,256,667,926 of the Budget cut.

29. Tr., p. 8005.
30. JCC, Dec. 6, 1945.
31. APH, p. 44; JCC, Ex. 5.
32. JCC, Nov. 15, 1945, Ex. 5, pp. 11-12.
33. APH, pp. 40-41, 44.
34. *Ibid.*, p. 44.
35. BR, p. 34.
36. *Ibid.*, p. 58.
37. *Ibid.*, p. 90.
38. Tr., p. 6230.
39. BR, p. 60.
40. *Ibid.*, p. 50. (Adm. Inglis testified Nov. 15, 1945, that the Navy fired 1,685 rounds of 5-inch/.38 caliber anti-aircraft ammunition during the attack, 1,523 rounds of 5-inch/.25 caliber AA, 1,741 rounds of 3-inch/.50 caliber AA, and 275,807 rounds of machine gun ammunition.)
41. CT, Jan. 11, 1946, 6:2.
42. JCC, Jan. 26, 1946.
43. NCI, p. 65.
44. JCC, Feb. 18, 1946.
45. *They Call It Pacific* (Viking, 1943), p. 306.
46. APH, p. 22.
47. Kimmel, p. 24.
48. JCC, Nov. 19, 1945.
49. Kimmel, p. 24.
50. NCI, p. 67.
51. *Ibid.*, p. 74.
52. *Ibid.*, p. 82.
53. *Ibid.*, p. 85.
54. Kimmel, p. 25.
55. NCI, p. 74.
56. Tr., pp. 6223-25.
57. JCC, Dec. 15, 1945.

NOTES ON CHAPTER VII: *BACK DOOR TO WAR*

1. Papers, 1936, p. 206.
2. Papers, 1937, pp. 406-11.
3. *Vital Speeches of the Day*, Dec. 15, 1938, p. 147.
4. Papers, 1939, p. 3.
5. Denied by Roosevelt: Papers, 1939, pp. 114-15.
6. Papers, 1939, p. 212.
7. *Ibid.*, p. 557.
8. Chron., p. 223.
9. Papers, 1940, p. 263.
10. NYT, June 21, 1940, 1:1.
11. Papers, 1940, pp. 673-74.
12. Chron., p. 254.
13. Address to Commons, Aug. 20, 1940.
14. NYT, Aug. 29, 1940, 1:7.
15. Chron., p. 255; Papers, 1940, pp. 391-407.
16. Papers, 1940, pp. 428-31.
17. *Ibid.*, p. 517.
18. *Ibid.*, p. 563.
19. JCC, Nov. 19, 1945.
20. Papers, 1940, p. 607.

21. *Ibid.*, pp. 633-44.
22. Radio address, Feb. 9, 1941.
23. NYT, Jan. 25, 1941, 1:8.
24. Chron., p. 273.
25. CT, June 15, 1946, 2:4.
26. *How War Came,* p. 187; Chron., p. **277.**
27. Chron., p. 283; NYT, May 30, 1941, p. **5.**
28. Fed. Reg., Vol. 6, p. 2897; Chron., p. **284.**
29. NYT, June 25, 1941, p. 1.
30. Chron., p. 288.
31. *How War Came,* p. 286.
32. Chron., p. 293; Peace, pp. 717-20.
33. *World Almanac,* 1942, p. 88.
34. Peace, pp. **737-43.**
35. *Ibid.*, pp. 767-72.
36. *Ibid.*, pp. 787-88.
37. Chron., p. 304.
38. JCC, Jan. 3, 1946.
39. *Ibid.*, Dec. 31, 1945.
40. Tr., pp. 6149-50.
41. JCC, Ex. D-2, Nov. 23, 1945.
42. JCC, Jan. 3, 1946.
43. *Ibid.*
44. Atlantic, pp. 35-37; Saturday Evening Post (Feb. 26, 1944), p. **16.**
45. JCC, Jan. 3, 1946; Tr., p. 6152.
46. JCC, Jan. 3, 1946.
47. *Ibid.*, Dec. 31, 1945.
48. *Ibid.*, Jan. 3, 1946.
49. Tr., p. 6150.
50. *Ibid.*, p. 6151.
51. *Ibid.*, pp. 6155-56.
52. *Ibid.*, p. 6286.
53. JCC, Dec. 6, 1945.
54. *Ibid.*, Nov. 30, 1945.
55. *Ibid.*, Nov. 29, 1945.
56. *Ibid.*, Feb. 12, 1946.
57. Tr., p. 6287.
58. JCC, Jan. 29, 1946.
59. Kimmel, p. 16.
60. JCC, Dec. 6, 1945.
61. Kimmel, p. 16.
62. JCC, Jan. 16, Jan. 18, 1946.
63. *Ibid.*, Nov. 16, 1945.
64. Tr., p. 6237.
65. JCC, Dec. 6, 1945.
66. CT, Oct. 19, 1944, 1:3.
67. NYT, Dec. 27, 1941, **1:1.**
68. APH, p. 34.
69. NCI, p. 62.
70. *Ibid.*
71. Kimmel, p. 15.
72. AP dispatch in CT, May 9, 1946, 13:4.
73. John T. Flynn, *The Truth about Pearl Harbor,* p. **14.**
74. Grew, pp. 402-3.
75. Intercepts, pp. 200-202.

75a. Chicago Daily News, Sept. 30, 1946, 5:3, 4.
76. *Ibid.,* pp. 228-29.
77. NYT, Dec. 9, 1941, 1:7.
78. *How War Came,* p. 315.
79. NYT, Nov. 30, 1941, 1:5.
80. *Time,* Aug. 7, 1939.
81. Chron., p. 256.
82. *Ibid.,* p. 289.
83. NYT, Dec. 2, 1941, p. 6.
84. For. Rel. II, p. 531.
85. Peace, p. 696.
86. For. Rel. I, pp. 517-63.
87. Peace, p. 422.
88. *Ibid.,* p. 475.
89. Grew, p. 295.
90. For. Rel. II, pp. 211-15.
91. *Ibid.,* pp. 216-18.
92. *Ibid.,* pp. 218-19.
93. *Ibid.,* p. 222.
94. *Ibid.,* pp. 222-23.
95. *American Metal Market,* Vol. LI, No. 215 (Nov. 4, 1944).
96. For. Rel. II, p. 224.
97. *Ibid.,* p. 225.
98. Chron., p. 258.
99. NYT, Dec. 1, 1940, p. 1.
100. Peace, pp. 623, 626.
101. *Ibid.,* pp. 631-37.
102. NYT, April 26, 1941, p. 7; *ibid.,* Jan. 24, 1941, p. 4.
103. Peace, pp. 704-5.
104. NYT, July 26, 1941, p. 5.
105. Fed. Reg., Vol. 6, p. 3825.
106. Chron., p. 295.
107. NYT, July 19, 1941, 2:8; Dec. 21, 1941, 27:3.
108. *Ibid.,* July 13, 1941, 14:6.
109. *Ibid.,* June 29, 1941, 9:1.
110. For. Rel. II, pp. 263-64.
111. *Asia and the Americas,* special section, Vol. XLV, No. 12 (December, 1945).
112. JCC, Jan. 21, 1946.
113. *Ibid.,* Nov. 24, 1945.

NOTES ON CHAPTER VIII: *A, B, C, D's*

1. NYT, Dec. 7, 1941, 1:7.
2. CT, Dec. 7, 1941, 10:3.
3. *Ibid.*
4. JCC, Feb. 12, 1946.
5. *Ibid.,* Nov. 19, 1945.
6. *Ibid.,* Dec. 10, 1945.
7. *Ibid.,* Nov. 19, 1945.
8. Tr., pp. 6207-9.
9. JCC, Dec. 6, 1945, Ex. 49, B-1.
10. *Ibid.,* Ex. 50, B-2.
11. *Ibid.,* Jan. 5, 1946.
12. In his campaign speech at the Navy Yard at Bremerton, Washington, August 12, 1944, President Roosevelt said, "We were not allowed to fortify Guam nor did we fortify Wake or Midway or Samoa."

Representative Keefe, in his statement of additional views attached to the majority report of the Joint Congressional Committee (pp. 266-V and W), states:

"Another subject that has been bandied about the country for a number of years relates to what has been frequently referred to as the failure or refusal of Congress to fortify the island of Guam. The contention has been made that Congress refused to appropriate money to fortify the island of Guam and that as a result of such failure the entire war in the Pacific in its initial stages was lost to the Japanese.

"The fact is that no proposal was ever submitted to the Congress involving the fortification of Guam. The Navy did request an appropriation of five million dollars for the purpose of dredging the harbor at Guam (Stark testimony, Tr., pp. 6546-47). The first request of the Navy was rejected by the Congress. Thereafter, the appropriation requested by the Navy was passed with only one vote against it. The dredging operation was being carried on when war broke out with Japan.

"It is interesting to note that 'Rainbow No. 5,' which is the Joint Chiefs of Staff world-wide war plan, placed the island of Guam in Category 'F' (Tr., p. 6535). The following questions and answers tell the story:

Mr. KEEFE. Now, I would like to ask a question which bothered me with respect to your Rainbow No. 5, which places the island of Guam in what is called Category F.

Adm. STARK. I have the category here.

Mr. KEEFE. Now will you state for the record what Category F means?

Adm. STARK. Yes, sir. We have that, I am sure. This is out of Joint Action, Army and Navy, and refers to degrees of preparation, and they are put in categories of defense, A, B, C, D, E, and F.

Mr. KEEFE. Well, take Guam to start with. That is in F. Now give us what Category F means.

Adm. STARK. Category F: "Positions beyond the continental limits of the United States which may be subject to either minor or major attack for the purpose of occupation but which cannot be provided with adequate defense forces. Under this category the employment of existing local forces and local facilities will be confined principally to the demolition of those things it is desirable to prevent falling into the hands of the enemy."

Mr. KEEFE. Then, so far as Guam was concerned, at the time this basic war plan was devised it was the considered opinion of both the Army and Navy that it could not be defended and it therefore was placed in Category F that required those on the island, through demolition or otherwise, to destroy anything of value to the enemy and to permit it to be taken?

Adm. STARK. Yes, sir.

Mr. KEEFE. And to surrender?

Adm. STARK. Yes, sir.

Mr. KEEFE. That is right, is it not?

Adm. STARK. That is correct, yes, sir (Tr., p. 6537).

Mr. KEEFE. Now, at the time of the attack on Guam and the capture of Guam by the Japs were improvements on the harbor being made at that time or had they been completed?

Adm. STARK. They had not been completed. Of course, I recall very clearly the legislation with regard to that. I do not know just what their status was at this moment. I had obtained from Congress the appropriation, I believe it was $6,000,000, for certain improvements to the harbor. You recall the first year I lost it by six votes, and the following year it went through almost unanimously, only one vote being opposed to it. Just how far we had gotten along with that I do not recall at the moment.

Mr. KEEFE. With those improvements completed, Guam would still be in Category F, would it not?

Adm. STARK. In the same category, Category F. The improvements were not such as improved the defense of Guam but very little.

Mr. KEEFE. Even with the improvements that were requested and contemplated the Island of Guam, in the opinion of the Joint Army and Navy Board, could not be successfully defended due to the power that Japan had in the mandated islands surrounding it, is that right?

Adm. STARK. That is correct (Tr., p. 6547).

"These simple facts as disclosed to the public for the first time in these hearings should effectively dispose of the contention that 'Congress refused to fortify the Island of Guam, and hence the United States suffered tremendous loss in the initial stages of the war with Japan.'"

13. p. 245.
14. JCC, Ex. 49, B-1, p. i.
15. Tr., pp. 5573-74.
16. JCC, Feb. 12, 1946.
17. Of these agreements the majority report of the Joint Congressional Committee (pp. 168-71) remarks:

"A great deal of inquiry was made during the course of proceedings to determine whether the government of the United States had entered into an agreement with Great Britain and the Netherlands committing this nation to war upon Japan in the event British or Dutch possessions were attacked by the Japanese. It is clear from evidence before the committee that no agreement was entered into in this regard. The President and his Cabinet, while momentarily expecting an attack by Japan, recognized and observed the constitutional mandate that this government could only be committed to war by a declaration of the Congress.

"Recognizing the inevitable consequences of the tripartite pact, representatives of the War and Navy departments participated during 1941 in a series of staff conversations with military and naval experts of Great Britain, Canada, and the Netherlands. The first of these meetings, initiated by the chief of naval operations and limited to American and British representatives, was held in Washington from Jan. 29 to March 27, 1941. The official report of the conversations, referred to as 'ABC-1,' points out specifically that the discussions were held with a view 'to determine the best methods by which the armed forces of the United States and British Commonwealth, with its present allies, could defeat Germany and the powers allied with her, *should the United States be compelled to resort to war.'* The report states clearly that the plans to accomplish this purpose, as embodied in the report, were subject to confirmation by the highest military authorities in the United States and Great Britain and by the governments of both countries as well. This was in accord with the joint statement of the position the American representatives would take, made by the chief of naval operations and the chief of staff on January 27 at the outset of the conversations.

"'ABC-1' was approved by the chief of naval operations and the Secretary of the Navy and by the chief of staff and the Secretary of War, thereafter being submitted to the President on June 2, 1941. On June 7 the President returned 'ABC-1' without formal approval, pointing out that since the plan had not been finally approved by the British government, he would not approve it at that time but that in case of war the report should be returned to him for approval.

"Shortly after the staff conversations in Washington military and naval representatives of the United States, Great Britain, and the Netherlands conferred in April of 1941 at Singapore in order to draft a plan for the conduct of operations in the Far East based on 'ABC-1.' In the instructions sent the commander-in-chief of our Asiatic fleet prior to the Singapore conversations it was emphatically pointed out that the results of such conversations were likewise subject to ratification by the governments concerned and were to involve no political commitment by the United States. The report of the conversations, referred to as 'ADB,' explicitly recognized that no political commitments were implied. Nevertheless, the chief of naval operations and the chief of staff withheld their approval feeling that some of the statements in the report had political implications. One of the proposals of the Singapore conference, however, was subsequently incorporated *as a recommendation* in the joint memoranda of Nov. 5 and 27 which the chief of staff and the chief of naval operations submitted to the President; i. e., that military counter-action should be undertaken in the event Japan attacked or directly threatened the territory or mandated territory of the United States, the British Commonwealth, or the Netherlands East Indies, or if the Japanese moved forces into Thailand west of 100° east or south of 10° north, Portuguese Timor, New Caledonia, or the Loyalty Islands. . . .

"From all of the evidence, as earlier indicated, there is no basis for the conclusion that an agreement had been effected committing the United States to war against Japan in the event of an attack by her upon the British or the Dutch. It is indisputable that the President and his Cabinet contemplated presenting the problem to the Congress should our position in the Far East become intolerable. Further, the reports of the 1941 staff conversations contain clear disclaimers of any political commitments and the voluminous records relating to these conversations will be searched in vain for any suggestion that an agreement binding the United States to go to war was made. Additionally, all the witnesses who were questioned on the point—including the ranking military and naval leaders of the country at the time—testified that *in these meetings the constitutional prerogative of the Congress to declare war was scrupulously respected.* The preliminary planning done at these conferences manifested commendable foresight and indeed our military leaders would have been inexcusably negligent had they not participated in these conversations in the face of the clear pattern of conquest mapped out by the Axis. This planning saved precious time and lives once Japan struck.

"While no binding agreement existed, it would appear from the record that the Japanese were inclined to the belief that the United States, Britain, and the Netherlands would act in concert. . . ."

The reader may compare this easy dismissal of the effect of the agreements with the findings of the minority (pp. 12-14):

"There is additional evidence for the conclusion that in January, 1941, President Roosevelt then became convinced that the war was a global war and that his decisions as chief executive and commander-in-chief must thenceforward be made with reference to that conviction. This evidence is as follows: Beginning in January, 1941, representatives of the American armed forces and representatives of British and Dutch armed forces on the suggestion of the United States started a series of conversations in respect of cooperation against Japan in the Far East. Out of these subsequent conversations were developed American-British-Dutch war plans for combined operations against Japan if Japanese armed forces started hostile actions against British, Dutch, *or* American possessions in the Far East. President Roosevelt approved these plans, 'except officially,' as Adm. Stark testified.

"The President's commitment to Great Britain was foreshadowed by understandings previously reached between American, British, and Dutch military authorities. In a memorandum to the President dated Nov. 27, 1941 (Ex. 17), Gen. Marshall and Adm. Stark stated:

" 'After consultation with each other, United States, British, and Dutch military authorities in the Far East agreed that joint military counteraction against Japan should be undertaken only in case Japan attacks or directly threatens the territory or mandated territory of the United States, the British Commonwealth, or the Netherlands East Indies, or should the Japanese move forces into Thailand west of 100° East or south of the 10° North, Portuguese Timor, New Caledonia, or the Loyalty Islands.'

"The agreement referred to by Adm. Stark and Gen. Marshall, was reached at conferences in Singapore in April, 1941, between United States, British, and Dutch military authorities in the Far East. . . .

"While the President did not approve written agreements on these understandings he and the high authorities in Washington acted with the British and Dutch just as if a binding pact had been made. Likewise the Japanese acted upon the same belief that the United States, Britain, and Netherlands East Indies were working together. There is ample evidence in the record to this effect. (Ex. I, p. 205— Tokyo to Berlin dispatch: Id. p. 227, Washington to Tokyo dispatch.)

"Subsequent American diplomatic negotiations with Japan were based upon the principle of cooperation with Great Britain, the Dutch Netherlands, China, and Australia. No separate over-all plan for the simple defense of American possessions against Japan was developed by the armed forces of the United States between January, 1941, and Dec. 7, 1941, with a view to safeguarding American interests separately. After the Japanese attack on Dec. 7, American, British, Dutch, and Australian operations in the Pacific theater were conducted on the cooperative principle which had governed the military and naval conversations and planning between January and December, 1941. . . ."

18. Kimmel, p. 9.
19. *Ibid.;* JCC, Ex. 44 E.
20. Kimmel, p. 10.
21. JCC, Dec. 5, 1945.
22. Tr., p. 8555.
23. *Ibid.,* p. 8557.
24. Kimmel, p. 41.
25. JCC, Dec. 31, 1945.
26. Tr., p. 6321.
27. JCC, Dec. 10, 1945.
28. Tr., p. 6291.
29. *Ibid.,* pp. 6312-14; JCC, Dec. 20, 1945.
30. Tr., p. 6315.
31. JCC, Feb. 20, 1946.
32. Tr., p. 6198.
33. *Ibid.,* p. 6204.
34. Intercepts, p. 111.
35. *Ibid.,* p. 227.
36. *Ibid.,* p. 173.
37. *Ibid.,* p. 192.
38. *Ibid.,* p. 238.
39. Address to Commons, NYT, Jan. 28, 1942, 1:4.
40. Radio address, NYT, Feb. 16, 1942, 1:3.
41. AP dispatch from London, June 21, 1944, in CT, same date, 1:2.

NOTES ON CHAPTER IX: *MEETING AT SEA*

1. JCC, April 9, 1946.
2. Welles's "Memorandum of Conversation," upon which this account of the Atlantic conference is based, was introduced before the JCC as Exhibits 22-B, 22-C, and 22-D on Nov. 23, 1945.
3. *How War Came,* p. 10.
4. The minority report of the Joint Congressional Committee (pp. 14-15) emphasizes a subsidiary agreement reached at the Atlantic conference:

"The danger of war with Japan formed a principal theme of discussion between President Roosevelt and Prime Minister Churchill at the Atlantic conference in August, 1941, and agreements or understandings reached by President Roosevelt and Prime Minister Churchill at that conference were based on a common program for dealing with Japan and close cooperation between the United States and Great Britain in diplomatic, military, and naval affairs in respect of the Far East as well as the Atlantic. Their chief understandings as thus far disclosed by official records were three in number:

"(1) Common diplomatic actions warning Japan against taking any further steps in dominating neighboring countries by force or threat of force.

"(2) Occupation of the Azores by the armed forces of the United States with protective assistance by British armed forces in guarding against a possible Nazi thrust from the mainland.

"(3) Cooperation between the United States and Great Britain in 'the policing of the world' during a transition period following the close of the war. . . .

"It is scarcely thinkable that in his discussions with Prime Minister Churchill at the Atlantic conference in August, 1941, President Roosevelt would have assumed that the United States was to cooperate with Great Britain in 'the policing of the world' for a transition period after the war unless he was then certain that at some stage in the development of the war the United States would become involved in it."

5. Peace, p. 714.
6. JCC, Nov. 24, 1945.
7. Ibid., Dec. 15, 1945.
8. Radio address, NYT, Aug. 25, 1941, 1:8.
9. NYT, Nov. 11, 1941, 1:1.
10. Grew, p. 478.
11. Tr., pp. 6298-6303.
12. The majority report of the Joint Congressional Committee (pp. 304-5) debates this question inconclusively:

"The evidence before the committee does not show whether or not the British government took 'parallel action' to the warning given Japan by President Roosevelt. Undersecretary Welles testified before the committee that he took it for granted that the British government took such parallel action and that the records of the State Department would probably show that (Tr., p. 1279), but Secretary Hull testified, and the State Department has advised the committee, that its files contain no record of any such action (Tr., p. 14, 306; 4480). Furthermore, as late as Nov. 30 (Washington time), Prime Minister Churchill sent a message to the President saying that 'one important method remains unused in averting war between Japan and our two countries, namely a plain declaration, secret or public as may be thought best, that any further act of aggression by Japan will lead immediately to the gravest consequences. . . . We would, of course, make a similar declaration or share in a joint declaration' (Ex. 24); and the evidence further shows that on Dec. 7 the Prime Minister submitted to President Roosevelt a draft of a proposed warning to Japan (Tr., pp. 13738-40). On the other hand, on Aug. 25, 1941, in an address reporting to Parliament on the Atlantic conference, the Prime Minister said:

"'But Europe is not the only continent to be tormented and devastated by aggression. For five long years the Japanese military factions, seeking to emulate the style of Hitler and Mussolini, taking all their posturing as if it were a new European revelation, have been invading and harrying the 500,000,000 inhabitants of China. Japanese armies have been wandering about that vast land in futile excursions, carrying with them carnage, ruin and corruption, and calling it "the Chinese incident." Now they stretch a grasping hand into the southern seas of China. They snatch Indo-China from the wretched Vichy French. They menace by their movements Siam, menace Singapore, the British link with Australasia, and menace the Philippine Islands under the protection of the United States.

"'It is certain that this has got to stop. Every effort will be made to secure a peaceful settlement. The United States are laboring with infinite patience to arrive at a fair and amicable settlement which will give Japan the utmost reassurance for her legitimate interests. We earnestly hope these negotiations will succeed. But this I must say: That if these hopes should fail we shall, of course, range ourselves unhesitatingly at the side of the United States (Tr., 1355-56; 4480-4481).'

"While Secretary Hull testified that he knew of no parallel action taken by the British other than this address (Tr., 14306), which was broadcast by radio, Undersecretary Welles testified that in his opinion this address did not constitute 'parallel action' of the kind proposed by Mr. Churchill to the President, and that in Mr. Welles's judgment such action would necessarily have had to have been in the form of an exchange of diplomatic notes (Tr., 1356)."

Again (p. 302) the majority report says:

"The evidence before the committee is conflicting as to whether or not Prime Minister Churchill promised President Roosevelt that the British government would take action parallel to that to be taken by the United States government.

"The only contemporaneous records of the Atlantic conference before the committee are three memoranda prepared by Undersecretary Welles (Ex. 22-B, 22-C, 22-D). Those memoranda show that the procedure outlined by President Roosevelt differed substantially from that envisaged in Prime Minister Churchill's proposal. As there described by Mr. Welles, the President's procedure did not call for parallel action by either the British or Dutch governments, or for keeping Russia informed, as Mr. Churchill had proposed. Nor, as in the case of Mr. Churchill's proposal, was the precise phraseology of the warning to Japan prescribed, it being left entirely up to the President. Mr. Welles testified that the promise given by the President to Mr. Churchill 'was limited to the fact that a warning would be given' (Tr., p. 142), and that the only agreement reached between the President and the Prime Minister was 'that the President made the promise to Mr. Churchill that the government of the United States, in its own words and in its own way, would issue a warning to the Japanese government of the character which actually was made by the President on Aug. 17' (Tr., p. 1428).

"While it is true that Mr. Welles testified that the promise made by President Roosevelt was to 'take parallel action with the British government in warning the Japanese government' (Tr., p. 1235-6) and that he 'took it for granted Mr. Churchill must have made that statement' (i. e., promised to make a parallel warning) to the President (Tr., 1446), it is also true that when asked directly whether the President had told him that Mr. Churchill had promised to make a parallel warning, Mr. Welles said, 'The President in his conversation with me, so far as I remember, did not make that specific statement' (Tr., p. 1446). Moreover, as previously noted, the Welles' memoranda neither state nor indicate that any such promise was made by Mr. Churchill (Ex. 22-B, 22-C, 22-D), and there is no evidence before the committee showing that action parallel to the President's warning to Japan was ever taken by the British government. On the other hand, both 'Peace and War' (Ex. 28, p. 129) and 'Foreign Relations of the United States, Japan 1931-1941' (Ex. 29, vol. II, p. 345) refer to an 'agreement' to take parallel action made by President Roosevelt and Prime Minister Churchill, though, of course, neither of these purports to be a contemporaneous account of the Atlantic conference. Likewise, in his testimony before the committee, Secretary Hull referred to such an 'agreement,' though again Secretary Hull did not attend the Atlantic conference (Tr., p. 1116)."

13. JCC, Nov. 24, 1945.
14. *Ibid.,* Nov. 27, 1945.
15. Intercepts, p. 197. (In this message Nomura used the phrase "on the 17th of this month," but evidently was referring to the warning of Aug. 17. Neither the account in For. Rel. II (pp. 740-43) or in Intercepts (pp. 141-43) of the conversation of the Japanese emissaries and Roosevelt on Nov. 17 shows the President to have voiced any additional warning.)
16. For. Rel. II, p. 139.
17. *Ibid.,* p. 143.

18. JCC, Nov. 28, 1945.
19. *Ibid.*, Dec. 21, 1945.
20. For. Rel. II, pp. 525-26.

NOTES ON CHAPTER X: *THE LAST OF THE JAPANESE MODERATES*

1. Grew, p. 446.
2. *Ibid.*, p. 359.
3. *Ibid.*, p. 361.
4. *Ibid.*, p. 362.
5. *Ibid.*, p. 363.
6. JCC, Nov. 27, 1945.
7. Grew, p. 369.
8. *Ibid.*, p. 365.
9. For. Rel. II, pp. 388-89.
10. *Ibid.*, p. 391.
11. *Ibid.*, p. 331.
12. *Ibid.*, pp. 398-402.
13. *Ibid.*, p. 407.
14. *Ibid.*, pp. 420-22.
15. *Ibid.*, pp. 428-34.
16. *Ibid.*, p. 440-41.
17. *Ibid.*, p. 447.
18. *Ibid.*, pp. 454-55.
19. *Ibid.*, pp. 486-92.
20. *Ibid.*, p. 485.
21. *Ibid.*, p. 509.
22. NYT, July 17, 1941, 1:5; July 19, 1:4.
23. For. Rel. II, p. 496.
24. *Ibid.*, p. 267.
25. Grew, p. 334.
26. Peace, pp. 569-72.
27. JCC, Nov. 27, 1945.
28. Tr., pp. 6339-40.
29. *Ibid.*, pp. 6341-42.
30. *Ibid.*
31. Peace, p. 88.
32. Tr., p. 6353.
33. *Ibid.*, pp. 6344-53.
34. For. Rel. II, pp. 516-20.
35. *Ibid.*, p. 525.
36. *Ibid.*, pp. 533-34.
37. *Ibid.*, p. 526.
38. *Ibid.*, p. 529.
39. *Ibid.*, pp. 534-35.
40. *Ibid.*, p. 549-50.
41. *Ibid.*, pp. 552-53.
42. *Ibid.*, pp. 554-55.
43. *Ibid.*, p. 402.
44. *Ibid.*, p. 550.
45. *Ibid.*, p. 553.
46. *Ibid.*, p. 565.
47. *Ibid.*, p. 568.
48. *Ibid.*, pp. 572-73.

49. *Ibid.*, p. 571.
50. *Ibid.*, p. 576.
51. *Ibid.*, pp. 576-77.
52. *Ibid.*, p. 592.
53. *Ibid.*, p. 588.
54. AP dispatch from Tokyo Dec. 19, 1945, in CT, Dec. 20, 1945.
55. For. Rel. II, p. 628.
56. Intercepts, pp. 33-36.
57. Peace, p. 754.
58. For. Rel. II, pp. 645-50.
59. Grew, p. 444.
60. For. Rel. II, pp. 352-54.
61. *Ibid.*, p. 662.
62. Grew, p. 456.
63. For. Rel. II, p. 692.
64. Grew, p. 481-82.
65. *How War Came,* p. 287.
66. AP dispatch from Tokyo, Dec. 16, 1945, in CT Dec. 17, 5:3.

NOTES ON CHAPTER XI: *DIPLOMACY FOR D-DAY*

1. The ambitious designs of the Japanese militarists were described in the majority report of the Joint Congressional Committee (pp. 295-6) as follows:

"On June 22, 1941, Germany had invaded Russia. The German attack upon Russia had precipitated a series of events in Japan which were to have far-reaching effects upon Japanese-American relations. It had quickened the appetites of those in the Japanese government who believed that then, or never, Japan's destiny was in her own hands. Intensive consideration had immediately been given in Tokyo to the question whether Japan should not attack Russia at once (Ex. 173, Konoye Memoirs, p. 16). Foreign Minister Matsuoka in particular had urged this course. According to the memoirs of Prince Fumimaro Konoye, the Japanese Premier at the time, the attention of the government became so centered upon this question that the American counter-proposal of June 21, which by that time had been received in Tokyo from the Japanese ambassador in Washington, became completely side-tracked until after an Imperial Conference with Emperor Hirohito on July 2 (Japan time) (Ex. 173, Konoye Memoirs, pp. 16, 18). At that conference the question of war with Russia had been temporarily shelved in favor of 'an advance into the southern regions,' and it had been decided that, first of all, the plans 'which have been laid with reference to French Indo-China and Thai will be prosecuted, with a view to consolidating our position in the southern territories' (Ex. 173, Konoye Memoirs, p. 70; cf. Ex. 1, pp. 1-2). It is now known that at the Imperial Conference on July 2 (Japan time) it was also decided that, in case the diplomatic negotiations with the United States should break down, 'preparations for a war with England and America will also be carried forward;' that all plans, including the plan to use Japan's military strength to settle the Soviet question if the German-Russian war should develop to Japan's advantage, were to be carried out—

" 'in such a way as to place no serious obstacles in the path of our basic military preparations for a war with England and America';
and that—

" 'In case all diplomatic means fail to prevent the entrance of America into the European war, we will proceed in harmony with our obligations under the tripartite pact. However, with reference to the time and method of employing our armed forces we will take independent action' (Ex. 173, Konoye Memoirs, p. 71).

"The following report of the Imperial Conference on July 2 (Japan time) had been cabled by the Japanese foreign minister to the Japanese ambassadors in the United States, Germany, Italy, and Russia, the same day:

" '(National Secret)

" 'At the conference held in the presence of the Emperor on July 2 "The Principal Points in the Imperial Policy for Coping with the Changing Situation" were decided. This Policy consists of the following two parts. The first part "The Policy" and the second part "The Principal Points." (I am wiring merely the gist of the matter.) Inasmuch as this has to do with national defense secrets, keep the information only to yourself. Please also transmit the content to both the naval and military attachés, together with this precaution.

" 'The Policy.

" '1. Imperial Japan shall adhere to the policy of contributing to world peace by establishing the Great East Asia Sphere of Co-prosperity, regardless of how the world situation may change.

" '2. The Imperial Government shall continue its endeavor to dispose of the China incident, *and shall take measures with a view to advancing southward* in order to establish firmly a basis for her self-existence and self-protection.

" 'The Principal Points.

" 'For the purpose of bringing the CHIANG Régime to submission, *increasing pressure shall be added from various points in the south,* and by means of both propaganda and fighting plans for the taking over of concessions shall be carried out. Diplomatic negotiations shall be continued, and various other plans shall be speeded with regard to the vital points in the south. *Concomitantly, preparations for southward advance shall be re-enforced and the policy already decided upon with reference to French Indo-China and Thailand shall be executed.* As regards the Russo-German war, although the spirit of the Three-Power Axis shall be maintained, every preparation shall be made at the present and the situation shall be dealt with in our own way. In the meantime, diplomatic negotiations shall be carried on with extreme care. Although every means available shall be resorted to in order to prevent the United States from joining the war, if need be, *Japan shall act in accordance with the Three-Power Pact and shall decide when and how force will be employed* (Ex. 1, pp. 1-2).'

"It is worthy of note that this intercepted Japanese message, which was translated and available in Washington on July 8 (Washington time), did not mention the decisions at the Imperial Conference respecting the United States.

"Commencing immediately after the Imperial Conference, Japan had proceeded with military preparations on a vast scale, calling up from one to two million reservists and conscripts, recalling Japanese merchant vessels operating in the Atlantic Ocean, imposing restrictions upon travel in Japan, and carrying out strict censorship of mail and communications."

Although Ambassador Nomura described the occupation of Indo-China as necessary to safeguard Japan's food supplies and to frustrate foreign powers bent upon encircling Japan, a diplomatic message of July 14, 1941, from Canton to Tokyo (Ex. 1, p. 2) stated:

"Subsequent information from the military officials to the Attachés is as follows:

"1. The recent general mobilization order expressed the irrevocable resolution of Japan to put an end to Anglo-American assistance in thwarting her natural expansion and her indomitable intention to carry this out, if possible, with the backing of the Axis but, if necessary, alone. Formalities, such as dining the expeditionary forces and saying farewell to them, have been dispensed with. That is because we did not wish to arouse greatly the feelings of the Japanese populace and because we wished to face this new war with a calm and cool attitude.

"2. The immediate object of our occupation of French Indo-China will be to achieve our purposes there. *Secondly, its purpose is, when the international situation is suitable, to launch therefrom a rapid attack.* This venture we will carry out in spite of any difficulties which may arise. We will endeavor to the last to occupy French Indo-China peacefully but, if resistance is offered, we will crush it by force, occupy the country and set up martial law. *After the occupation of French Indo-China, next on our schedule is the sending of an ultimatum to the Netherlands Indies. In the seizing of Singapore the Navy will play the principal part.* As for the Army, in seizing Singapore it will need only one division and in seizing the Netherlands Indies, only two . . ."

2. Grew, p. 460.
3. For. Rel. II, p. 697.
4. AP dispatch from Tokyo Dec. 18, 1945, in CT Dec. 19.
5. For. Rel. II, pp. 703-4.
6. *Ibid.*, p. 704.
7. *Ibid.*, p. 679.
8. AP dispatch from Tokyo Sept. 6, 1945, in CT Sept. 7; AP dispatch from Tokyo Sept. 20, 1945, in CT Sept. 21, 3:3.
9. Grew, p. 470.
10. Paul V. Horn, "Effects of Allied Economic Blockade on Japan," *The Conference Board Economic Record*, III: 22 (Nov. 25, 1941), 509-12.
11. For. Rel. II, p. 705.
12. *Ibid.*, p. 706.
13. *Ibid.*, pp. 709-10.
14. *Ibid.*, p. 716.
15. *Ibid.*, pp. 710-14.
16. *Ibid.*, p. 710.
17. *Ibid.*, p. 718.
18. *Ibid.*, p. 720.
19. *Ibid.*, pp. 731-34.
20. *Ibid.*, pp. 736-37.
21. *Ibid.*, pp. 740-43.
22. *Ibid.*, p. 745.
23. *Ibid.*, p. 746.
24. *Ibid.*
25. *Ibid.*, p. 747.
26. *Ibid.*, pp. 759-61.
27. *Ibid.*, p. 789.
28. *Ibid.*, p. 757.
29. *Ibid.*, p. 756.
30. *Ibid.*, pp. 754-55.
31. *Ibid.*, p. 760.
32. *Ibid.*, pp. 763-64.
33. JCC, Nov. 23, 1945.
34. Grew, p. 483.
35. *Ibid.*, p. 486.
36. For. Rel. II, pp. 148-49.
37. *Ibid.*, pp. 377-78.
38. JCC, Nov. 23, 1945.
39. Stimson, p. 47.
40. JCC, Nov. 23 1945.
41. *Ibid.*
42. *Ibid.*
43. *Ibid.*, Nov. 24, 1945.
44. APH, p. 51.
45. The terms of this proposed agreement were:

"1. The government of the United States and the government of Japan, both being solicitous for the peace of the Pacific, affirm that their national policies are directed toward lasting and extensive peace throughout the Pacific area and that they have no territorial designs therein.

"2. They undertake reciprocally not to make from regions in which they have military establishments any advance by force or threat of force into any areas in Southeastern or Northeastern Asia or in the southern or the northern Pacific area.

"3. The Japanese government undertakes forthwith to withdraw its forces now stationed in southern French Indo-China and not to replace those forces; to reduce the total of its force in French Indo-China to the number there on July 26, 1941; and not to send additional naval, land, or air forces to Indo-China for replacements or otherwise.

"The provisions of the foregoing paragraph are without prejudice to the position of the government of the United States with regard to the presence of foreign troops in that area.

"4. The government of the United States undertakes forthwith to modify the application of its existing freezing and export restrictions to the extent necessary to permit the following resumption of trade between the United States and Japan in articles for the use and needs of their peoples:

"(a) Imports from Japan to be freely permitted and the proceeds of the sale thereof to be paid into a clearing account to be used for the purchase of the exports from the United States listed below, and at Japan's option for the payment of interest and principal of Japanese obligations within the United States, provided that at least two-thirds in value of such imports per month consist of raw silk. It is understood that all American owned goods now in Japan, the movement of which in transit to the United States has been interrupted following the adoption of freezing measures shall be forwarded forthwith to the United States.

"(b) Exports from the United States to Japan to be permitted as follows:

"(i) Bunkers and supplies for vessels engaged in the trade here provided for and for such other vessels engaged in other trades as the two governments may agree.

"(ii) Food and food products from the United States subject to such limitations as the appropriate authorities may prescribe in respect of com-modities in short supply in the United States.

"(iii) Raw cotton from the United States to the extent of $600,000 in value per month.

"(iv) Medical and pharmaceutical supplies subject to such limitations as the appropriate authorities may prescribe in respect of commodities in short supply in the United States.

"(v) Petroleum. The United States will permit the export to Japan of petroleum, within the categories permitted general export, upon a monthly basis for civilian needs. The proportionate amount of petroleum to be exported from the United States for such needs will be determined after consultation with the British and the Dutch governments. It is understood that by civilian needs in Japan is meant such purposes as the operation of the fishing industry, the transport system, lighting, heating, industrial and agricultural uses, and other civilian uses.

"(vi) The above stated amounts of exports may be increased and additional commodities added by agreement between the two governments as it may appear to them that the operation of this agreement is furthering the peaceful and equitable solution of outstanding problems in the Pacific area.

"5. The government of Japan undertakes forthwith to modify the application of its existing freezing and export restrictions to the extent necessary to permit the resumption of trade between Japan and the United States as provided for in paragraph 4 above.

"6. The government of the United States undertakes forthwith to approach the Australian, British, and Dutch governments with a view to those governments taking measures similar to those provided for in paragraph 4 above.

"7. With reference to the current hostilities between Japan and China, the fundamental interest of the government of the United States in reference to any discussions which may be entered into between the Japanese and the Chinese governments is simply that these discussions and any settlement reached as a result thereof be based upon and exemplify the fundamental principles of peace, law, order, and justice, which constitute the central spirit of the current conversations between the government of Japan and the government of the United States and which are applicable uniformly throughout the Pacific area.

"8. This *modus vivendi* shall remain in force for a period of 3 months with the understanding that the two parties shall confer at the instance of either to ascertain whether the prospects of reaching a peaceful settlement covering the entire Pacific area justify an extension of the *modus vivendi* for a further period." (JCC, Ex. 18).

46. Stimson, p. 46; APH, p. 51.
47. Stimson, p. 49.
48. Tr., pp. 6161-67.
49. *Ibid.*, pp. 6171-72.
50. *Ibid.*, p. 6173.
51. Stimson, p. 51.
52. Tr., pp. 6181, 6184-85.
53. *Ibid.*, pp. 6191-93.
54. *Ibid.*, p. 6194.
55. *Ibid.*
56. *Ibid.*, p. 6196.
57. *Ibid.*, pp. 6199-6201.
58. *Ibid.*, pp. 6201-3.
59. The influence of other governments upon the decision to reject the *modus vivendi* was discussed by Secretary Hull as follows:

"The Chinese government violently opposed the idea. The other interested governments were sympathetic to the Chinese view and fundamentally were unfavorable or lukewarm. Their cooperation was a part of the plan. It developed that the conclusion with Japan of such an arrangement would have been a major blow to Chinese morale" (Tr., p. 1146).

The minority report of the Joint Congressional Committee says of these events:

"A *modus vivendi* was under discussion with Japan in November 1941 to run for three months. This had been strongly urged by the War and Navy authorities in order to supply absolutely essential time for preparation. Secretary Stimson and Knox went over the terms of this document and advised Secretary Hull that it adequately protected our interest.

"Suddenly the *modus vivendi* was dropped from the agenda and there was substituted the Hull message which was followed shortly after by the attack on Pearl Harbor.

"Early on the morning after the delivery of the Hull message Lord Halifax arrived at the State Department. He found Mr. Welles in charge and asked him what has become of the *modus vivendi*. Mr. Welles replied that it was dropped because of Chinese lack of interest. Lord Halifax intimated a continuing British interest and Mr. Welles significantly replied: 'That is not the way London sounded yesterday.'

"The message from Churchill of the preceding day certainly bears out the Welles observation. The committee was told by the State Department that there is no record of any telephone conversations between Mr. Churchill and President Roosevelt. This certainly invites inquiry.

"The Halifax early morning visit in apparent ignorance of the Churchill message of the day before and of the decision to drop the *modus vivendi* is not in tune with usual British diplomatic procedure.

"Whether or not the Japanese would have accepted the *modus vivendi* must remain a matter of opinion.

"Whether or not it should have been submitted is a matter on which light might well be shed.

"Particularly is this the case when we have the testimony of Gen. George C. Marshall that a delay by the Japanese from December, 1941, into January, 1942, might have resulted in a change of Japanese opinion as to the wisdom of the attack because of the collapse of the German front before Moscow in December, 1941.

"Whether or not such a development would have been one to be desired must remain for future investigation when more of the diplomatic history of the closing months of 1941 can be more thoroughly explored" (Min., pp. 7-8).

A more extended comment on the *modus vivendi* follows:

"Besides the President's instructions or suggestions, Secretary Hull had before him the 'outline of a proposed basis for agreement between the United States and Japan,' which had been carefully prepared by Henry Morgenthau, Jr., secretary of the treasury. Henry Morgenthau's 'outline' with a covering note, dated Nov. 19, 1941, was presented to Secretary Hull, initialled M. M. H. (Maxwell M. Hamilton, chief of the division of Far Eastern affairs). The covering note informed Secretary Hull that all the senior officers of the division concurred with Mr. Hamilton in the view that 'the proposal is the most constructive one I have seen.' Mr. Hamilton urged Secretary Hull to give most careful consideration to the proposal promptly, and suggested that the Secretary make copies of the proposed 'outline' available to Adm. Stark and Gen. Marshall and arrange to confer with them as soon as they had had an opportunity to examine the 'outline' (Exhibits 18, 168).

"With the President's instructions or suggestions and Secretary Morgenthau's 'outline' before him, Secretary Hull considered the terms of a possible agreement with Japan as the basis of a general settlement or an indefinite continuation of negotiations in connection with the Japanese proposal for a *modus vivendi*. This is no place to give a fifty-page summary of the record of the events connected with Secretary Hull's operations. Nor is it necessary to discuss the merits of the case. But the following recital of facts illustrates the confusion and lack of cooperation that prevailed in administration circles.

"Secretary Hull drafted a memorandum for at least a kind of truce with Japan.

"Secretary Hull discussed his proposals with British, Dutch, and Australian representatives in Washington.

"Secretary Hull had a conference on the proposals with Secretary Stimson and Secretary Knox at his office on Nov. 25. Of this conference Secretary Stimson noted in his diary:

'Hull showed us the proposal for a three months' truce, which he was going to lay before the Japanese today or tomorrow. It adequately safeguarded all our interests, I thought as I read it, but I don't think there is any chance of the Japanese accepting it, because it was so drastic' (Tr., Vol. 70, p. 14417).

"The next day, Nov. 26, Secretary Hull told Secretary Stimson over the telephone that he had about made up his mind not to give the proposal for the three months' truce to the Japanese but 'to kick the whole thing over.' Under pressure coming from Chiang Kai-shek, Winston Churchill, and others, relative to the *modus vivendi,* Secretary Hull refrained from making an independent decision on this important step and it appears he was led to decide it without thought of the military capacities necessary to back up our diplomatic position. On that day, Nov. 26, Secretary Hull, with the approval of President Roosevelt, kicked the whole thing over and sent to the Japanese the now famous memorandum which Japan treated as an ultimatum. In taking this action Secretary Hull gave no advance notice to

Gen. Marshall and Adm. Stark, who were then preparing their second careful memorandum to the President begging for a postponement of war with Japan until the Army and Navy could make better preparation for waging it. Moreover, it should be noted that Secretary Hull did not give to the British and Australian representatives any advance information about his sudden decision 'to kick the whole thing over.'

"When Secretary Hull, with the approval of President Roosevelt, made this decision on Nov. 26 and handed his memorandum to the Japanese ambassadors on Nov. 26, he was practically certain that the Japanese government would reject his proposals and that a break in relations would be a highly probable consequence of his action.

"For this statement there is sufficient evidence from Secretary Hull himself. In his account of the meeting with the Japanese representatives, when he presented the memorandum to them, Secretary Hull reported that, after reading the document, Mr. Kurusu said 'that when this proposal of the United States was reported to the Japanese government, that government would be likely to "throw up its hands"; that this response to the Japanese proposal (the so-called *modus vivendi* proposal from Tokyo) could be interpreted as tantamount to the end of the negotiations.' So certain was Secretary Hull of the coming breach that, according to his account, he declared on Nov. 25 and Nov. 28 at a meeting of 'high officials' that 'the matter of safeguarding our national security was in the hands of the Army and Navy' (*Peace and War, 1931-1941* [1943, p. 144]). Some exchanges with the Japanese occurred after Nov. 27, 1941, but none of these exchanges altered in any respect the situation created by Secretary Hull's memorandum of Nov. 26 to Japan" (Min., pp. 7-8).

In a fuller development of its views on this subject, the minority report (pp. 67-69) said:

"Of the many instances showing failures of Washington authorities to cooperate and keep one another duly informed when such acts of duty were vital to the interests of the United States, none was more fateful than actions on the so-called *modus vivendi* proposed by Japan on Nov. 20, 1941.

"Item 1 of the Japanese proposal read:

" 'Both the governments of Japan and the United States undertake not to make any armed advancement into any of the regions in the Southeastern and Southern Pacific area excepting the part of French Indo-China where Japanese troops are stationed.'

"Item 2 read:

" 'The Japanese government undertakes to withdraw its troops now stationed in French Indo-China upon either the restoration of peace between Japan and China or the establishment of an equitable peace in the Pacific area.'

"Wholly apart from the merits or demerits of these and other items in the Japanese proposal of Nov. 20, here was an opportunity at least to prolong 'the breathing spell' for which Gen. Marshall and Adm. Stark were pleading in their efforts to strengthen the armed forces of the United States for war. On Nov. 5, Gen. Marshall and Adm. Stark presented a strong plea to the President begging for time in which to make the Army and Navy ready for war. While the Japanese proposal for a *modus vivendi* was under consideration by the President and Secretary Hull, Gen. Marshall and Adm. Stark prepared another plea for the postponement of the breach with Japan so that the Army and Navy could be made stronger in striking or defensive power. They did not ask for any surrender of American principles; they merely called for delay.

"The Japanese proposal for a *modus vivendi* offered an opportunity to stop for a few weeks the advance of Japanese armed forces into the Southeastern and Southern area—the advance which, according to American war plans, made in cooperation with British and Dutch officers, provided for American action against

Japan or American participation in a war against Japan. It is true that President Roosevelt had not committed the United States officially to these plans but, according to the testimony of Adm. Stark, 'the President, except officially, approved of' the basic principles of these plans (Tr., Vol. 35, pp. 6370-72). American official War Plan WPL 46 was based on them. Whether written in binding agreements or not, American, British, and Dutch authorities acted in concert just as if binding pacts had been made. The Japanese, as Washington clearly learned from the intercepts, also acted upon the assumption that American, British, and Dutch agreements for concerted action existed.

"President Roosevelt evidently deemed it both feasible and desirable to reach some kind of *modus vivendi* with Japan with a view to a possible settlement in general or in any event a prolongation of negotiations with Japan until American armed forces were better prepared for war. Proof of this was found in a pencilled memorandum written by the President for the Secretary of State 'not dated but probably written shortly after Nov. 20, 1941,' that is, after the receipt of the Japanese proposal (Exhibit 18).

"President Roosevelt's memorandum for Secretary Hull with regard to the possible terms of the *modus vivendi* with Japan read:

" '6 MONTHS

" '1. U. S. to resume economic relations—some oil and rice now—more later.

" '2. Japan to send no more troops to Indo-China or Manchurian border or any place South (Dutch, Brit. or Siam).

" '3. Japan not to invoke tripartite pact even if the U. S. gets into European war.

" '4. U. S. to introduce Japs to Chinese to talk things over but U. S. to take no part in their conversation.

*   *   *   *   *

" 'Later in Pacific agreements.' "

60. For. Rel. II, pp. 768-70.
61. *How War Came*, p. 308.
62. For. Rel. II, pp. 764-6.
63. *Ibid.*, pp. 770-1.
64. *Ibid.*, p. 777.
65. Peace, pp. 816-17.
66. AP dispatch from Tokyo Oct. 25, 1945, in CT Oct. 26.
67. For. Rel. II, p. 779.
68. *Ibid.*, p. 780.
69. *Ibid.*, p. 782.
70. *Ibid.*, p. 783.
71. John Chamberlain, "The Man Who Pushed Pearl Harbor," *Life* (April 1, 1946), p. 94.
72. JCC, Nov. 26, 1945; NYT, Nov. 27, 1945, 4:1; Grew, pp. 493, 497.
73. For. Rel. II, pp. 784-86.
74. NYT, Dec. 8, 1941, 1:2.
75. For. Rel. II, p. 385.
76. *Ibid.*, pp. 786-87.
77. *Ibid.*, pp. 787-92.
78. *Ibid.*, p. 787.
79. *Ibid.*, p. 793.
80. *Ibid.*, pp. 793-94.
81. That Roosevelt's policy of never holding out anything but the promise of war when the peaceful elements of the now defeated enemy nation were begging for conciliation had a powerful influence in determining Japan's resolution to fight was implicitly admitted by an American spokesman at the Tokyo war crimes trial. Frank S. Tavenner, deputy prosecutor, said that Germany for months had been egging on Japan to seize Singapore so that Britain would be weakened in her war

with Hitler. The Germans, before their own invasion of Russia, also sought to induce the Japs to attack Russia. Tavenner asserted, however, that there was suspicion and distrust between Germany and Japan.

Early in 1941, Tavenner said, the Japs not only postponed a decision on the Nazi request to fight Russia in the north, but went so far as to notify Hitler that Japan would not fight immediately even if the United States entered the war in Europe. Some time after July, 1941, Tavenner stated, "something as yet undisclosed" prompted a change in policy in Tokyo. The Japanese decided to strike at the United States. Instead of adopting Singapore as the initial objective in a Pacific war and leaving American territory inviolate, the Japanese concluded that they must launch their attack upon Pearl Harbor.

Thus, the American government through an official spokesman subscribes to the thesis that as late as the end of July—four months and a week before the Pearl Harbor attack—there was still a strong chance that peace could be kept between the United States and Japan. Tavenner contends that "something as yet undisclosed" changed the mind of the Japanese, but it requires no great prescience to achieve the explanation which the American prosecutor says has eluded him.

Near the end of July American policy toward Japan stiffened until it bordered on belligerency. Welles' statement of July 23 that there was "no longer any basis" for a peaceful solution was followed by the drastic measures of the oil embargo and credit freeze of July 25. Then Roosevelt met with Churchill at sea and adopted the "parallel action" policy. That was followed by Roosevelt's refusal to meet with Konoye, and by the fall of the Konoye government. The Hull ultimatum of Nov. 26 was the finishing touch. These disclosed facts account for the change in Japanese policy which led to Pearl Harbor. (See CT, Sept. 20, 1946, 22:1.)

82. Dispatch from London April 25, 1946, in CT April 26, 1:2.
83. Peace, p. 843.

NOTES ON CHAPTER XII: *MAGIC*

1. APH, pp. 36-37.
2. 79th Congress, 1st session, Calendar No. 159, Report No. 161.
3. CT, Oct. 26, 1945, 1:6.
4. CR, Nov. 6, 1945, pp. 10606-11.
5. JCC, Nov. 15, 1945, Ex. 1.
6. Intercepts, p. 9.
7. *Ibid.*, p. 14.
8. *Ibid.*, p. 17.
9. *Ibid.*, p. 34.
10. *Ibid.*, p. 20.
11. *Ibid.*, p. 47.
12. *Ibid.*, pp. 50-51.
13. *Ibid.*, pp. 57-58.
14. *Ibid.*, p. 66.
15. *Ibid.*, pp. 72-73.
16. *Ibid.*, pp. 73-74.
17. *Ibid.*, p. 78.
18. *Ibid.*, p. 76.
19. *Ibid.*, p. 79.
20. *Ibid.*, p. 81.
21. *Ibid.*, p. 83.
22. *Ibid.*, pp. 86-87.
23. *Ibid.*, p. 90.
24. *Ibid.*, pp. 92-93.
25. *Ibid.*, p. 98.

26. *Ibid.*, p. 100.
27. *Ibid.*, pp. 97, 101.
28. *Ibid.*, p. 101.
29. *Ibid.*, pp. 113-16.
30. *Ibid.*, pp. 119-22.
31. *Ibid.*, p. 123.
32. *Ibid.*, pp. 126-27.
33. *Ibid.*, pp. 127-29.
34. *Ibid.*, p. 127.
35. *Ibid.*, pp. 131-34, 136.
36. *Ibid.*, p. 137.
37. *Ibid.*, pp. 137-38.
38. *Ibid.*, pp. 141-43.
39. *Ibid.*, p. 145.
40. *Ibid.*, p. 148.
41. *Ibid.*, pp. 150-52.
42. *Ibid.*, p. 154.
43. *Ibid.*, p. 155.
44. *Ibid.*, p. 158.
45. *Ibid.*, p. 165.
46. For. Rel. II, p. 647.

NOTES ON CHAPTER XIII: *THE WRITING ON THE WALL*

1. Intercepts, p. 168.
2. *Ibid.*, p. 173.
3. *Ibid.*, p. 174.
4. *Ibid.*, p. 175.
5. *Ibid.*, p. 178.
6. *Ibid.*, pp. 179-80.
7. *Ibid.*, p. 182.
8. *Ibid.*, p. 183.
9. *Ibid.*, pp. 186-88.
10. *Ibid.*, pp. 190-91.
11. *Ibid.*, p. 193.
12. *Ibid.*, p. 195.
13. *Ibid.*, pp. 195-96.
14. *Ibid.*, p. 198.
15. *Ibid.*, pp. 200-202.
16. *Ibid.*, p. 204.
17. *Ibid.*, pp. 205-6.
18. *Ibid.*, pp. 206-7.
19. *Ibid.*, p. 208.
20. *Ibid.*, pp. 208-9.
21. *Ibid.*, p. 209.
22. *Ibid.*, pp. 209-10.
23. *Ibid.*, pp. 210-12.
24. *Ibid.*, p. 212.
25. *Ibid.*, p. 215.
26. *Ibid.*, pp. 215-16.
27. *Ibid.*, pp. 216-21.
28. *Ibid.*, p. 224.
29. *Ibid.*, pp. 224-25.
30. *Ibid.*, p. 227.
31. *Ibid.*, p. 228.

32. *Ibid.,* pp. 228-29.
33. *Ibid.,* p. 230.
34. *Ibid.,* p. 231.
35. *Ibid.,* pp. 232-33.
36. *Ibid.,* p. 233.
37. *Ibid.,* p. 234.
38. *Ibid.,* p. 234.
39. *Ibid.,* p. 236.
40. *Ibid.,* p. 237.
41. *Ibid.,* p. 236.
42. *Ibid.,* p. 237.
43. *Ibid.,* pp. 238-39.
44. JCC, Feb. 1, 1946.
45. Intercepts, pp. 245-46.
46. *Ibid.,* p. 246.
47. *Ibid.,* p. 247.
48. JCC, Dec. 17, 1945.
49. For. Rel. II, p. 792.
50. Intercepts, p. 245.
51. JCC, Dec. 12, 1945.
52. Intercepts, p. 248.
53. *Ibid.,* p. 248.
54. *Ibid.,* p. 249.
55. *Ibid.,* pp. 249-51.
56. *Ibid.,* p. 252.

NOTES ON CHAPTER XIV: *EAST WIND RAIN*

1. Intercepts, p. 154.
2. APH Top Secret Testimony, released to press by Senator Barkley December 11, 1945. The majority report of the Joint Congressional Committee is at pains to dispute the evidence that a "winds" message was intercepted before December 7. Among its rather equivocal conclusions (Maj., pp. 469-86) are the following:

"Significantly, a check of the Army file of intercepts for the period Dec. 3-5, 1941, reflected that the Navy file contains all intercepts that are in the Army file.

"Conceding for purposes of discussion that a winds execute message was received in the form alleged by Safford, it will be noted that such message would not indicate *where* or *when* Japan would strike but merely her possible purpose to go to war. Bearing in mind the rather frank admission by Army and Navy officials that they knew war was imminent in the days before Dec. 7, credence could scarcely be placed in the theory that the message was deliberately destroyed when it contained no information that was not admittedly already possessed. . . .

"From consideration of all evidence relating to the winds code, it is concluded that no genuine message, in execution of the code and applying to the United States, was received in the War or Navy Department prior to Dec. 7, 1941. It appears, however, that messages were received which were initially thought possibly to be in execution of the code but were determined not to be execute messages. In view of the preponderance weight of evidence to the contrary, it is believed that Capt. Safford is honestly mistaken when he insists that an execute message was received prior to Dec. 7, 1941. Considering the period of time that has elapsed, this mistaken impression is understandable.

"Granting for purposes of discussion that a genuine execute message applying to the winds code was intercepted before Dec. 7, it is concluded that such fact would have added nothing to what was already known concerning the critical character of our relations with the empire of Japan."

3. "Secretary of War Henry L. Stimson announced on Dec. 1, 1944, that the report of the Army Pearl Harbor Board had been submitted to him, and that: 'In accordance with the opinion of the judge advocate general, I have decided that my own investigation should be further continued until all the facts are made as clear as possible, and until the testimony of every witness in possession of material facts can be obtained, and I have given the necessary directions to accomplish this result.' By memorandum dated Feb. 6, 1945, for Army personnel concerned, Secretary Stimson stated that 'Pursuant to my directions and in accordance with my public statement of 1 December, 1944, Maj. Henry C. Clausen, JAGD, is conducting for me the investigation supplementary to the proceedings of the Army Pearl Harbor Board.' This investigation was commenced on Nov. 23, 1944, and was concluded on Sept. 12, 1945. The record of its proceedings and exhibits covers 695 printed pages" (Maj., pp. 270-71).

4. JCC, Feb. 12, 1946.

5. Ibid., Dec. 13, 1945.

6. Ibid., Dec. 11, 1945.

7. Ibid., Dec. 13, 1945.

8. APH, p. 59.

9. JCC, Dec. 12, 1945.

10. Ibid.

11. Ibid.

12. "The investigation conducted by Col. Carter W. Clarke 'regarding the manner in which certain Top Secret communications were handled' was pursuant to oral instructions of Gen. George C. Marshall, chief of staff, United States Army. Col. Clarke was appointed by Maj. Gen. Clayton Bissell, chief of the military intelligence division, War Department, under authority of a letter dated Sept. 9, 1944, from the adjutant general. This investigation was conducted from Sept. 14 to 16, 1944, and from July 13 to Aug. 4, 1945. Testimony was taken concerning the handling of intercepted Japanese messages known as Magic, the handling of intelligence material by the military intelligence division, War Department, and the handling of the message sent by Gen. Marshall to Lieut. Gen. Walter C. Short at Hawaii on the morning of Dec. 7, 1941. The record of the proceedings of this investigation, together with its exhibits, covers 225 printed pages" (Maj., p. 270).

13. CT, Dec. 2, 1945, 16:5.

14. "The Marshall-Dewey Letters," Life, Dec. 17, 1945, p. 19; JCC, Dec. 7, 1945.

15. JCC, Dec. 18, 1945.

16. Ibid., Dec. 19, 1945.

17. "The inquiry conducted by Adm. H. Kent Hewitt, United States Navy, was initiated under precept dated May 2, 1945, from Secretary of the Navy James Forrestal to conduct 'Further investigation of facts pertinent to the Japanese attack on Pearl Harbor, Territory of Hawaii, on 7 December 1941.' The precept stated that upon review of the evidence obtained by the examinations conducted by Adm. Thomas C. Hart and by the Navy Court of Inquiry, 'the Secretary (of Navy) has found that there were errors of judgment on the part of certain officers in the naval service, both at Pearl Harbor and at Washington. The Secretary has further found that the previous investigations have not exhausted all possible evidence. Accordingly he has decided that the investigation directed by Public Law 339 of the 78th Congress should be further continued until the testimony of every witness in possession of material facts can be obtained and all possible evidence exhausted. . . . You are hereby detailed to make a study of the enclosures (Proceedings of Hart inquiry and Navy Court of Inquiry) and then to conduct such further investigation, including the examination of any additional persons who may have knowledge of the facts pertinent to the said Japanese attack, and to reexamine any such person who has been previously examined, as may appear necessary, and to record the testimony given thereby.' This inquiry commenced on May 14, 1945,

and was concluded on July 11, 1945. The record of its proceedings and exhibits covers 1,342 printed pages" (Maj., p. 271).

18. JCC, Feb. 2, 1946.
19. CT, Feb. 4, 1946, 1:2.
20. JCC, Feb. 2, 1946.
21. *Ibid.*
22. *Ibid.*
23. Safford, p. 1. (Tr., pp. 9622-54.)
24. The minority report of the Joint Congressional Committee (p. 46) observes:

"In the lower, operating echelons of the Army and Navy, on the other hand, men seemed to see or to sense the gathering crisis and even the immediate danger to Hawaii. They tried to take steps to meet it but were discouraged by their superiors. This was notably evident in the testimony of Capt. Arthur McCollum, chief of the Far Eastern section of naval intelligence. Alarmed by conditions on Dec. 4, 1941, he prepared a dispatch to fully alert the fleets in the Pacific. He tried to get permission to send this dispatch at a meeting attended by Admirals Stark, Ingersoll, Turner, and Wilkinson but was discouraged from doing so on the ground that the messages of Nov. 24 and 27 to Admiral Kimmel were sufficient. He protested that they were not sufficient and that he would like to send his Dec. 4 dispatch anyway. The dispatch he prepared and wanted to send was never sent, and the result was tragic. (See testimony of Capt. McCollum, Tr., Vol. 49, p. 9132 ff.)"

25. The following dispatch was sent on April 1, 1941, from the chief of naval operations addressed to the commandants of all naval districts:

PERSONNEL OF YOUR NAVAL INTELLIGENCE SERVICE SHOULD BE ADVISED THAT BECAUSE OF THE FACT THAT FROM PAST EXPERIENCE SHOWS THE AXIS POWERS OFTEN BEGIN ACTIVITIES IN A PARTICULAR FIELD ON SATURDAYS AND SUNDAYS OR ON NATIONAL HOLIDAYS OF THE COUNTRY CONCERNED, THEY SHOULD TAKE STEPS ON SUCH DAYS TO SEE THAT PROPER WATCHES AND PRECAUTIONS ARE IN EFFECT (JCC, Ex. 37, p. 1).

26. All of the foregoing is quoted from Safford statement supra.

NOTES ON CHAPTER XV: *"IMPRISON'D IN THE VIEWLESS WINDS"*

1. NCI testimony introduced before JCC Feb. 5, 1946.
2. *Ibid.*
3. *Ibid.*
4. JCC, Feb. 5, 1946.
5. *Ibid.,* Feb. 6, 1946.
6. *Ibid.,* Feb. 7, 1946.
7. *Ibid.,* Feb. 8, 1946.
8. NCI, p. 86.
9. JCC, Feb. 9, 1946.
10. *Ibid.,* Feb. 10, 1946.
11. *Ibid.,* Feb. 11, 1946.
12. NYT, Feb. 12, 1946, 15:3.
13. JCC, Feb. 11, 1946.
14. *Ibid.,* Feb. 15, 1946.
15. *Ibid.,* Feb. 16, 1946.
16. *Ibid.,* Feb. 2, 1946.
17. *Ibid.*
18. *Ibid.,* Feb. 1, 1946.
19. *Ibid.,* Feb. 16, 1946.

20. *Ibid.*, Dec. 20, 1945.
21. *Ibid.*, Jan. 30, 1946.
22. *Ibid.*, Feb. 2, 1946.
23. Memorandum of Gen. Cramer, dated Nov. 23, 1944, introduced before JCC Jan. 26, 1946: Tr., Vol. 46, pp. 8621-28.
24. *Ibid.*, p. 8627.
25. *Ibid.*
26. Kimmel, p. 97.
27. Cf. minority views of the Joint Congressional Committee (Min., pp. 31-32):

"Although the knowledge gained from these and other items of information [Japanese spy and diplomatic intercepts] was sufficient to warn high authorities in Washington that Japan was on the verge of starting hostilities, reference should be made in this connection to the so-called 'winds' messages concerning which there had been much dispute and no little mystery. The story, though long, may be abbreviated here.

"Col. Otis Sadtler testified before the Army Pearl Harbor Board that about Nov. 20, 1941, a Japanese message was intercepted notifying nationals that another message was to come indicating whether war, if launched, would be against the United States, Great Britain, or Russia or any combination of them. The first message stated that the second or 'activating' message to come would indicate by reference to the directions of the winds and weather the names of the countries against which war would be started. The Army Pearl Harbor Board also had evidence to the effect that the second or 'activating' message from Japan had come and that it meant 'War with England, War with America, Peace with Russia.' According to the board's report:

" 'This original message has now disappeared from the Navy files and cannot be found. It was in existence just after Pearl Harbor and was collected with other messages for submission to the Roberts Commission. Copies were in existence in various places but they have all disappeared' (Top Secret, p. 8).

"The evidence before this committee bearing on the interception of the activating message from Tokyo and on the contention that it indicated hostilities between Japan and the Anglo-American combination covers hundreds of pages. Admittedly the evidence is confusing and conflicting, but after reviewing it, Adm. Royal E. Ingersoll, deputy to Adm. Harold Stark, testified before the Hart inquiry to questions 68 and 69:

" '68. Q. During November or December, '41, were you cognizant of a special code which the Japanese had arranged, under which they were to inform their nationals concerning against what nations they would make aggressive movements, by means of a partial weather report?

" 'A. Yes; I do recall such messages.

" '69. Q. Do you recall having seen, on or about 4 December, the broadcast directive, thus given, indicating that the Japanese were about to attack both Britain and the United States?

" 'A. Yes.'

"Adm. Ingersoll, deputy to Adm. Harold Stark at Washington, and Adm. Turner, Navy operations officer at Washington, both stated they did not know until 1945 about the allegation that there had been no wind execute message. Even if the wind execute message they saw was a false one they believed it true at the time and should have acted accordingly.

"If, however, the receipt of the activating 'winds' message be wholly discounted, such discounting in no way affects the other items of unmistakable evidence which demonstrate that high authorities in Washington had sufficient knowledge of Japanese designs to convince them before the attack that war with Japan was an imminent certainty."

28. Memorandum by William D. Mitchell, CR, Nov. 6, 1945, p. 10431.

APPENDIX

NOTES ON CHAPTER XVI: *"DO-DON'T" WARNINGS*

1. APH, p. 22.
2. *Ibid.*, p. 23.
3. JCC, Ex. 37, p. 18; Kimmel, pp. 38-39; Tr., Vol. 42, p. 7923.
4. Hart Report, p. 423; Tr., Vol. 46, p. 8535.
5. JCC, Dec. 20, 1945.
6. Tr., Vol. 42, p. 7923.
7. Kimmel, p. 41; JCC, Ex. 37, p. 32.
8. JCC, Ex. 106.
9. Kimmel, p. 42; JCC, Ex. 37, p. 36.
10. Tr., Vol. 42, pp. 7927-28; JCC, Ex. 32, p. 7.
11. APH, pp. 27-28.
12. *Ibid.*, p. 27.
13. *Ibid.*
14. *Ibid.*
15. *Ibid.*, p. 28; Tr., pp. 4247, 4270.
16. APH, p. 27.
17. *Ibid.*, p. 28; Tr., pp. 4251-52.
18. JCC, Dec. 11, 1945.
19. The minority report of the Joint Congressional Committee (p. 42) states:

"Two points in the message of Nov. 27 to Gen. Short deserve special consideration. It informed him that 'the United States desires Japan to commit the first overt act,' if hostilities cannot be avoided. And it also informed him that such measures as he deemed necessary to adopt 'should be carried out so as not to alarm the civil population or disclose intent.' A limitation on dissemination was to 'minimum essential officers.'

"As to 'overt act,' it is to be emphasized that an all-out alert for defense against a possible or probable attack by an enemy is not an overt act of war. Nor did the government of the United States regard it as such, for, on the basis of reports respecting a probable Japanese attack, Gen. Marshall, on June 17, 1940, instructed Gen. Herron, the commanding general in Hawaii, to order an all-out, full, war alert and the armed forces were set in motion immediately and kept alerted for six weeks (testimony Tr., Vol. 17, pp. 2775 ff.)."

Representative Keefe (Maj., p. 266-K) adds:

"The message sent to Gen. Short by Gen. Marshall on Nov. 27, 1941, shows the other feature of the administration's plan of action—to make sure that the Japanese would strike first so that the offensive by the fleet would be approved by the American public."

20. APH, p. 28.
21. JCC, Dec. 31, 1945.
22. APH, p. 29.
23. *Ibid.*
24. *Ibid.*
25. *Ibid.*, p. 54.
26. As to the psychology of this cautious attitude, Representative Keefe (Maj., pp. 266 M and N) observes:

"On Nov. 27, 1941, the information which Gen. Marshall had showed a far more severe crisis in Japanese-American relations than existed in June of 1940. As his letter to Gen. Herron shows, he felt that this all-out alert in Hawaii in 1940 may have discouraged the Japanese from attacking that area. Yet he did not repeat on Nov. 27, 1941, his message of June 17, 1940, to Hawaii with its clear-cut order: *'Immediately alert complete defensive organization to deal with possible trans-Pacific raid.'* He assigned as a reason for not doing so, the fact that in the message of Nov. 27, 1941, 'you had to include instructions of the President regarding overt acts' (Tr., p. 3975).

"Mr. Stimson describes the preparation of the Army message of Nov. 27 to Gen. Short as follows:

" 'If there was to be war, moreover, we wanted the Japanese to commit the first overt act. On the other hand, the matter of defense against an attack by Japan was first consideration. In Hawaii because of the large numbers of Japanese inhabitants, it was felt desirable to issue a special warning so that nothing would be done, unless necessary to defense, to alarm the civil population and thus possibly precipitate an incident and give the Japanese an excuse to go to war and the chance to say that we had committed the first overt act' (Stimson statement, pp. 21-22). . . .

"The same fear of publicity, alarm, or anything which might savor of a first overt act by the United States, rather than by Japan, is reflected in the President's message to High Commissioner Sayre in the Philippines on Nov. 26, 1941. After describing the crisis in Japanese-American relations, the President directed Mr. Sayre to impress upon the president of the Philippines 'the desirability of avoiding public pronouncement or action since that might make the situation more difficult' (Tr., pp. 13861-62)."

27. Tr., p. 7928. Representative Keefe in statement of additional views appended to majority report of Joint Congressional Committee (p. 266-I) says:

"I have pointed out that during the critical period prior to the attack, the administration in Washington made certain over-all policy decisions as to how to deal with the Japanese crisis. One decision was that Japan should commit the first overt act against the United States and thus resolve the dilemma in which the administration's secret diplomacy had placed it. The other was to be in instant readiness to strike at Japan to check her further aggression against the British and Dutch in Far East Asia. Certainly the information and orders sent to Gen. Short and Adm. Kimmel prior to the attack reflected the policy adopted in Washington.

"Gen. Short and Adm. Kimmel were not informed about the most important diplomatic steps in 1941. They were not informed of the parallel action agreement at the Atlantic conference or the warning to Japan which followed. They were not informed of the significant terms of the American note to Japan of Nov. 26. They were not informed of the commitment made to Great Britain, as set forth in the Brooke-Popham telegram of Dec. 6. [See Chap. XIX.] They did not receive the vital intercepted Japanese messages or any condensation or summary of them."

28. Tr., pp. 7928-29.
29. JCC, Ex. 32, p. 10.
30. *Ibid.*, p. 12.
31. The minority report of the Joint Congressional Committee states of the failure of Washington officials to react to Gen. Short's message:

"The chief of the war plans division of the Army, Gen. Leonard T. Gerow, saw Gen. Short's reply, noted, and initialed it (Ex. 46). Gen. Marshall saw Gen. Short's reply, initialed the document to which it was appended, and routed it to the Secretary of War (Ex. 46) (Tr., Vol. 22, pp. 3722-23). The Secretary of War saw, noted, and initialed Gen. Short's reply (Ex. 46). . . .

"To Gen. Short's response, the War Department made no answer whatever. The President's commission on Pearl Harbor took note of this failure on the part of the War Department and placed it among the contributory causes of the catastrophe. In their testimony before this committee, Gen. Marshall and Gen. Gerow admitted that the failure to inform Gen. Short immediately as to the insufficiency of his anti-sabotage alert was a mistake on their part and Gen. Marshall took full responsibility upon himself for this failure (Tr., Vol. 19, pp. 3126 and 3164). Reasonably conclusive evidence that the war warning messages which had been sent to Gen Short and Adm. Kimmel on Nov. 27 were insufficient to constitute a proper and adequate war warning is provided by Gen. Marshall's decision to send another warning message to Gen. Short on the morning of Dec. 7, despite the insistence of other high authorities in Washington that the previous messages were sufficient. . . .

"The fact is that the War Department and Navy Department did not instruct Gen. Short and Adm. Kimmel to put into effect an all-out war alert, and the War Department was informed by Gen. Short that he had actually put into effect the alert against sabotage. . . .

"The War Department failed to reply to Gen. Short's anti-sabotage report. It failed to give him further instructions for a stronger alert. These failures, it is reasonable to say, contributed heavily to the unpreparedness existing at Pearl Harbor when the Japanese struck.

"It could reasonably follow from this failure that the Army airplanes, instead of being scattered, were bunched together wing to wing; ammunition, except that near the fixed anti-aircraft guns, was in storehouses; anti-aircraft artillery and two combat divisions were in their permanent quarters and not in combat positions. . . .

"This was known to the War Department by Gen. Short's reply to the message of Nov. 27, but the department took no action.

"The President's lack of power under the Constitution to meet the Japanese menace by an attack without a declaration of war by Congress increased the responsibility of high authorities in Washington to use the utmost care in putting the commanders at Pearl Harbor on a full alert for defensive actions before the Japanese attack on Dec. 7, 1941. This they did not do."

32. Tr., pp. 7930-31.
33. *Ibid.*, p. 7931.
34. JCC, Ex. 32, p. 13.
35. Tr., p. 8660.
36. JCC, Ex. 32, p. 17.
37. Tr., pp. 7993-94.
38. *Ibid.*, p. 7969.
39. *Ibid.*, p. 7994.
40. JCC, Ex. 37, p. 14.
41. JCC, Ex. 32, p. 19.
42. Tr., p. 7934.
43. JCC, Nov. 29, 1945.
44. Kimmel, pp. 42-44.
45. Hart inquiry, pp. 40-41.
46. Kimmel, pp. 44-47.
47. Tr., pp. 7935, 8656-57.
48. Kimmel, pp. 53, 55.
49. *Ibid.*, p. 55.
50. JCC, Ex. 78, p. 2.
51. Kimmel, p. 47.
52. *Ibid.*, p. 48.
53. JCC, Ex. 80.
54. JCC, Dec. 21, 1945.
55. Kimmel, p. 49.
56. JCC, Jan. 21, 1946.
57. APH, p. 31.
58. *Ibid.*
59. R, Section IX.
60. APH, p. 32.
61. *Ibid.*
62. JCC, Dec. 8, 1945.
63. APH, p. 32.

64. The minority report of the Joint Congressional Committee (pp. 33-34) comments:
    "The fact that Gen. Marshall decided on the basis of the intercepts of Japanese messages made available on or before 11:25 o'clock on the morning of Dec. 7, to send an urgent war warning to the outpost commanders is itself evidence that, despite previous messages to outpost commanders, Washington authorities recognized that their knowledge of these intercepts and their minute direction of affairs placed an obligation on them to convey precise information to outpost commanders and to make sure that they were on an all-out alert for war. Owing to inexcusable delays in Washington this final warning to Gen. Short did not reach him until after the Japanese attack.
    "Gen. Marshall failed to use the scrambler telephone on his desk to call Gen. Short in Hawaii on Sunday morning, Dec. 7, nearly two hours before the attack, and give him the same information which he sent in the delayed telegram which reached Gen. Short after the attack. Gen. Marshall testified that among the possible factors which may have influenced him against using the scrambler telephone was the possibility that the Japanese could construe the fact that the Army was alerting its garrisons in Hawaii as a hostile act (Tr., Vol. 20, pp. 3389-3390).
    " 'The Japanese would have grasped at most any straw to bring to such portions of our public that doubted our integrity of action that we were committing an act that forced action on their part' (Tr., Vol. 19, p. 3193).
    "This explanation is no excuse for the failure to put the Hawaiian commanders on the full alert for defense. Such an alert could not be considered a hostile or aggressive act on the part of the United States."
65. Tr., pp. 5676 and 8682.
66. APH, p. 32.
67. Tr., pp. 8529-30.

NOTES ON CHAPTER XVII: *"KNOWN IMPENDING WAR"*

1. APH, p. 36.
2. Kimmel, p. 54.
3. NCI, p. 66.
4. *Ibid.*, p. 70.
5. APH, p. 54.
6. NCI, p. 69. Representative Keefe states: "Despite the elaborate and labored arguments in the [majority] report and despite the statements of high ranking military and naval officers to the contrary, I must conclude that the intercepted messages received and distributed in Washington on the afternoon and evening of Dec. 6 and the early hours of Dec. 7, pointed to an attack on Pearl Harbor" (Maj., p. 266-F).
7. The majority report of the Joint Congressional Committee (p. 47) concedes the importance of "Magic," stating, "This material not only indicated what Japan and her ambassadors were *saying* but literally what they were *thinking.*"
    The minority report (pp. 20-21) said of this information:
    "Through the Army and Navy intelligence services extensive information was secured respecting Japanese war plans and designs, by intercepted and decoded Japanese secret messages, which indicated the growing danger of war and increasingly after Nov. 26 the imminence of a Japanese attack.
    "With extraordinary skill, zeal, and watchfulness the intelligence services of the Army Signal Corps and Navy office of naval communications broke Japanese codes and intercepted messages between the Japanese government and its spies and agents and ambassadors in all parts of the world and supplied the high authorities in Washington reliable secret information respecting Japanese designs, decisions, and operations at home, in the United States, and in other countries. Although there were delays in the translations of many intercepts, the intelligence

services had furnished to those high authorities a large number of Japanese messages which clearly indicated the growing resolve of the Japanese government on war before Dec. 7, 1941.

"Incidentally, it was a matter of great imprudence for the State and War Department to permit so large a number (200) of Japanese consular representatives at so important a naval base as Hawaii. Much of the espionage involved in the intercepts emanated from this consular group in Hawaii.

"Four volumes laid before the committee contain hundreds of these messages —including in some cases comment and interpretations:

"(1) *Pearl Harbor: Intercepted Diplomatic Messages.* Ex. 1 (253 pp.);

"(2) *Japanese Messages Concerning Military Installations, Ship Movements,* etc. (of the United States) (mimeograph, Ex. 2); and

"(3) *Army Pearl Harbor Board: Top Secret Testimony, Report and Official Memoranda* (mimeograph).

"(4) *The Navy Court of Inquiry Top Secret Testimony and Report.*

"No person has any intellectual or moral right to pass judgment on the question of responsibility for Pearl Harbor who has not read, compared, studied, and interpreted all of these documents. . . .

"There was abundant evidence in the intercepted messages that Japan intended to attack the United States. . . ."

8. Kimmel, p. 78.
9. *Ibid.,* pp. 78-9.
10. *Ibid.,* pp. 79-80.
11. *Ibid.,* p. 80.
12. *Ibid.,* pp. 80-81.
13. *Ibid.,* p. 81.
14. *Ibid.*
15. *Ibid.* The minority report of the Joint Congressional Committee (Conclusion 12, pp. 36-38) states:

"*Inasmuch as the knowledge respecting Japanese designs and operations which was in the possession of high authorities in Washington differed in nature and volume from that in the possession of the Pearl Harbor commanders it was especially incumbent upon the former to formulate instructions to the latter in language not open to misinterpretation as to the obligations imposed on the commanders by the instructions.*

"Since Washington authorities knew that vital information in their possession —diplomatic, military, and naval—was not being sent to Gen. Short and Adm. Kimmel, and that this was because of Washington's own decision, it was obligatory for them to give particular care to the formulation of messages to the commanders which revealed the growing war tension, the menacing imminence of the breach in American-Japanese relations, and the resolve of those high authorities to wait for an attack, while still carrying on maneuvering.

"The increasing assumption of the detailed direction of affairs by high authorities in Washington added to the obligation of those high authorities to give precise instructions to the outpost commanders. . . .

"But it is beyond all question that Washington authorities had a large volume of information, particularly as to vital diplomatic decisions and Japanese intentions which was not transmitted to the Hawaiian commanders. This withholding of information from Gen. Short and Adm. Kimmel was in part due to a general policy adopted in Washington. . . .

"The exceptional practice of sending the substance in some messages was stopped in July, 1941, and Gen. Miles testified that, so far as he knew, Gen. Short and Adm. Kimmel were not notified of this change—this discontinuance of sending even the substance of some intercepts (Tr., Vol. 13, pp. 2140-42). . . .

"From among the numerous items of crucial information in possession of Navy intelligence and Washington authorities and *not* transmitted to Gen. Short one may be selected as particularly pertinent to Pearl Harbor. Through its intelligence sources in the Fourteenth Naval District at Pearl Harbor and in Washington, the Navy discovered the presence at Jaluit, in the Marshall Islands, of a Japanese fleet composed of aircraft carriers and other vessels, but lost track of it about Dec. 1. Jaluit is 1,500 miles nearer to Pearl Harbor than is the mainland of Japan. The Japanese fleet there was a strong force capable of attacking Hawaii. Information about this Japanese fleet was delivered to the War Department, but it was not transmitted to Gen. Short. Gen. Short testified during the Army Board hearings on Pearl Harbor that knowledge of the Japanese fleet at Jaluit would have materially modified his point of view and actions."

16. JCC, Ex. 15.
17. Kimmel, p. 34.
18. JCC, Ex. 52, p. 1.
19. Kimmel, pp. 36-38. The obligation of Roosevelt and his official circle to warn the outpost commanders on the basis of information in their exclusive possession is stated in the minority report of the Joint Congressional Committee (Conclusion 10, p. 30) as follows:

   "*The knowledge of Japanese designs and intentions in the hands of the President and the Secretary of State led them to the conclusion at least ten days before Dec. 7 that an attack by Japan within a few days was so highly probable as to constitute a certainty and, having reached this conclusion, the President, as Commander-in-Chief of the Army and Navy, was under obligation to instruct the Secretary of War and Secretary of the Navy to make sure that the outpost commanders put their armed forces on an all-out alert for war.*

   "Besides the knowledge of Japanese designs and operations which the President and the Secretary of State acquired from their diplomatic negotiations with Japan, they also had the knowledge of Japanese designs and operations made available to them by the Army and Navy intelligence services. This additional knowledge could only serve to fortify the conviction already reached as early as Nov. 25, namely, that a Japanese attack was near at hand, or, to use President Roosevelt's own words, 'we were likely to be attacked perhaps as soon as Monday' (Dec. 1)."

20. Kimmel, pp. 43, 54-55.
21. JCC, Ex. 2, p. 12.
22. *Ibid.*, p. 13.
23. *Ibid.*
24. *Ibid.*, p. 15.
25. *Ibid.*, p. 14.
26. *Ibid.*, p. 15.
27. *Ibid.*
28. JCC, Ex. 2.
29. *Ibid.*, p. 29.
30. *Ibid.*, p. 27.
31. The minority report of the Joint Congressional Committee (Conclusion 15, pp. 44-45) states:

   "*The failure of Washington authorities to act promptly and consistently in translating intercepts, evaluating information, and sending appropriate instructions to the Hawaiian commanders was in considerable measure due to delays, mismanagement, nonco-operation, unpreparedness, confusion, and negligence on the part of officers in Washington.*

   "The record before this committee is crowded with items of evidence which sustain this conclusion.

   "As to delays, take for example section B of *Japanese Messages Concerning Military Installations, Ship Movements, Etc.* [Ex. 2]. Pages 16-29 give 'messages translated after Dec. 7, 1941.' Here are messages exchanged by the Japanese government and its agents which were intercepted by American intelligence services before Dec. 7, *but not translated until after Dec. 7*. Special attention should be drawn to the message from a Japanese agent in Honolulu to Tokyo on Dec. 6, 1941, listing the ships at anchor in Pearl Harbor on that day and reporting to Tokyo: 'It appears that no air reconnaissance is being conducted by the fleet air arm—' a fact with which high authorities in Washington were not acquainted, if the testimony before this committee is accepted as accurate and comprehensive."

32. JCC, Feb. 13, 1946.
33. *Ibid.*, Feb. 11, 1946; Ex. 2, p. 22.
34. Tr., pp. 8691-92.
35. Kimmel, pp. 84-85; Tr., pp. 6779-80.
36. JCC, Dec. 4, 1945.
37. *Ibid.*, Jan. 19, 1946.
38. Tr., p. 7989. The minority report of the Joint Congressional Committee says of these intercepted spy messages:

"The probability that the Pacific fleet would be attacked at Pearl Harbor was clear from the 'bomb plot' available in Washington as early as Oct. 9, 1941, and related Japanese messages.

"The 'bomb plot' message, and those messages relating to Pearl Harbor which followed it, meant that the ships of the Pacific fleet in Pearl Harbor were marked for a Japanese attack. No other American harbor was divided into sub-areas by Japan. And no other American harbor had such a large share of the fleet to protect.

"In no other area did Japan seek information as to whether two or more vessels were alongside the same wharf. Prior to the 'bomb plot' message Japanese espionage in Hawaii was directed to ascertain the general whereabouts of the American fleet, whether at sea or in port. With the 'bomb plot' message Japan inaugurated a new policy directed to Pearl Harbor and to no other place, in which information was no longer sought merely as to the general whereabouts of the fleet, but as to the presence of particular ships in particular areas of the harbor. In the period immediately preceding the attack Japan required such reports even when there was no movement of ships in and out of Pearl Harbor. The reports which Japan thus sought and received had a useful purpose only in planning and executing an attack upon the ships in port. These reports were not just the work of enthusiastic local spies gathering meticulous details in an excess of zeal. They were the product of instructions emanating from the government of Japan in Tokyo. Officers of the high command in Washington have admitted before us that the 'bomb plot' message, if correctly evaluated, meant an attack on ships of the Pacific fleet in Pearl Harbor (Tr., Vol. 18, p. 3026; Vol. 23, p. 4014; Vol. 27, p. 4874; Vol. 12, p. 2100-2102; Vol. 59, p. 11313-11314; Vol. 35, p. 6390, 6394; Vol. 30, p. 5378). . . .

"Military intelligence through Col. Bratton delivered the 'bomb plot' message to the Secretary of War, the chief of staff, and the chief of the war plans division (Tr., Vol. 62, p. 12083). The message was discussed several times by Col. Bratton, chief of the Far Eastern section, military intelligence division, War Department general staff, with his opposite numbers in the Navy Department (Tr., Vol. 62, p. 12105). They discussed possible significance of the message, as indicating a plan for an air attack on ships in Pearl Harbor (Tr., Vol. 62, p. 12105). In the course of these discussions officers in naval intelligence stated that the Japanese were wasting their time in getting such meticulous detail about the location of ships in Pearl Harbor because the fleet would not be in Pearl Harbor when the emergency arose.

"Simple reason in evaluating these bomb plot messages should have discovered their significance.

"1. Such meticulous detail was not needed to enable Japan to keep track of the American fleet for general purposes.

"2. The messages were sent to *Tokyo* obviously for use originating from there—air or sea attack.

"3. The messages couldn't be for sabotage. Sabotage is an on-the-spot affair. Saboteurs have to be in Hawaii. They get their information direct by local observation. Therefore, they needed no bomb plot.

"4. The only purpose could be for air attack, submarine attack, direct invasion—all external operations.

"5. Had Washington so evaluated this bomb plot, it could have seen this significance and warned the commanders at Hawaii. Washington authorities failed to do so or if they did in fact evaluate it, they failed to pass the information on to the Hawaiian commanders.

"The commander of a fleet (in this case Adm. Kimmel) has custody of the fleet; he is at all times materially interested in its safety. The commander of a naval base (in this case Gen. Short) has the duty of protecting the fleet when it is at his base. Any information showing specific hostile interest in that fleet or in the harbor where the fleet is anchored is basic information for the commander of the fleet and the commander of the naval base.

"In Washington, long prior to Dec. 7, 1941, Army and Navy intelligence officers, the chief of naval operations, the Army chief of staff, and other high authorities gained vital information (the bomb-plot messages) from intercepted Japanese communications affecting the fleet and the defense of the naval base at Hawaii. They gained it from sources of information not available to Adm. Kimmel and Gen. Short.

"In these circumstances, it was the express duty of the Washington authorities to pass this information in its original form on to Adm. Kimmel and Gen. Short. The information was of such a specific character and so directly related to the fleet and naval base that Washington authorities were not justified in keeping it to themselves or in evaluating it in any manner which would dilute or generalize the significance of the messages in their original form. Washington authorities failed in this, a prime responsibility in their relations with the outpost commanders.

"In the days immediately preceding Pearl Harbor, Japan made no effort to conceal the movements or presence of her naval forces in South East Asia (Tr., Vol. 3, p. 453). The movements of her troops in Indo-China at that time were the subject of diplomatic exchanges between the United States and Japan (Foreign Relations of the United States, Japan, 1931-41, II, p. 779). Yet the intercepts showed that some Japanese plan went into effect automatically on Nov. 29, from which Japan hoped to divert American suspicion by a pretext of continued negotiations. The Pearl Harbor 'bomb plot' messages gave some hint of what might follow 'automatically.'

"Only the President and his top advisers in Washington had this information."

The majority report (p. 190) contains the following remarks:

"It cannot be forgotten that a surprise attack by air on Pearl Harbor had been listed and understood, both in Washington and Hawaii, as the greatest danger to that base. We must assume that military men realized that in order to execute successfully such an attack the Japanese would necessarily need detailed information as to dispositions at the point of attack. It would seem to be a natural consequence that if Japan undertook an attack on Pearl Harbor she would seek to acquire such detailed information and in point of time as nearly as possible to the hour of such attempt.

"We are unable to conclude that the berthing plan and related dispatches pointed directly to an attack on Pearl Harbor, nor are we able to conclude that the plan was a 'bomb plot' in view of the evidence indicating it was not such. We are of the opinion, however, that the berthing plan and related dispatches should have received careful consideration and created a serious question as to their significance. Since they indicated a particular interest in the Pacific fleet's base this intelligence should have been appreciated and supplied the commander in chief of the Pacific fleet and the commanding general of the Hawaiian Department for their assistance, along with other information and intelligence available to them, in making their estimate of the situation."

Representative Keefe observes (Maj., p. 266-E):

"The reports which Japan thus sought and received had a useful purpose only in planning and executing an attack upon the ships in port. Those reports were not just the work of enthusiastic local spies gathering meticulous details in an excess of zeal. They were the product of instructions emanating from the government of Japan in Tokyo. Officers of the high command in Washington have admitted before us that this message, if correctly evaluated, meant an attack on ships of the Pacific fleet in Pearl Harbor (Tr., pp. 3036, 4014; 4874; 2100-2102; 11313-14; 6390, 6394; 5378)."

39. APH, p. 6. The minority report of the Joint Congressional Committee (Conclusion 8, p. 27) says relevant of this consideration:

"*Judging by the military and naval history of Japan, high authorities in Washington and the commanders in Hawaii had good grounds for expecting that in starting war the Japanese government would make a surprise attack on the United States.*

"There is no evidence in the record before the committee that President Roosevelt, Secretary Hull, Secretary Stimson, and/or Secretary Knox expected at any time prior to Dec. 7 a formal declaration of war on the United States by Japan in case the diplomatic negotiations came to a break. Indeed, all the evidence bearing on expectations in Washington as to Japan's probable methods of making war point to the belief of the administration that Japan would begin with a surprise attack.

"For example, Secretary Hull on Nov. 25 and Nov. 28 at a meeting of 'high officials,' when he stated that the matter of safeguarding our national security was in the hands of the Army and Navy, 'expressed his judgment that any plans for our military defense would include the assumption that the Japanese might make the element of surprise a central point in their strategy, and also might attack at various points simultaneously with a view to demoralizing efforts of defense and of coordination for purposes thereof' (Peace and War, p. 144).

"Speaking to Ambassador Halifax on Nov. 29, Secretary Hull said that it would be a—

" 'serious mistake . . . to make plans of resistance without including the possibility that Japan may move suddenly and with every possible element of surprise . . . that the Japanese recognize that their course of unlimited conquest . . . is a desperate gamble and requires the utmost boldness and risk' (*Peace and War*, pp. 144-45).

"Ambassador Grew reported to Hull on Nov. 3—

" 'Japan may resort with dangerous and dramatic suddenness to measures which might make inevitable war with the United States' (*Peace and War*, p. 775)."

40. Testimony by Adm. Kimmel before Roberts Commission, supplied to JCC Dec. 31, 1945.

41. JCC, Dec. 18, 1945.

42. Testimony by Gen. Short before Roberts Commission, supplied to JCC Dec. 31, 1945.

43. Kimmel, pp. 101, 104.

44. Tr., p. 8706.

45. Tr., pp. 7965-66.

46. Tr., p. 3713.

47. Tr., pp. 1420-22.

48. Tr., pp. 2726-29.

49. Tr., pp. 3727-28.

50. Tr., p. 8007. Representative Keefe in his statement added to the majority report (pp. 266-L and M) remarks:

"Subsequently, in the same examination (printed record pp. 1422-1423) Gen. Marshall stated that Gen. Gerow had a direct responsibility in this matter and that he had full responsibility as chief of staff. Gen. Marshall was very fair. He admitted that a tragic mistake had been made, and while it was the direct responsibility of Gen. Gerow, chief of war plans, to have 'caught' Gen. Short's reply and to have immediately advised his chief of staff, yet Gen. Marshall as chief of staff did assume over-all responsibility for failure of the Washington headquarters to interpret and evaluate Gen. Short's reply and to see to it that he was on an all-out alert in accordance with the command directive issued in the message from Marshall to Short on Nov. 27. The Secretary of War saw, noted and initialed Gen. Short's reply (Ex. 46). It was the responsibility of Gen. Marshall to see that Gen. Short was properly alerted (Tr., p. 3723). Gen. Short, after being ordered to report his state of readiness to Gen. Marshall, was entitled to assume that his state of readiness was satisfactory to the chief of staff unless he heard to the contrary (Tr., p. 3443). Neither Gen. Marshall, Gen. Gerow, nor Secretary of War Stimson made any criticism or suggestion to Gen. Short about the condition of his alert in Hawaii in the ten-day period prior to the attack. Because of their silence Gen. Short was led to believe that the chief of staff approved his alert against sabotage. I believe that Secretary Stimson, and Generals Marshall and Gerow, understood the nature of his alert which was plainly indicated in the reply itself. I further believed they were satisfied with Gen. Short's alert until the blow fell on Hawaii."

51. Tr., p. 7953.
52. Tr., p. 2888.
53. JCC, Ex. 53, pp. 1-3.
54. Tr., pp. 7996-98.
55. Tr., pp. 8539-42.
56. Tr., pp. 8542-44.

NOTES ON CHAPTER XVIII: *THE LIGHT THAT FAILED*

1. FM 100-5, dated May 22, 1941, p. 40.
2. Tr., p. 7981.
3. JCC, Nov. 29, 1945.
4. Tr., p. 7985.
5. JCC, Jan. 24, 1946.
6. *Ibid.*, Nov. 29, 1945. The minority report of the Joint Congressional Committee (Conclusion 7, pp. 26-27) says:

   "Army and Navy information which indicated growing imminence of war was delivered to the highest authorities in charge of national preparedness for meeting an attack, among others, the President, the Secretaries of State, War, and Navy, and the chief of staff and the chief of naval operations.

   "The 'Magic' intelligence was regarded as preeminently confidential and the policy with respect to its restricted distribution was dictated by a desire to safeguard the secret that the Japanese diplomatic codes were being broken. Delivery of the English texts of the intercepted messages was limited, within the War Department, to the Secretary of War, the chief of staff, the chief of the war plans division, and the chief of the military intelligence division; within the Navy, to the Secretary of the Navy, the chief of naval operations, the chief of the war plans division, and the director of naval intelligence; to the State Department; and to the President's naval aide for transmittal to the President. By agreement between the Army and Navy in Washington, the Army was responsible for distribution of 'Magic' within the War Department and to the State Department; the Navy for distribution within the Navy Department and to the White House.

"The President requested the original raw messages in English, examining them personally, and on Dec. 6 had his naval aide on special night duty to receive and deliver them to him.

"The dissemination of 'Magic' materials did not include the commanders at Hawaii, but on a few occasions material derived therefrom was dispatched by the Navy Department to Adm. Kimmel. The War Department did not send the 'Magic' to the field. A large amount of other intelligence obtained from various sources within and without the country was not sent to either of the commanders in Hawaii."

7. JCC, Feb. 8, 1946.
8. Tr., pp. 2091-92.
9. APH, p. 32.
10. JCC, Nov. 29, 1945.
11. *Ibid.*, Nov. 30.
12. *Ibid.*, Jan. 29, 1946.
13. *Ibid.*
14. The minority report of the Joint Congressional Committee (pp. 59, 62, 63) states:

"Evidence set forth in this report in detail is ample to show that in the period approximately from May, 1940, to Dec. 7, 1941, the high authorities at Washington assumed so much of the direction of affairs at Hawaii as to remove many of the basic responsibilities from the commanders in the field. The result was to reduce the discretion of the commanders in the field by those things which they were ordered to do by directions from Washington and not to do certain things unless they were so ordered from Washington. Another result of this practice was to lull the commanders in the field into awaiting instructions from Washington.

"Being charged with the responsibility attaching to the highest command in Washington and having taken so much of the responsibility and direction of affairs away from the commanders in the field, the high authorities in Washington themselves failed in the performance of their responsibilities, as the evidence in the conclusions of this report clearly shows. . . .

"High Washington authorities took over so much of the detailed direction of affairs respecting operations of the Pacific fleet and of the Hawaiian naval base as to limit narrowly the discretion and freedom allowed to the Hawaiian commanders. Having thus weakened the individual obligations of the Hawaiian commanders and having failed correspondingly to provide them with clear and adequate orders, high Washington authorities reduced the responsibility of the Hawaiian commanders in the defense of Pearl Harbor. . . .

"Having assumed so much of the detailed direction of affairs relating to Hawaiian defense, Washington authorities had the obligation to correct all wrongful decisions at Hawaii which had been made in response to Washington orders. A crucial decision of this kind was made by Gen. Short when he alerted his command only against sabotage in response to orders in the message of Nov. 27, 1941. With superior knowledge of impending danger and having the immediate obligation to correct Gen. Short's error of judgment, Washington authorities, particularly Gen. George C. Marshall and Gen. Leonard T. Gerow, did not do so but permitted Gen. Short to assume that he had done all that had been required of him. This error, as later proved, left the defenses at Hawaii particularly vulnerable to external attack."

15. JCC, Jan. 29, 1946.
16. Cramer report of Nov. 25, 1944: JCC, Dec. 12, 1945.
17. Tr., pp. 8000-8001.
18. APH, p. 56.
19. Tr., pp. 8585-87.
20. Peace, p. 136.
21. *How War Came,* p. 303.

22. The minority report of the Joint Congressional Committee (pp. 15-16) points out that, once having taken the decision to abandon a *modus vivendi* and to submit to Japan conditions which were known to be inacceptable, it was more than ever incumbent upon high authorities in Washington to put into effect an all-out war alert:

"On Nov. 26, 1941, Secretary Hull, with the approval of President Roosevelt, rejected the Japanese proposal of Nov. 20 for a temporary agreement, sometimes called a *modus vivendi*, and presented to Japan his memorandum of that date. The secretary recognized, and said, that there was then 'practically no possibility of an agreement being achieved with Japan.' Having reached this conclusion, the secretary, according to his account of what happened, declared on Nov. 25 and on Nov. 28, at meetings of high officials of this government, 'that the matter of safeguarding our national security was in the hands of the Army and Navy' (Peace and War, 1943, p. 144). This was presumptively a warning to the War Department and the Navy Department to make ready for war. Accepting it as such the two departments sent to Gen. Short and Adm. Kimmel messages which, the departments claimed, ordered the commanders to put into effect a due alert for war —a possible Japanese attack.

"The President, the Secretary of State, the Secretary of War, and the Secretary of the Navy were, therefore, certainly bound by the duties of their respective offices to be on the alert day and night after Nov. 26, 1941, for the receipt of any word or message from Japan and for the receipt of any intercepts or other information respecting Japanese designs and intentions that were indicative of a breach of relations and war. They were also bound by their duties to alert and to keep on the alert for sudden attack their immediate subordinates and the outpost commanders having duties in connection with war operations."

23. JCC, Feb. 15, 1946.
24. *Ibid.*, April 9, 1946.
25. *Ibid.*, May 31, 1946.
26. John T. Flynn, "The Final Secret of Pearl Harbor," p. 9.
27. JCC, April 9, 1946.
28. *Ibid.*, Dec. 11, 1945.
29. Representative Keefe inquires (Maj., pp. 266 H and G):

"Why did the high command in Washington fail to disclose promptly to Adm. Kimmel, Gen. Short, and other American commanders in the field the information available in Washington, Saturday night and early Sunday morning? In seeking the answer to this question we have encountered failures of memory and changes in sworn testimony. . . . .

"Gen. Marshall, chief of staff of the Army, had the 'pilot message' available to him on the afternoon of Saturday, Dec. 6. This placed on him an obligation to make sure he would promptly receive the subsequent information which the pilot message indicated would be soon forthcoming. He did not do so. In placing himself outside of effective contact with his subordinates for several hours on Sunday morning, he failed to exercise the care and diligence which his position required.

"The alleged failure of the chief subordinates of Adm. Stark and Gen. Marshall to furnish them promptly with the intercepted messages on Saturday night was unusual for two reasons. First, it was a departure from the usual routine for the distribution of intercepts. Second, these two were the only usual recipients of intercepts who testified that the messages were not brought to their attention on Saturday night. Neither Adm. Stark nor Gen. Marshall made any effort thereafter to ascertain why such a colossal breakdown should occur in the functioning of their staffs on the eve of war" (Tr., pp. 3490-91, 6215).

30. APH, p. 52.
31. NYT, Oct. 11, 1945, 1:7.

32. APH, p. 53.
33. *Ibid.*, p. 36. One of the remarkable features of the Pearl Harbor story is that, almost without exception, those who played the administration's side in the controversy prospered, while everyone who showed a less accommodating spirit failed to win promotion and pay.

Adm. Standley, member of the Roberts Commission, was decorated with the distinguished service medal by President Roosevelt after signing the report against Kimmel and Short. Later he was appointed ambassador to Russia.

Adm. Reeves, a member of the Roberts Commission, was retired as a rear admiral in 1936. Five and one-half years later, and five months after signing the report, he was advanced to admiral for "eminent and conspicuous service in the Spanish-American war." Mr. Roosevelt discovered his heroic contributions forty-four years after they were made.

Gen. McCoy, a member of the Roberts Commission, subsequently was appointed chairman of the Far Eastern advisory commission.

Col. McNarney, a member of the commission, was shortly promoted to lieutenant general. After serving as chairman of the War Department reorganization committee in 1942, he was appointed Assistant Chief of Staff to General Marshall. At the end of the war he had been promoted four grades and installed as Commanding General of American Occupation Forces in Germany.

When a new classification of five-star generals of the Army was devised, Chief of Staff Marshall headed the list.

When five-star admirals of the fleet were created at the same time, Adm. King, who blamed the American people for Pearl Harbor, became one of them.

Adm. Ingersoll, deputy to Adm. Stark in naval operations, later was appointed commander of the Western Sea Frontier.

Col. Clarke, who carried the Marshall message to Gov. Dewey, was promoted to Brigadier General.

Adm. Stark, after serving as chief of naval operations, was given an assignment as commander of United States Naval Forces in Europe and was decorated with his second distinguished service medal by Roosevelt.

Gen. Gerow, who was castigated in three different Pearl Harbor reports for his conduct of the war plans division of the War Department, was, nevertheless, promoted from Brigadier General to Lieutenant General, placed in command of the 15th Army in Europe, and, at the end of the war, appointed Commandant of the Command and General Staff School at Fort Leavenworth.

Roosevelt, of course, got a fourth term.

Secretary of State Hull, whose diplomacy hurried the country into war, received the most ironic award. The Nobel Peace Prize and the large cash award that goes with it were conferred upon him in 1945.

Cols. Bratton and Sadtler and Capt. Safford, in comparison with these gentlemen, did not get ahead in the world.

34. JCC, Dec. 17, 1945.
35. *Ibid.*, Jan. 19, 1946.
36. *Ibid.*, Jan. 29, 1946.
37. *Ibid.*, Feb. 5, 1946.
38. Tr., pp. 6223, 6245.
39. JCC, Feb. 14, 1946.
40. APH, p. 6.
41. Min., p. 27.
42. JCC, Feb. 6, 1946.
43. APH, p. 6.
44. Tr., Vol. 69, p. 13988.
45. *Ibid.*, p. 13989.
46. Maj., p. 266-J.

47. JCC, April 11, 1946.
48. *Ibid.*
49. JCC, Feb. 14, 1946.
50. *Ibid.*, Dec. 17, 1945.
51. *Ibid.*, Jan. 30, 1946.
52. Cramer report submitted to JCC Dec. 12, 1945.
53. Tr., p. 6223.
54. JCC, Feb. 6, 1946.
55. See CT, Nov. 7, 1945, 1:7; Nov. 9, 1945, 11:3; Nov. 15, 1945, 1:1. Capt. Kramer for almost a month before the opening of the congressional investigation was confined in the neuropsychiatric ward at the naval hospital at Bethesda, Md. Representatives Keefe and Gearhart, members of the committee, asserted on the floor of the House that he had been "badgered and grilled" into a nervous breakdown by high Navy officers who sought to make him change his testimony about events in Washington preceding the Pearl Harbor attack. Kramer was retired by the Navy shortly after the end of regular daily hearings by the congressional committee.
56. The shilly-shallying in Washington on the morning of December 7 is emphasized in the minority report of the Joint Congressional Committee (p. 35):
   "In the early morning of Dec. 7, 1941, about 5:00 A.M. Washington time, the message fixing the hour for delivery of the Japanese note as 1:00 P.M., Washington time, was available in the Navy Department in Washington (Tr., Vol. 56, pp. 10694-10701). This was 8½ hours before the attack on Pearl Harbor. Adm. Stark and his principal subordinates have testified before us that they had knowledge of this message about 10:30 A.M. (Tr., Vol. 26, p. 4675; Vol. 49, pp. 9146-48; Vol. 55, p. 10469). This was 5½ hours after it had been received in the Navy Department. It was about 3 hours before the attack.
   "The relation of 1:00 P.M. Washington time to early morning in Hawaii was pointed out to Adm. Stark (Tr., Vol. 49, pp. 9146-48, 9154-56, 9236-54; Vol. 26, pp. 4679, 4685). It meant dawn in Hawaii—the strategic time at which to launch an attack. Adm. Stark was urged by the director of Naval intelligence to send a warning to the fleet (Tr., Vol. 26, p. 4673). The chief intelligence officers of the Army had the '1:00 P.M. message' by 9:00 A.M. Washington time, immediately appreciated its significance, but did not succeed in bringing it to Gen. Marshall's attention until nearly several hours later (Tr., Vol. 62, pp. 12077-78, 12079-81). Marshall was horseback riding in Virginia. No action was taken by the Army until he saw and read the 1:00 P.M. message and related intercepts, at which time he sent a message to Gen. Short which went over commercial facilities and was received after the Pearl Harbor attack (Tr., Vol. 18, pp. 2935-39, Vol. 45, p. 8396). Adm. Stark took no action on this information except to agree to the inclusion in the belated Army message of instructions to Gen. Short to advise Adm. Kimmel of its contents (Tr., Vol. 32, pp. 5814-16).
   "Mr. Hull, Mr. Stimson, and Mr. Knox had the 1:00 P.M. message at their conference about 10:30 A.M. Washington time, Dec. 7 (Tr., Vol. 55, p. 10473). The relation of Washington time to time in Hawaii and the Philippines was brought to their attention (Tr., Vol. 55, pp. 10473-75)."
57. Tr., p. 7943.
58. *Ibid.*, pp. 7943-44.
59. APH, p. 32. The assertion that Gen. Marshall warned the Philippines by scrambler telephone was made by Gen. Short before the Roberts Commission (R., p. 310). It was accepted by the Army Pearl Harbor Board. The majority report of the congressional committee (p. 225) says that Marshall considered calling Gen. MacArthur, but did not use the phone at all.
60. *Ibid.*
61. Tr., pp. 8523-27.
62. Tr., p. 8530.

63. JCC, Dec. 10, 1945.
64. APH, p. 27.
65. Tr., pp. 7949-50.
66. JCC, Dec. 10, 1945.
67. Tr., pp. 8680-84.
68. *Ibid.*, pp. 8682-83.
69. *Ibid.*, pp. 8685-89. Of the manifest failures in Washington, the minority report of
the Joint Congressional Committee (pp. 62-65) observes:

"High Washington authorities did not communicate to Adm. Kimmel and
Gen. Short adequate information of diplomatic negotiations and of intercepted
diplomatic intelligence which, if communicated to them, would have informed
them of the imminent menace of a Japanese attack in time for them to fully alert
and prepare the defense of Pearl Harbor. . . .

"In the critical hours from the afternoon of Dec. 6 to 10:30 A.M. on Dec. 7,
Washington authorities failed to take the instant action called for by their special
knowledge of Japanese messages on those days, which would have placed the
Hawaiian commanders on the specific alert for probable danger to Hawaii. . . .

"In extenuation of failures on the part of high authorities in Washington two
statements were often made by witnesses who appeared before the committee. First,
it is easy to see *now* the mistakes and failures made by high authorities but this
is merely 'hindsight.' Second, those high authorities were busy men carrying heavy
burdens in their respective offices—burdens so heavy that many failures on their
part must be excused.

"Undoubtedly, hindsight is often easier and better than foresight. But the exercise of prudence and foresight with reference to knowledge in his possession is
a bounden duty imposed on every high authority in the government of the United
States by the powers and obligations of his office. For every failure to exercise
prudence and foresight with reference to knowledge in his possession he must bear
a corresponding burden of responsibility for the consequences that flow from that
failure. By virtue of his office he is presumed to have special competence and
knowledge; to act upon his special knowledge, and to be informed and alert in
the discharge of his duties in the situation before him.

"The introduction of hindsight in extenuation of responsibility is, therefore,
irrelevant to the determination of responsibility for the catastrophe at Pearl Harbor.

"The question before this committee is: What did high authorities in Washington know about Japanese designs and intentions; what decisions did they make on
the basis of their knowledge; and what actions did they take to safeguard the
security of the American outposts?

"With regard to Gen. Marshall and Adm. Stark, they were certainly carrying
heavy burdens in preparing the armed forces of the United States for war; in making war plans; in building up an Army and Navy (which they knew were not yet
ready for war), and in struggling for a postponement of the war until the Army
and Navy were better prepared to cope with the foe. With regard to the President,
the Secretary of State, the Secretary of War, and the Secretary of the Navy, it may
be said justly that they were carrying heavy burdens also. But all these officials,
as Secretary Stimson's diary demonstrates, spent many days before Dec. 7 in general discussions which led to no decisions. This they did at a time when they
possessed special knowledge of Japanese designs and were acquainted with their
own intentions and resolves and certainly had the leisure to do the one obvious
duty dictated by common sense—that is, draw up a brief plan for telling the
outpost commanders just what to do in a certain contingency on receipt of orders
from Washington.

"That contingency was a Japanese attack on American possessions somewhere.
Secretary Stimson records that 'the question (during those days) was how we (the
President, Secretary Hull, Secretary Stimson, Secretary Knox, Gen. Marshall, and

Adm. Stark) should maneuver them (the Japanese) into the position of firing the first shot without allowing too much damage to ourselves.' In any event, inasmuch as the President decided against appealing to Congress for a declaration of war on Japan, they were all waiting for the Japanese to fire the first shot,* and in those circumstances it was their duty to prepare definite plans and procedures for action in meeting that attack.

"This is exactly what they did not do at any time before Dec. 7. They had plans for action or actions by the armed forces of the United States *if* Congress declared war or *if* by some process the United States got into or entered the war. War plans (for example, Rainbow No. 5 which was WPL 46) were to go into operation only after war had begun and were not intended for preparation in meeting a surprise attack.

"They prepared no plan giving the outpost commanders instructions about the measures they were to take in preparing for and meeting a Japanese attack on American possessions when and if it came. This plan could have been drawn up in a few hours at most and set down in two or three typewritten pages at most. With modifications appropriate to the various outposts this plan could have been sent to the respective commanders by couriers or swifter means of communication. And a procedure could have been adopted for instructing the commanders by one word in code, or a few words, to put plans for meeting Japanese attack into effect. No such plan was drawn up or at 'all events no such plan was sent to the commanders. No procedure for giving them the code word or words for action under any plan or procedure was ever adopted by the authorities in Washington whose official duty it was to prepare, with all the resources at their command, for meeting the Japanese attack which they privately recognized as an imminent menace."

NOTES ON CHAPTER XIX: *JAPAN SOLVES THE DILEMMA*

1. JCC, Ex. 16-A.
2. *Ibid.*, Dec. 10, 1945.
3. APH, p. 27.
4. *Ibid.*, p. 51.
5. *Ibid.*, p. 27.
6. Tr., pp. 6173-80.
7. *Ibid.*, pp. 14421-23.
8. APH, p. 56.
9. Stimson, p. 11.
10. *Ibid.*, p. 49.
11. *Ibid.*, p. 52.
12. JCC, Ex. 45.
13. Stimson, p. 48.
14. *Ibid.*, p. 49.
15. *Ibid.*, p. 50.
16. *Ibid.*, p. 51.
17. The minority report of the Joint Congressional Committee (p. 44) says: "Notwithstanding their apparent ignorance of the full meaning of Japanese movements in the Southeastern Pacific, Washington authorities knew or should have known from their understandings of parallel action with the British and Dutch, that a Japanese attack on the Philippines, Thai, or the Kra Peninsula meant war with America."
18. Tr., p. 8536; Hart Report, p. 428, question No. 49.
19. *How War Came*, p. 267.
20. JCC, Ex. 50, p. 13.
21. Peace, p. 714.
22. NYT, Nov. 25, 1941, 8:4.

*See Chap. XIX.

23. JCC, Dec. 10, 1945.
24. Tr., pp. 14435-36.
25. Stimson, p. 4.
26. *Ibid.*, pp. 18-19.
27. *Ibid.*, pp. 54-55.
28. *Ibid.*, pp. 9-10.
29. *Ibid.*, pp. 21-22.
30. *Ibid.*, pp. 46-47.
31. Tr., p. 7928.
32. Min., pp. 17-18.
33. Stimson, p. 15.
34. *Ibid.*, p. 12.
35. *Ibid.*, p. 42.
36. *Ibid.*, pp. 47-48.
37. *Ibid.*, pp. 26-27.
38. *Ibid.*, p. 28.
39. *Ibid.*, p. 56.
40. *Ibid.*, pp. 28-29.
41. Maj., p. 397. The proposed message consisted of some twenty typewritten pages, excerpts from which follow:

"GENTLEMEN OF THE CONGRESS: I have come before you to report to you on serious danger which is threatening this country and its interests in the Far East. Relations between the United States and the Japanese empire have reached a stage where I consider it incumbent upon me to lay before you the essential facts of the situation and their extremely serious implications."

It said of Japanese movements:

"Today they are openly threatening an extension of this conquest into the territory of Thailand. That step, if taken, would place them where they would directly menace, to the north, the Burma Road, China's lifeline, and, to the south, the port and Straits of Singapore through which gateway runs the commerce of the world, including our own, between the Pacific and the Indian Ocean.

"To the eastward of the Philippines, Japan has extended her threatening activities through the Caroline and Marshall Islands where, in violation of the mandate under which she received the custody of those islands, she has been secretly establishing naval and air bases and fortifications directly on the line between the United States and the Philippines.

"By these steps Japan has enveloped with threatening forces the western, northern, and eastern approaches to the Philippines. Should this process go further, it will completely encircle and dangerously menace vital interests of the United States. . . .

"This situation, precipitated solely by Japanese aggression, holds unmistakable threats to our interests, especially our interest in peace and in peaceful trade, and to our responsibility for the security of the Philippine Archipelago. The successful defense of the United States, in a military sense, is dependent upon supplies of vital materials which we import in large quantities from this region of the world. To permit Japanese domination and control of the major sources of world supplies of tin and rubber and tungsten would jeopardize our safety in a manner and to an extent that cannot be tolerated. Along with this would go practical Japanese control of the Pacific.

"Unless the present course of events in the Far East is halted and considerations of justice, humanity, and fair dealing are restored, we will witness in that region of the world precisely what has already transpired throughout the continental limits of Europe where Hitler seeks dominion by ruthless force. . . .

"If the Japanese should carry out their new threatened attacks upon, and were to succeed in conquering, the regions which they are menacing in the southwestern

Pacific, our commerce with the Netherlands East Indies and Malaya would be at their mercy and probably cut off. Our imports from those regions are of vital importance to us. We need those imports in time of peace. With the spirit of exploitation and destruction of commerce which prevails among the partners in the axis alliance, and with our needs what they are now in this period of emergency, an interruption of our trade with that area would be catastrophic."

The message concluded with an expression of confidence that "it is within our capacity to withstand any attack which any one may make upon us . . ." (JCC, Ex. 19).

42. JCC, May 23, 1946.
43. *Ibid.*, Ex. 19.
44. Stimson, p. 58.
45. Tr., p. 14631.
46. *Ibid.*, pp. 13741-42.
47. United States News, April 19, 1946, p. 28.
48. Stimson, p. 6.
49. NYT, Dec. 3, 1941, 1:8.
50. *Ibid.*, Dec. 4, 1941, 4:3.
51. *Ibid.*, Dec. 6, 1941, 3:1.
52. *Ibid.*
53. JCC, Feb. 12, 1946.
54. *Ibid.*, Feb. 13, 1946.
55. CR, Dec. 4, 1941, pp. 9407-11, 9413; Dec. 5, 1941, p. 9502.
56. JCC, Jan. 19, 1946.
57. Stimson, p. 5.
58. *Ibid.*, p. 21.
59. *Ibid.*, p. 29.
60. *Ibid.*
61. JCC, Ex. 37, p. 39.
62. Maj., p. 266-P.
63. *Ibid.*, pp. 266-N, 266-O.
64. JCC, Ex. 21.
65. *Ibid.*, Dec. 10, 1945.
66. *Ibid.*, Ex. 21.
67. Maj., p. 425, Note 1.
68. Tr., p. 5507.
69. *Ibid.*, p. 6213.
70. Infantry Journal, June, 1946, p. 27.
71. JCC, Feb. 14, 1946.
72. *Ibid.*, Ex. 79, p. 12.
73. *Ibid.*, April 9, 1946.
74. CT, Dec. 7, 1941, 10:3.
75. Tr., pp. 14631-32, 13738.
76. *Ibid.*, pp. 13738-40.
77. Stimson, p. 59.
78. *Ibid.*, pp. 59, 65-68.
79. *Ibid.*, p. 30.
80. *Ibid.*, pp. 59-60.
81. *Ibid.*, p. 62.
82. United States News, April 19, 1946, p. 27.
83. *Ibid.*, p. 28.
84. See the remarks of Edward Samuel Corwin, McCormick professor of jurisprudence at Princeton University, who delivered the William W. Cook Foundation Lectures at the University of Michigan. These were reported in the *Chicago Daily Law Bulletin*, March 19, 1946.

NOTES ON CHAPTER XX: *WHO WAS GUILTY?*

1. APH, p. 56. The board said:

"The extent of the Pearl Harbor disaster was due primarily to two causes:

"1. The failure of the Commanding General of the Hawaiian Department adequately to alert his command for war, and

"2. The failure of the War Department, with knowledge of the type of alert taken by the Commanding General, Hawaiian Department, to direct him to take an adequate alert, and the failure to keep him adequately informed as to the developments of the United States–Japanese negotiations, which in turn might have caused him to change from the inadequate alert to an adequate one.

"We turn now to responsibilities:

"1. The Secretary of State—the Honorable Cordell Hull. The action of the Secretary of State in delivering the counter-proposals of November 26, 1941, was used by the Japanese as the signal to begin the war by the attack on Pearl Harbor. To the extent that it hastened such attack it was in conflict with the efforts of the War and Navy departments to gain time for preparations for war. However, war with Japan was inevitable and imminent because of irreconcilable disagreements between the Japanese empire and the American government.

"2. The Chief of Staff of the Army, General George C. Marshall, failed in his relations with the Hawaiian Department in the following particulars:

"(*a*) To keep the Commanding General of the Hawaiian Department fully advised of the growing tenseness of the Japanese situation which indicated an increasing necessity for better preparation for war, of which information he had an abundance and Short had little.

"(*b*) To send additional instructions to the Commanding General of the Hawaiian Department on Nov. 28, 1941, when evidently he failed to realize the import of General Short's reply of Nov. 27, which indicated clearly that General Short had misunderstood and misconstrued the message of Nov. 27 (472) and had not adequately alerted his command for war.

"(*c*) To get to General Short on the evening of Dec. 6 and the early morning of Dec. 7, the critical information indicating an almost immediate break with Japan, though there was ample time to have accomplished this.

"(*d*) To investigate and determine the state of readiness of the Hawaiian Command between Nov. 27 and Dec. 7, 1941, despite the impending threat of war.

"3. Chief of the War Plans Division, War Department General Staff, Major General Leonard T. Gerow, failed in his duties, in the following particulars:

"(*a*) To keep the Commanding General, Hawaiian Department, adequately informed on the impending war situation by making available to him the substance of the data being delivered to the War Plans Division by the Assistant Chief of Staff, G-2.

"(*b*) To send to the Commanding General of the Hawaiian Department on November 27, 1941, a clear, concise directive; on the contrary he approved the message of November 27, 1941, (472) which contained confusing statements.

"(*c*) To realize that the state of readiness reported in Short's reply to the November 27th message was not a state of readiness for war, and he failed to take corrective action.

"(*d*) To take the required steps to implement the existing joint plans and agreements between the Army and Navy to insure the functioning of the two services in the manner contemplated.

"4. Commanding General of the Hawaiian Department, Lieut. Gen. Walter C. Short, failed in his duties in the following particulars:

"(*a*) To place his command in a state of readiness for war in the face of a war warning by adopting an alert against sabotage only. The information which he had was incomplete and confusing but it was sufficient to warn him of the tense relations between our government and the Japanese empire and that hostilities might be momentarily expected. This required that he guard against surprise to the extent possible and make ready his command so that it might be employed to the maximum and in time against the worst form of attack that the enemy might launch.

"(b) To reach or attempt to reach an agreement with the Admiral commanding the 14th Naval District for implementing the Joint Army and Navy plans and agreements then in existence which provided for joint action by the two services. One of the methods by which they might have become operative was through the joint agreement of the responsible commanders.

"(c) To inform himself of the effectiveness of the long-distance reconnaissance being conducted by the Navy.

"(d) To replace inefficient staff officers."

2. APH, p. 60.

3. NCI, p. 86. This view that the American people were to blame had previously been asserted by Adm. King. "It is true," he said (NCI, p. 77), "that the country as a whole is basically responsible in that the people were unwilling to support an adequate Army and Navy until it was too late to repair the consequences of past neglect in time to deal effectively with the attack that ushered in the war." The same view was echoed before the joint congressional committee by Rear Adm. Inglis (Tr., Vol. 2, pp. 197-200). Cf. his examination by Senator Ferguson:

"Senator Ferguson: Do you think the people were to blame?

"Admiral Inglis: My opinion is that they did contribute to some extent to the Pearl Harbor attack.

"Senator Ferguson: Well, now, you explain how that contributed to the Pearl Harbor attack.

"Admiral Inglis: Because the armed forces were not as strong as they might have been had the country been unified and had the appropriations been larger for the Army and Navy."

4. Ibid., p. 71. The court expressed belief that Adm. Stark "failed to display the sound judgment expected of him in that he did not transmit to Adm. Kimmel . . . during the very critical period 26 November to 7 December, important information which he had regarding the Japanese situation and, especially, in that, on the morning of 7 December, 1941, he did not transmit immediately information which appeared to indicate that a break in diplomatic relations was imminent, and that an attack in the Hawaiian area could be expected soon."

The court absolved Adm. Kimmel, stating, "The court is of the opinion that Admiral Kimmel's decision, made after receiving the dispatch of 24 November, to continue the preparations of the Pacific fleet for war, was sound in the light of the information then available to him." It asserted that the "war warning" message of November 27 "directed attention away from Pearl Harbor rather than toward it."

5. Ibid., pp. 78, 86.

6. Kimmel, pp. 105-08.

7. Ibid.

8. Tr., p. 8549.

9. Ibid., pp. 8549-53.

10. Ibid., pp. 8601-2.

11. Ibid., pp. 8602-13. The charges and Short's responses to them follow:

"1. Failure to provide an adequate inshore aerial patrol.

"Short: Not guilty. I did have an adequate patrol. The air people were satisfied and had full control. The purpose was anti-submarine defense, and the patrol was not designed for air defense. We had one observation squadron, six planes, in commission, and we were operating them several hours a day. I would say we were using them all we should use them. In addition to that, there was a lot of observation that accomplished the same thing because our pursuit training was all over Oahu, pretty much around the perimeter, and they were all given to understand that they should learn to observe for submarines.

"2. Failure to provide adequate anti-aircraft defense.

"Short: Not guilty. We would have had an adequate anti-aircraft defense if the War Department had given us the equipment, and had given us the information which indicated imminent attack. Or, if they had replied to my report and indicated any desired modification.

"3. Failure to set up an interceptor command.

"Short: Not guilty. We were training personnel as fast as we could to operate an effective interceptor command, and it was set up and operating as effectively as it could. (The general might have added that the Army high command, having given tacit approval by its silence to his report that he had decreed an alert only against sabotage, was itself responsible for the fact that few of his planes were able to get into the air Dec. 7, because they had been grouped wing-tip to wing-tip, according to the most recent Army studies of the best means of defense against sabotage.)

"4. Failure to provide a proper aircraft warning service.

"Short: Not guilty. We were training our personnel as fast as we could to set up an effective aircraft warning service. It was in operation. [Short testified elsewhere that the warning service picked up the Jap attacking formation 132 miles from Oahu, but that the warning was disregarded by a young Army Air Corps officer who, under the Army's curious system of recognizing merit, was subsequently promoted from second lieutenant to lieutenant colonel. Short further testified that this mistake was occasioned by the fact that the officer at the radar information center assumed that the planes shown on the radar screen were B-24's coming in from the mainland, although they were far off course. He stated that, inasmuch as all of our planes were equipped with radio, this error in judgment could have been obviated if the Army radio had simply contacted the planes and asked them whether they were enemy or friend. Short also testified that radar installations at strategic sites selected by Signal Corps officers had been held up for ten months because Secretary Ickes' Department of the Interior insisted that the design of buildings going into the national parks must agree with its standards for preserving scenic beauty.]

"5. Failure to provide for the transmission of appropriate warnings to interested agencies.

"Short: Not guilty. We were restricted by direct order from Marshall from transmitting the Nov. 27 warning to any other than the minimum essential officers.

"6. Failure to establish a proper system of defense by co-operation and co-ordination with the Navy.

"Short: Not guilty. We had full, complete plans for defense in co-operation with the Navy which had been approved by Gen. Marshall and Adm. Stark, and they would have been carried out 100 per cent if they [Marshall and Stark] would have given us the information they had.

"7. Failure to issue adequate orders to his subordinates as to their duties in case of sudden attack.

"Short: Not guilty. I could not tell subordinates to expect a sudden attack which neither I nor the War Department nor anyone else expected. Our information regarding impending possible action was, by direction of the chief of staff, limited to the minimum essential officers. Our standard operating procedure of Nov. 5, 1941, prescribed fully the duties of all personnel in event of any sudden attack. [This extended to the length, Short said, that the legislature of Hawaii had passed M-day legislation governing the conduct of the entire civilian population in the event of war. It was put into effect eleven hours after the attack on Dec. 7.]

"8. Failure to take adequate measures to protect the fleet and naval base at Pearl Harbor.

"Short: Not guilty. I took every measure I thought necessary to protect the fleet and naval base against sabotage. I so reported to the War Department. Marshall testified that I was reasonable in assuming that I was doing exactly what he wanted, because otherwise he would have notified me that he wanted more measures taken.

"9. Failure to have his airplanes dispersed in anticipation of a hostile attack, after having been warned of the danger thereof.

"Short: Not guilty. I was never warned of any imminent danger of an air attack. The planes were therefore grouped for more adequate protection against hostile action in the form of sabotage.

"10. Failure to have his airplanes in a state of readiness for attack.

"Short: Not guilty. My aircraft were not in a state of readiness for a surprise attack, but were protected against sabotage as directed by the War Department in the sabotage-alert messages of Nov. 27 and 28, and as reported to the War Department by me. If they had been equipped with ammunition, grouped as they were, and a sabotage attack had been made, there would have been much more damage by exploding ammunition.

"11. Failure to provide for the protection of military personnel, their families, etc., and of civilian employees on various reservations.

"Short: We made a quite elaborate plan for evacuating the families of civilians on the military reservation. We asked the War Department for money to establish a camp some 4 miles east of Schofield. I wrote a personal letter to the chief of staff and told him that we were asking for the money to establish these camps on the basis of recreation camps, and the different units, different families, would be assigned to different locations, but our real purpose was to get ready for a possible attack and this would give us a chance to acquaint everybody with the details without advertising what we were doing. He answered my letter and stated that funds were needed worse for other purposes.

" 'I notice,' said Ferguson, 'that you left out the words "Not guilty" to this last one. Is there any reason?'

" 'No, sir. I plead not guilty.' "

12. *Ibid.*, p. 8590.
13. *Ibid.*, pp. 8590-91.
14. *Ibid.*, pp. 8591-93.
15. JCC, Ex. 140; Tr., p. 8599.
16. Tr., p. 8599.
17. *Ibid.*, pp. 8599-8600.
18. *Ibid.*, pp. 8692-93.
19. *Ibid.*, pp. 8617-18.
20. *Ibid.*, pp. 8618-19.
21. *Ibid.*, pp. 8614-16.
22. Min., prefatory note.
23. Maj., pp. 251-52. The report states:

"Specifically, the Hawaiian commands failed—

"(*a*) To discharge their responsibilities in the light of the warnings received from Washington, other information possessed by them, and the principle of command by mutual co-operation.

"(*b*) To integrate and co-ordinate their facilities for defense and to alert properly the Army and Navy establishments in Hawaii, particularly in the light of the warnings and intelligence available to them during the period Nov. 27 to Dec. 7, 1941.

"(c) To effect liaison on a basis designed to acquaint each of them with the operations of the other, which was necessary to their joint security, and to exchange fully all significant intelligence.

"(d) To maintain a more effective reconnaissance within the limits of their equipment.

"(e) To effect a state of readiness throughout the Army and Navy establishments designed to meet all possible attacks.

"(f) To employ the facilities, matériel, and personnel at their command, which were adequate at least to have greatly minimized the effects of the attack, in repelling the Japanese raiders.

"(g) To appreciate the significance of intelligence and other information available to them.

"The errors made by the Hawaiian commands were errors of judgment and not derelictions of duty.

"The War Plans Division of the War Department failed to discharge its direct responsibility to advise the commanding general he had not properly alerted the Hawaiian Department when the latter, pursuant to instructions, had reported action taken in a message that was not satisfactorily responsive to the original directive.

"The Intelligence and War Plans Divisions of the War and Navy Departments failed:

"(a) To give careful and thoughtful consideration to the intercepted messages from Tokyo to Honolulu of Sept. 24, Nov. 15, and Nov. 20 (the harbor berthing plan and related dispatches) and to raise a question as to their significance. Since they indicated a particular interest in the Pacific Fleet's base this intelligence should have been appreciated and supplied the Hawaiian commanders for their assistance, along with other information available to them, in making their estimate of the situation.

"(b) To be properly on the *qui vive* to receive the 'one o'clock' intercept and to recognize in the message the fact that some Japanese military action would very possibly occur somewhere at 1:00 P.M., Dec. 7. If properly appreciated, this intelligence should have suggested a dispatch to all Pacific outpost commanders supplying this information, as Gen. Marshall attempted to do immediately upon seeing it.

"Notwithstanding the fact that there were officers on twenty-four hour watch, the committee believes that under all of the evidence the War and Navy Departments were not sufficiently alerted on Dec. 6 and 7, 1941, in view of the imminence of war."

The majority report submitted twenty-five principles for increased efficiency in national defense to preclude a repetition of Pearl Harbor (Maj., pp. 253-66). They were:

"1. Operational and intelligence work requires centralization of authority and clear-cut allocation of responsibility.

"2. Supervisory officials cannot safely take anything for granted in the alerting of subordinates.

"3. Any doubt as to whether outposts should be given information should always be resolved in favor of supplying the information.

"4. The delegation of authority or the issuance of orders entails the duty of inspection to determine that the official mandate is properly exercised.

"5. The implementation of official orders must be followed with closest supervision.

"6. The maintenance of alertness to responsibility must be insured through repetition.

"7. Complacency and procrastination are out of place where sudden and decisive action are of the essence.

"8. The co-ordination and proper evaluation of intelligence in times of stress must be insured by continuity of service and centralization of responsibility in competent officials.

"9. The unapproachable or superior attitude of officials is fatal; there should never be any hesitancy in asking for clarification of instructions or in seeking advice on matters that are in doubt.

"10. There is no substitution for imagination and resourcefulness on the part of supervisory and intelligence officials.

"11. Communications must be characterized by clarity, forthrightness, and appropriateness.

"12. There is great danger in careless paraphrase of information received and every effort should be made to insure that the paraphrased material reflects the true meaning and significance of the original.

"13. Procedures must be sufficiently flexible to meet the exigencies of unusual situations.

"14. Restriction of highly confidential information to a minimum number of officials, while often necessary, should not be carried to the point of prejudicing the work of the organization.

"15. There is great danger of being blinded by the self-evident.

"16. Officials should at all times give subordinates the benefit of significant information.

"17. An official who neglects to familiarize himself in detail with his organization should forfeit his responsibility.

"18. Failure can be avoided in the long run only by preparation for any eventuality.

"19. Officials, on a personal basis, should never countermand an official instruction.

"20. Personal or official jealousy will wreck any organization.

"21. Personal friendship, without more, should never be accepted in lieu of liaison or confused therewith where the latter is necessary to the proper functioning of two or more agencies.

"22. No considerations should be permitted as excuse for failure to perform a fundamental task.

"23. Superiors must at all times keep their subordinates adequately informed and, conversely, subordinates should keep their superiors informed.

"24. The administrative organization of any establishment must be designed to locate failures and to assess responsibility.

"25. In a well-balanced organization there is close correlation of responsibility and authority."

David Lawrence (*Chicago Daily News,* July 23, 1946, 10:3) comments:

"Despite the impressions which the concluding part of the report seeks to establish, the headings of the document fix responsibility as plainly as if names had been called. . . . Future historians cannot fail to read those tell-tale headings, for each one states an impersonal conclusion out of which only one inference can be made—namely, that the persons who had the responsibility for each task and did not perform it efficiently are being blamed.

"Thus there is language in the conclusion of the report itself, signed by the majority, which absolves certain individuals, but there is no such evasiveness in the headings. . . . Particularly significant are Nos. 17, 23, 24, and 25. . . .

"All that the historian of tomorrow needs to do is find out who, on Dec. 7, 1941, was chief of staff of the Army, chief of naval operations and in command of subordinate positions in the War and Navy Departments, and who was commander-in-chief of the Army and Navy and then read the main headings of the report on Pearl Harbor.

"He will find that Republicans and Democrats were unanimous about the headings, but politeness, courtesy, and deference caused the omission of the names of the personalities involved, in the case of the majority who signed the report, whereas the minority just named those responsible."

24. Maj., p. 251, Conclusions 4 and 5:

"4. The committee has found no evidence to support the charges, made before and during the hearings, that the President, the Secretary of State, the Secretary of War, or the Secretary of Navy tricked, provoked, incited, cajoled, or coerced Japan into attacking this nation in order that a declaration of war might be more easily obtained from the Congress. On the contrary, all evidence conclusively points to the fact that they discharged their responsibilities with distinction, ability, and foresight and in keeping with the highest traditions of our fundamental foreign policy.

"5. The President, the Secretary of State, and high government officials made every possible effort, without sacrificing our national honor and endangering our security, to avert war with Japan."

25. Min., pp. 78-79.
26. *Ibid.*, Conclusion 16, pp. 46-49.
27. *Ibid.*, Conclusion 11, p. 36.
28. *Ibid.*, Conclusion 5, pp. 19-20.
29. *Ibid.*, Conclusion 19, pp. 70-71.
30. *Ibid.*, Conclusion 21, pp. 76-78.
31. "Conclusions of Fact and Responsibility" as set forth in the minority report of the Joint Congressional Committee (pp. 9-12) are as follows:

"1. The course of diplomatic negotiations with Japan during the months preceding Dec. 7, 1941, indicated a growing tension with Japan and after Nov. 26 the immediate imminence of war.

"2. By Nov. 7, 1941, President Roosevelt and his Cabinet had reached the unanimous conclusion that war tension had reached such a point as to convince them that 'the people would back us up in case we struck at Japan down there (in the Far East).' They then took under consideration 'what the tactics would be' (Tr., Vol. 70, p. 14415). Unless Japan yielded to diplomatic representations on the part of the United States, there were three choices on tactics before the President and the Cabinet; they could wait until Japan attacked; they could strike without a declaration of war by Congress; or the President could lay the issue of peace or war before Congress (Tr., Vol. 70, p. 14415 ff.).

"3. So imminent was war on November 25, that the President in a conference with Secretary Hull, Secretary Knox, Secretary Stimson, Gen. Marshall, and Adm. Stark, 'brought up the event that we were likely to be attacked perhaps (as soon as) next Monday' (Dec. 1); and the members of the conference discussed the question 'How we should maneuver them (the Japanese) into the position of firing the first shot without allowing too much danger to ourselves' (Tr., Vol. 70, p. 14418).

"4. Having considered without agreeing upon the proposition that a message on the war situation should be sent to Congress, the President and the Secretary of State, the Secretary of War, and the Secretary of the Navy, pursued from Nov. 25 to Dec. 7 the tactics of waiting for the firing of 'the first shot' by the Japanese.

"5. The appropriate high authorities in Washington had the organization for working in such close co-operation during the days immediately prior to the Japanese attack on Dec. 7 that they had every opportunity to make sure that identical and precise instructions warranted by the imminence of war went to the Hawaiian commanders.

"6. Through the Army and Navy Intelligence Services extensive information was secured respecting Japanese war plans and designs, by intercepted and decoded Japanese secret messages, which indicated the growing danger of war and increasingly after Nov. 26 the imminence of a Japanese attack.

"7. Army and Navy information which indicated growing imminence of war was delivered to the highest authorities in charge of national preparedness for meeting an attack, among others, the President, the Secretaries of State, War, and Navy, and the chief of staff and the chief of naval operations.

"8. Judging by the military and naval history of Japan, high authorities in Washington and the commanders in Hawaii had good grounds for expecting that in starting war the Japanese government would make a surprise attack on the United States.

"9. Neither the diplomatic negotiations nor the intercepts and other information respecting Japanese designs and operations in the hands of the United States authorities warranted those authorities in excluding from defense measures or from orders to the Hawaiian commanders the probability of an attack on Hawaii. On the contrary, there is evidence to the effect that such an attack was, in terms of strategy, necessary from the Japanese point of view and in fact highly probable, and that President Roosevelt was taking the probability into account—before Dec. 7.

"10. The knowledge of Japanese designs and intentions in the hands of the President and the Secretary of State led them to the conclusion at least 10 days before Dec. 7 that an attack by Japan within a few days was so highly probable as to constitute a certainty and, having reached this conclusion, the President, as Commander-in-Chief of the Army and Navy, was under obligation to instruct the Secretary of War and the Secretary of the Navy to make sure that the outpost commanders put their armed forces on an all-out alert for war.

"11. The decision of the President, in view of the Constitution, to await the Japanese attack rather than ask for a declaration of war by Congress increased the responsibility of high authorities in Washington to use the utmost care in putting the commanders at Pearl Harbor on a full alert for defensive actions before the Japanese attack on December 7, 1941.

"12. Inasmuch as the knowledge respecting Japanese designs and operations which was in the possession of high authorities in Washington differed in nature and volume from that in the possession of the Pearl Harbor commanders it was especially incumbent upon the former to formulate instructions to the latter in language not open to misinterpretation as to the obligations imposed on the commanders by the instructions.

"13. The messages sent to Gen. Short and Adm. Kimmel by high authorities in Washington during November were couched in such conflicting and imprecise language that they failed to convey to the commanders definite information on the state of diplomatic relations with Japan and on Japanese war designs and positive orders respecting the particular actions to be taken—orders that were beyond all reasonable doubts as to the need for an all-out alert. In this regard the said high authorities failed to discharge their full duty.

"14. High authorities in Washington failed in giving proper weight to the evidence before them respecting Japanese designs and operations which indicated that an attack on Pearl Harbor was highly probable and they failed also to emphasize this probability in messages to the Hawaiian commanders.

"15. The failure of Washington authorities to act promptly and consistently in translating intercepts, evaluating information, and sending appropriate instructions to the Hawaiian commanders was in considerable measure due to delays, mismanagement, nonco-operation, unpreparedness, confusion, and negligence on the part of officers in Washington.

"16. The President of the United States was responsible for the failure to enforce continuous, efficient, and appropriate co-operation among the Secretary of War, the Secretary of the Navy, the chief of staff, and the chief of naval operations, in evaluating information and dispatching clear and positive orders to the Hawaiian commanders as events indicated the growing imminence of war; for the Constitution and laws of the United States vested in the President full power, as

Chief Executive and Commander-in-Chief, to compel such co-operation and vested this power in him alone with a view to establishing his responsibility to the people of the United States.

"17. High authorities in Washington failed to allocate to the Hawaiian commanders the material which the latter often declared to be necessary to defense and often requested, and no requirements of defense or war in the Atlantic did or could excuse these authorities for their failures in this respect.

"18. Whatever errors of judgment the commanders at Hawaii committed and whatever mismanagement they displayed in preparing for a Japanese attack, attention to chain of responsibility in the civil and military administration requires taking note of the fact that they were designated for their posts by high authorities in Washington—all of whom were under obligation to have a care for competence in the selection of subordinates for particular positions of responsibility in the armed forces of the United States.

"19. The defense of Hawaii rested upon two sets of interdependent responsibilities: (1) The responsibility in Washington in respect of its intimate knowledge of diplomatic negotiations, widespread intelligence information, direction of affairs and constitutional duty to plan the defense of the United States; (2) the responsibility cast upon the commanders in the field in charge of a major naval base and the fleet essential to the defense of the territory of the United States to do those things appropriate to the defense of the fleet and outpost. Washington authorities failed in (1); and the commanding officers at Hawaii failed in (2).

"20. In the final instance of crucial significance for alerting American outpost commanders, on Saturday night, Dec. 6, and Sunday morning, Dec. 7, the President of the United States failed to take that quick and instant executive action which was required by the occasion and by the responsibility for watchfulness and guardianship rightly associated in law and practice with his high office from the establishment of the Republic to our own times.

"21. The contention coming from so high an authority as President Truman on August 3, 1945, that the 'country is as much to blame as any individual in this final situation that developed in Pearl Harbor,' cannot be sustained because the American people had no intimation whatever of the policies and operations that were being undertaken."

The body of the report reviews these conclusions with supporting evidence.
32. Stimson, pp. 31-33.

INDEX

INDEX

417

Hart, Admiral, inquiry conducted by, into Pearl Harbor disaster, 347-48

Hawaiian commanders, choosing of, by Roosevelt, 321. *See also* Kimmel; Richardson; Short

Hawaiian defenses: alerting of, against sabotage and subversive activities, 229–31, 232–33, 257; on all-out alert in June and July, 1940, 53–54, 229, 246, 247, 387; proposal to weaken, to provide defense for Wake, Midway, and other islands, 233–35. *See also* Pearl Harbor defenses

Hewitt, Admiral, and Pearl Harbor investigations, 202 ff., 384–85

Hirohito, Emperor, reply of, to Roosevelt's appeal of December 6, 1941, 164–65

Hitler: desire of, not to engage United States in war, 90, 94, 283; informed by Japan of imminence of war, 326; military fraud of, on the Japanese, 96–97, 189

Hopkins, Harry, allocation by, of patrol bombers, to Britain, 93

Hull, Secretary of State: belief of, in imminence of war with Japan, 266, 273; complaint of, on Japanese treachery, 190; criticisms of, in "appeasing" Japan, 157–60; deception by, in reporting progress of peace negotiations with Japan, 299; demands of, on Japan, 11; on fleet at Pearl Harbor as deterrent to Japan, 60; on Japanese reply to American proposals of November 26, 1941, 166; *modus vivendi* of: abandonment of, 154–59, 287–88, 377, Chinese opposition to, 155–59, 287, 288, 377, to effect three months' truce with Japan, 154, 286; terms of, 375–77, 380; on possibility of surprise attack by Japan, 273, 274; proposals of, to Japan, on November 26, 1941, 152–53, 160–61, 186, 187, 285, 310, 377–80; *see* Japanese diplomatic note, final, to United States; on proposed Roosevelt-Konoye meeting, 139–40; responsibility of, for diplomacy leading to Pearl Harbor disaster, 319; on treachery of Pearl Harbor attack, 166

Iceland, America assumes garrisoning of, 87

Indo-China: Japanese occupation of, 98, 115, 137, 173; proposed neutralization of, 120–21

Ingersoll, Admiral, testimony of, on "winds" message, 215

Intelligence, importance of, to conduct of war, 260–61, 281–82

Italy, declaration of war by, as "stab in back" of France, 86

Japan: American proposals to, November 26, 1941, 160–61, Japanese reply to, 165–66; blockade of, by United States, 59, 60; and China, 11; economic sanctions against, American program of, 99, 119, 132–37, 147, 148, 283, 310; final proposals of, for understanding with United States, 150–51; first overt act by, as desire of- Roosevelt administration, 271, 292–93, 387, 388, 402; first overt act by, simultaneous with declaration of war, 253, 395; foreign assets of, freezing of, 11, 132, 147, 148, 173, 179–80, 284; foreign policy of, in November, 1941, 180; "incident" on part of, as object of Roosevelt, 301–4; *modus vivendi* of November 20 and 21, 1941, 150–51; oil embargo against, 134–36; "parallel declarations" to, by United States, Britain, and Holland, 117–25, 188; policy of, to keep peace with United States, 174; policy of totalitarian expansion of, in South Seas, 98; position of, in Far East, just before Pearl Harbor attack, 177–78; relations with United States, deterioration of, 98–103; seizure by, of Indo-China, 98; surplus population of, problem of, 101–2; surprise attack by, anticipation of, by high officials in Washington, 273, 395; surprise attack by, forecast of, for weekend or holiday, 210-11, 385; surprise attack by, prophecies of, 163; and tripartite alliance, *see* Tripartite alliance; ultimatum to, by Roosevelt, in August, 1941, 122–23, 125; ultimatums to, by United States, 125–26

Japanese aggression in Far East: and A B C D powers, 105–16; and "parallel declarations" of United States, Britain and Holland, 117–25; "deadlines" for, established by agreement of United States, Britain, and Holland, 289–92, 335 (map)

Japanese diplomatic note, final, to United States, 165–66, 188, 192, 194–196, 253, 269, 275

Japanese expeditions in Far East, probable objectives of, 291–92

Japanese fleet: at Pearl Harbor attack, 16; en route to Pearl Harbor, 163

Japanese fourteen-part note, *see under* Hull, Secretary of State

Japanese militarists, ambitious designs of, 144, 373

Japanese naval situation, Navy intelligence report on, dated December 1, 1941, 236–37

FOR
REFERENCE
ONLY
DO NOT REMOVE
FROM
LIBRARY